"PROFESSOR STOUT addresses a major need in Cather studies, and she does so with impeccable scholarship and critical acumen." —Susan J. Rosowski, author of *Birthing a Nation: Gender, Creativity, and the West in American Literature.*

An infamous clause in Willa Cather's will, forbidding publication of her letters and other papers, has long caused consternation among Cather scholars. There is a lot to be learned from reading an author's letters. For Cather, a complex and private person who seldom made revelatory public pronouncements, personal letters provide – or would provide – an especially valuable key to understanding. But because of the terms of her will, that key is not readily available. Cather's letters will not come into public domain until the year 2017. Until then, even quotation, let alone publication in full, is prohibited.

Janis P. Stout has gathered over eighteen hundred of Cather's letters – all the letters currently known to be available – and provides a brief summary of each, as well as a biographical directory identifying correspondents and a multisection index of the widely scattered letters by location, by correspondent, and by names and titles mentioned. This book will be an essential resource for Cather scholars.

Janis P. Stout is a professor of English at Texas A & M University. She is the author of numerous books, including *Through the Window, Out the Door: Women's Narratives of Departure, from Austin and Cather to Tyler, Morrison, and Didion,* and *Willa Cather: The Writer and Her World.*

A Calendar of the Letters of

Willa Cather

edited by Janis P. Stout

University of Nebraska Press

Lincoln and London

Publication of this book was assisted by a grant
from the Department of English, Texas A & M
University.

Library of Congress Cataloging in Publication Data
Cather, Willa, 1873–1947.
A calendar of the letters of Willa Cather; edited by
Janis P. Stout.
p. cm. Includes index ISBN 0-8032-4293-X (cloth:
alkaline paper)
1. Cather, Willa, 1873–1947 – Correspondence –
Catalogs. 2. Novelists, American – 20th cen-
tury – Correspondence – Catalogs. I. Stout,
Janis P.
PS3505.A87 Z48 2002 813'.52 – dc21 [B] 2001034723

To the many scholars interested in the mind and art of Willa Cather and her resonance of the times in which she lived, in the hope that it will facilitate their work.

Contents

Acknowledgments

WITH WARM THANKS to Ann Romines, Deborah Williams, Bruce Baker, and other Cather scholars who encouraged me in this project, especially Susan Rosowski. Thanks also to John McDermott and Craig Kallendorf, who first suggested that I consider making my work on the letters available in this way; to Robert Thacker, who shared with me his transcriptions of a number of letters; to John Murphy, who saved me from a dreadful blunder; to Mark Madigan, whose work on Cather's "The Profile" and Evelyn Osborne saved me other blunders; to the incomparable Kari Ronning, who greatly enriched the biographical information given here and caught several errors; to Yessica Garces and especially Molly McBride for their research assistance at Texas A&M University, the results of which are evident in the biographical directory, the dating of several undated letters, and various bracketed notes incorporated into the letter summaries themselves; and to Juli Parrish, Mark Heineke, and Alena Amato Ruggerio, who helped with research at Carnegie Mellon University, Georgetown University, and Indiana University, respectively. Special thanks are also owed to Sherrill Harbison, who shared with me in manuscript her listing and summaries of nineteen letters to Sigrid Undset discovered at a private estate in Lillehammer, Norway, in February 1999 and now archived at the Oslo Division of the National Library of Norway; my listing here follows Dr. Harbison's dating, and my summaries are compressions of hers. Special thanks also to Mary Weddle, who allowed me access to letters to Mrs. George P. Cather, through the intermediation of Sue Rosowski.

The identification of George Woodberry, in the biographical dictionary, is from John P. Anders, *Willa Cather's Sexual Aesthetics and the Male Homosexual Literary Tradition* (1999).

Textual and historical information provided in the Willa Cather Scholarly Edition has been helpful in a great variety of ways, ranging from the date of the newspaper story reporting a rumor that the Cathers were hiding Marjorie Anderson (the *Argus*, October 30, 1924, per Kari A. Ronning, "Historical Essay," *Obscure Destinies*) to the first name of Ferris Greenslet's secretary, Miss Bishop (Helen, per Charles W. Mignon with Kari A. Ronning, "Textual Commentary," *My Ántonia*). Thanks are owed by all Cather scholars, now and in the future, to those who envisioned and have labored to produce these editions.

Introduction

WHEN WILLA CATHER DIED on April 24, 1947, her Last Will and Testament included a provision that has severely hampered the study of her work: a prohibition on publishing her letters, either in whole or in part. Such a prohibition is enforced not only by respect for the author's wishes (which might, after the lapse of more than half a century, be discounted in the interests of scholarship) but by the copyright laws of the United States. Until an unpublished work reverts to the public domain upon the expiration of the copyright period, the copyright (as distinct from the physical document) remains the property of its creator or heirs, as represented by an executor. Cather's executors have steadfastly held to her wishes and refused to grant permission for publication or quotation.

Under the Copyright Act of 1976 the period of protection for unpublished materials was set at fifty years after death, but that provision was not to take effect until January 1, 2003. Cather's letters were scheduled, then, to become part of the public domain (at which time the scholar wishing to quote from them would need only the permission of the library holding the document, not the executor) on January 1, 2003, fifty-five years, eight months, and eight days after her death. But in 1998 Congress passed, and the president subsequently signed, what is commonly known as the Copyright Extension Act, extending the term of protection for unpublished material to seventy years beyond death. That means Cather's letters will not enter the public domain until 2017.

What is to be done in the meantime to satisfy the demand for knowledge generated by the flourishing state of Cather scholarship? The usual answer is paraphrase, which is both permissible under the law and customary according to normal standards of scholarly ethics. Paraphrase, of course, carries its own problems: How is one to steer between the Scylla of coming too close, thereby violating the prohibition on quoting, and the Charybdis of giving too wide a berth, thus failing to represent accurately? But how can even a very close paraphrase ever convey the full meaning of a writer's own words? After all, words are not interchangeable tokens.

Mark Twain long ago derided tone-deaf writers who do not care whether they use the right word or its second cousin. Then there is the problem of subjectivity: Since the words of a paraphrase are chosen by individual human beings with their own interpretive purposes, how can even the most scrupulous of writers be sure they are not distorting the author's meaning in favor of their own? If the scholar attempts to provide a precise rendition by intermingling some of Cather's own words into the paraphrase, readers cannot know which words are whose. Present Cather scholarship, citing the letters more and more often, provides evidence of all of these problems.

Even before one can face the problem of paraphrase, however, one must face the problem of access. If we choose to go read the letters themselves, so as to know exactly what Cather said even if we cannot quote it, we face a costly and time-consuming project. Indeed, how do we even know where to go? Since Cather did not want her letters to be read, she did not donate them to any library. There is no single or even principal collection of the papers of Willa Cather. Instead, there is a scattering of the papers of various correspondents, including sometimes one, sometimes two, or in some cases a treasure-trove of the precious letters. To know where these are we must rely on lists of references in various publications, on word of mouth, or on guesswork. Margaret Anne O'Connor's article "A Guide to the Letters of Willa Cather," *Resources for American Literary Study* 4 (1974): 145–72, is a good starting place, but additional letters have continued to come to light since it was published. As recently as 1999 Georgetown University discovered a letter (listed here as no. 918) between the pages of a book in its collection. Six letters to Louise Imogen Guiney at the College of the Holy Cross are presently unavailable because misplaced. Surely they will be located! A group of letters to Stephen Tennant was purchased by a private collector when the Tennant estate was sold at Sotheby's and was then resold to a dealer. Perhaps these letters are even now in cataloging at some university's library. There may be many such stories, and in truth, a compilation such as this one can never be said with confidence to be complete.

This calendar of letters, representing an effort of collection extending over a period of several years, will go at least some distance toward solving these problems.

Certainly Cather scholars before me consulted and transcribed various of Cather's letters. But my efforts, unlike those of most of my predecessors, were facilitated by the use of a laptop computer, a tool that has transformed archival research. Until only a decade or so ago scholars undertaking research in unpublished manuscripts went armed with pencils and pads of paper. A laptop makes all the difference, both in the time required to collect a large quantity of material and in the accessibility of information, through search processes, once it is collected. Traveling to libraries with Cather holdings, I transcribed letters on site word for word, that is, to the extent that I could read them, for as anyone who has ever tried knows, Cather's handwriting is far from easy to read. A few libraries (actually, only two that I know of) prohibit even hand-transcription, an understandable if extreme stance, since different libraries' lawyers will naturally read the will's prohibition on publication differently and define "publication" differently. Some libraries are glad to provide photocopies (for a price), obviating the need to go there physically in order to make transcriptions. Even when I was able to obtain photocopies, however, I transcribed them into the computer in order to be able to search them and in order to construct a chronological sequence. My files include the full texts of all letters listed here except for a few that I have only in paraphrase because of library restrictions.

Which returns us to the problem of how to make an accurate paraphrase without coming too close. I have struggled with it as best I could.

Another problem is chronology. Many of Cather's letters, even business letters, bear only partial dates or none at all. Like many of us, she often headed her letters only by day of week ("Wednesday") or month and day without year ("June 13"). In such cases the scholar becomes a detective, following whatever clues present themselves. It is easier when a letter is headed, say, "Wednesday, June 13," since a perpetual calendar, available in standard almanacs, reduces the range of possibilities by telling us the years in which June 13 fell on a Wednesday. Internal evidence provides additional clues. To take an easy example, a letter written on stationery printed "Number Five Bank Street" was almost certainly written between January 1913 and August 1927, the period when Cather lived at that address. (The scholar knows this because she or he has, of course, compiled a chronology of known dates, partly on the basis of letters that *are* dated.) Or the range of possibilities may be reduced because of known biographical data about the person being addressed; thus a particular letter couldn't have been written after such-and-such year because I know from the New York Times obituaries that so-and-so died then. Or there may be continuities with other letters. Especially if one has both sides of a correspondence (which is true of much of the correspondence with Ferris Greenslet, at the Houghton Library, Harvard, but generally not otherwise) one can track query and response. Or the same statement, couched in much the same terms, may appear in several letters, presumably written about the same time. Here again the computer makes all the difference. With some eighteen hundred letters to examine, a large portion of them undated, the scholar-detective would have to be very astute indeed to make such linkages on the strength of memory and persistence alone.

Through a combination of these techniques, I have been able to establish dates or approximate dates for most of the undated letters. Those that remain undated are listed in a separate section at the end of the calendar. Perhaps readers will notice clues that will establish dates for some of these, or additional letters may become available that will provide the missing clues. Probably some will always remain undated. Fortunately, most of the intransigently undated ones are short and trivial notes that could have been written almost anytime, and it probably does not matter much.

In some ways the most interesting of Cather's letters are the earliest ones. The child's mind, so important to what it grows into, is the most inaccessible to us. We can be glad that Mrs. Helen Stowell, about whom we know very little (but see the biographical directory), kept three letters written by the fifteen- and sixteen-year-old Willa, or "William," Cather. The only earlier document written by Cather that I have seen is not a letter at all but a little composition on the subject of dogs, apparently done while she was being home-schooled. (It is signed "William" in what would appear to be a preadolescent hand, contrary to theories that she began to call herself William in adolescence.) We can be doubly glad that Mariel Gere, whom Cather met when she went to Lincoln to attend a preparatory year at the Latin School before matriculating in the University of Nebraska proper, kept so many of the letters written to her by her friend, who emerges from these pages as having been notably mercurial, especially in her youth.

As the years go on we can trace Cather's struggles to find a vocation, a career, and establish herself in it. We see the beginning, the quick blossoming, and the sad end of her acquaintance with Sarah Orne Jewett, a mentor whose influence had profound effects on what came after. We see the early traces of Cather's major works and her subsequent reflections on them. One of the most interesting of these traces, to me, was the discovery that the first visible germ of *One of Ours* came while Cather was still working intently on *My Ántonia*. To what extent did the Great War weigh on her mind and imagination while she produced that richly nurturant book, often taken as her defining work? The concern with the Great War becomes, indeed, one of the most important ongoing threads in the letters, extending far beyond the Armistice, tying into her foreboding over the coming of World War II and her keen distress and then weariness with that even greater war.

Another important theme in the letters is Cather's involvement in the production side and business side of her work. Susan Rosowski, especially, has studied these matters, through the correspondence with Alfred A. Knopf and the significance of that interaction. The even longer correspondence with Ferris Greenslet, Cather's editor at Houghton Mifflin, is more various but equally enlightening, not least in what it shows us about the making of *My Ántonia* as a visual text. Another theme, this one launched even before Cather left Nebraska for Pittsburgh to begin her career in journalism, is religion. In this, as in other respects, the letters are interesting both for what they say and for what they do not say.

In some ways Cather's letters are disappointingly inexpressive. She knows Mrs. Franz Boas but never says a word about her husband's profoundly influential anthropological work, or for that matter about his brilliant student Elsie Clews Parsons, who went to the Southwest the same year Cather did, 1912, knew some of the same people Cather knew, including Mabel Dodge Luhan, and was a much talked-of presence in New York during at least three decades of Cather's residence there, but never makes an appearance in the letters. Nor does Georgia O'Keeffe, despite their conspicuously shared interests and the fact that Cather (who was in New York when the Armory Show burst on the art world but never mentions it) took a real interest in the visual arts. It is puzzling.

Another major theme in the letters is, of course, Nebraska and, intertwined with Nebraska, the idea of home itself. We see Cather telling her friends that she can never be really happy living anywhere else while she goes on living in New York and traveling to Europe. We see, too, her surprising absence from Nebraska during the last fifteen years of her life and the shifting reasons she gives for that absence. Again and again she tells Carrie Miner Sherwood, her very first friend in Red Cloud and a faithful one, that she will be there for Christmas or at some other specified time, only to write and say she can't come. Usually she cites illness, but sometimes the reasons are transparent dodges and must have struck Carrie that way, especially the time Cather writes that she has returned from summer vacation and found the apartment very dusty, so she must stay and clean house, as if she couldn't simply let it stay dusty a little longer. Finally the letters give the real reason: that she was suffering from emotional debilitation and any emotional strain, even of happiness, caused her to lapse into uncontrollable weeping. The condition was so severe that she sought medical advice. She admitted to fearing both the powerful emotions that might be aroused by a visit to Red Cloud and the possibility that people she knew there, many of whom she had come to regard as enemies, would see her weakness and make insulting conjectures about it.

In these and other ways, the letters help us understand this writer whose art is so elusive and so rich that it continues to elicit study, criticism, and devotion. A calendar of the letters is a poor substitute for the letters themselves, but it may help to fill the gap caused by their unavailability for publication, giving readers at least a sense of what they say and serving as a guide to further research.

Format of Entries and List of Abbreviations

THE FORMAT of all listings is this: name of person to whom addressed (with missing first or last names supplied where possible), date (with any surmised or supplied elements shown in brackets), sometimes the place from which written, description of the document (such as "postcard"), and the collection in which the letter was found. The paraphrased text of the letter follows, with only a minimum of bracketed amplification or information supplied. The mode of signature used by Cather is indicated, and summaries of any postscripts follow the signature.

Repositories are referred to using the following short forms.

AAAL	American Academy of Arts and Letters, New York
Allegheny	Pelletier Library, Allegheny College, Meadville, Pa.
Amherst	Amherst College, Amherst, Mass.
Arkansas	University of Arkansas, Fayetteville, Ark.
Baltimore	Enoch Pratt Free Library, Baltimore, Md.
Beinecke	Beinecke Library, Yale University, New Haven, Conn.
Berkeley	The Bancroft Library, University of California, Berkeley, Calif. (copies; originals at the Masaryk Institute in Prague)
BPL	Boston Public Library, Boston, Mass.
Bryn Mawr	Bryn Mawr College, Bryn Mawr, Pa.
Buffalo	Buffalo and Erie County Public Library, Buffalo, N.Y.
BYU	L. Tom Perry Special Collections Library, Harold B. Lee Library, Brigham Young University, Provo, Utah
Chicago	The University of Chicago Library, Chicago, Ill.
CMU	Carnegie Mellon University, Pittsburgh, Pa.
Colby	Miller Library, Colby College, Waterville, Maine
Columbia	Columbia University, New York
Cornell	Carl A. Kroch Library, Cornell University, Ithaca, N.Y.
Dartmouth	Dartmouth College, Hanover, N.H.
Duke	Duke University, Durham, N.C.
Emporia	Emporia State College, Emporia, Kans.

First Church	First Church of Christ, Scientist, Boston, Mass.
GU	Georgetown University, Washington, D.C.
Harvard	Houghton Library, Harvard University, Cambridge, Mass.
HRC	Harry Ransom Humanities Research Center, University of Texas, Austin, Tex.
HSNeb	Nebraska State Historical Society, Lincoln, Nebr.
HSW	Historical Society of Wisconsin, Madison, Wisc.
Huntington	Huntington Library, San Marino, Ca.
Indiana	Lilly Library, Indiana University, Bloomington, Ind.
Jaffrey	Jaffrey, N.H., Public Library
Kentucky	Margaret I. King Library, University of Kentucky, Lexington, Ky.
Knox	Seymour Library, Knox College, Galesburg, Ill.
LC	Library of Congress, Washington, D.C.
LincCity	Lincoln, Nebr. City Libraries, Jane Pope Geske Heritage Room of Nebraska Authors
Manhat	Manhattanville College, Purchase, N.Y.
Michigan	Bentley Historical Library, University of Michigan, Ann Arbor, Mich.
Middlebury	Middlebury College, Middlebury, Vt.
Mills	Mills College, Oakland, Calif.
Newark	Newark Public Library, Newark, New Jersey
Newberry	Newberry Library, Chicago
NHHS	New Hampshire Historical Society, Concord, N.H.
Notre Dame	University of Notre Dame, Notre Dame, Ind.
NYPL	New York Public Library
Oslo	National Library of Norway, Oslo Division
Penn	Van Pelt-Dietrich Library, University of Pennsylvania, Philadelphia, Pa.
Penn. State	Pennsylvania State University, State College, Pa.
Phil-Ex	Phillips Exeter Academy, Exeter, N.H.
PM	Pierpont Morgan Library, New York [Note: Photocopies of most of the letters to Elizabeth Shepley Sergeant located at the PM are held at Alderman Library, University of Virginia.]
Princeton	Firestone Library, Princeton University, Princeton, N.J.
Richmond	Boatwright Memorial Library, University of Richmond, Richmond, Va.

Stanford	Stanford University, Stanford, Calif.
Sweet Briar	Sweet Briar College, Sweet Briar, Va.
TWU	Texas Woman's University, Denton, Tex.
UNC	University of North Carolina, Chapel Hill, N.C.
UNH	University of New Hampshire, Durham, N.H.
UNL	Love Library, University of Nebraska-Lincoln
USC	University of Southern California, Los Angeles, Calif.
UVa	Alderman Library, University of Virginia, Charlottesville, Va.
UVt	Bailey-Howe Library, University of Vermont, Burlington, Vt.
VTech	Virginia Polytechnic Institute and State University, Blacksburg, Vt.
WCPM	Willa Cather Pioneer Memorial, Red Cloud, Nebr.
Weddle	Private Collection of Mary Weddle
Wellesley	Margaret Clapp Library, Wellesley College, Wellesley, Mass.
WRHS	Western Reserve Historical Society, Cleveland, Ohio
Yale	University Library, Yale University, New Haven, Conn.
Yongue	Private Collection of Patricia Lee Yongue

Postmark is abbreviated as pm.

A few short inscriptions have been quoted in full, and longer letters paraphrased, from published sources, referenced as follows.

Bohlke	Brent Bohlke, ed. *Willa Cather in Person: Interviews, Speeches, and Letters.* Lincoln: Univ. of Nebraska Press, 1986.
Butcher	Fannie Butcher, *Many Lives One Love.* New York: Harper & Row, 1972.
O'Brien	Sharon O'Brien, *Willa Cather: The Emerging Voice.* New York: Oxford Univ. Press, 1987.

A Calendar of the Letters of Willa Cather

1. **To Mrs. Helen Stowell,** Aug. 31, 1888, from Red Cloud, Nebr.; WCPM.
   Hopes Mrs. Stowell will soon come to town for another visit. School will start soon, and she will have to leave her dissecting laboratory and father's office, where she is in charge. Yesterday father thwarted an attempted scam. Carrie Miner gone to college. A nearby married couple not happy. Another couple as romantic as characters in a Ouida novel. Wm. Cather.

2. **To Mrs. Helen Stowell,** May 31, 1889, from Red Cloud, Nebr.; WCPM.
   Won Latin prize at end of school year. Grades of 90 in rhetoric, 95 in Latin, and 100s in physics, astronomy, and ancient history. Teacher wrote a message in report card praising her literary interests. Has fixed up a room at father's office as a library. Is reading the Latin Bible, astronomy, geology, history, Homer, Milton, Swinburne, Ouida, and George Sand. Sister Jessie in school musicale yesterday. Mother, Mrs. Wiener, Mrs. Garber, and husbands had a picnic. Longs to go to Europe. Mary Miner doing well at piano. William Cather, Jr. P.S.: As usual, Cather house is a gathering place for young people to flirt.

3. **To Mrs. Helen Stowell,** Aug. 28, 1889, from Red Cloud, Nebr., on father's letterhead; WCPM.
   Has been studying Greek and reading Bulwer-Lytton and Dickens. Brothers Roscoe and Douglass competed in the Firemen's State Tournament. Is serving as a reporter for the *Republican*, edited by Dr. McKeeby. Has been to picnics in the Garbers' grove. Local couple flirting ridiculously. Jessie, Roscoe, and Douglass singing in cantata. Is going to baseball game in Superior, Nebraska, with Mary and Hugh Miner. Is going to dance at platform in the Garbers' grove tonight. Willa Cather.

4. **To Mariel Gere,** July 16, 1891, from Red Cloud, Nebr.; WCPM.
   Why did Mariel buy the disreputable Sappho? Kit [Katherine Weston] and Mr. Myres flirting. Is feeling lonely but takes refuge in French history, George Eliot, and long horseback rides. Was at Mrs. Garber's on Sunday. Kit loaned her copy of Sappho to a church woman—how depraved! Is doing

vivisection on frogs. Mariel could set up lab at newspaper office. Willa Cather.

5. **To Mariel Gere**, Sept. 5, 1891, from Red Cloud, Nebr.; WCPM.
Thanks for invitation, but has promised to go to Louise's when she gets to Lincoln. Is packing. William Cather, Jr.

6. **To Mrs. Charles Gere**, n.d. [Oct. 1891?]; WCPM.
Enclosing first issue of the *Lasso* [an alternative literary paper at the university]. Has marked her own articles with asterisks. Willa Cather.

7. **To Louise Pound**, n.d. [probably fall 1891], from 1029 L Street, Lincoln; Duke.
Please drop by her room alone on Wednesday evening. Willa Cather.

8. **To Mariel Gere**, n.d., note imitating a centered formal invitation, transcription by Bernice Slote; UNL.
Please come to an informal supper at the rooms of William Cather, Jr., on November 26, 1891.

9. **To Louise Pound**, [May?] 1892, poem in Cather's hand; Duke.
[Titled "After-Glow." Six quatrains describing an intensely emotional experience in a theater setting. Accompanying letter referred to in subsequent letter is not in the file.]

10. **To Louise Pound**, n.d. [June 15, 1892, according to note signed by Olivia Pound], from Lincoln; Duke.
Is writing after midnight, having left her for the last time before summer vacation. Felt overcome by the sight of Louise in her new dress. After much thought, chose the Rubáiyát [of Omar Khayyám, in popular translation by Edward FitzGerald] as a going-away gift. Reason she was not very sociable was prospect of parting. Wanted to make the traditional gesture of goodbye but feared Louise might be revolted. Not fair that friendships between women are regarded as not natural. Letter may be even more foolish than one left unsent in March. William.

11. **To Louise Pound**, Aug. 6, 1892, from Red Cloud, Nebr.; Duke.
Is returning some books whose presence makes her unhappy. Louise may throw them away or do whatever she chooses with them. William.

12. **To Mariel Gere,** June 1, 1893, from Red Cloud, Nebr., on father's letterhead; WCPM.
Had to leave without saying goodbye because of grandmother's illness. Brother James has the measles. Sister Elsie prates of Willie and "Willwese" [for Louise]. Louise dislikes the name Willa but will not call her Love in front of others. Could Mariel and her sisters come to visit? Louise may do so. Mrs. Wiener's health has improved, and Mrs. Garber is her pleasant self. W. Cather.

13. **To Louise Pound,** June 29, 1893, from Red Cloud, Nebr.; Duke.
Has been feeling depressed. Has written a story about a tippling prima donna. Doubts Louise reads letters carefully, if at all. As to Louise's question about the word "bassoon," got it out of Ella Wheeler Wilcox, *Poems of Passion*. The school year was a trial. Interesting times around Red Cloud recently, with murders and suicides. Has tried a translation of "Wallenstein" [as follows; from Friedrich Schiller]. Glad Mariel and sisters are coming to visit, to cheer her up. Still disappointed Louise didn't come and will put off the Gere sisters if she might. Has been writing papers on Shakespeare. Willa Cather. P.S.: Has received her note. If she does not come, things will be different next year. It has been too one-sided anyway. Please come and show forgiveness or else it is goodbye.

14. **To Mariel, Ned [Ellen], and Frances Gere,** June 30, 1893, from Red Cloud, Nebr.; WCPM.
Please come visit July 10 and see the harvest. Won't talk about Louise all the time. Can promise her [Cather's] brothers will be fun and there will be whipped cream with dessert. Is totally in charge at father's office. Is reading Caesar with Roscoe and will include the two younger girls in her lessons if they want. William.

15. **To Mariel Gere,** Aug. 1, 1893, from Red Cloud, Nebr.; WCPM.
Has been lonely since Louise's visit. Tried to bribe James [brother] to leave them alone. Spent a few days at uncle's home near other families from Virginia. Aunt hosted a "literary" at which a truly atrocious singer did twelve songs. Climbed the windmill in the evening and enjoyed the sight of moonlight glistening on ponds and corn tassels. Had to pull off skirts to climb down when a storm approached. Roscoe away haying, but when he gets back they will go up the river to their island. Baby brother Jack has

been ill. Please greet a certain blonde [Louise?] if she sees her. Drove her about the countryside with one hand or none, but she didn't object. Still dreams about it. Don't read that part to Ned [Ellen] and Frances. Cather.

16. **To Mariel Gere,** Sept. 11, 1893, from Red Cloud, Nebr.; WCPM.
Expects to arrive in Lincoln Friday afternoon [Sept. 15]. Cather.

17. **To Mariel Gere,** June 16, 1894, from Red Cloud, Nebr.; WCPM.
Children were all dressed up for her homecoming. Is reading Virgil and botanizing. Mr. Wiener now boarding at Mrs. Garber's. Thanks for being mainstay during past winter and spring, when she [Cather] was despairing over the loss of what she had lived for. Appreciates her patience these past years while she raved over a certain girl's beauty, charm, and talent; rhapsodized over merely touching that person's hand; and suffered through the loss of love. Loving too much is a mistake. Hopes they can meet in Crete [Nebr.]. Douglass may come, too. Willa.

18. **To Grace [Broady],** Aug. 29, 1894, from Red Cloud, Nebr.; WCPM, copy also at LincCity.
Is sending clipping from the *Auburn Granger,* so scathing she may never be able to go to Brownville again. Pictures were excellent, especially those of the Episcopal church after they piled the prayer benches into the aisle. Such fun! School grind starting again soon. Will be in Lincoln about September 20. Willa Cather.

19. **To Ellen and Frances Gere,** July 30, 1895, from Red Cloud, Nebr.; WCPM.
Has returned home from Beatrice [Nebr.], where she had a good time. Country around Red Cloud very green and fresh. Hopes they will come to visit. Has enjoyed riding her bicycle ["wheel"]. Needs Mariel's address. Willa.

20. **To Mariel Gere,** Dec. 27, 1895, from Beatrice, Nebr., fragment; WCPM.
Has been visiting Katharine [Weston] and her brother. Please send trunk keys she left. Why no letters? [Breaks off.]

21. **To Mariel, Ellen, and Frances [Gere], Allie [Althea Roberts], and Maysie [Mary Ames],** Jan. 2, 1896, from "Siberia"; WCPM.
Enjoyed visiting Katharine [Weston] and her brother, who is more charming than ever. Quoted Ella Wheeler Wilcox to each other. Attended New

Year's dance with Douglass—a rustic event. Could Mariel retrieve her [Cather's] copy of Daudet's *Sapho* from Sarah Harris? Doesn't know when she will be back in Lincoln. Here in the country might as well be dead. Is indifferent to everything, even suicide. Willa.

22. **To Mariel Gere,** Mar. 12, [1896], from Red Cloud, Nebr.; WCPM.
Feels exiled. Why doesn't Mariel write? Cooks sometimes to relieve boredom. Rides bicycle when weather permits. Planned and orchestrated a wedding breakfast for her [Cather's] cousin and Hugh Miner. Looked after the children the previous week while parents went to Hastings. Enjoys playing cards and going visiting with Douglass and Roscoe, when he comes to town. Has been reading *Arabian Nights* and *Alice in Wonderland* to James. Willa.

23. **To Charles Gere,** Mar. 14, 1896, from Red Cloud, Nebr.; WCPM.
Enclosing a letter to Professor Adams. Has been to see Regent Kaley, who says decision on new instructor to replace Professor Bates rests with regents and chancellor. Please speak to them about it. Is confident she can stay in the job if she gets temporary appointment. Age and sex are against her, but would take it at lower rank and less pay than a man. Willa Cather.

24. **To Mariel Gere,** May 2, 1896, from Red Cloud, Nebr.; WCPM.
Appreciates her help getting through scrapes during years at the university. Now another one. Keeps making a fool of herself! Keeps trying on personas (the scholarly, the bohemian)! Would consider suicide but knows her stupidities spring from liking someone too well. People always watching her, waiting for her to do something unusual. Feels superficial and useless where she is. Little brother Jack is the one consolation. Has been to a dance with Douglass and actually enjoyed it. Miner girls there. Met a Miss [Anna] Gayhardt and talked all night. Can't talk like this to Katharine [Weston], of course. Hopes to get up to Lincoln soon. Professor Bates very happy in his new job. Willa.

25. **To Mariel Gere,** Friday [July 1896], from Pittsburgh; WCPM.
Has been in this grimy city only a few hours. Began feeling happier when she got east of Chicago and started seeing hills and clear streams and trees. Conductor asked if she was going home. Was met by Mr. Axtell. For now, is staying at the Axtells' gloomy house, where the only ornament is a draw-

ing of someone's grandfather. At least their library has some novels (tame ones), and Mrs. Axtell has *Harper's* magazine. Using daughter's room while she is away; room has three Bibles and an E. P. Roe novel. Willa.

26. **To Mrs. Charles Gere**, July 13, [1896], from Pittsburgh; WCPM.
Why don't the girls write? Is lonely, not during work days but at night. Has her own stenographer and entire responsibility for the first issue, even overseeing layout. Is arranging for material for September issue [of *Home Monthly*]. Wants to do article on Mrs. William Jennings Bryan and Mrs. William McKinley. Please help get personal details about Mrs. Bryan. Magazine not much as literature, but hopes to make a success of it. Is behaving. Willa.

27. **To Ned [Ellen] Gere**, Monday [c. July 27, 1896], from Pittsburgh; WCPM.
Presbyterian Axtells not so stern as first thought, but not much fun. Their social life limited to fellow church members! Summoned the Baptist minister from next door as soon as they learned the Cathers were Baptists. Has been to an organ recital at Carnegie music hall, which shares a building with library and art museum; theater next door. Between going to church and pretending to know Wild West stories, is losing all standards of truth. Magazine is dull stuff, but is practically the managing editor, with her own desk. Willa.

28. **To Mariel Gere**, Aug. 4, 1896, from Pittsburgh; WCPM.
Has received letter. How could she believe she [Cather] was really a bohemian? Only visits in Bohemia, doesn't live there. Plans to abash her enemies by showing she can succeed. Only wildness these days is racing streetcars on bicycle. Believes more firmly than ever that the one God is Art. Likes her work, though hard. Editor of *Cosmopolitan* admired "The Count of Crow's Nest," but must use it in *Home Monthly*. Willa. P.S.: Has her own stenographer.

29. **To Mariel Gere**, Aug. 10, 1896, on *Home Monthly* letterhead; WCPM.
Sorry for previous letter. Ironic to be called bohemian, considering present hardworking life. Has been on a picnic to Erie and an excursion on the river; returning by moonlight, admired the glow of the steel furnaces and was serenaded by a Princeton boy. Recited college composition on Carlyle at an afternoon tea and was at once welcomed into the social set. Axtells are kind but not warm; resemble the Pounds. Willa.

30. **To George Seibel,** Oct. 2, 1896, on *Home Monthly* letterhead; WCPM.
    Will use his article on Richard Wagner. Willa Cather.

31. **To Mariel Gere,** Oct. 4, 1896, from Pittsburgh; WCPM.
    Is Katharine [Weston?] still in Montana, or has she come home? Hasn't
    heard from her since August 1. Willa.

32. **To George Seibel,** Nov. 16, [1896], on *Home Monthly* letterhead; WCPM.
    Would Friday do this week instead of Thursday? Willa Cather.

33. **To Mrs. George Seibel,** Nov. 20, 1896, on *Home Monthly* letterhead; WCPM.
    Won't be able to come on Thursday, as it is Thanksgiving and already has
    a commitment. Will visit next week. Willa Cather.

34. **To Will Owen Jones,** Jan. 15, 1896 [actually 1897], from Pittsburgh; WCPM.
    Won't be able to send material for newspaper until next week. Has met
    W. A. Magee, managing editor of two Pittsburgh newspapers and politi-
    cal boss of the city. Had a letter of introduction from an actress friend.
    Magee's office crowded with people, but he had a kind word for each, gave
    letters to several to help them get jobs. It was hard to ask a stranger for a
    job, but he encouraged her to come back. Asked her into his private office,
    said he would take some articles and there might be a job coming open
    on the evening paper. Willa Cather.

35. **To George Seibel,** Jan. 29, 1896 [actually 1897], on *Home Monthly* letterhead;
    WCPM.
    Enclosing check for $6 for his article on the Star of Bethlehem. "A Higher
    Critic" will be in March issue, also for $6. Willa Cather.

36. **To Mrs. George Sibel [Seibel],** n.d. [Feb. 1897?]; WCPM.
    Is sending a valentine written by Ella Golden [?] in dialect. Willa S. C.

37. **To Mariel Gere,** Apr. 25, 1897, on *Home Monthly* letterhead; WCPM.
    Why hasn't she written? Is lonely since visit by Dorothy Canfield. Dorothy
    likes the young doctor who wants to marry her [Cather]. Would be a good
    match, but doesn't care for him. Magazine is trashy, but is doing her job
    as instructed. Social life going well, with none of the old problems (short
    hair, Dr. Tyndale, bohemianism) to mess her up. Willa.

38. **To Mr. and Mrs. George Seibel,** June 21, 1897, on *Home Monthly* letterhead;
    WCPM.

Enjoyed Saturday evening. Probably will not see them again before she leaves. Jack will enjoy the brownies [rubber stamp] being sent by Erna [Seibels' baby]. Willa Cather.

39. **To Mariel Gere,** June 21, 1897, from Pittsburgh; WCPM.
Would like to stop off in Lincoln before going on home. So much to tell! Willa. P.S.: Will be at the Canfields' in Columbus on the way.

40. **To Mrs. George Seibel,** July 23, 1897, from Red Cloud, Nebr.; WCPM.
Probably will not go back to Pittsburgh until September. Magazine has been sold. Will try to get a newspaper job. Afraid Mr. Seibel has not been paid. Jack enjoying the brownies [rubber] stamp. Is going hunting with older brother in August. Is sending Erna [Seibels' baby] a spoon. Willa Cather. P.S.: Has been reading Charles Lamb's *Dramatic Essays.*

41. **To Mr. and Mrs. George Seibel,** Aug. 9, 1897, from Red Cloud, Nebr.; WCPM.
Has received Erna's picture. Is impressed that Mr. Seibel has acquired a complete set of Hugo, but they will envy her "Thistle" Stevenson. Has not yet retrieved manuscripts from Axtell and Orr. Beware of Christians! But is attending church with her family. Leaving on hunting trip today. Has a cold. Willa Cather.

42. **To Will Owen Jones,** Tuesday [Sept. 7, 1897], from Red Cloud, Nebr.; WCPM.
Has just that day been hired by the *Pittsburgh Leader* at $75 a month. To report next week. Has been writing stories, but must take this opportunity. Socializes too much in Pittsburgh, but can't resist [Emma] Calvé and [Sarah] Bernhardt.

43. **To Mariel Gere,** Wednesday [pm. Sept. 8, 1897], from Red Cloud, Nebr.; WCPM.
Has been called back to Pittsburgh by the *Leader.* Will be in Lincoln Friday to Tuesday. Willa.

44. **To Mariel Gere,** Sept. 9, 1897, from Red Cloud, Nebr.; WCPM.
Please send several yards of braid trimming to match enclosed swatch. Willa.

45. **To Mariel Gere,** Sunday [Sept. 19, 1897?], from Pittsburgh; WCPM.
Felt like jumping off train when it left Lincoln. Likes her work as telegraph editor, writing headlines for all telegraph material received during

day shift. Writes theater reviews for extra pay. Will not stay away from Nebraska so long next time. Was never really a bohemian. Hopes Mariel will come visit at Christmas. Willa.

46. **To Louise Pound,** Oct. 13, 1897, from Pittsburgh; Duke.

Not fair to accuse her of keeping her address a secret. Had not expected to be daytime telegraph editor when she accepted the *Leader* job, but when it became available applied and got it, despite youth and sex. Work is like running a race, but hours are short. Hard to write distinctive headlines for a dozen suicides at a time. Has received *A Portrait of a Lady* [James]. Mr. Farrar has come to call, so must break off. Willa Cather.

47. **To Mariel Gere,** Jan. 10, 1897 [actually 1898], from Pittsburgh; WCPM.

Roscoe has been ill, but needs money worse than he needs her presence. How nice it is to have independence! Life has a lot of variety these days. Mr. Farrar broke his leg but is still capable of fun. Mrs. Canfield and Dorothy visited during Christmas. Turned the tables by introducing *them* to society. Many parties, including a dinner for Ethelbert Nevin. Has met interesting people – Anthony Hope Hopkins, F. Marion Crawford, Fridtjof Nansen. Went shopping with Nevin today, and he bought her a bunch of violets. Willa.

48. **To Mariel Gere,** March 7, 1898, from Pittsburgh; WCPM.

Has been to Homestead, Pennsylvania, to see Mary Esther Robbins, now engaged to a German professor of science. Was in New York in February; had lunch with Madame [Helena] Modjeska. Willa.

49. **To Frances Gere,** June 23, 1898, from Pittsburgh; WCPM.

Glad to hear Fritz Westermann has gone off to the [Spanish-American] war. Has been writing headlines about the blockade of Santiago Harbor. Sorry not to come to her commencement. Dorothy [Canfield] will be visiting in early July. Has been in Washington with her cousin Professor Gore, who was preparing for a polar expedition. His Norwegian wife, Lillian Thekla Brandthall, is glamorous and impressive. Looking forward to getting back to Nebraska. Willa.

50. **To Fred [Winifred Richardson, later Garber],** Aug. 15, 1898, from Red Cloud, Nebr.; WCPM.

Writing on family's behalf. Will be at home until first of October; having lots of fun. Is leaving for a ten-day hunting trip near Big Horn with Roscoe. Douglass handsomer than ever. Would like to demonstrate what good gin cocktails she can make. Hopes to produce a book of essays about the theater next winter. Plans to return to Pittsburgh because of job. Refused offer from the *New York Sun* that would have meant night work. Has had a happy year. Willa Cather.

51. **To Mrs. George Seibel,** Aug. 20, 1898, from Holdrege, Nebr.; WCPM.
Is off on a hunting trip with Roscoe through South Dakota to Laramie, Wyoming. Having a lot of fun. Douglass has been hired as a cashier on the B&M Railroad. Was having lots of parties at home. Hates having to live away. Never reads newspapers these days. Willa Cather.

52. **To Fred [Winifred Garber?],** n.d. [Sept. 1898?]; WCPM.
Wanted to ask about her future plans, but never had a chance to talk freely. Please explain to Mr. McNeny why she has been so little at his office — because wanted to spend as much time as possible with family. Willa.

53. **To Mariel Gere,** n.d. [pm. Oct. 20, 1898], from Columbus, Ohio, joint letter with Dorothy Canfield; WCPM.
Canfield: Willa has been ill with grippe but is better, her cough not so deep. Has also been sick herself. Expects to graduate in June. Cather: Took refuge with the Canfields because of prolonged grippe and overwork. Leaving tomorrow for Pittsburgh. Canfield: Family sends regards. Mrs. Flavia Canfield: Seconds Dorothy's invitation for Mariel to join them in Europe next year. Cather: Dorothy's brother has just left to take his fiancée home. Will write again from Pittsburgh.

54. **To Mariel Gere,** n.d. [Dec. 7, 1898], excerpt transcribed by Bernice Slote; UNL.
Dorothy Canfield is the "Real Thing." [allusion to story by Henry James.]

55. **To [?],** n.d. [prob. 1897 or 1898], excerpt transcribed by Bernice Slote; UNL.
Enjoyed Thanksgiving visit to Columbus. Canfields away, leaving house to Dorothy, Jim and fiancée, and herself. Many parties. Is spending much of her leisure time with Ethelbert Nevin, a lovable man. Has been reading Kipling's poetry, as she used to at the university.

56. **To William V. Alexander,** at *Ladies Home Journal,* Jan. 11, 1899; UVa.
Has interviewed Nevin for the article she is doing. He told her about his writing of *Narcissus.* Is returning photographs. Willa Sibert Cather.

57. **To Mariel Gere,** Aug. 2, 1899; WCPM.
How lucky Mariel is! [See no. 53.] Is traveling home the long way, by the Great Lakes, but will be in Lincoln the next Sunday. Is worried about her mother, who has been ill. Willa.

58. **To Dorothy Canfield,** Oct. 10, 1899, from 1176 Murray Hill, Pittsburgh; UVt.
Is studying Greek and being treated like a goddess. Hasn't seen the Nevins, but they have phoned and he has sent a copy of Shakespeare's sonnets. In Chicago had dinner with Mr. Dooley [Dunne]. He and the Peatties encouraged her to come there to work. Mrs. Peattie's new story in *Atlantic* ["The Man at the Edge of Things," reviewed by Cather Nov. 4] establishes her as a writer. Was met at the train station by Isabelle, looking beautiful. They have been walking in the hills and going to concerts. Has read all of Dorothy's letters from Paris. Had a nice visit with May Willard last night. Willa. P.S.: Will tell her about Alfred next time.

59. **To William V. Alexander,** at *Ladies Home Journal,* Nov. 25, 1899; UVa.
Will revise article on Ethelbert Nevin. Willa Sibert Cather.

60. **To William V. Alexander,** Jan. 17, 1900; UVa.
Returning proofs of her article on Nevin with inserts Alexander suggested. Willa Sibert Cather.

61. **To Mrs. George Seibel,** n.d. [Mar. 1900?], on *Pittsburgh Leader* letterhead; WCPM.
Could not visit last night because had to serve as a last-minute substitute reviewer of an orchestra concert. May go to Paris next month. Has a poem in the March *Critic.* ["Grandmither, Think Not I Forget" was in the April 1900 *Critic.*] Willa Cather.

62. **To Will Owen Jones,** Sept. 29, 1900, from Pittsburgh; UVa.
Has accepted a temporary position with the *Library.* Parents may move to Lincoln. Will be there to help around the first of November and will stay through the winter. Would be interested in some work on the *Journal.* Has to work, or will begin to resemble Herbert Bates. Has some new prose and poetry being published in the fall. Willa Cather.

63. **To George Seibel,** Monday [Nov. 1900?]; WCPM.
Wondering where Omar is. Please send it. Willa S. Cather.

64. **To Mrs. George Seibel,** Dec. 19, 1900, from Washington, D.C.; WCPM.
Unsure whether she will get back to Pittsburgh for Christmas. Here's a hug for Erna. Omar has been accepted. Willa.

65. **To George Seibel,** Jan. 4, 1901, from Washington, D.C.; WCPM.
Very pleased about the acceptance of his play based on Omar. Now he should write a comedy for Julia Marlowe, so she could stop acting melodrama. Willa Cather.

66. **To William V. Alexander,** Feb. 21, 1901, from Washington, D.C.; UVA.
Ethelbert Nevin died last Sunday. Would like to have the photographs she sent that he did not use. Willa Sibert Cather.

67. **To William V. Alexander,** Feb. 29, 1900 [actually 1901], from Washington, D.C.; UVA.
Appreciates his returning the photographs. Willa Sibert Cather.

68. **To Dorothy Canfield,** n.d. [Mar. 1901], from Pittsburgh; UVT.
Has finished first month of teaching, but may quit and go home to Red Cloud. So much effort, if one is serious about it, for so little pay. The "letters" have been rejected [projected book of open letters to actors]. Just as well; they were overwritten and not of lasting interest. Maybe some can be placed in the *Critic,* with Dorothy's help. "Jack-a-Boy" in the *Saturday Evening Post* with good illustrations. Has been reading Lemaître. McClungs have moved into new house. Would like to discuss the Pittsburgh novel. Willie. [Two poems are enclosed: "Caliban" and "The Inexorable."]

69. **To Mrs. Charles Gere,** Sunday [July 7, 1901?], from Red Cloud, Nebr.; WCPM.
Children not so changed as she expected; mother better than reports had indicated. Very hot; doubts she can work. Mrs. Garber doesn't go out any more. Hopes Mariel is better. Willa.

70. **To George Seibel,** July 17, 1901, from Red Cloud, Nebr.; WCPM.
Has been home about two weeks, feeling tired out. Mother better than in years. Hopes he will read her story in the June *New England Magazine* ["El Dorado: A Kansas Recessional"]. Another to be in August or September *Scribner's* [?]. Hoping for cooler weather. Willa.

71. To Dorothy Canfield, n.d. [pm. Dec. 13, 1901], from Pittsburgh; UVt.
Hopes she can schedule her visit earlier, as school begins January 2. English now a major subject because of her, and must uphold responsibility. But come any time. Very eager to see her. Willa.

72. To Dorothy Canfield, n.d. [May 1902]; UVt.
Examinations to begin soon. Will sail the 14th from Philadelphia, be in England until mid- to late July, depending on when she can meet them in Paris. Why has Dorothy been reading old *Hesperians?* Is not proud of her writing in them. Was not happy during that time. Hopes she likes new verses ["Lament for Marsyas" and "Hawthorn Tree"]. Willa. P.S.: Plan to go to Shropshire.

73. To Dorothy Canfield, July 6, 1902, from Ludlow, Shropshire, England; UVt.
[Begins with lines from A. E. Housman, "The Recruit."] Is looking forward to seeing her in Paris. After Liverpool went to Chester, then to Shrewsbury. [Inserts four lines from Housman's "The Welch Marches."] Saw football being played [two lines from "(Is my team ploughing?)"] and went to Shrewsbury jail [four lines from "(On moonlit heath)"]. Tracing scenes of *A Shropshire Lad.* Has found out Housman's London address from his publisher. Ludlow Castle delightful, with its associations with both Housman and Sir Philip Sidney. [Inserts three stanzas of her own poem "Poppies on Ludlow Castle."] Willie.

74. To George Seibel, July 21, 1902, from Scotland; WCPM.
Having a delightful trip. Willa Cather.

75. To Dorothy Canfield, Thursday [pm. Aug. 9, 1902], from American Express office in Paris, postcard; UVt.
Has taken pictures to be developed, shopped with Miss [Evelyn] Osborne for underclothes, and overeaten on Mme Sibut's excellent fish. Please scold the laundress who failed to return a set of underwear. Willa.

76. To Mariel Gere, Aug. 28, [1902], from Paris; WCPM.
Has been there four weeks; meant to write sooner. She and Isabelle like the Sibuts, at whose pension they are staying. Disagree as to whether they like Mlle Céline [Sibut]. Dorothy spent three weeks with them in London and accompanied them to Paris but now has gone back to Scotland. Went to Barbizon with a school friend of Dorothy's. Will soon leave for a walk-

ing tour of Provence and the Mediterranean coast. Enjoyed a walking tour to the Oise Valley. Willa.

77. **To Dorothy Canfield,** Sept. 24, 1902, from Liverpool; UVt.
Enjoyed their day at Oxford. Jealousy on the part of the two people in Paris must have been what caused the grief. She seemed strange there as well. Willie.

78. **To George Seibel,** n.d. [Dec. 1902?]; WCPM.
Tell Mrs. Seibel will be there Monday to spend the night. Hopes they can start decorating the tree then, as per their custom. Will help the McClungs trim a tree on Wednesday. Willa Cather.

79. **To Will Owen Jones,** Jan. 2, [1903?], from 1180 Murray Hill, Pittsburgh; UVa.
Please return letters from France. Will have a volume of poems published in the spring. Would like to borrow a Lincoln directory to get addresses to send advertising circulars. Willa S. Cather.

80. **To Dorothy Canfield,** Saturday [pm. Mar. 29, 1903], from Pittsburgh; UVt.
Sorry to cancel visit, but must keep at work on stories, then going to New York to try to arrange book publication. Still regrets misunderstanding in the fall. Some of the stories good, but "Paul's Case" shows haste and "Pilgrim Joy" has to be discarded and replaced. Cycle will be two painter stories, one actor, one sculptor, one musician, one musical study, one writer, and one case of an artistic temperament without talent, and Fulvia. Title to be *The Troll Garden*, with epigraph from Charles Kingsley to explain. So wishes to come see her. Please apologize to parents. Wants her and Mrs. Canfield to read Phaedra story. Willie. P.S.: Mrs. McClung has been ill. Has scarcely had an evening to herself to work.

81. **To George Seibel,** Apr. 28, [1903]; WCPM.
Appreciates his review of the poems. Looking forward to his visit on Thursday. Willa S. Cather.

82. **To George Seibel,** Tuesday [Apr. 30, 1903?]; WCPM.
Appreciates his generous review. Willa S. C.

83. **To George Seibel,** n.d. [c. May 1, 1903?]; WCPM.
Has been called to New York. Please advise what journals might review the book of poems. Hopes *McClure's* bodes well. W. S. C.

84. **To Will Owen Jones,** May 7, 1903, from 1180 Murray Hill, Pittsburgh; UVa.
Thanks for launching her with S. S. McClure. Had a telegram from him
and has been to New York to see him. Feeling elated, as if her life is now
more valuable than before. McClure to run her stories in the magazine,
then publish as a book. Will place for her any he does not use. At the
McClure house met wife of Robert Louis Stevenson, who had read the
stories. Greatly appreciates his help. Other plans afoot. Willa S. Cather. P.S.:
Doesn't seem to be able to reach Sarah Harris.

85. **To Dorothy Canfield,** n.d. [c. May 15-20, 1903]; UVt.
As a result of Dorothy's having written to her [Cather's] mother, has had
the first letter from her that she could bear to read in two years. They may
yet make peace. Isabelle and Edith [McClung] away on a fishing trip to
West Virginia. Sarah Harris has written denouncing the "animalism" of
April Twilights – must be crazy. Is tired from parties and work. Is Mrs. Can-
field painting? Has she read "The Better Sort" [volume of short stories by
Henry James, pub. 1903]? Very complex and obscure. Willie.

86. **To Dr. James Hulme Canfield,** May 21, 1903, from Pittsburgh; UVt.
Appreciates his bringing her book to people's attention. Enjoyed visiting
with Mrs. Canfield and Dorothy in New York. Willa S. Cather.

87. **To Mrs. Charles Gere,** June 10, 1903, from 1180 Murray Hill, Pittsburgh;
WCPM.
Is sending a picture, the best she ever had made. Wishing to see everyone
at home. Willa.

88. **To Viola Roseboro',** June 14, [1903], from 1180 Murray Hill, Pittsburgh; Harvard. Typed note by Witter Bynner indicates that Roseboro' gave him the
letters.
Yes, certainly knows *A Shropshire Lad.* Don't her own poems show it? Traced
Housman in Shropshire, where he seems unknown. Visited him in a
boardinghouse in a dreary London suburb. He looked gaunt, seemed bit-
ter, but is the only English poet now active whose work will endure.
Though an instructor in Latin, he writes strictly from the level of a country boy. Willa S. Cather.

89. **To Viola Roseboro',** n.d., from 1180 Murray Hill Avenue, Pittsburgh in-
complete; bears a headnote by Witter Bynner; Harvard.

Hard to believe he [Housman] refused the money. What nobility! Still remembers, from when she paid that call along with two American friends, the holes in his shoes and in the carpet, couch with broken springs, his uneasiness. Manner stern and patrician. They all cried on the way back.

90. **To Dorothy Canfield,** July 13, 1903, from Cheyenne, Wyo.; UVt.
She and Douglass have been enjoying their visit, but can feel the difference the years make. Has been made head of the English department at Allegheny High School at $1400 a year. Had to take a competitive exam. Hasn't been to Red Cloud yet. Willie.

91. **To Dorothy Canfield,** Nov. 6, 1903, from Pittsburgh; UVt.
Why didn't she tell her Dr. Canfield was in town? Has been shut in with a cold. Enjoys teaching but would prefer lower-class students who were used to working. When will Dorothy's children's story be published? Is her brother's new baby a boy or a girl? Edith [Isabelle's sister] is having coming-out parties. Willie.

92. **To Dorothy Canfield,** Friday [Nov. 27, 1903]; UVt.
Still sorry not to have seen her father. Has seen Minnie Maddern Fiske in *Hedda Gabler* [Ibsen], with Isabelle. Has been to many concerts. Can't be up past ten on a school night or won't be any good in the classroom. Many parties for Edith [McClung]. Has written about 40,000 words of a new manuscript; not ready to talk about it yet. Had a happy Thanksgiving dinner last night; Judge McClung away. Willie.

93. **To Dorothy Canfield,** Thursday [Feb. 1904?]; UVt.
Is something wrong? Is she ill? Isabelle had diphtheria while in Boston in January and is still weak. Please write. Hopes to have a finished manuscript to ask her to read soon. Willie.

94. **To Dorothy Canfield,** n.d. [Mar. 1904]; UVt.
Sorry they have had a misunderstanding. Sorry to be so often cross and ungracious; behaved badly two years ago in Europe. Felt inferior, not understanding French. Teaching wears on her disposition. Has not written a line of poetry in months. Others say she has become unfeeling. Has been to a doctor to see if there is a physical cause. Is paying now for not tearing away from happiness in Pittsburgh four years ago. Appreciates comments on "A Wagner Matinee" [*Everybody's Magazine*, Feb. 1904]. Spirits low; escapes by

working. Please wait until these low spirits are gone before eloping with a tenor, if that's what she wants! Sorry to have written such a self-revealing letter all about feelings, but is trying to be honest. Willie. P.S.: Can't talk about the McClung household, of course, but it is wearing, too.

95. **To Will Owen Jones,** Mar. 6, 1904, from Pittsburgh; UVa.
Comments about "A Wagner Matinee" in his column were biting. Family is offended by the story, too. Didn't mean to disparage Nebraska. Story reflects past times and a particular mood. *The Troll Garden* won't be out until fall. Willa S. Cather.

96. **To Dorothy Canfield,** n.d. [Mar. 1904?]; UVt.
Generous of her to say she understands that incoherent letter. Likes the first part of Dorothy's boy story better than the last, where it spells things out too much. "A Wagner Matinee" has stirred up a hornet's nest, led by Will Jones. Will write another and make them even madder. Willie.

97. **To Dorothy Canfield,** Saturday [Mar. or Apr. 1904]; UVt.
Thanks for sharing what Miss Roseboro' said about the stories. Roseboro's own are a sentimental muddle. Best wishes for Dorothy's doctoral exam in May. Hopes to get to Vermont this summer. Will mainly be in New York near or with Edith Lewis. Hopes to finish novel there. Might take an English course at Columbia, if there is one in the summer. Isabelle still droopy from bad throat. Parents [Cather's] have just moved into a new, roomier house and want her to come help select furnishings, but she needs to finish the novel for McClure. Willie.

98. **To Dorothy Canfield,** Sunday [May 1904]; UVt.
Sorry not to have been more sensitive about the doctoral exam, but doesn't understand Ph.D.s. Now realizes it was an ordeal. Expects to be in New York about June 28 and hopes she can come down. Hasn't decided whether the novel is worth rewriting. Hopes to go abroad with Isabelle again next year. May yet go to Red Cloud this summer. Has had two nice visits with the Willards. Exams to begin soon at school, so will be busy. Willie.

99. **To Mariel Gere,** Oct. 7, 1904, from 1180 Murray Hill, Pittsburgh; WCPM.
Has just heard about Mr. Gere's death. Can hardly imagine them without him. Shares their bereavement. Willa.

100. **To Dorothy Canfield,** Sunday [Dec. 18, 1904]; UVt.

Has received her telegram about "The Profile." Character resembles Miss Osborne only in that she has a scar, not uncommon. Miss Osborne shouldn't take it as a reference to herself. Sorry Dorothy is upset. Willa.

101. **To Dorothy Canfield,** n.d. [c. Jan. 5, 1905]; UVt.

Can't withdraw the story without canceling the entire volume, which is already in type. Doubts Miss Osborne will ever see it, let alone take it to heart. Does not agree it is a portrait of her. Isabelle, who has a strong moral sense, does not see anything wrong. This has spoiled the pleasure in her first book of fiction. Wouldn't ask such a thing of anyone. Is very hurt by Dorothy's attitude. Willa.

102. **To Otto Lichtenberg,** Feb. 2, [1905]; UVa.

Appreciates his writing about her story. A volume is being published. (Miss) Willa Sibert Cather.

103. **To Viola Roseboro',** n.d. [Feb. 1905?], transcription by Bernice Slote; WCPM.

Thanks for the photo of herself. Is getting over the feeling of being disgraced with the firm. Can't understand why some people think she has done something terrible. Hopes to go to New York last week of March. Has been feeling very low. Willa Sibert Cather.

104. **To Kate McPhelim Cleary** [of Hubbell, Nebr.], Feb. 13, 1905, from Pittsburgh; WCPM.

Appreciates her letter to McClure about story in January issue ["The Sculptor's Funeral"]. Glad someone besides herself knows it is accurate, not exaggerated. A volume of stories to be out soon. Willa Sibert Cather. [not signed]

105. **To Witter Bynner,** June 7, 1905; Harvard.

Writes about life in the West out of personal experience. Realizes stories are rather grim. Some details in "A Wagner Matinee" remembered from Cather ranch. Recalls how she and her brothers loved the few trees that grew along a nearby creek, the bleakness of the first Christmas, the drought during early college years, when there were suicides among their neighbors. Things are better there now. Willa Sibert Cather.

106. **To Flavia [Mrs. James Hulme] Canfield,** n.d. [c. June 15, 1905?], from 1180 Murray Hill, Pittsburgh; UVt.

Understands why she did not come with Dorothy last week. Not surprising she would feel angry toward anyone who hurt Dorothy. Willa Cather.

107. **To Mariel Gere,** n.d. [Sept. 30, 1905?]; WCPM.
Appreciated her long letter. Missed Mr. Gere during her visit to Lincoln. Spent a week in Cheyenne with Douglass and a week camping in the Black Hills with Roscoe, then four weeks in Red Cloud helping her father around the new house. Jessie [sister] expecting a baby. Mrs. Garber still charming but sad from missing Mr. Garber, though he was a care. Wishes she could live in the West. Getting settled into school work again. Love to Mrs. Gere and to Ellen and Frances, and greetings to the Joneses and others. Willa.

108. **To Mariel Gere,** n.d. [Jan. 1, 1906?]; WCPM.
Thanks for the picture. Isabelle sends greetings. Love to her mother, Frances, and Ellen. Willa.

109. **To unidentified recipient** [prob. Witter Bynner; first part of letter missing], n.d. [c. Jan. 15, 1906]; Harvard.
Agrees the story is rather chilly and impersonal, but it doesn't warrant amplification. Looks forward to visit so they can talk. Will try again on *The Golden Bowl* [James, 1904]. Didn't manage to penetrate it last year. Wonders what new Kipling story is about. Willa Sibert Cather.

110. **To Witter Bynner,** Feb. 24, [1906?]; Harvard.
Has revised the story but done nothing with the novel. Appreciates his calling her book to [Henry?] James's attention; very pleased with James's letter. Would be disappointed if he and a couple of others did not think the way he says. Feels nervous at the thought of his considering her writing further. Willa Sibert Cather.

111. **To Mrs. Elizabeth Moorhead Vermorcken,** Mar. 7, [1906], from 1180 Murray Hill Avenue, Pittsburgh; PM.
Read her new story along with several friends, and all enjoyed it. The central character is quite compelling. Congratulations. Willa Sibert Cather.

112. **To Students of Allegheny High School, Pittsburgh,** June 6, 1906; quoted in Bohlke.
Will not return to the school in the fall, though expected to when she told them goodbye. Is going to New York to engage in work she enjoys even more than teaching. Wishes them well in their senior year. Willa Cather.

113. **To H. G. Dwight,** Saturday [June 23, 1906], on *McClure's* letterhead; Amherst.
Sorry to have missed him. Felt ill and left early. Can they have an appointment July 2 or 3? Willa S. Cather.

114. **To H. G. Dwight,** July 3, 1906, on *McClure's* letterhead; Amherst.
Will publish "The Valley of the Mills" as is if he can't revise it. Would like to see "Mortmain" again if he can sharpen its point. S. S. McClure, per W. S. C.

115. **To H. G. Dwight,** July 20, 1906; Amherst.
Watching for "The Valley of the Mills" from Mr. Reynolds. Will be glad to give "Mortmain" another reading. Regrets he is taking an ironic tone. Why read and talk at all if one can't be candid? Willa Sibert Cather.

116. **To H. G. Dwight,** Oct. 9, 1906, on *McClure's* letterhead; Amherst.
Liked "The Valley of the Mills" enough to buy it, but believes his work can be stronger. Would like to talk with him about some descriptive articles on the Mediterranean. Going to Pittsburgh on Friday [Oct. 12] to stay until November 1. Will be living at no. 60 South Washington Square upon return. Please drop by the office. Willa Sibert Cather

117. **To H. G. Dwight,** Friday [Nov. 2, 1906?], on *McClure's* letterhead; Amherst.
Envies his getting away and wishes him luck. He seems to think she wants to exploit his work as Witter Bynner might, but as a fellow writer, is simply interested and will give his stories fair consideration. Hopes he brings back literary spoils. Willa Sibert Cather.

118. **To H. G. Dwight,** Nov. 21, 1906, on *McClure's* letterhead; Amherst.
S. S. McClure has reread "The Valley of the Mills" and hopes to see more work from him. Please send his address so she won't have to write through Reynolds. Willa Sibert Cather.

119. **To Mrs. S. S. McClure,** n.d. [Dec. 1906?]; Indiana.
Appreciates her comforting words. Very worried about father, but news today seems encouraging. Willa Cather.

120. **To Charles F. Cather,** n.d. [Dec. 17, 1906?], on *McClure's* letterhead; UVa.
Sorry not to get home for Christmas, especially when he is ill, but can't desert McClure in this difficulty. Must get the March article out [on Mary

Baker Eddy]. Did not work on the January one, began with February. Hopes to be home by New Year's. Willie.

121. **To William L. Graves** [of Columbus, Ohio], Dec. 17, 1906, on *McClure's* letter-head; UVa.
Will take his poem "The Road at Night." He may recall they met some time ago and shared an admiration for Miss Guiney. Hopes he liked Guiney's "Wood-Doves" in the October issue. Willa Sibert Cather. Enclosed: $20 check.

122. **To Carrie Miner,** Dec. 22, [1906?]; WCPM.
People seem to prefer lying to telling the truth. Knew Oley Iverson in Bladen as a hired boy for uncle George Cather. He was married then. Willie.

123. **To Mrs. Charles Miner,** n.d. [Dec. 22, 1906?], Christmas card; WCPM.
Sends love and greetings. Willie.

124. **To Ida Tarbell,** Friday [prob. Jan. 4 or 11, 1907], from New York; Allegheny.
Has read the tariff articles while at home with a cold and was surprised to find them interesting. Truly important magazine writing. Willa Cather. [Tarbell's tariff articles appeared in *American Magazine* from 1906-1911; in book form 1911.]

125. **To H. G. Dwight,** Jan. 12, [1907?], from 60 Washington Square, New York; Amherst.
Envies his being in Italy. Is working on the material about Eddy, after three men failed with it. It drives out every trace of an imaginative idea. Why doesn't he like [Pierre] Loti – afraid of real imagination? He covers up his own with slang and imitations of Kipling. Or maybe he fears being sentimental. McClure has paid $500 for illustrations for "The Valley of the Mills." Was in Pittsburgh a couple of months ago and saw the Willards. Only music saves her in New York. Please ask Mr. Reynolds to send her his work personally. Willa S. Cather.

126. **To S. S. McClure,** Thursday [Jan. 17, 1907?], from Boston; Indiana.
Glad to have his letter along saying he has confidence in her. Has started to work. Needs to have the April article to the printer in two weeks. Mr. McKenzie very helpful and a born editor. Willa S. Cather.

127. **To S. S. McClure,** Monday [prob. early 1907]; Indiana.
Has held up illustrations for the first article. In a rush to get out *Harper's Weekly* with shortage of staff. Won't lose much time, as still has some Boston material. W. S. C.

128. **To Mr. Gilder** [*Century Magazine*], June 5, [1907]; NYPL.
Story enclosed ["The Willing Muse," *Century* August 1907], with all grammatical errors found (she hopes) and corrected. Willa Sibert Cather.

129. **To the Hon. William E. Chandler,** July 16, 1907, from Boston; NHHS.
Will need to treat the current litigation in the last chapter of the *History of Christian Science*. Wants to approach it by way of Eddy's relationship with her son, George Glover. Is going to Nebraska in late July, would like to see Mr. Glover while in the West. He could edit the article to safeguard Glover's interests in the suit. Would he like to borrow her copy of the 1881 edition of *Science and Health*? Willa Sibert Cather.

130. **To Hon. William E. Chandler,** Aug. 1, 1907, from Boston; NHHS.
Understands he cannot give permission to interview the Glovers. Willa Sibert Cather.

131. **To Hon. William E. Chandler,** Oct. 17, 1907, from Boston; NHHS.
Found his September 13 letter when she returned. Hopes to see him about the Eddy matter. Willa Sibert Cather.

132. **To Hon. William E. Chandler,** Nov. 29, 1907, from Pittsburgh; NHHS.
Is it true he has a diary kept by Dr. E. J. Foster that quotes many of Mrs. Eddy's sayings? May she have access to it? Would quote only with his approval. Willa Sibert Cather.

133. **To Witter Bynner,** Feb. 4, [1908?], from Boston; Harvard.
Thanks for his book of poems. Received one by Ford Madox Hueffer [Ford] the same day. Particularly likes the "Harvard Ode" and "The Fruits of the Earth." Willa Sibert Cather.

134. **To Mrs. [Augustus] Saint-Gaudens,** Tuesday [pm. Feb. 4, 1908], from Boston; Dartmouth.
Would be happy to meet her if she is in Boston. Believes a better title for her book of poems "Songs of Pain and Renunciation." Willa Sibert Cather.

135. **To Annie Adams Fields,** Wednesday [early 1908?], from The Parker House, Boston; Huntington.

Looks forward to seeing her this afternoon. Sorry to have telephoned so persistently. Has long wanted to know her and Miss Jewett. Willa Sibert Cather.

136. **To Annie Fields,** Wednesday night [April 1908?]; Huntington.

Enjoyed seeing Mrs. Gardener's house last week, with daffodils in bloom. Has returned library books and asked them to keep her card in case she comes back. Came to Boston in pursuit of Mrs. Eddy and likes the city better and better. In New York, feels under siege. Wishes Mr. McClure had come and introduced her last year, but is glad they finally met. Her friendship and Jewett's make the year's work worthwhile. Willa Sibert Cather.

137. **To Mrs. Alice E. D. Goudy,** May 3, [1908], from Naples, Italy; WCPM.

Has just returned from a week in the Apennines. Spent two days in Pompeii and is enjoying the Pompeiian collection at the Naples Museum, also the beautiful Bay of Naples. The classical world seems close at hand. Has regained enough Latin to read Tacitus and Suetonius. Remembers seeing a picture of the bust of Caesar in a textbook when Mr. Goudy was her teacher, and now has seen it at the museum. Farmers working their fields just as in Virgil's *Georgics.* Goes on to Rome next week. Willa.

138. **To Sarah Orne Jewett,** May 10, 1908, from Ravello, Italy; Harvard.

What a beautiful place! Camellias and roses in bloom all around. Room overlooks the Gulf of Salerno, as blue as the water in a [Pierre] Puvis de Chavanne painting. Yesterday a festival celebrating the arrival of the skull of St. Andrew in Amalfi seven hundred years ago, but enjoyment interrupted by the arrival of some people she used to know in Nebraska. [Alice] Meynell's essays about Italy in the book Jewett gave her are very fine, but A. E. Housman writes with equal truthfulness. The "White Heron" and the Dunnet ladies [references to copies of books by Jewett] are always with her. Willa Cather.

139. **To Elizabeth Moorhead Vermorcken,** Sept. 25, [1908]; PM.

Very sorry to hear of the death of her father. Another sorrow after such a hard two years. Must be very hard for her mother. Hopes to see her in Pittsburgh some time this fall. Sends condolences. Willa Cather.

140. To Sarah Orne Jewett, Oct. 24, [1908], from 82 Washington Place, New York; Harvard.

Is pleased that she and Mrs. Fields liked the first part of Mrs. Ward's story; will send the outline of the rest. Mrs. Fields the only person left who evokes the dignity of the New England past. Has been enjoying Fields's poems. She and Edith Lewis liking their apartment. Get their own dinner three evenings a week and go to the Brevoort [Hotel] the other nights. Fears Jewett won't like her story in the December issue ["On the Gulls' Road"]. Willa.

141. To Ferris Greenslet, Oct. 1908, from 82 Washington Place, New York, transcription by E. K. Brown; Beineke.

Enjoyed reading the Aldrich book [?] on the train. Willa S – C – (William).

142. To Guglielmo Ferrero, Nov. 28, 1908, on *McClure's* letterhead; Columbia.

Would he write three articles, two on Julius Caesar and one on Antony and Cleopatra, with an option for two more after the first is published? $300 per article. Willa Sibert Cather.

143. To Guglielmo Ferrero, Nov. 30, [1908]; Columbia.

Understands his thinking the three articles too general. Would he do the two on Julius Caesar for $500 each? Willa Sibert Cather.

144. To Jessie Cather Auld, Dec. 17, 1908, on *McClure's* letterhead; TWU.

Is sending a present for Peter Rabbit. Don't open until Christmas! Will send books for Mary Virginia as soon as she and Miss Lewis (with whom she is partners in housekeeping) have read them. Found these nice children's books from England in a local book shop. Willie.

145. To Sarah Orne Jewett, Dec. 19, [1908], from New York; Harvard.

Has read her letter many times. These past few years has felt confused, tired, drained of energy by the job and has felt cut off from her self. Mr. McClure wants her to become another Ida Tarbell; he doesn't believe she will ever be much of a writer of fiction. Feels as much a beginner in her writing as she ever did, as if she hadn't learned at all. Doesn't even have the feeling of learning about other things, as when she was a teacher. Hectic pace is giving her a bad temperament. Glad to have her salary; needs to help out the family now and then; but could quit now and have enough in the bank to live on for three or four years. Has reread "Martha's Lady," such a beautiful story. Will hope to get up to Boston after Christmas. Willa.

146. **To Guglielmo Ferrero,** Dec. 28, 1908, on *McClure's* letterhead; Columbia. Would like to discuss illustrations for the articles on Julius Caesar. Willa Sibert Cather.

147. **To Guglielmo Ferrero,** Jan. 11, 1909; Columbia. Unable to send new copies of the Standard Oil book [by Ida Tarbell], as the book business has been sold, but Mr. McClure is sending copies from his personal library. Willa Sibert Cather.

148. **To Guglielmo Ferrero,** Jan. 14, 1909, on *McClure's* letterhead; Columbia. Would like to publish some of the lectures he has delivered in the U.S. Willa Sibert Cather.

149. **To Guglielmo Ferrero,** Jan. 15, 1909, on *McClure's* letterhead; Columbia. Would he arrange with *Putnam's* to let them see the rest of his lectures, after the two *Putnam's* are taking? Willa Sibert Cather.

150. **To Guglielmo Ferrero,** Jan. 19, 1909, on *McClure's* letterhead; Columbia. Obtained the pictures they spoke of. Greetings to Mrs. Ferrero. Willa Sibert Cather.

151. **To Zoë Akins,** Jan. 27, 1909, on *McClure's* letterhead; Huntington. Great to hear from her. Enjoyed the story about the droll Negroes – a people rich in imagination. Can't use the poems. Wonders when Zoë will settle down to serious work for theater. Her own interest in theater has waned. Best wishes in her work, whatever it is. Willa Sibert Cather.

152. **To Zoë Akins,** n.d. [early 1909?], from 82 Washington Place, New York; Huntington. Sorry for the tactless letter. Still not used to having to reject things. Glad she likes *April Twilights*. Thinks "The Palatine," published in *McClure's* the previous summer, is better than poems in the book. Suggests Zoë study Miss Guiney's work as a model of richness combined with restraint. Willa Sibert Cather.

153. **To Perceval Gibbon [in Mortlake, England],** Feb. 2, 1909, on *McClure's* letterhead; UVa.

Have not seen any of his work for some time. Please ask Mr. Pinker [his agent?] to send some. Can promise a quick reading. Willa Sibert Cather.

154. **To A. F. Jaccaci,** Feb. 2, 1909, on *McClure's* letterhead; AAAL.
Is trying to find out for Mr. McClure who wrote the article on [James] Whistler published in the September, 1896, *McClure's*. Hopes he will have that information. Willa Cather.

155. **To James B. Pinker [in London],** Feb. 20, 1909, on *McClure's* letterhead; UVa.
Mr. Gibbon is the best paid of any of their story writers. Please state expectation when sending stories. Sorry Mr. McClure sometimes misplaces manuscripts or is slow to return them, but if sent to her personally they will get prompt attention. Willa Sibert Cather.

156. **To Guglielmo Ferrero,** Apr. 4, 1909, on *McClure's* letterhead; Columbia.
Will need the two articles in translation by July 1 and July 15. [Ida] Tarbell is glad to hear of his interest in the Standard Oil book. Mr. McClure would join her in sending greetings, but is in Paris. Willa Sibert Cather.

157. **To Flavia [Mrs. James Hulme] Canfield,** Apr. 15, 1909, from 82 Washington Place, New York; UVt.
Very sorry to hear about Mr. Canfield's death. Was delayed in learning of it because in the hospital with mastoiditis. Willa Sibert Cather.

158. **To Dorothy Canfield Fisher,** Apr. 15, 1909, from New York; UVt.
So very sorry about her father. Sorry Dorothy was away during his illness, but had been a constant happiness to him. Willa Cather.

159. **To E. J. Overing, Jr. [President of the Red Cloud Board of Education],** Apr. 30, 1909 [letter read at 1909 commencement exercises and published in the *Red Cloud Chief* May 27, 1909]; WCPM, also Bohlke.
Had hoped to be there for commencement, but is leaving for London on business. Has kept up with Red Cloud schools through brothers and sisters. Remembers with love Mr. and Mrs. A. K. Goudy and Mr. and Mrs. O. C. Case. Mrs. Case, then Miss King, was principal when she first entered the school. Remembers her first teacher and some of her fellow pupils. Always tried to please Miss King, who helped and advised her all through high school—even tried to teach her algebra, an impossibility. Hard to believe it has been nineteen years since she graduated. Best wishes to the new

graduates. They should try to live up to their teachers' goals for them. Willa Cather.

160. **To Mrs. S. S. McClure,** May 18, 1909, from Thackeray Hotel, London; WCPM.
Thanks for her letter. Will start back after George Meredith's funeral. Willa Cather.

161. **To Mrs. Ford Madox Hueffer,** May 20, 1909, from Thackeray Hotel, London; Cornell.
Apologizes for having caused Mrs. Hueffer the irritation of a complaint from Joseph Conrad about Cather's attempt to see him. Believed Mr. Hueffer [pseud. Ford Madox Ford] had assured her of welcome. Had hoped to obtain something for publication in *McClure's*. Is leaving for Paris Saturday [the 22nd] but hopes to see her when she returns. Willa Sibert Cather.

162. **To Annie Adams Fields,** June 27, 1909, from London; Harvard.
Learned of their terrible loss [of Sarah Orne Jewett] yesterday. Cannot accept that Jewett is not still there. Knows how fearful Jewett had been of losing Fields; had loved her so dearly for so long. Sailing next week. Will let her know as soon as she lands in New York. Shares her grief. Willa.

163. **To Annie Adams Fields,** July 13, [1909], from aboard the *Kaiser Wilhelm der Grosse*; Harvard.
Her letter was a comfort, especially the account of how peaceful Jewett was. Keeps dreaming they are both still there together. Receipt of this letter will show she has landed. Willa.

164. **To Mary Virginia Auld,** n.d. [pm. Nov. 5, 1909], postcard; WCPM.
A picture of New England children with pumpkins. Isabelle helping her fix up her house [?]. Aunt Willie.

165. **To Orson Lowell,** Nov. 15, 1909, on *McClure's* letterhead; UVa.
Keeps hoping they can get some of his work into the magazine. Hopes the rumor that he does not want to work for *McClure's* is false. Has some stories on hand they would like to turn over to him [for illustration?]. Willa Sibert Cather.

166. **To Orson Lowell,** Nov. 18, 1909, on *McClure's* letterhead; UVa.
Glad to receive his reassuring letter. Willa Sibert Cather.

167. **To Flavia [Mrs. James Hulme] Canfield,** Jan. 4, 1910, from 82 Washington Place, New York; UVt.

Glad to receive her invitation and hopes she will stop by the office when in town. Willa Cather.

168. **To Mrs. George P. Cather [Aunt Franc],** Jan. 5, 1910, from 82 Washington Place, New York; Weddle.

Wishing her a belated happy New Year. Has been managing the magazine by herself since returning to New York in the fall. Has been unwell, so has had not only little time but little energy. Isabelle McClung with her from early November through Christmas; helped a great deal with shopping and the training of a new maid, so the apartment is now very pleasant. Always feels homesick at Christmas; seems everyone in New York suffers from homesickness then. Last year went to the children's service at Trinity Church on Christmas Eve and people were crying all around her. Probably wishing to be back at some small town. Is glad Jack and Elsie put out holly and evergreens in the cemetery for her at Christmas. Both such nice children. Elsie will be nicer when she gets older and not so sure of herself. Enjoys thinking of Bessie [Elizabeth Seymour] and Auntie [Sarah Andrews, sister of Mary Virginia Cather] being together and less burdened by care. Used to find it so hard not being able to do anything for them. Mother seems in better spirits lately. Is anticipating a Grand Jury investigation as a result of *McClure's* articles on Tammany and prostitution. Expects to go to London again in a few months but hopes to get back to Nebraska in the summer. Hopes to have as nice a visit as this past summer, when Mother did not seem to begrudge her visiting in the country. Please let her known if Bess and Auntie need anything. Sends love and best wishes. Willie.

169. **To Elizabeth Shepley Sergeant,** Jan. 26, 1910, on *McClure's* letterhead [bears notes taken by Sergeant regarding McClure's preferences for the magazine]; PM.

Received her letter this morning. Will be in the office tomorrow and expects to see her about nine. Willa Sibert Cather.

170. **To Prof. Hugo Munsterberg,** Mar. 4, 1910, on *McClure's* letterhead; BPL.

Mr. McClure hopes he will do some articles on Germany while there. Especially interested in something on German railroads. Hopes to see him in Boston in two weeks. Willa Sibert Cather.

171. **To Amy Lowell,** Mar. 8, 1910, on *McClure's* letterhead; Harvard.
Can't use article on Harden [?]. Mr. McClure has commissioned one from William Archer. Appreciates her thinking of them. Willa Sibert Cather.

172. **To Prof. Hugo Munsterberg,** Mar. 14, 1910, on *McClure's* letterhead; BPL.
Mr. McClure will be in the office March 25 to April 5. Please stop by if in town. Will be in Boston April 6–14 and could see him then. Glad for him to write whatever he wishes about Germany. Perhaps the schools? Willa Sibert Cather.

173. **To Elizabeth Shepley Sergeant,** Apr. 5, 1910, on *McClure's* letterhead; PM.
Her article only needs a little cutting. Will mark cuts and other suggested changes and send by Monday. Check for $200 in a few days. No need to postpone sailing. Willa Sibert Cather.

174. **To Prof. Hugo Munsterberg,** Apr. 27, 1910, on *McClure's* letterhead; BPL.
Can offer a four article series, one dealing with German education, one on municipal government, and two others on whatever he thinks important about German civilization. Series title might be "When I Came Home." Will run in four consecutive numbers. All right to do something on German theater for a literary magazine such as *Atlantic*. Willa Sibert Cather.

175. **To Prof. Hugo Munsterberg,** May 6, 1910, on *McClure's* letterhead; BPL.
Agrees to $2000 for series of four or five articles, no less than twenty thousand words total. Would appreciate his providing appropriate illustrations. Please send photograph of himself other than the one they have already used, plus biographical sketch. Want to give the series good advance promotion. Willa Sibert Cather.

176. **To Prof. Hugo Munsterberg,** May 13, 1910, on *McClure's* letterhead; BPL.
Sorry he found title frivolous, but would like to strike a personal note if possible. Doesn't believe the American Institute in Berlin would have wide enough interest. Willa Sibert Cather.

177. **To George Seibel,** May 17, 1910, on *McClure's* letterhead; WCPM.
Sorry she used such a foolish title. Hasn't seen Francis Hill lately. Will pay

for however much ginger ale he can drink, though not a popular choice in New York. Willa Sibert Cather.

178. To Witter Bynner, May 19, 1910, on *McClure's* letterhead; Harvard.
Is glad to send the verses he asked for. Gives permission to reprint. Willa Sibert Cather.

179. To Elizabeth Shepley Sergeant, May 31, 1910, on *McClure's* letterhead; PM.
Sorry the proofs went astray, but proofed the article thoroughly herself. Can't use more than one article about the Labor Congress. Emphasis should be on developments abroad for protection of workers. Can pay $150 for article and photographs. If Sergeant gets to Berlin might visit Permanent Exposition for the Welfare of Workingmen and feature some of the exhibits there. Miss Wyatt preparing article on the working girl, so not sure they could use another on French working girls. Seems as if the whole city is being demolished and rebuilt these days. Willa Sibert Cather.

180. To Prof. Hugo Munsterberg, June 27, 1910; BPL.
Will have "The Case of the Reporter" set in type soon and send proofs to Danzig. Glad he likes the article on the German emperor. Can meet him at the office between four and five on Friday [July 1]. Would be good to talk things over before he sails. Willa Sibert Cather.

181. To Elizabeth Shepley Sergeant, July 6, 1910, on *McClure's* letterhead; PM.
Sending an item from the *New York Evening Post* that casts doubt on accuracy of her article. With [Josephine] Goldmark, is taking it up with the Child Labor Commission. Wonderful Sergeant got this notice. Still wondering what she thinks of the workmen's museum idea. Can pay $200 for the article plus $50 toward travel expenses. Willa Sibert Cather.

182. To Norman Foerster, July 20, 1910, on *McClure's* letterhead; UNL.
Is pleased to see his success. Looking forward to his article on Gilbert White. Always expected him to write well, if he could get beyond youthful egoism. Since they have no book publishing now, can't consider his book of nature essays. Suggests Doubleday Page, which bought them out, or Houghton Mifflin. Ferris Greenslet there an old friend. For the magazine, more interested in content and a style more scientific than literary, designed to convey information. Willa Sibert Cather. P.S.: Has been running

the magazine alone past six months, as Mr. McClure has been ill. Will be going abroad this winter.

183. **To Norman Foerster,** Saturday [July 24, 1910?], from Plainfield, N.H.; UNL.
Liked his paper on White. Glad he's no longer trying to imitate Pater and Swinburne. Willa Sibert Cather.

184. **To Robert U. Johnson,** Aug. 30, 1910, on *McClure's* letterhead; NYPL.
Would like to change the title of the story she recently revised for him, from "Nellie Deane" to "The Flower in the Grass." Willa Sibert Cather. ["The Joy of Nelly Deane," *Century,* October 1911]

185. **To Norman Foerster,** Oct. 1, 1910, on *McClure's* letterhead; UNL.
Has he thought of topics for articles? Sorry if letter from Plainfield seemed too bossy. Willa Sibert Cather.

186. **To S. S. McClure,** Nov. 7, 1910, on *McClure's* notecard; Indiana.
Please clarify how far she should go in making arrangements with Miss Jessie Wilcox Smith for pictures. Willa Sibert Cather.

187. **To Elizabeth Shepley Sergeant,** Friday [early 1911?]; PM.
Not feeling well, and now Miss Lewis isn't also. She had better not come. W. S. C.

188. **To Mrs. George P. Cather [Aunt Franc],** Feb. 22, 1911; Weddle.
Another busy winter. Elsie made her first visit to New York at Christmas; they had a wonderful time except for worrying about Mother, who'd hurt herself in a fall. Elsie liked the apartment and the colored maid, who has taken over all housekeeping cares. Health is better this winter, though working all summer while Mr. McClure was ill in Europe wore her down. Had some time away to recuperate in the fall. Saw Mr. Wiener a few weeks ago; he is still himself, in spite of having made so much money. Isabelle visiting and sends her greeting. Hears from Howard Gore that he is going to the coronation of the king of Siam, whom he knew years ago. Wishes he wouldn't pursue aristocrats, but vanity seems endemic to Washington. Hears that Bessie and Auntie are well, and that she and Uncle George are too. May have to go to England in April. Hopes to receive a letter from her before going. Willie.

189. To George Kennan, Mar. 3, 1911, on *McClure's* letterhead; LC.

Mr. McClure cabled from London asking if Kennan can sail next week and saying he has settled the Russian matter. Not clear what he means. Thinks the magazine will pay his passage. Willa Sibert Cather.

190. To Louise Pound, May 9, 1911, from New York; UVa.

Elsie [sister] enjoying studies, but learned more with her. Please visit if in town. What does Louise think of Arnold Bennett? He may be overly documentary, but is at any rate substantial. Willa Cather.

191. To Sara Teasdale, May 9, 1911; UVa.

Sorry to have been away when she was in town; would have enjoyed seeing her. Liked her poem in the May *Scribner's*. Will stop off in St. Louis someday to see her and [Zoë] Akins. Willa Sibert Cather.

192. To Prof. Hugo Munsterberg [in Berlin], May 13, 1911; BPL.

The four articles too much like essays for *McClure's*. Rejected the idea for a piece on German theater for that very reason. Mr. McClure believes German methods superior to those of the U.S. and wants something informative along that line. Perhaps after he returns, he can provide that kind of thing? Willa Sibert Cather.

193. To Roberts Walker [at 115 Broadway, New York], May 15, 1911; Indiana.

Is sending this by messenger, along with a letter from William Archer, who was in Mexico to do a story and has been stranded on his way back to New York aboard the *Merida*. Please send a letter she can send to Mr. Archer. Willa Sibert Cather.

194. To Mrs. George P. Cather [Aunt Franc], May 16, 1911; Weddle.

Has just seen a report of G. P.'s accident in the Red Cloud newspaper. It appears he is out of danger but must be in a lot of pain. Has always been afraid of automobiles, and gasoline seems inherently dangerous. Only a week ago an explosion a couple of blocks away caused several apartment buildings to burn down. G. P. is a very strong young man, but this is a terrible ordeal. Elsie is enjoying Northampton. Hopes to see her next week during a trip to Boston. Willie.

195. To Elizabeth Shepley Sergeant, Sunday [pm. June 4, 1911], from New York; PM.

Thanks for the box of candy. Someone from Hull House was at the office and said Miss Wyatt is obsessed with white slavery these days. Too bad she can't see anything amusing in humanity. Miss McClung to be in town soon and Miss Goldmark not long after. Wishes Sergeant could be there to meet Isabelle, who also dislikes people obsessed with social reform. Willa Cather.

196. **To Louise Pound,** June 6, 1911, from 82 Washington Place, New York; UVa.
Sorry to hear of her loss [father?]. Willa Sibert Cather.

197. **To DeWolfe Howe,** June 10, 1911, on *McClure's* letterhead; Harvard.
Manuscript too biographical for *McClure's*, not focused enough. Sorry appointment was cut short, but needed to see Mr. Mackenzie, the business manager, before he left town. Willa Sibert Cather.

198. **To Christine Ladd Franklin,** June 20, 1911, from 82 Washington Place, New York; Columbia.
Has been called to Portland, Maine, so will have to miss seeing her. Willa Sibert Cather.

199. **To Elizabeth Shepley Sergeant,** June 27, 1911, from South Berwick, Maine; PM.
So glad she liked the stories. They now seem distant and ill tempered. But appreciates the good words. Here, can forget the present and its troubles. Returning tomorrow. Willa Cather.

200. **To William Stanley Braithwaite [in Boston],** June 29, 1911, on *McClure's* letterhead; UVa.
His outline might work up into an interesting article, but they never publish literary criticism. Specialize in sociological and economic issues. Willa Sibert Cather.

201. **To Prof. Hugo Munsterberg [in Berlin],** July 17, 1911, on *McClure's* letterhead; BPL.
Mr. McClure will decide about the articles when he gets back. Expects him in a few days. Willa Sibert Cather.

202. **To H. G. Dwight,** Aug. 24, 1911, on *McClure's* letterhead; Amherst.
Poem is beautiful but too long for *McClure's*. A terrible summer in New

York. Leaving at the end of September for a six-month vacation to set herself straight. Willa Sibert Cather.

203. **To H. G. Dwight,** Sept. 6, 1911, on *McClure's* letterhead; Amherst.
Verses he sent are too intellectual for *McClure's*. Poetry they use must be more pictorial or narrative or emotional. Eager to leave, but hopes to see him before she goes. Willa Sibert Cather.

204. **To Norman Foerster,** Sept. 6, 1911, on *McClure's* letterhead, fragment; UNL.
Sorry she didn't get the invitation to his wedding. Heard he was married, but not that he was in Wisconsin. A good place to teach. *McClure's* never uses literary articles. Might try *Atlantic Monthly*. A lot of trash written about Robert Browning, but he remains popular because behind his hectic style are strong ideas fairly near common sentiment. [Breaks off]

205. **To S. S. McClure,** Oct. 21, 1911, from Cherry Valley, N.Y.; Indiana.
Glad he is coming. Has enjoyed the rainy weather and is sleeping well. Willa Cather.

206. **To Robert U. Johnson,** Oct. 22, 1911, from Cherry Valley, N.Y.; NYPL.
Will be glad to write some articles [for the *Century*] after December 1. Will send a short story in a few days. Willa Sibert Cather.

207. **To [Cameron] Mackenzie,** Nov. 3, 1911, from Cherry Valley, N.Y.; Indiana.
Glad Miss McClung was able to clear up misunderstanding caused by her [Cather's] earlier letter. Willa Cather.

208. **To S. S. McClure,** Nov. 5, 1911, from Cherry Valley, N.Y.; Indiana.
So glad to get his two letters. Wishes he could have stayed longer. Is working on a story about the length of the bridge-builder one. So good to be writing again. Not even thinking about magazine work. Willa Cather.

209. **To S. S. McClure,** Nov. 17, 1911, from Cherry Valley, N.Y.; Indiana.
Glad to receive his note. Can assess his needs when he gets back from Europe. Has plenty to do. Hasn't felt this good in years. Greetings to Mrs. McClure. Willa Cather.

210. **To Mrs. William [Jessie Cather] Auld,** Dec. 18, [1911], from Cherry Valley, N.Y.; UNL.
Sorry not to be sending Christmas gifts to the children. Has only some

little handkerchiefs for Mary Virginia. Nothing to buy here. Hears from mother that the new baby is pretty. Willie.

211. **To Zoë Akins**, Feb. 6, 1912, from Boston; Huntington.
Hasn't received her book of poetry. Has been in the hospital. Now with Margaret Deland, reading proofs flat in bed. Willa Sibert Cather.

212. **To Fanny Butcher**, Feb. 16, [1912?]; Newberry.
So glad to get Fanny's letter and to hear she is opening a book shop. Would be pleased to have her [Cather's] picture displayed in it. Going abroad in late spring, but must go see parents first. Knows handwriting is hard to read, but wanted to send a personal message. Willa Cather. P.S.: Will come by to see the shop if possible.

213. **To Elizabeth Shepley Sergeant**, n.d. [pm. Mar. 1, 1912], from New York; PM.
Has sold the Bohemian Girl story for $500. Was offered $750, but that was too much. How can she [Cather] leave *McClure's* when they are so nice to her? Mr. Mackenzie already wanting to advertise the opera singer story, when she hasn't even written it. Thinks she caught the germ of selling manuscripts from her! It was a good one to catch. Is staying in town for the dinner for William Dean Howells. W. S. C.

214. **To Elizabeth Shepley Sergeant**, n.d. [pm. Mar. 2, 1912]; PM.
Wishes she were there to go on top of a bus with her to the park. A fine day. Enjoyed last Saturday. Enclosing a note from Mrs. Fields. W. S. C.

215. **To Pauline Goldmark**, n.d. [Mar. 6, 1912?];. UVa.
Sorry she has had bad news. Mr. McClure turned up unexpectedly last week. Leaving for Pittsburgh tomorrow. Elsie Sergeant saved her sanity while she [Cather] was in Boston. Willa Sibert Cather.

216. **To Elizabeth Shepley Sergeant**, Tuesday [pm. Mar. 13, 1912], from 1180 Murray Hill, Pittsburgh; PM.
It was hard to get away from New York, because Mr. McClure had arrived. Isabelle's mother is very ill, unconscious following a stroke. Has been able to keep from getting tense and nervous so far. Would be glad for her to come to Arizona, but doesn't know when she will leave, how long she will stay with her mother, or anything at all about Winslow. Was just called to Mrs. McClung's side for a brief interval of consciousness. W. S. C.

217. To S. S. McClure, Wednesday [Mar. 13, 1912?]; Indiana.

Mrs. McClung had a stroke Saturday night and was unconscious until Tuesday afternoon. Now has some body movement and dim consciousness. Seems to have a chance. Is resting, but the fright of this illness has caused her [Cather] to regress somewhat. Glad he likes "Spanish Johnny," who was a real person she knew as a child. When will he sail? Willa Cather.

218. To Zoë Akins, Mar. 14, 1912, from Pittsburgh; Huntington.

Both copies of Zoë's poems have arrived. Appreciates the inscription. Sorry to have been cross at times, but was worn out. Will never let herself be so worn down again. Likes "City and Country" best, also "Where Joy Passed By" and "Ask Me No More." Hates the pictures for "Alexander." The book will look better. Hopes she will like "The Bohemian Girl," a much better story though probably few will like it as well. Willa Sibert Cather.

219. To Elizabeth Shepley Sergeant, Sunday [pm. Mar. 26, 1912]; PM.

Mrs. McClung had a relapse on Saturday that seems serious. Has been taking refuge in Michelet; just finished the third volume. Recommends Richard Wagner's autobiography; it is so honest and direct. W. S. C.

220. To Elizabeth Shepley Sergeant, n.d. [pm. Apr. 19, (1912)] postcard; PM.

Has reached Winslow. Is worried about Elsie's news. W. S. C.

221. To Elizabeth Shepley Sergeant, Apr. 20, [1912], from Winslow, Ariz.; PM.

Has been knocking about the West for two weeks. Sorry to hear she is ill. Hopes she will rest up so she can get back to writing. The West so big it is almost frightening. Used to fear she would never escape it. Visited the Bohemian area while in Red Cloud and believes the story catches it just right. Winslow is unattractive; not so nice as New Mexico. Houses are flimsy, her brother's is tiny. Can't write there. Believes she [Cather] could work in Albuquerque. Please try to write clearly when she writes. It is often hard to read her script. Willa S. C.

222. To S. S. McClure, Apr. 22, [1912], from Winslow, Ariz.; Indiana.

Will be glad to assist with autobiography. Is enjoying her trip, especially seeing pueblos and cliff dwellings. A wonderful part of the world. Planning to see a Moki [Hopi] snake dance and go into Mexico with Douglass. News of the *Titanic* is shocking. Willa Cather.

223. **To Mariel Gere,** Apr. 24, 1912, from Winslow, Ariz.; WCPM.
Has just learned of Mrs. Gere's death. Hard to believe. Can still hear her laughter at the pretensions of young people. Benefited from that laugh when she was an unpolished country girl. Always coveted Mrs. Gere's good opinion. Health is better; is visiting Douglass. Willa Cather.

224. **To Elizabeth Shepley Sergeant,** Apr. 26, 1912, from Winslow, Ariz.; PM.
People are ultimately more interesting than scenery. Feels restless when the wind keeps her from going riding. Douglass has been on a run for three days, leaving her with a brakeman named Tooker, who keeps house and goes off drinking at night. A big talker. Has been target-shooting with a pistol and may use Tooker for a target if he doesn't drop the poly-syllabics. Mainly enjoying the Mexicans in the area, who live south of the train tracks in a delightful village. Hopes to go to Flagstaff and see cliff dwellings tomorrow. W. S. C.

225. **To Elizabeth Sergeant [in North Carolina],** May 2, [1912], postcard; PM.
Yes, does remember springtime in the South. Has gotten over her loneli-ness. Won't get to Mexico after all. W. S. C.

226. **To Carrie Miner,** May 10, [1912], from Winslow, Ariz.; WCPM.
Is sending a letter she may want for the autograph. [No identification.] Willie.

227. **To Mrs. George Seibel,** May 12, 1912, from Winslow, Ariz. [but pm. Albu-querque], postcard; WCPM.
Mr. Seibel should come see the cliff dwellings and the Spanish missions. Willa Sibert Cather.

228. **To Elizabeth Shepley Sergeant,** May 12, [1912], postcard with printed text about Hopi; UVa.
Has been out with a priest visiting his Indian missions. Some Mexicans came and played for her, and a young man as beautiful as Antinous sang. W.

229. **To Elizabeth Shepley Sergeant,** May 21, [1912], from Bright Angel Camp, Grand Canyon; PM. Note by Sergeant indicates that Edith Lewis asked her to withhold this letter from the library.
So much has happened, no time to write. The beautiful young man she

met when riding to the missions with the priest is named Julio, pronounced hu-lio. Has been camping in canyons with Tooker and doing some pretty daring climbing. Went down a cliff using hand-holds. Spent a day in the Painted Desert with Julio and could hardly get over it. Now the Grand Canyon. Wonderful how unspoiled it is, not a single souvenir shop. New Mexico is wonderful but expensive. Elsie would love it, but her money would go and she would take up with a sweetheart who would take all her attention. Has been asked to a Mexican dance when back in Winslow, and then if she can tear herself away from Julio will go to Albuquerque with Douglass. Didn't mean to go on and on about Julio – it's just that he's so fascinating. People would be fighting over him as an artist's model in New York. W. S. C.

230. **To Elizabeth Shepley Sergeant,** May 30, [1912], postcard with printed text about Acoma; PM.
The expanse of the country, along with the cost of hiring horses, has worn her out. Will start for Red Cloud on Sunday [June 2]. W.

231. **To Irene Miner Weisz,** n.d. [pm. May 30, 1912], from Albuquerque, postcard; Newberry.
Likes the old part of Albuquerque. Has had a wonderful time. W. S. C.

232. **To Elizabeth Shepley Sergeant,** June 2, [1912], postcard with printed text about Isleta [largest of the Rio Grande pueblos]; PM.
Sorry she has discovered that book of bad poetry [*April Twilights*]. She shouldn't waste good money buying a copy. W. S. C.

233. **To S. S. McClure,** June 9, 1912, from Lamy, N.M.; Indiana.
Has just returned from a long trip in the desert and found his letters. Sorry to hear Mrs. McClure is ill. How can he do magazine work here when she is abroad? Sounds as though finances are another worry. Hopes the problem will be short-term. Did he find prospects for a magazine in London? Hard to believe, with his ability and experience, his career will end. Will do anything she can to help. He can write to her in Red Cloud, though she may be in Colorado or Wyoming for several months. Willa Cather.

234. **To Irene Miner Weisz,** n.d. [pm. June 11, 1912, at El Paso, Tex.], postcard with picture of Laguna Pueblo; Newberry.
[No message.]

235. **To S. S. McClure,** June 12, [1912], from Red Cloud, Nebr.; Indiana.
Wrote to him from New Mexico, but he may not have received letters. Sorry to hear about Mrs. McClure's illness and his business troubles. People should be as generous to him as he has always been to others. Contracts have been changed so much it is hard to know what his share of the company now is. Will help with autobiography without charge for friendship's sake. Hopes she can write the articles as he wants them. He will recall that she couldn't hit what he wanted in some parts of the Christian Science series. Hasn't written a bit since she left New York, but is suntanned and healthy and in good humor again. Hopes people will forget how cross she was. It was from fatigue. Will never let little things bother her so much again. Willa Cather.

236. **To Elizabeth Shepley Sergeant,** June 15, [1912], from Red Cloud, Nebr.; PM.
Got away from the desert, but may yet go back and get Julio. Sorry to hear she is no better. Would like to go to France with her. Knows she will like Avignon. A good place to work. Enclosing a translation of a serenade Julio sang to her, which is not proper for a woman to sing to anyone but her lover or her husband. ["Serenata Mejicana," which ends "The heart of night is still – / Beloved, sleep!"] W. S. C.

237. **To Annie Adams Fields,** June 27, 1912, from Red Cloud, Nebr.; Huntington.
Mother has had surgery but is recovering well. Will go see the Bohemians' wheat harvest next week. She wouldn't believe how hot Nebraska is now. Looks forward to telling her about Arizona. Willa.

238. **To Louise Pound,** June 28, [1912], from Red Cloud, Nebr.; UVa.
Hasn't answered her letter because traveling. Spent two adventurous months with Douglass. Probably won't get to Lincoln. Needs to return to New York as soon as possible after her brother Roscoe comes to visit. Was ill most of the winter but quite well now. She shouldn't bother reading "Alexander," but may like "The Bohemian Girl." Willa Cather.

239. **To Elizabeth Shepley Sergeant,** July 5, [1912], from Red Cloud, Nebr.;. PM.
Hopes to hear she is better. Is going to the Bohemian area to see the wheat harvest next week. Leaving for Pittsburgh in about two weeks. Will work on a story to be called "The White Mulberry Tree" that will alarm Ferris Greenslet. W. S. C. [Enclosure: poem "Prairie Spring"]

240. **To Annie Adams Fields,** July 24, 1912, from Red Cloud, Nebr.; Huntington.
Has been seeing the wheat harvest in the French and Bohemian country. Attended French mass at the Church of Saint Anne. Must get to work
when she gets to Pittsburgh. Feeling well. Willa.

241. **To Elizabeth Shepley Sergeant,** Aug. 14, [1912], from Pittsburgh; PM.
Enjoyed her long letter. Hopes voyage will be restful. Enjoyed reading her
paper about France in *Scribner's*. Glad to be back from the West; feeling
worn out by its vastness. Couldn't exchange all of civilization for Julio.
Reading vol. 9 of Michelet with Isabelle. W.

242. **To Elizabeth Shepley Sergeant,** Sept. 12, [1912], from 1180 Murray Hill, Pittsburgh; PM.
Spent two weeks in New York getting the winter's work set. Promised the
magazine two stories before Christmas. Wants to lengthen the Swedish
story and merge it with the other to make a two-part pastoral. British edition of *Alexander* looks much better than the American. Has been reading
Balzac and the disgusting *Idiot* by Dostoevsky. Thought the first two parts
of *Creative Evolution* [Bergson] were splendid. Everyone seems to be celebrating "The Bohemian Girl" except a reader who thought it immoral.
W. S. C.

243. **To Harriet Monroe,** Sept. 15, 1912, from Pittsburgh; Chicago.
Appreciates her invitation to submit a poem or poems for *Poetry*, but does
not have anything to send at present. Looks forward to seeing the first
issue. Willa Sibert Cather.

244. **To Elizabeth Shepley Sergeant,** Oct. 6, [1912], from Pittsburgh; PM.
Postcards from London are plenty. Has moved into the ideal apartment at
no. 5 Bank Street. But wishes she [Cather] were in London. W. S. C.

245. **To Literary Editor,** *Chicago Evening Post,* Oct. 16, 1912, from Pittsburgh;
Newberry.
Appreciates the astute review of *Alexander's Bridge* on June 21. Reviewer
understood what she was doing. Willa Sibert Cather.

246. **To Zoë Akins,** Oct. 31, [1912?], from Pittsburgh; UVa.
Don't overwork while running a temperature. Glad she likes "The Bohemian Girl." Feels pretty good about it. Is doing a longer story with the

same setting; actually, setting is the main character. Saw Arnold Bennett's *Milestones* in New York. Wishes the office would quit interrupting her work. W. S. C.

247. **To Zoë Akins,** Nov. 27, [1912?], from Pittsburgh; Huntington.
Enjoyed reading her one-act play and her sonnets, but doesn't really like poems about artistic endeavor. "Rain, Rain!" and "Amen" are very good. Was in New York in October working on an article on the play openings. W. S. C.

248. **To H. L. Mencken,** Dec. 6, [1912?], from no. 5 Bank Street [handwritten], New York; NYPL.
Appreciates his letter with comments about *Alexander's Bridge*. Willa Sibert Cather.

249. **To Elizabeth Shepley Sergeant,** Dec. 7, [1912], from Pittsburgh; PM.
Enjoyed her letter. Has nearly finished new story. Can't write when she is gathering material; the two processes are separate. Recommends Chekhov's *The Cherry Orchard*. Wants to write more, but very busy with holiday season plus writing the murder in her story. W. S. C.

250. **To Elizabeth Shepley Sergeant,** n.d. [early 1913? per E. S. S. note], from no. 5 Bank Street [handwritten], New York; PM.
Has been getting settled in the new apartment, including floors being painted. Thanks for the Christmas present. Has been hearing a lot of music. New book twice as long as *Alexander*. Has taken her themes from the long grass, as Dvořák did in the *New World* Symphony (which was not made from Negro songs as people say). Nervous about the new story, though it is just what she has been wanting to write. Probably very few people will like it. Willa Cather.

251. **To Elizabeth Shepley Sergeant,** Feb. 2, [1913], from no. 5 Bank Street [handwritten], New York; PM.
When is she coming home? Hopes she will like the apartment. W. S. C.

252. **To Elizabeth Shepley Sergeant,** n.d. [1913?], from no. 5 Bank Street [handwritten], New York; PM.
Being back in New York and going to the opera makes her want people around. Wishes they could have a good visit. Won't she come for a visit

when she gets back? May go to Virginia in May. Sending "Pioneers" for her to read. Be honest. W. S. C.

253. **To Jessie B. Rittenhouse,** Tuesday, [1913?]; Newberry.
Has made several changes in the poem ["Grandmither, Think Not I Forget"]. Willa Sibert Cather. [Reprinted in *The Little Book of Modern Verse*, 1913, ed. Rittenhouse.]

254. **To Mrs. George P. Cather [Aunt Franc],** Feb. 23, 1913, from no. 5 Bank Street [written in above *McClure's* letterhead], New York; Weddle, copy at UNL.
Thanks for the letter. Has just finished a new novel, having reduced her work for the magazine by half. Is settling into new apartment, which had to have considerable refurbishing but was worth it, spacious and quiet. Has bought four Persian rugs. The same colored maid as for the past four years is still keeping life in order. Agrees that *Alexander* is morally flimsy, but goodness in characters does not necessarily make strong fiction. Believes she will like the new novel better. Elsie [sister] is enjoying her teaching. Finds that one of the rewards of nearing forty years old is feeling more comfortable with older relatives, who always used to seem rather intimidating. Not so much Aunt Franc and Father as others. Willie.

255. **To Elinor Wylie,** n.d. [Apr. 1913?]; Beinecke.
Glad to learn they are neighbors. Hopes she will come to tea. Willa Cather.

256. **To Elizabeth Shepley Sergeant,** Apr. 14, [1913?], from no. 5 Bank Street [handwritten]; PM.
Would have liked to go to France with her. Proofs of *Pioneers* coming in. Not so pleased with it as at first. Is getting acquainted with Olive Fremstad, who is rather overwhelming. W. S. C.

257. **To Elizabeth Shepley Sergeant,** Apr. 22, [1913]; PM.
Has not succeeded in getting *Outlook* to commit to a publication date for her article. Would she please edit the French in *Pioneers*? So glad she likes it. Understands she would like a more distinct structure, but that wouldn't suit the country. Mr. Greenslet likes it. Still, wishes to do something different. Would like to be able to write what is in Fremstad's mind. Saw her after she had sung Kundry in *Parsifal* [Wagner] yesterday, and she looked exhausted. Isabelle is visiting. Misses her. W.

258. **To Elizabeth Shepley Sergeant,** Apr. 25, [1913]; PM.
Is going to Boston to visit Mrs. Fields for a week. Hopes she will come to visit when she gets back [from France]. *Pioneers* to be out in June. Has been reading proofs and feels happier with it again. Wants to tell her about the Swedish girl who was the model for the frontispiece; also about Fremstad. W. S. C.

259. **To Zoë Akins,** June 11, [1913?], from no. 5 Bank Street, New York; Huntington.
Will be there until July 15. W. S. C.

260. **To Elizabeth Shepley Sergeant,** July 4, [1913]; PM.
Weather has been very hot since she left. New Hampshire must be better. Enjoyed their two days together. Was not able to describe Elsie's French clothes adequately to Isabelle. Plans to take Kronstall's wardrobe from advertisements. W. S. C.

261. **To Elizabeth Shepley Sergeant,** Monday [pm. Aug. 5, 1913]; PM.
Sorry she and her family saw such a terrible accident. Enclosing a review just in from Chicago [by Floyd Dell]. W.

262. **To Elizabeth Shepley Sergeant,** Sunday [Aug. 1913?]; PM.
Hates the bright blue paper she [Cather] is writing on. Stuck in this heat trying to write an article on ballet that she promised *McClure's*. Reviews are wonderful. Going to Virginia in September. W.

263. **To Irene Miner Weisz,** n.d. [Aug. 1913?]; Newberry.
[A review of O *Pioneers!* enclosed.] Doesn't want to be blamed for this! Willie.

264. **To Elizabeth Shepley Sergeant,** Sept. 12, 1913, from Winchester, Va., UVa.; PM.
Traveled from Pittsburgh to Virginia via Lake Erie. Winchester is dull. Doesn't really care about the people there anymore. Food is terrible. Would like to go up to Chocorua [N.H.] but needs to get back to New York and work. Why didn't she send her novel manuscript? Willa.

265. **To Elizabeth Shepley Sergeant,** Sept. 22, [1913], from Gore, Va., UVa.; PM.
Trip has been worthwhile after all. Has been walking a lot in the moun-

tains. Fremstad has invited her up to her camp in Maine to visit. English reviews are wonderful. Willa S. C.

266. **To Elizabeth Shepley Sergeant,** Oct. 11, 1913, from 1180 Murray Hill, Pittsburgh; PM.

Will go to New York next week, then back here. Has been reading phone directories from various cities – L, K, and O in Minneapolis. Isabelle's sister Edith getting married. W. S. C.

267. **To Elizabeth Shepley Sergeant,** Sunday [1913?]; PM.

Likes many things about the manuscript [see no. 264] but does not like the epistolary form. Even the best fiction in that form has a certain artificiality about it. Heroine is necessarily too talky. It gets in the way of one's gaining a real sense of her. W. S. C. P.S.: May be incoherent because of headache.

268. **To Ferris Greenslet,** Thursday [prob. 1913], from no. 5 Bank Street, New York; Harvard.

Telephone number is 2036 Chelsea. Wants to see him and Mr. Sadler. W. S. C.

269. **To [William] Winter,** Nov. 5, [1913?], on no. 5 Bank Street printed stationery; Colby.

His letter rewards her for the work of writing the book. Glad it makes him remember the prairie. Willa Sibert Cather.

270. **To Elizabeth Shepley Sergeant,** Nov. 19, [1913], from New York; PM.

Swedish cousin has died in Paris. Spent a few days in Washington with her cousin's husband after he returned bringing the body. Is settling back into the apartment. Did about 28,000 words on new novel while in Pittsburgh. Has she seen the article about singers in the December *McClure's*? Fremstad likes it. Has been invited to Boston to visit Mrs. Fields, but can't go until after Christmas. Wishes she [Sergeant] were there to go to the ballet tonight. W. S. C. P.S.: Mrs. Fields's primness about a nude figure on the magazine cover is funny.

271. **To Mr. or Mrs. McClure,** n.d. [Dec. 10, 1913?], from New York; Indiana.

Glad he is pleased with the autobiography. Has heard he provided excellent illustrations. Glad to hear his health is good. Willa Cather.

272. **To Zoë Akins,** Friday [Jan. 1914?]; Huntington.

Has been in Boston. Doesn't like her story, which seems to have been written only to be clever. It has no feeling. Zoë can't work up to her potential until she gets out of this manner. W. S. C.

273. **To Ferris Greenslet,** Monday [Jan. 12, 1914], from New York; Harvard.

Is pleased to have the Adams book [prob. Henry Adams, *Mont-Saint-Michel and Chartres*, 1904; reissued by Houghton Mifflin in 1913]. Tell Nancy Moore her serial will get a quick reading by Mackenzie [at *McClure's*]. Willa Cather.

274. **To Zoë Akins,** Saturday [Feb. 1914?], from New York; Huntington.

Sorry to have missed her. Was getting her head x-rayed. Is having a temperature every afternoon and head pains. Doctors can't seem to find what is wrong. Thanks for the flowers. Could Zoë come by Monday for tea? W. S. C.

275. **To [William Lyon?] Phelps,** Feb. 11, [1914?], from New York; UVa.

Many thanks for the kind letter. Glad the story pleases someone who really knows the area. Spent her childhood in Nebraska. Willa Sibert Cather.

276. **To Elizabeth Shepley Sergeant,** n.d. [pm. Feb. 13, 1914]; PM.

Somehow got a painful infection from a scratch on the back of the head. Now has a poultice on it, is bandaged up, and is taking morphine. So addled she can scarcely read a letter. W. S. C.

277. **To Elizabeth Shepley Sergeant,** Feb. 24, 1914, from Roosevelt Hospital, New York; PM.

Has been in the hospital a week. Back of head shaved. Treatments may take as much as three months. Mutilation is such a grotesqueness. What a loss of time, not to mention personal dignity! W. S. C.

278. **To Elizabeth Shepley Sergeant,** Sunday [pm. Mar. 2, 1914]; PM.

Got home yesterday. Doesn't know why she felt so dismal in the hospital. Fremstad came and cheered her up, showed her how to wear her hair to hide the disfigurement. Blood poisoning seems to affect one's mind. W.

279. **To Elizabeth Shepley Sergeant,** Mar. 19, 1914; PM.

Has received her two letters, but had such lassitude, couldn't write. Sees the doctor every other day. Is trying to work a little. Has been to the opera twice; missing hair not so conspicuous at night. Isabelle stayed almost a month. Willa.

280. **To Elizabeth Shepley Sergeant,** Tuesday [pm. Apr. 30, 1914]; PM.
Thanks for the cheery letter. Is free of bandages now. Went to Atlantic City for a few days and got sidetracked from her [Cather's] story, but is back on it now. Writing a lot about the mechanics and politics of opera. Is getting acquainted with the Hoyts. Wishes events in Mexico would settle down so she could go see the cities there. Going to Pittsburgh soon. W.

281. **To Ferris Greenslet,** May 2, [1914], from New York; Harvard.
Glad the book is selling fairly well. How did the Heinemann edition do? Is going to Pittsburgh in a few days. Miss Lewis sailing for Naples toward the end of the month. W. S. C.

282. **To Elizabeth Shepley Sergeant,** May 26, [1914], from Pittsburgh; PM.
She is a sport to go fishing with Greenslet. Henry James's latest book, "Brothers and Son" [*Notes of a Son and Brother,* 1914], is too mannered, with too little substance, to be worth reading. Tortured with afterthoughts and retraction. Hears from Greenslet that Elsie is not going to marry a cubist after all – he seems to have taken the joke seriously. Glad to be away from New York. Will probably go visit Fremstad in Maine some time in June. Is not pushing herself. Enjoying the weather and resting a lot. W.

283. **To Will Owen Jones,** May 29, [1914], from Pittsburgh; UVa.
Enjoyed doing McClure's autobiography. Put down the facts as he remembered them. No, doesn't hold a grudge about his reaction to her early stories. Is going to Wyoming this summer and of course to Red Cloud. Willa Cather.

284. **To Elizabeth Shepley Sergeant,** Tuesday [pm. June 23, 1914], from Pittsburgh; PM.
Went to Maine June 7 and returned home yesterday. Had a wonderful time with Fremstad and then visited Mary Jewett. With Fremstad, was active every minute, fishing, rowing, hiking, and cooking. What a vigorous woman! Thornton Oakley would do good illustrations for a book on Provence. Scribner's would be a good publisher for it. Going to Wyoming soon. Isabelle will probably go to Italy during that time. W.

285. To Elizabeth Shepley Sergeant, Aug. 10, [1914], from Red Cloud, Nebr.; PM.
Just back from two weeks in the French and Bohemian area watching the harvest. Saw some old friends, like fictional characters whose story she [Cather] keeps reading. Weather very hot. Surely she will not go abroad with the Kaiser acting like another Napoleon. Will get back to work in about a month in Pittsburgh. W. S. C.

286. To Elizabeth Shepley Sergeant, Sept. 11, [1914], postcard with picture of Fisher's Peak [near Trinidad, Colo.]; PM.
Back on old paths, a big, beautiful country, all golden-brown. W. S. C.

287. To Elizabeth Shepley Sergeant, Sunday [pm. Sept. 28, 1914], from Pittsburgh; PM.
Back from an active summer. Brought along her twenty-year-old brother [Jack], who is enrolled at Carnegie Technical. Couldn't put the war out of her mind even when she was in the Sangre de Cristo Mountains [in northern New Mexico]. Shouldn't hear any more about suffrage and such for a while. Recent issues of *Punch* make one realize how solid England is. Kipling's recent speech was splendid. Will be in New York in October but only for a week; wants to keep working on her book in Pittsburgh until the first of the year. Willa.

288. To Elizabeth Shepley Sergeant, n.d. [pm. Nov. 13, 1914], from Pittsburgh; PM.
Just a hello. Sorry to have missed her in New York. Won't be back until January. Enjoyed seeing Fremstad when she came to Pittsburgh for a concert. Hopes to find a good apartment in New York. Hears there is starvation in Belgium. W. S. C.

289. To Mrs. George P. Cather [Aunt Franc], Nov. 17, [1914], from Pittsburgh; Weddle, copy at WCPM.
Has been working well. Expects to be in Pittsburgh until Christmas. Jack doing well at school; sees him often. War occupies all conversation. A friend from Belgium, Mme Flahant, is in New York and says her family members in Brussels are starving. The Belgian Relief Committee in London says that only the U.S. can sustain Belgium through the winter. Germans allow no food in that comes through England or France. Will donate to the relief fund instead of sending Christmas presents. America will have to answer to history if it fails Belgium. Willie.

290. To Elizabeth Shepley Sergeant, Dec. 5, [1914], from Pittsburgh; PM.
Will go to New York about mid-January by way of Washington. Working well here. Won't get to Boston before late winter. The new book great fun but awfully long! Please return *The Idiot* [Dostoevsky], if it was she to whom she lent it. Is reading *The Awkward Age* [James] with Isabelle. W. S. C.

291. To Ferris Greenslet, Dec. 13, [1914], from Pittsburgh; Harvard.
Will finish the novel by summer at the latest. It will be twice as long as *O Pioneers!* and more interesting. How about calling it *The Song of the Lark?* Willa Cather.

292. To Ferris Greenslet, Dec. 21, [1914], from Pittsburgh; Harvard.
Making record progress on the book. Not going to New York until February 1. Hopes he can indeed stop the war while he is in England! Willa Cather.

293. To Zoë Akins, Feb. 1, [1915?], from Pittsburgh; Huntington.
Going to Washington for a week, then to New York by February 12. Novel has reached 200,000 words. W. S. C.

294. To Marguerite Wilkinson, Feb. 11, [1915?], from New York; Middlebury, copy at WCPM.
May use "Grandmither, Think Not I Forget" as she wishes. Willa Sibert Cather.

295. To Ferris Greenslet, March 28, 1915, from no. 5 Bank Street, New York; Harvard.
Is sending most of the novel. About 20,000 words yet to write. Believes it is very good. Feels envious of Doubleday's sales methods. Houghton Mifflin ought to push this book more than they did *O Pioneers!*. Parts of the story are drawn from her early years, including the death of the railroad man, which happened when she was about thirteen. Story is full of the West. Has hit it with this one! Willa Cather.

296. To Ferris Greenslet, Tuesday [prob. Apr. 6, 1915], from New York; Harvard.
Will change "billiards" to "pool" and refrain from making Dr. Archie governor. Sorry he objects to the diminishing scale of the book, but that was her plan, to emphasize Thea's youth. Hopes he can come see her this weekend. Can't phone; has no telephone. Willa Cather.

297. **To Ferris Greenslet,** Thursday [prob. Apr. 8, 1915], from New York; Harvard.
Will expect him Sunday. W. S. C.

298. **To Ferris Greenslet,** n.d. [c. Apr. 15, 1915]; Harvard.
Only the epilogue in Moonstone yet to do. Please return all the "ten years later" part if he wants Archie rewritten. W. S. Cather.

299. **To Ferris Greenslet,** Apr. 22, [1915]; Harvard.
Is enclosing two postcards of Breton's *The Song of the Lark*; prefers the one in brown tones. How does he like the later chapters of the book? Can't revise until she gets a short story done for *McClure's* and gets her brother sent back to Pittsburgh. W. S. C.

300. **To Ferris Greenslet,** Apr. 28, [1915], from New York; Harvard.
Enclosing a first draft of the epilogue. Worried he is not satisfied with the book. Can call off the contract if he wishes. Willa Cather. P.S.: If they go ahead she wants three pulls of each galley proof, one of which will go to a musical expert for checking.

301. **To Mrs. C. E. Perkins,** Apr. 29, [1915?]; Newberry.
Glad she likes the little book, and will hope to meet her when she is in Boston. Willa Sibert Cather.

302. **To Ferris Greenslet,** Sunday [prob. May 1, 1915], from New York; Harvard.
Feels reassured by his letter [of Apr. 29]. He was right about the tide in Venice. Wishes he could have been there for the dinner party she gave for Olive Fremstad. W. S. C.

303. **To R. L. Scaife,** May 10, [1915], from New York; Harvard.
When will she receive proofs? Doesn't want to stop work on some stories and articles until there are enough proofs that she can stick with them. Willa S. Cather.

304. **To R. L. Scaife,** May 12, [1915], from New York; Harvard.
Please have foreign words set in italics. Copyeditor didn't in *O Pioneers!*. Also names of operatic roles. Hopes he has a proofreader who is fluent in Spanish and someone who can check the German used in the music lessons. Willa S. Cather.

305. **To Glendinning Keeble,** n.d. [prob. between May 15, 1915, and July 19, 1915]; CMU.

Is offering a revision of the character of Jessie Darcey [singer Thea Kronborg accompanies in *The Song of the Lark*] and will be glad to revise more. Thea has control over her own fortune; was a liar and was lied to. She expected to marry Fred, despite the fact that her Methodist childhood would not have led her to expect it. She ended up punishing Fred for what she did herself. Won't make all this entirely clear, because doesn't want character of Thea to alienate readers. Isabelle is going away for a few days to rest.

306. **To R. L. Scaife,** May 18, [1915], from New York; Harvard.
Sending about half the corrected proofs to the press today. Please remember to provide three pulls of the galleys. Willa S. Cather.

307. **To Miss Van Tuyll [at Houghton Mifflin],** May 24, [1915], from New York; Harvard.
Very pleased that she likes the story. Doesn't want a picture of herself published unless she gets a good one this summer at the cliff dwellings. Will get one taken by a photographer if she must, but it will only be disillusioning to the public. Willa S. Cather.

308. **To Ferris Greenslet,** Sunday [May 23 or 30, 1915], from New York; Harvard.
Glad to have eliminated the governorship for Dr. Archie. Has made a suggestion about the jacket to Miss Van Tuyll. Also, has returned thirty-three pages of proof. It's pretty rough. Willa S. Cather.

309. **To Mrs. George P. Cather [Aunt Franc],** June 16, [1915]; Weddle.
Is sending a chain letter for her to pass on to three friends. Is correcting proofs for new book to be published in the fall. Expects to be in Nebraska in September and will come for a visit. Willie.

310. **To Elizabeth Shepley Sergeant,** June 27, [1915], from New York; PM.
Has just read her essay on Provence in *Century*. Is busy with proofs. Jack is off in Maine. A musical critic is reading galleys and is enthusiastic, especially about the singing lessons. Would have felt bad if those hadn't been right! Has she seen Henry James's article about Mrs. Fields in the June *Atlantic*? Isn't she disappointed in Owen Wister's novel? [*Pentecost of Calamity*, 1915] Willa. P.S.: Loves her khaki outfit for the cliff dwellings – reminds her of Kurt's outfit in *Fidelio* [Beethoven].

311. **To Ferris Greenslet,** June 30, [1915], from New York; Harvard.
Likes the jacket, but the copy is wrong—Moonstone, Colorado, not Arizona. Also, Thea and Fred go to Mexico, not New Mexico. Wishes it could say something about her artistic growth in the cliff dweller ruins. Actually, not so *very* happy with the cover. Couldn't it be more like British edition of *Pioneers*? Henry James seems patronizing in his essay on the Fieldses. Willa Cather.

312. **To Ferris Greenslet,** Tuesday [prob. July 13, 1915], from New York; Harvard.
Can't let him use the snapshot of her with Olive Fremstad, but has had some new photos taken. Should capitalize on current interest in cliff dwellings in advertising the book. Willa Cather.

313. **To Glendinning Keeble,** Monday [prob. July 19, 1915], from New York; CMU.
Appreciates his returning proofs quickly; couldn't finish until she got his help. Isabelle will be leaving for Pittsburgh in a few days and she will follow. In the meantime she and all of New York interested in a group of eight morris dancers staying across the street from her who are causing trouble for their stage manager due to having lost all their gear en route.

314. **To Ferris Greenslet,** Wednesday [prob. July 21, 1915], from New York; Harvard.
Will send the epilogue next week. There isn't a prologue. Leaving for Pittsburgh tomorrow, so send proofs to 1180 Murray Hill. Leaving for Colorado and New Mexico on August 6. Please send a sample of the new cover before then. Willa Cather.

315. **To Ferris Greenslet,** Saturday [prob. July 24, 1915], from Pittsburgh; Harvard.
For three days has been on the verge of sailing for Bergen, then to Germany to interview German leaders. Since S. S. McClure was going, there had to be someone else, so Isabelle was going. All off when Judge McClung decided he didn't want her to take the risk. Will get back onto the page proofs. It was a more appealing project financially than the novel will be. Would have needed to be tactful in order to be accurate without being or at least seeming pro-German. Willa Cather.

316. To Ferris Greenslet, Monday [pm. July 26, 1915], postcard; Harvard.
Mailed the epilogue yesterday. W. S. Cather.

317. To Elizabeth Shepley Sergeant, July 28, [1915], from Pittsburgh; PM.
Was about to sail for Germany when Judge McClung decided Isabelle
must not go. Will start for Durango August 6. Proofs are finished. Even
the page proofs needed a lot of correction. Loves *North of Boston* [Frost],
so bare and strong. Knowing real poetry is being written enables her to
tolerate even the likes of Witter Bynner. W. S. C.

318. To R. L. Scaife, Aug. 3, [1915], from Pittsburgh; Harvard.
New cover is fine. Leaves for Durango on Friday [August 6]. Uncertain
where she'll be the next few weeks. Willa Cather.

319. To Elizabeth Shepley Sergeant, Aug. 20, [pm. Aug. 22, 1915], postcard with
picture of Spruce Tree House, Mesa Verde, Colo.; PM.
Lingering at Mesa Verde. Ruins are a marvel. W. S. C.

320. To Elizabeth Shepley Sergeant, Aug. 31, 1915, from Lamy, N.M., postcard
with picture of a Pueblo Indian; PM.
Had a wonderful week at Taos, with good horses to ride and good canta-
loupes to eat. W. S. C.

321. To Ferris Greenslet, Sept. 5, [1915], from Denver; Harvard.
Will be in Red Cloud for a month starting September 10. Going to Wyo-
ming first. Is Heinemann bringing out the book in England? Willa Cather.
P.S.: What is the publication date? W. S. C.

322. To Ferris Greenslet, Sept. 13, [1915], from Red Cloud, Nebr.; Harvard.
Good work on the publicity booklet and poster. Thanks for the advance
copy. Likes the cover, jacket, and type. Has excellent photos of Mesa Verde
provided by the Denver and Rio Grande Railroad, also of Taos and the
pueblos near Santa Fe. Would he still like to have a book about the Southwest? Might be able to travel for free on Santa Fe next summer to gather
additional material. Unfortunately, has gained six pounds while climbing
and riding. Edith lost weight. W. S. C.

323. To Elizabeth Shepley Sergeant, Sept. 21, [1915], from Red Cloud, Nebr.; PM.
Just got her letter. Gained five pounds at Mesa Verde. Had a bad time in the
worst canyon in Colorado; got some bruises. Has received an advance copy

of the book – terrible proofreading. Surely a good proofreader would have caught the errors she missed herself. Has learned a lesson about hurrying a book. Has marvelous photos of the Southwest. Has Elsie seen *A Boy's Will* [Frost]? It's even better than *North of Boston*. W.

324. **To Ferris Greenslet,** Sept. 26, [1915], from Red Cloud, Nebr.; Harvard.
Curtis Brown won't do much for her book due to resentments left from *McClure's* days, when she got the magazine out of bad agreements made by McClure. How about advertising at women's colleges? Girls will like the aggressive careerism. Willa Cather.

325. **To Ferris Greenslet,** Oct. 25, [1915], from Pittsburgh, telegram; Harvard.
OK to cut out reference to Lily Langtry. Will write again tomorrow. Willa Cather.

326. **To R. L. Scaife,** Oct. 27, [1915], from Chicago; Harvard.
Stores in Lincoln say they are unable to get copies. One has never heard of the book or the poster either. W. S. Cather.

327. **To Ferris Greenslet,** Oct. 28, 1915, from Pittsburgh; Harvard.
OK to cut the Lily Langtry sentences. Will write again tomorrow. W. S. Cather.

328. **To Will Owen Jones,** Oct. 29, 1915, from Pittsburgh; UVa.
Is enclosing the article from the *Nation* [a review of *The Song of the Lark*] hoping he will reprint it. Believes it would be of interest to people there. Willa S. Cather.

329. **To R. L. Scaife,** Oct. 30, [1915], from Pittsburgh; Harvard.
Thinks the ad is unexciting. Why not quote some of the really live statements in reviews? Has redone the ad proposing some other quotations. [Encloses example.] Has sent her *Nation* to Will Owen Jones for reprint. Willa Cather.

330. **To Ferris Greenslet,** Nov. 1, [1915], from Pittsburgh; Harvard.
Has written to McClure about providing a sketch, but he is away in Texas. Will try to write the article for *Book News* if he will send more specific instructions. Let Mr. Scaife know about the quotable reviews in the *Boston Advertiser* and the *New Bedford Standard*. Willa Cather. P.S.: Wondering if it will be reviewed in the *Atlantic*.

331. To Ferris Greenslet, n.d. [Nov. 2, 1915?]; Harvard.
Wants a half dozen of the *Song of the Lark* brochures. W. S. C.

332. To Ferris Greenslet, Nov. 4, [1915], from Pittsburgh; Harvard.
Likes the idea of the college contest. W. S. C.

333. To Irene Miner Weisz, Nov. 5, [1915], from Pittsburgh; Newberry.
She should try to see Fremstad as Isolde later this month. Willie.

334. To Emma Mills, Nov. 8, [1915], from New York; NYPL.
Is going to Philadelphia tomorrow. Will come to the Book and Play Club
luncheon if she is back. Willa Cather.

335. To Ferris Greenslet, Nov. 17, [1915], from Pittsburgh; Harvard.
Enclosing an article for *Book News*. Isabelle's father has died. Has had to
forgo going to Chicago with Fremstad, who seems to like the book. Glad
the reviews haven't mentioned her. Hasn't heard from McClure. W. S. C.

336. To Ferris Greenslet, Nov. 20, 1915, from Pittsburgh, postcard; Harvard.
Why not use [H. W.] Boynton's article in the *New York Evening Post* in place
of the one he hoped to get from S. S. McClure? W. S. Cather.

337. To Ferris Greenslet, Nov. 24, [1915], from Pittsburgh; Harvard.
No longer feels he was disappointed with the book. Some of the advertising has been effective. W. S. C.

338. To H. W. Boynton, Dec. 6, 1915; UVa.
Appreciates his understanding her purposes in the book [*The Song of the
Lark*]. Was encouraged to undertake it by his review of *Pioneers*. Willa Sibert
Cather.

339. To Ferris Greenslet, Dec. [6, 1915?], from Pittsburgh; Harvard.
Could he use just a paragraph from McClure? Won't return to Bank Street
until after the holidays. W. S. C.

340. To Elizabeth Shepley Sergeant, Dec. 7, [1915], from Pittsburgh; PM.
Judge McClung died three weeks ago. Wishes she had reviewed the book.
Misses Thea's company. Had feared Fremstad might be angry about the
book, but she liked it exceedingly. W.

341. **To Emma Mills,** Friday [Dec. 10, 1915]; Mills.

Appreciates her interest in *The Song of the Lark*. Will plan on speaking at the luncheon on Wednesday. Willa Sibert Cather.

342. **To Ferris Greenslet,** Dec. 10, 1915, from Pittsburgh, postcard; Harvard.

Is going to New York tonight, to stay until the 19th. Mr. McClure went on the *Peace Ship*. What a group to go off with! W. S. C.

343. **To Mrs. George P. Cather [Aunt Franc],** Dec. 25, 1915, from Pittsburgh; Weddle.

Is sending her love on this special day. Since Isabelle McClung has lost her father as well as her mother and this house (which has been almost a home to her [Cather] for fifteen years) is to be sold, it is her last Christmas there. May never feel so secure in any other house. Even her apartment in New York, pleasant as it is, is not a home in the way this was. Has been spending some time with Jack during the school vacation. New book enjoying good sales as well as favorable reviews. Is eager to get to work on a new one. Willa.

344. **To Ferris Greenslet,** Saturday [1915?]; Harvard.

Copy enclosed. He can make cuts. W. S. C.

345. **To Ferris Greenslet,** n.d. [prob. 1915]; Harvard.

Please send a copy of *The Song of the Lark*. What does he think of the enclosed ad? W. S. C.

346. **To Ferris Greenslet,** Jan. 22, [1916]; Harvard.

Thanks for the gift book about Boston. Is going to New York next week for the rest of the winter. When will British edition be out? W. S. C.

347. **To Ferris Greenslet,** Monday [Jan. 1916?]; Harvard.

Will be glad to see him Wednesday evening. Still resisting telephone. W. S. C.

348. **To Ferris Greenslet,** Monday [Jan. 31, 1916?]; Harvard.

Sending H. L. Mencken's article [in *Smart Set* January 1916?]. Has he seen Hugh Walpole's article in *Bookman*? Willa Sibert Cather.

349. **To Mrs. George Seibel,** Jan. 31, [1916?], from New York; Harvard.

Is very pleased by her letter praising the book. Someone wanted to know if the piece-picture was made up. Mrs. Seibel will remember that it hung in the fitting room of a tailor for women. Except when hospitalized with blood poisoning, writing went steadily. Glad she believes in her. Willa Sibert Cather.

350. **To Mr. Bridges,** Feb. 28, [1916?], from New York; Princeton.
Hopes he will like the enclosed poem [not identified]. Willa Sibert Cather.

351. **To Dorothy Canfield Fisher,** Mar. 15, [1916?]; UVt.
The Song of the Lark was fun to write, but shows carelessness. Cut out several chapters set in Germany to keep it focused on the Moonstone perspective. They would have spoiled the unity. A few negative reviewers have wished it were a tragedy rather than a success story. The title is a weakness, it's true. Hasn't been up to starting a new book this winter, with Judge McClung's death, the closing of the house, and prospect of Isabelle's marriage [April 3, 1916]. Doesn't get along well with Jan Hambourg. Loss of Isabelle is a severe one. Also, Annie Fields died last winter. So much misery in the world in general, with the war. Wishes they could have a long talk. Willa.

352. **To Zoë Akins,** Wednesday [prob. late Mar., 1916]; Huntington.
Excited about her play [*The Magical City* opened at the Bandbox Theater in mid-March 1916]. Sets wonderful, characters wonderful. Poet character a true ass. Shows what a clear sense of theater she has. Sorry for the poor handwriting, but is in bed with grippe. Hoping to sail for Italy in early June unless submarines get too active. W. S. C.

353. **To Carrie Miner Sherwood,** Apr. 18, [1916?], from New York; WCPM.
Enclosing letters from Mrs. [Peorianna] Sill. Needs to go visit her. Willie.

354. **To Houghton Mifflin Co.,** Apr. 18, [1916?], from New York; Harvard.
Do not send any more mail to 1180 Murray Hill Avenue, Pittsburgh. Delete that address from their records. Willa S. Cather.

355. **To H. L. Mencken,** May 2, [1916?], from New York; NYPL.
Enclosing the story she had told him about. Hopes he doesn't object to an indirect method of narration. Appreciates his review of *The Song of the Lark*. Willa Sibert Cather.

356. **To Ferris Greenslet,** May 2, [1916?], from New York; Harvard.

Is outraged by the $166.73 charge for changes in proof. This is 14 percent of her royalties! Very pleased with the reviews. Has had a terrible winter and has written very little. Willa Cather.

357. **To H. G. Dwight,** Thursday [May 4, 1916?], from New York; Amherst.

Please come to dinner on Saturday, May 6. Willa Cather.

358. **To H. L. Mencken,** May 12, 1916, from New York; NYPL.

True, the story ["The Diamond Mine"] suggests Lillian Nordica, though there are only two specifics that resemble her life, the shipwreck and the dispute over the will. Yes, her last husband, George Young, is still alive. Let her know by mail if he is going to be in town, as she has had her telephone disconnected. Willa S. Cather. P.S.: Truly doesn't see how Young could object to the story.

359. **To Ferris Greenslet,** June 30, [1916?], from Brown Palace Hotel, Denver; Harvard.

Paul Reynolds sold the clumsy story she told him about for $600. Is on her way to Taos. Hopes he will remember she still wants to do a book about the Southwest and will not commit to anyone else for one. W. S. C.

360. **To Paul R. Reynolds,** July 10, 1916, from Taos, N.M.; Columbia.

Has received the $540 check for "The Diamond Mine." Hopes to have some new material for him in the fall. Willa Sibert Cather.

361. **To H. G. Dwight,** July 10, 1916, from Taos, N.M.; Amherst.

The Columbian Hotel in this wonderful place is pink adobe, the owner a dark Mexicana. Enjoys taking horseback rides and stopping at people's houses. Sorry she didn't invite him another day and arrange for him to bring his friends, but reached the point where she had to leave. Hopes he will visit in the fall. Has taken Paul Reynolds as agent, and he has sold a story she would never have tried to place with a magazine. Willa Cather.

362. **To Paul R. Reynolds,** July 12, 1916, from Taos, N.M.; Columbia.

Sending a photo of herself. Willa Sibert Cather.

363. **To Elizabeth Shepley Sergeant,** Aug. 3, [1916]; PM.

Came up to Wyoming from New Mexico two weeks ago. Hard to advise her where to go in the West. Taos probably the best. Will be off to Red

Cloud in about two weeks. Hasn't done any writing. Has sold the Nordica story to McClure's for a good price. W.

364. **To Elizabeth Shepley Sergeant,** n.d. [prob. 1916], first page and possibly last page missing; UVa.
Isabelle's marriage still hard to accept, but the world looks brighter now. Is enjoying being with Roscoe and his wife in the mountains. Glad that Elsie is working well on her book. Will be in Red Cloud by the end of August. Recommends she go to Taos, though there is a good dude ranch near here in Wyoming.

365. **To Ferris Greenslet,** Aug. 22, [1916], from Red Cloud, Nebr.; Harvard.
Has been in the Wind River Mountains in Wyoming. Has he seen Alice Meynell's review in the *Manchester Guardian?* Will have another book ready by the end of the year, probable title "The Blue Mesa." The book on the Southwest to come after that. Is shutting last year behind her. Glad to receive his check. W. S. C.

366. **To Dorothy Canfield Fisher,** Sept. 2, [1916]; UVt.
Just reached Red Cloud after a summer in New Mexico and Wyoming. Enjoyed Roscoe and his family, especially the twins. Made a talk about *The Bent Twig* [Canfield Fisher's novel, 1915] to a bridge club. Interesting that they both used the same kind of treatment for such different material. Sympathizes with the character who fled moral restrictions. The mother reminds her of a stalwart woman who came to visit Fremstad when she was in Maine – such wisdom. They have different groups of readers in Lincoln. Dorothy's think Cather immoral, and her own think Dorothy boring. All of Dorothy's readers want to believe Thea didn't live with Fred out of wedlock. Willa.

367. **To Paul R. Reynolds,** Sept. 25, [1916?]; Columbia.
Sorry not to have anything to send him yet. Will get back to New York in November and start to work. Glad to see the story in McClure's ["The Diamond Mine," Oct. 1916], but they should have let her cut it as she did "My Little Sister" [by Elizabeth Robins, pub. Dec. 1912 and Jan. 1913]. Willa Sibert Cather.

368. **To Ferris Greenslet,** Oct. 1, [1916], from Red Cloud, Nebr.; Harvard.
Please send a copy of *The Song of the Lark* to Ruth St. Denis in Los Angeles,

who has just written her about "The Diamond Mine." W. S. C. P.S.: Has been asked to do some long stories for New York magazines. Would he be interested in book publication of a group of three or four?

369. **To Ferris Greenslet,** Oct. 23, [1916], from Red Cloud, Nebr.; Harvard.
Should she buy the plates to *Troll Garden*? Did he see the article where she is said to write like [Edith] Wharton? Does not want to. Has heard George Young may sue over "The Diamond Mine," but doesn't believe he will. Mother has been ill. Willa Cather.

370. **To Ferris Greenslet,** Nov. 4, [1916?], from Red Cloud, Nebr.; Harvard.
Pleased at the statement he just sent, showing steady sale of *The Song of the Lark*. Will be in New York by the 25th. W. S. C.

371. **To Paul R. Reynolds,** Nov. 9, 1916, from Red Cloud, Nebr.; Columbia.
Pleased with his success with this last story ["A Gold Slipper"]. Please ask *Harper's* to let her have the manuscript back to do a little revision. Willa Cather.

372. **To Elizabeth Shepley Sergeant,** Nov. 13, [1916?], from Red Cloud, Nebr.; PM.
Mother has been ill since September 1. Has been keeping house and cooking. Has a dear servant [Marjorie] who helps but doesn't cook. Has finally learned to make good pastry. Will go to Arizona in two weeks. Glad to hear she went to Walnut Canyon. Has read her "French Perspectives" and found it very pleasing. Still distressed about poor proofreading in *Lark*. Maybe they will see each other in New York after Christmas. W. S. C.

373. **To Paul R. Reynolds,** Dec. 11, 1916; Columbia.
Can have lunch with him on Monday the 18th. May have a manuscript for him. Willa Cather.

374. **To H. G. Dwight,** Saturday [Dec. 16, 1916], from New York; Amherst.
Can he come to dinner on Thursday Dec. 21 at seven? S. S. McClure and Isabelle McClung Hambourg will be there. Enjoyed his poem in the *Atlantic*. Willa Cather.

375. **To Ferris Greenslet,** Dec. 16, [1916], from New York; Harvard.
People she knows from Sweden and Norway have indicated possible interest there in translations of *O Pioneers!* and *The Song of the Lark*. Could he

take it up with publishers, perhaps enclosing a copy of Edward Garnett's article in last February's *Atlantic*? Is enclosing a list of the best people to write. He can get their attention by mentioning that reviewers have thought Thea Kronborg was modeled after Olive Fremstad. Please send three dozen copies of the advertising booklet for her to send to people who inquire. Finishing some short stories for Reynolds to place, but will start on the next book soon. Hopes he can come to New York to discuss the Scandinavian possibilities. Will have a phone in soon and send him the number. Might he be there next Thursday [Dec. 21] for dinner with the Hambourgs, S. S. McClure, and Harry Dwight? McClure will tell everyone about the war. Willa S. C.

376. **To Mary Rice Jewett,** Dec. 29, [1916], from New York; Harvard.
So glad she had her poems printed. Delighted to receive a copy. Spent six months in the West this year and is in very good health. Is going to the dock today to see Arthur Foote's daughter off to join the ambulance service in France. Real happiness impossible until the war is over. Has not heard from Miss Guiney for a long time. Please write soon. Willa.

377. **To Ferris Greenslet,** Jan. 21, 1917, from New York; Harvard.
Has heard people are having trouble finding copies of *O Pioneers!*. Latest statement seems to indicate they are letting it go out of stock. Since it is selling a few hundred a year in its fourth year, would think they would want to keep it available. Certainly an author wants that. Willa Cather.

378. **To Ferris Greenslet,** Saturday [Feb. 1917?]; Harvard.
Phone number is 7955 Chelsea. Hopes he will visit while in town. First few chapters of Mr. McClure's book [about war] are exciting. Her story in *Harper's* [prob. "A Gold Slipper," January 1917] has been praised more than it deserves. W. S. C.

379. **To Mary Austin,** n.d., calling card printed Miss Edith Lewis, Number Five Bank Street; Huntington.
Is disappointed to have missed her. Will call again next week.

380. **[To Mary Austin],** n.d., calling card printed Miss Willa Sibert Cather, Fridays, Number Five Bank Street; Huntington.
Will be at home on Fridays in February from four to seven.

381. [To ?], n.d., calling card printed Miss Willa Sibert Cather, Fridays, Number
     Five Bank Street; NYPL.
     Is at home on Fridays in February, four to seven.

382. **To R. L. Scaife,** Mar. 8, 1917, from New York; Harvard.
     Has set aside "The Blue Mesa" to work on a novel with western setting
     about the same length as *O Pioneers!*. Is about half through the first draft.
     How late could she get manuscript in to have a fall publication date? May
     have it by end of May or middle of June. If a fall publication this year not
     possible, will probably set it aside and do more stories. Reynolds can get
     $700 each for them. Willa Sibert Cather.

383. **To R. L. Scaife,** Mar. 13, [1917]; Harvard.
     Will try to finish the manuscript in time for fall publication. Doesn't want
     illustrations unless she can find just the right person. Would like a cover
     of dark blue with perhaps a bright yellow jacket. Willa Cather.

384. **To R. L. Scaife,** Apr. 7, [1917], from New York; Harvard.
     Will be glad to help with Albertieri's book about dance, but doubts he will
     split the manuscript into two. Rather than the illustrators he suggested,
     believes Benda might do something for the new book. Willa S. Cather.

385. **To Carrie Miner Sherwood,** Sunday [1917?] from New York; WCPM.
     Enclosing the best war book she has read, by a woman from Poland. Hon-
     est account of the terrible things she witnessed and experienced. Easy to
     see why the French fear German domination so. Willie.

386. **To Ferris Greenslet,** Saturday [prob. Apr. 28, 1917], from New York; Harvard.
     Glad he is back from London. Has been socializing with Fremstad and
     with the Hambourgs lately, so not much writing. W. S. C.

387. **To Elizabeth Shepley Sergeant,** June 23, [1917?], from Red Cloud, Nebr.;
     PM.
     Can't suggest anything new to read. Most new books disappointing. Elsie
     might try Mary Austin's *The Ford*. Came to Nebraska to receive an hon-
     orary doctorate. Edith Abbott, Jane Addams's assistant, awarded honorary
     degree at the same time, the first given by the University of Nebraska
     to women. Then more than a week of visiting, until tea parties became
     repetitious and tiresome. Nebraska is in a heat wave plus burning with
     patriotism. Is going to Wyoming soon. W. S. C.

388. To Ferris Greenslet, June 25, [1917], from Red Cloud, Nebr.; Harvard.
Came west to receive an honorary degree from the University of Nebraska.
Now at home. Will go on to Wyoming soon, or may join Isabelle in New
Hampshire. Nebraskans are very pro-war. Willa S. C.

389. To Mrs. George P. Cather [Aunt Franc], Saturday [pm. July 14, 1917], from
Red Cloud, Nebr.; Weddle.
Father so enjoyed listening to Will Andrews's new Victrola that they stayed
too late to get by Bladen before going home. It was almost dark when they
got back to Red Cloud. Will come to visit next week, before Jack has to
leave. Willie.

390. To Mrs. George P. Cather [Aunt Franc], Sept. 9, [pm. 1917], from the Shattuck Inn, Jaffrey, N.H.; Weddle.
Understands her regret that G. P. has enlisted, but he has always wanted
to be in the military and this is his chance. It's a time of return to basics:
men carrying guns. For herself, feels proud of him and glad he can go,
especially as an officer. Wishes Jack were going. Was sorry not to see her,
but the heat was debilitating and she and her friend fled back East. Was
too worn out to work for a while, but now is working every morning in
a tent about a mile from the inn. Douglass's reports about Mother are
disheartening. Wonders if she should go to California to see about her.
Address is at Hotel Garfield on O'Farrell Street in San Francisco. Elsie is
delighted with her school and with Albuquerque. On the whole, families
are pretty good things to have. Willa.

391. To Paul R. Reynolds, Sept. 14, [1917?], from Jaffrey, N.H.; Columbia.
Will take $350 for the stories. Suggests he try "Little Annie" on *McClure's*
and *Everybody's*. Did *Smart Set* reject "Scandal"? W. S. C.

392. To Mrs. George P. Cather [Aunt Franc], Sept. 19, [1917], from Jaffrey, N.H.;
Weddle, copy also at UNL.
Sending a letter from Elsie [sister] she will enjoy. Willa. P.S.: Will be home
on Bank Street about Oct. 1.

393. To Paul R. Reynolds, Sept. 19, [1917?], from Jaffrey, N.H.; Columbia.
Will be back to Bank Street Oct. 10. Making good progress on the novel.
Houghton Mifflin urging her to hurry. Sending a rough first draft of a
story called "Explosives." Willa S. Cather.

394. To Ferris Greenslet, Oct. 18, 1917, from New York; Harvard.

Glad to accept contract for Continental rights of the next book. Will certainly accept reduced royalties on O *Pioneers!* in a soldiers' edition. *Century* will start "Office Wives" series in January and wants the book rights. Trusts Houghton Mifflin will not mind. Wants to discuss the physical design of the novel when he comes to town. Will invite Benda to dinner and ask him about doing head and tail pieces. Otherwise, would prefer no illustrations. Has tried drawing her own. Willa Cather.

395. To Ferris Greenslet, Oct. 20, [1917], from New York; Harvard.

Won't make an agreement for "Office Wives" volume if he may want it. W. S. Cather.

396. To Carrie Miner, Oct. 29, [1917]; UVa.

Has been in New Hampshire and only now learned of Carrie's mother's death. It may have been a mercy. A character much like Mrs. Miner [Mrs. Harling] is in the novel she is working on. Book will be dedicated to Carrie and Irene. As one gets older, one's early impressions become clearer and more precious. Willie Cather.

397. To Ferris Greenslet, Wednesday [pm. Nov. 14, 1917], from New York; Harvard.

Should get copy to him Monday morning [Nov. 19]. W. S. C.

398. To Ferris Greenslet, Nov. 18, [1917?], from New York; Harvard.

Sending first two chapters. Should run no longer than 65,000 words. Wants same type as O *Pioneers!* on rough, cream-colored paper. Please send proofs of the pages they set for the dummy, so she can see the visual effect. Willa Cather. P.S.: Has no other copy of these pages, so don't lose them!

399. To Ferris Greenslet, Nov. 24, [1917], from New York; Harvard.

Has been too upset by Mr. Scaife's visit to work. Chose Benda on strength of earlier discussions with Scaife. Benda has put a lot of time into the project and has planned twelve drawings and completed three. Now Scaife says they will pay only $150 for the whole set. Can't ask him to do more than three for that amount. Misunderstanding is her fault; should have made a clear arrangement with Scaife sooner. Could they offer Benda $200 for eight or ten? Willa Cather. P.S.: Is *The Song of the Lark* out of stock?

400. To R. L. Scaife, Dec. 1, [1917], from New York; Harvard.
Chose Benda to do pen-and-ink drawings after seeing his drawings for Jacob Riis's *The Old Town*, for which Macmillan paid him $900. Expected to have about a third as many for her book. Benda will not do what they had decided on for the amount Houghton Mifflin is offering. Might do something simpler and easier for that amount. Will work with him on some new ideas. Is cutting the book so it will be very little longer than *O Pioneers!*. Willa S. Cather.

401. To Miss Van Tuyll [at Houghton Mifflin], Dec. 4, [1917]; Harvard.
The sample of heavy lettering is what she had in mind, but the accent over the initial "A" needs to be more distinct. Willa Cather.

402. To R. L. Scaife, Sunday 9 [Dec., 1917]; Harvard.
Sending two Benda drawings with size marked on the margins. Should be full page with wide margins, rather than tail-pieces. Print small on spacious page, all on recto, to give the effect of old wood cuts. Please send proofs of drawings when ready, as a guide to her and Benda in planning the rest. Willa S. Cather.

403. To Ferris Greenslet, Dec. 26, 1917, from New York; Harvard.
Sent fifty pages of the manuscript by registered mail today. Please send his impressions. Hopes for proofs of the drawings soon. W. S. C.

404. To Ferris Greenslet, Monday [1917? or 1918?]; Harvard.
Can give him more copy next week. W. S. C.

405. To R. L. Scaife, Jan. 16, [1918], from New York; Harvard.
Thanks for telling her about Miss Bishop [Helen Bishop, Ferris Greenslet's secretary]. Will expect her on Friday [the 18th]. Willa S. Cather.

406. To Ferris Greenslet, Jan. 17, [1918]; Harvard.
Will send another batch in about two weeks. W. S. C.

407. To Ferris Greenslet, Friday [c. Feb. 1, 1918]; Harvard.
Introduction will be nearly the last to be written. Will send back the dummy Miss Bishop left with her tomorrow. Looks good. Please remove the middle initial from her name on the title page. W. S. C. P.S.: Would be glad to have Miss Bishop again soon.

408. **To Miss Bishop,** Saturday [c. Feb. 2, 1918], from New York; Harvard.
Please see that the middle initial is cut out of name on title page. Please set illustrations a little lower on the page to give an effect of spaciousness overhead. Willa Cather.

409. **To Ferris Greenslet,** Friday [prob. Feb. 8, 1918]; Harvard.
French maid [Josephine Bourda] has been ill. Has been working on "Ántonia" with one hand and cooking with the other. Signed contract enclosed. Willa Cather.

410. **To Ferris Greenslet,** Feb. 28, [1918], from New York; Harvard.
Has he received the two drawings she sent this week? Has been ill for two weeks, and the maid ill for a month. Very behind in work. It will be hard to get the rest to him by April 1. Hadn't they better wait for fall publication? W. S. C.

411. **To Ferris Greenslet,** Mar. 7, [1918], from New York; Harvard.
Thanks for his support. Would rather plan for fall, not summer. Will send three more Benda drawings tomorrow, including one of Lena Lingard almost splitting her clothes. Will they please send Benda his money right away, also gift copies of *O Pioneers!* and *The Song of the Lark?* Now well and will send more copy soon. W. S. Cather.

412. **To Ferris Greenslet,** n.d. [Mar. 8, 1918?], from New York; Harvard.
Please send proofs of all cuts for "Ántonia" that have been set. W. S. C.

413. **To Ferris Greenslet,** Monday [1918]; Harvard.
Thanks for proofs of the drawings. Please do one over to make figure on horseback larger. W. S. C.

414. **To Carrie Miner Sherwood,** Mar. 13, 1919 [actually 1918], from New York; WCPM.
So glad to have her letter. Theirs is a lifelong friendship. Proud to hear of her work for the Red Cross. Has had a hard winter, with fuel shortage and illnesses, and the book will be delayed. Olive Fremstad helped get her through an attack of bronchitis; she wasn't working because there were no German operas this year. Is getting along well with Isabelle's husband now, having learned to like him. Was at the Wieners' house often before Mr. Wiener's death. A gracious family, unlike many wealthy Jews. Edith

sends regards. Winter was hard on her, too, but of course worst on the poor people of the city. Willie.

415. **To Zoë Akins,** May 4, [1918?]; Huntington.
Interested in her new efforts in play production. Looking forward to seeing her piece [probably "Did It Really Happen?"] in *Smart Set*. What is she going to do with the Spoon River poet [Edgar Lee Masters] in her anthology? [The "anthology" was a series by Akins published from Feb. 19 to Aug. 13, 1915, in *Reedy's Mirror*, St. Louis. The series was to have been published in book form but was not until 1994, under the title *In the Shadow of Parnassus: A Critical Anthology of Contemporary American Poetry*, edited by Catherine Parke.] He is beneath comment. W. S. C. P.S.: Sending some poems not in *April Twilights*. Novel finished and being set in type.

416. **To Paul Reynolds,** May 10, [1918?], from Washington, D.C., cable; Columbia.
Might sell "Little Annie" to this editor. W. S. C. [Retitled "Her Boss," the story was published in *Century*, August 1919.]

417. **To Ethel Marie Armes,** n.d. [? 1918], fragment; Knox.
Sends greetings from Howard Gore, whom she saw in May 1917. Does not want to be interviewed. Willa Sibert Cather.

418. **To Mrs. George P. Cather [Aunt Franc],** n.d. [June 6, 1918], from New York; Weddle.
Knows she must be thanking God for a son who could make them all so proud with his courageous deeds, showing he was a true man and not an inferior one. She and Uncle George are the only ones who deserve the glory he has brought to the family [referring to a newspaper notice of G. P.'s death on the parapet of a trench]. Willie

419. **To Mrs. George P. Cather [Aunt Franc],** June 12, [1918], from New York; Weddle.
Feels inadequate to write, but wants her to know that her loss [of Grosvenor] is present in her thoughts. Everything else seemed to fade into unreality when she saw G. P.'s name in the newspaper under the heading "killed in action" — a title that sets men apart in glory. Now feels she carries a name of honor because it was his name. It was Isabelle who showed her the newspaper notice. Somehow, had not believed he would be harmed in the war. Knows she must be glad he found his mission in

life. Remembers talking with him about the war news in August, 1914. He was not content on the farm; this great endeavor was the kind of effort he needed and craved. Very few men have both the courage and the ability to serve the country in this great challenge as he did. Sends love and sympathy. Willie.

420. **To Ferris Greenslet,** June 20, [1918], from New York; Harvard.
Is enclosing manuscript of introduction as well as all the rest. Is going to Jaffrey on the 25th for about three weeks. Will read proof there. Sending back twenty-seven corrected galleys. Please send proofs of the eight Benda drawings so she can mark where they come in the text. W. S. C.

421. **To Ferris Greenslet,** July 2, [1918], from the Shattuck Inn, Jaffrey, N.H.; Harvard.
Enclosing proofs of cuts with instructions. Progressing well with proofs. Why did the copyeditor change Mama to Mamma and eliminate subjunctives? Shouldn't be charged for restoring those. Did he see the notice that her cousin, Lt. Grosvenor Cather, was killed in action on May 28? W. S. C.

422. **To Houghton Mifflin Co.,** July 9, [1918], from Jaffrey, N.H.; Harvard.
Has not received proofs of the introduction. Willa S. Cather.

423. **To Ferris Greenslet,** July 11, [1918], from Jaffrey, N.H.; Harvard.
Has received proofs but is puzzled that there are no blank pages for the cuts. Wants them on same paper as text. Needs to see how they are set on the page. W. S. C. P.S.: Should she be writing to someone else about these production matters?

424. **To Ferris Greenslet,** July 17, [1918], from Jaffrey, N.H.; Harvard.
Art department plans to print cuts on inserts. Will they be bound into the places she indicated? They will not be effective if not placed properly. W. S. C. P.S.: Pictures should be considered part of the text.

425. **To Ferris Greenslet,** Saturday [July 20, 1918], from Jaffrey, N.H.; Harvard.
Feels reassured by his letter. W. S. C.

426. **To Houghton Mifflin Co.,** July 28, [1918], from Jaffrey, N.H.; Harvard.
Has returned 215 pages of proof to the Riverside Press, but still has not received all of the proofs. Willa S. Cather.

427. To Houghton Mifflin Co., Aug. 3, [1918], from Jaffrey, N.H.; Harvard.
Is reading and returning proofs as fast as possible, but the last of them still have not arrived. Had arranged to leave today but will stay until Tuesday [Aug. 6]. Please telegraph if proofs won't be there. Willa S. Cather.

428. To Ferris Greenslet, Saturday [Aug. 3, 1918], from Jaffrey, N.H.; Harvard.
Proofs have now arrived. Hambourgs have taken a cottage at Scarsdale, N.Y., and Josephine is there with them. W. S. C.

429. To Ferris Greenslet, n.d. [prob. late Aug. 1918], from Scarsdale, N.Y.; Harvard.
Is spending a week with the Hambourgs and will then go west by way of New York. Several musicians there who play chamber music every night. It's heavenly, but the quiet of corn fields will be a welcome rest. W. S. C.

430. To Ferris Greenslet, Sept. 6, [1918], from Red Cloud, Nebr.; Harvard.
Glad to hear advance orders are coming in well. Would he like a volume of stories about musicians and singers? Could include "The Diamond Mine" and "The Gold Slipper," as well as some new ones. Mother's health improving. Will return to New York in October. W. S. C.

431. To Ferris Greenslet, Sept. 15, [1918], from Red Cloud, Nebr.; Harvard.
Meant to say, would he want such a book of stories for spring, given present economic conditions? W. S. C.

432. To Ferris Greenslet, Sept. 19, [1918]; Harvard.
Yes, was wondering about the paper situation specifically. Will send the stories when she returns to New York. W. S. C.

433. To R. L. Scaife, Sept. 23, [1918], from Red Cloud, Nebr.; Harvard.
Thanks for the proof of the ad. Glad he thinks the book looks good. Willa Cather.

434. To R. L. Scaife, Sept. 30, [1918], from Red Cloud, Nebr.; Harvard.
Yes, her copies have arrived, but book shop in Red Cloud has not received its order. Likes the appearance of the volume, though she wishes the paper were a yellower cream color. Willa S. Cather.

435. To R. L. Scaife, Oct. 3, [1918], from Red Cloud, Nebr.; Harvard.
Local book shop received only twelve copies out of an order of twenty-five

and has sold out. Friends in Toronto [Hambourgs] report they can't get it there. Willa S. Cather.

436. **To Irene Miner Weisz,** Monday [pm. Oct. 14, 1918], from Red Cloud, Nebr.; Newberry.
Will get to Chicago at 9 A.M. Thursday [Oct. 17] and leave for Toronto at four that afternoon. Hopes they can visit for a few hours. Willa.

437. **To Ferris Greenslet,** Oct. 20, [1918], from Toronto; Harvard.
Staying with the Hambourgs for ten days, then on to New York. Book still not available here. W. S. C.

438. **To Irene Miner Weisz,** Oct. 26, [1918], from Toronto; Newberry.
Enclosing a review. Such a reader catches the whole better than those who concentrate on identifying originals for the characters. Please share with Carrie. Leaving for New York on the 30th. Willie.

439. **To Ferris Greenslet,** Nov. 3, [1918], from New York; Harvard.
Has received royalty check. Please send one copy each of *The Song of the Lark* and *My Ántonia* to Dr. Frederic Sweeney at Jaffrey. Willa Cather.

440. **To Mrs. George P. Cather [Aunt Franc],** Nov. 11, [1918]; Weddle, copy at UNL.
Thinking of her on this day of peace. For the first time in all history the sun rose on a world without monarchies. A fulfillment of Ralph Waldo Emerson's prediction that God would one day say He was tired of kings. Wishes Grosvenor had lived to see it, but he is now God's soldier, as the line in *Macbeth* says. The old is gone for good. Now more than ever the flag belongs in churches. Willie.

441. **To Ferris Greenslet,** Monday [Nov. 14, 1918?]; Harvard.
Please send her photo to the *Philadelphia Record*. Willa Cather.

442. **To Ferris Greenslet,** Dec. 2, [1918], from New York; Harvard.
Not interested in doing the book of short stories after all. Has begun two other new books. W. S. C. P.S.: Terrible about Elsie Sergeant's injury. Please send review copy of *Ántonia* to the *New York Globe*.

443. **To Elizabeth Shepley Sergeant [at American Hospital in Paris],** Dec. 3, [1918], from New York; PM.
Shocked by the news of her accident. Must have been very painful and the

explosion shocking. Is seeing a lot of returning soldiers and having some to her apartment for dinner. Ours are nicer than other countries' soldiers. So glad she likes *Ántonia*. Her own feelings about it have vacillated. Terrible how many American soldiers died in training camps [in influenza epidemic]. Do come home to recover, then go back to France to get back to work. What a strange world! — with Germany expecting relief first. Willa S. C.

444. **To R. L. Scaife,** Dec. 8, [1918]; Harvard.
Have copies been sent to *New Republic* and *Bookman?* What is the decision about Albertieri's book on dance? Willa S. Cather.

445. **To Lewis Gannett,** Dec. 16, [1918?]; Harvard.
Prefers to remain silent. [?] Willa Cather.

446. **To Ferris Greenslet,** Dec. 28, [1918?]; Harvard.
Can he advance her $200? W. S. C.

447. **To Ferris Greenslet,** Jan. 6, [1919?]; Harvard.
Thanks for the advance on her account. The *Globe* still hasn't received a review copy. Has he tried for a British edition? Has written four chapters on the soldier story. Feels like a medium through which the story writes itself. Willa Cather.

448. **To Ferris Greenslet,** Jan. 15, [1919], from New York; Harvard.
Is pleased to be nominated for the Pulitzer Prize. Willa Cather.

449. **To Mrs. George Seibel,** Feb. 2, [1919?], from New York; WCPM.
Appreciates her nice letter about the book. Surprising that it is so well received, since it avoids all the usual ingredients of a story. Enjoyed Mr. Seibel's romance of prehistory [*The Fall: Being a True Account of What Happened in Paradise, with a New Interpretation of Sacred History, Vindicating Snakes and Apples, 1918*]. Looking forward to her visit. Willa Cather.

450. **To Edgar Lee Masters,** Feb. 9, [1919?]; HRC.
Glad he likes "Grandmither." Seldom writes verse. Unfortunately, the poems [Harriet] Monroe included in her noted anthology [*The New Poetry*, 1917] were garbled. Sorry to have been without a telephone, so missed hearing from him when he was in town. Willa Cather.

451. To Ferris Greenslet, Feb. 11, [1919?], from New York; Harvard.

Thanks for relaying what Mary Austin wrote. Glad to have her esteem. Still hoping for an English edition. Elsie Sergeant writes that she is on crutches and hopes to be dismissed from the hospital soon. W. S. C.

452. To Carrie Miner Sherwood, Feb. 11, [1919], from New York; WCPM.

Sending some reviews; please share with Irene. The one in the *Dial* is the best. Former president of the Missouri Pacific Railroad, Edwin W. Winter, visited to tell her how he liked the book and now drops in like an old friend. Mostly feels glad that her father and Carrie like it. Willie.

453. To Ferris Greenslet, Mar. 2, [1919], from New York; Harvard.

When does he leave for England? Is sending a note from H. L. Mencken, in response to hers thanking him for his review. A Mr. Melchers, of some magazine for booksellers, has been urging her to stick with midwestern material, not shift to New York. W. S. C.

454. To Ferris Greenslet, Friday [Mar. 1919 or after]; Harvard.

Hugh Walpole's phrase in *Bookman* – "one of the very finest of all American novels" – might be good for the dust jacket along with Mencken's comment. W. S. C.

455. To Ferris Greenslet, Monday [1918?]; Harvard.

Miss Lewis did the enclosed. He may omit the second paragraph if he wishes. W. S. C.

456. To Ferris Greenslet, May 2, [1919], from New York; Harvard.

Glad Heinemann will publish an edition. Getting inquiries about serial rights on next novel, to be titled simply "Claude." Won't decide until they talk. Has sold two stories for good prices and two articles for *Red Cross Magazine*. Willa Cather. P.S.: What do Londoners think of [Woodrow] Wilson?

457. To H. L. Mencken, May 2, [1919?], from New York; Baltimore.

May be interested to know Heinemann will publish an English edition of *My Ántonia*. Perhaps he has friends who could call attention to it? Glad *O Pioneers!* got Edward Garnett's notice. Willa S. Cather.

458. To Ferris Greenslet, Sunday [prob. May 4, 1919]; Harvard.
Is he away on a fishing trip or at the office? Is sending a letter she wants to go into no one's hands but his. Willa Cather.

459. To Ferris Greenslet, Saturday [prob. May 10, 1919], from New York; Harvard.
Please send twenty-five reprints from *Chicago News*. Is Houghton Mifflin going to insert this item as a folder into new publications? Knopf has done that for Hergesheimer. Long letter to come soon. W. S. C.

460. To Ferris Greenslet, Tuesday [May 13, 1919?]; Harvard.
Will wait until Booksellers' Convention is over before sending her letter. W. S. C.

461. To Ferris Greenslet, May 19, [1919], from New York; Harvard.
Has many things to take up with him. Bill for corrections on proof has brought all this to a head. If Houghton Mifflin really valued her, wouldn't they absorb such costs? Three New York publishers have approached her recently. Houghton Mifflin has not used good reviews effectively to boost sales and has not been diligent about getting review copies out. One reviewer told her Houghton Mifflin seems unwilling to praise this book. Why are they reluctant to quote people who say things like "great writer"? Wishes they would advertise her as Knopf has Hergesheimer, but they do not seem to take a long-term interest in her books. Their stock of *The Song of the Lark* has dropped to eight copies and *O Pioneers!* to four. Hates to have books with two different publishers, but wants a press that will believe in her. Willa Cather.

462. To Will Owen Jones, May 20, 1919, from New York; UVa.
Used the device of the introduction in *My Ántonia* much as some Russian and French writers do, to set a tone. Wanted a male character's memory because it was from men that she learned the most interesting things about the women she was remembering. Wanted first person narrative to emphasize emotion rather than plot. Believes she learned to handle a male point of view by writing Mr. McClure's autobiography. Glad he likes the result. It took getting older to write simply and to be guided by memory. Willa Cather.

463. To H. L. Mencken, May 30, 1919, from New York; Baltimore.
Understands that he, too, thinks Joseph Conrad's latest book [*The Arrow*

of Gold] weak. Hard to believe how people think it's the real thing. Is working on a new novel. Willa Cather.

464. **To Ferris Greenslet,** May 30, [1919?]; Harvard.
Thanks for his letter [probably long letter dated May 23, 1919, trying to persuade her Houghton Mifflin did care about her books]. Now understands the proof charges and is content to pay half, but it seems that not much would change in the future. Who is doing the Swedish translation of *O Pioneers!*? Has been spending a lot of time with returning soldiers from Nebraska. Will not show "Claude" to anyone until fall. W. S. C.

465. **To Ferris Greenslet,** n.d. [c. June 12, 1919], from Toronto; Harvard.
Meant to ask him to keep secret that her new book will relate to the war. Looks as though 5 Bank Street is going to be torn down. Will have to rush back and find someplace to live. Looking forward to talking with him. W. S. C.

466. **To Zoë Akins,** June 26, [1919?]; UVa.
Feels generously treated in her anthology [series of articles Akins anticipated publishing in book form]. Agrees that *Spoon River* [Masters] is realistic, but it shouldn't have to be so harsh. Hates the syntax. W. S. C.

467. **To H. L. Mencken,** July 2, [1919], from Toronto; Baltimore.
Has only one story available [probably "Her Boss," *Smart Set* October 1919], and it has been declined by *Century*. He may have it for $100 if he wants it. Looking forward to seeing his book on the American language when she gets back to New York. Interesting that Conrad himself thinks the new book is weak. Willa Cather.

468. **To Ferris Greenslet,** July 10, [1919], from Toronto; Harvard.
Quite satisfied with the new jacket, but quotation is misattributed. Will leave here the end of July and spend August in Jaffrey, N.H. Edith Lewis is looking at apartments. Is working well and hates to stop. W. S. C.

469. **To Ferris Greenslet,** July 11, [1919], from Toronto; Harvard.
Please send a half-dozen of the nice new dust jacket. W. S. C.

470. **To Ferris Greenslet,** July 28, [1919?], from Toronto; Harvard.
Will arrive at Jaffrey, N.H., August 1. Could he drive out sometime the latter half of the month? Needs a new tent like the one she used to write

in. Please have a catalog sent to her at the Shattuck Inn in Jaffrey. Hopes
to get as far as she can on the novel before stopping to do some stories
she has promised. Hopes they will be better than the one in the current
Century ["Scandal"]. Only reason she does short stories is for the income.
Willa Cather.

471. To Ferris Greenslet, Aug. 4, [1919], from Jaffrey, N.H.; Harvard.
Has sent the tent company a description of what she wants. Hopes it will
be there by Saturday [Aug. 9]. Please let her know when he is coming. Avoid
Sunday; too much traffic. Willa Cather.

472. To Ferris Greenslet, Tuesday [Aug. 12, 1919], from Jaffrey, N.H.; Harvard.
Please try to find her a copy of Turgenev's letters. Tent has arrived. W. S. C.

473. To Ferris Greenslet, Sunday [prob. Sept. 21 or 28, 1919], from Jaffrey, N.H.;
Harvard.
Has had influenza for ten days. Expects to return to New York in about a
week. W. S. C.

474. To Mrs. S. S. McClure, Oct. 2, 1919, from Shattuck Inn, Jaffrey, N.H.; Indiana.
Has been ill; almost had pneumonia. Let Mr. McClure know why she has
not written. Can't undertake what he suggests. Hopes to return to 5 Bank
Street by the 10th. Willa Cather.

475. To Ferris Greenslet, Sunday [prob. Oct. 5, 1919], from Jaffrey, N.H.; Harvard.
Is enjoying the books he sent. Please send *A Year in the Navy* by James Husband. Miss Lewis has sketched out some good advertising ideas. Moving
back into 5 Bank Street on October 23. Same apartment but twice the rent.
W. S. C.

476. To Ferris Greenslet, Oct. 7, [1919], from Jaffrey, N.H.; Harvard.
Please try to get something quotable about her books from Hugh Walpole.
Knopf would do this if he were publishing her next book. Leaving Friday
[Oct. 10]. Willa S. C.

477. To Zoë Akins, Oct. 8, [1919], from Jaffrey, N.H.; Huntington.
Delighted to see the good review in yesterday's *Times* [of *Déclassée*, which
opened at the Empire Theatre on October 6 with Ethel Barrymore in the
lead]. Seems a triumph – a word that can only be used for the theater since

the advent of trench warfare. Confident the play has real quality, is not just what is usually popular. Will go see it as soon as she gets back to New York. Willa Cather.

478. **To Ferris Greenslet,** Friday [Oct. 10, 1919?], from Jaffrey, N.H.; Harvard.
Isn't she due a royalty statement? How about a report of sales in England? W. S. Cather.

479. **To Ferris Greenslet,** Oct. 11, [1919], from Jaffrey, N.H.; Harvard.
Going straight to New York on Monday to avoid the crowds. Seeing people from the *Century* on Tuesday. Got some good work done while at Jaffrey. When would he need the manuscript for spring publication? W. S. C.

480. **To Ferris Greenslet,** Oct. 18, [1919], from New York; Harvard.
The *Bookman* that he spoke of in his October 14 note has arrived. Likes the ad. Swedish edition of *O Pioneers!* has also arrived. When he reprints, will he please change the color of the binding? Let her know when she can phone him – doesn't have her own phone just now. Will get back to work on "Claude" Monday after this [October 27]. W. S. C.

481. **To Ferris Greenslet,** Nov. 2, [1919]; Harvard.
Thanks for statement and check. How many copies do they have in stock? Is saving a bottle of libation for his visit. Father was there for a week. Willa Cather.

482. **To Ferris Greenslet,** Sunday [1919?]; Harvard.
Still no telephone. Come in for tea and then a glass of cheer. No maid yet, so can't offer dinner. W. S. C.

483. **To Ferris Greenslet,** Nov. 17, [1919?], from New York; Harvard.
Can't they get into the *Times Book Supplement* a notice such as this one about Hergesheimer? Understands there will be a Czech translation of *Ántonia*. Still trying to get a phone. Willa Cather.

484. **To Ferris Greenslet,** Nov. 26, [1919]; Harvard.
Telephone company says that only new mothers can get a phone. That would be funny! Please send books she can send to [William Allen] White in Kansas. Nice he wants them. *Century* has made an offer she wants to discuss with him. W. S. C. P.S.: Nice of Mrs. Austin to go to the trouble [to write an article about her].

485. To Ferris Greenslet, Dec. 3, [1919], postcard; Harvard.
White still wanting the books; needs them by the 15th. W. S. C.

486. To William Allen White, Dec. 8, [1919], from New York; LC.
Sent the books today. So good of him to try to encourage people from the region. Willa Cather.

487. To Ferris Greenslet, Dec. 8, [1919], from New York; Harvard.
Got the books off to White. People from Boni and Liveright and from Collier's and *Ladies' Home Journal* came to tea and brought copies of the Tribune article by Mrs. Norris. Will send Mary Austin a copy of *The Troll Garden* if he didn't already. If Austin is bothering to use her big intellect on writing an article, she ought to have everything. W. S. C.

488. To Ferris Greenslet, Dec. 11, [1919]; Harvard.
Sending two books for him to send to [Mary] Austin. W. S. C.

489. To Ferris Greenslet, Dec. 28, 1919, from New York; Harvard.
Hopes he will be in New York before January 7. Please change the mustard-color binding of *O Pioneers!*. If the company doesn't want to bother with the book, how much would they want for the rights to it? Has agreed to let Knopf bring out a new edition of *The Troll Garden* in early spring. Will make sure it isn't at the same time as "Claude." Willa Cather. P.S.: The *Bookman* ad was the only time they were willing to make bold claims for the quality of her books.

490. To Ferris Greenslet, Jan. 7, 1920; Harvard.
Advertising *Ántonia* on the back of Capok's book on the Czechs was a good idea, but the name of the Bohemian who wrote the letter was not Sadiler, but Sadilek. It makes a difference. Another example of his publicity department's work. And they had an agreement that she was to see all advertising in proof! When he comes to see her, he'd better be prepared. Has just finished a good story that opens a new line she can follow when she chooses. Take note! W. S. C.

491. To Ferris Greenslet, Jan. 11, [1920]; Harvard.
Likes the new binding of *O Pioneers!*. Now how about a new jacket? Still no telephone. Could he come in next Saturday evening [Jan. 17]? He would also be welcome for tea on Friday, when she is customarily in for visitors. W. S. C.

492. **To Ferris Greenslet,** Jan. 12, [1920], from New York; Harvard.
Saturday afternoon will be all right if he can come then; she has excused herself from going to Fremstad's recital. W. S. C.

493. **To Ferris Greenslet,** Jan. 20, [1920]; Harvard.
Please send photo of her in striped vest and hat to address shown in enclosed letter. Other times they have failed to do so reviews had to appear without photo. Willa Cather.

494. **To Mr. Linscott,** Feb. 2, [1920], from New York; Harvard.
Enclosed is a better picture of her than the one he had. Willa S. Cather.

495. **To Ferris Greenslet,** Feb. 5, [1920], from New York; Harvard.
Sending quotation from [William Allen] White. Please return it. Miss Lewis has had a relapse and they couldn't get a nurse. What is the doctor calling the bug he has? Sorry he didn't see Knopf. Viola Roseboro' has been telling her she can't find a copy of *Ántonia*. Stores in Chicago have been unable to get copies, and Brentano's says its order hasn't been filled. Willa Cather.

496. **To R. L. Scaife,** Feb. 16, [1920], from New York; Harvard.
Brentano's has a good supply of *Ántonia*, after having been out for several weeks. Is Mr. Greenslet better? Willa Cather.

497. **To Fannie Butcher,** Feb. 16, 1920, from no. 5 Bank Street, New York, dedication written on photograph; Butcher.
"For Fannie Butcher, who wrote the first discriminating review of my first novel. (In this case my interest in the reviewer has outlasted my interest in the novel, for I don't think much of that book now!) With greetings and good wishes, Willa Sibert Cather."

498. **To Mary Virginia Auld,** Feb. 21, [1920?]; UNL.
Sending this note to Grandmother [Cather's mother] to keep for her. Recently a guest brought a marionette that walked in beside him and was so funny. Wanted a cigarette and fell down and sobbed when she said he was too young to smoke. Kissed her hand on the way out. Few real men are so charming. Has been going to operas with Zoë Akins. On Valentine's Day the apartment looked like a florist's shop. Aunt Willie.

499. To R. L. Scaife, Feb. 21, [1920]; Harvard.

Shocked that he would attribute the reports from Chicago to "investigators." They were people she knew. Will read Miss Singmaster's book when she can, but has seen many of her manuscripts in the past and they never had any particular interest. Willa Cather.

500. To Irene Miner Weisz, Mar. 4, [1920], from New York; Newberry.

Please encourage people to patronize Fanny Butcher's shop. Willie.

501. To Paul R. Reynolds, Monday [Mar. 15, 1920]; Columbia.

No, hasn't sold "Aphrodite," but has tried to. Sailing for France soon. W. C.

502. To Fanny Butcher, Mar. 19, [1920], from New York; Newberry.

Trying to get a passport. Will be abroad when *Youth and the Bright Medusa* comes out this fall. Hopes she will like it. Willa Cather.

503. To Ferris Greenslet, Mar. 24, [1920]; Harvard.

Has he recovered? Has been a hard winter. Sailing on May 19 if she can get a passport. Miss Roseboro' searched for four weeks before finding a copy of *Ántonia* for a gift. Willa Cather.

504. To Ferris Greenslet, Apr. 19, [1920]; Harvard.

Please ask Mr. Linscott to return the photograph she sent. Would appreciate receiving her semiannual royalty check now, before she goes abroad. Willa Cather. P.S.: Please send a copy of *My Ántonia* to Dr. Johan Bojer, to take back to Norway.

505. To William Allen White, Apr. 19, [prob. 1920], from New York; LC.

Has been ill, or would have written sooner. Has obtained a passport and will sail on May 19. Hopes [Herbert] Hoover will be nominated while she is away. Willa Cather.

506. To Ferris Greenslet, May 8, 1920; Harvard.

Was too ill after typhoid shot to write sooner to thank him for the check. Anticipates a good trip. Saw Hugh Walpole recently. W. S. C.

507. To Viola Roseboro', June 5, [1920], from Paris; UVa.

Had a wonderful voyage. Edith Lewis not so ill as usual. Enjoyed reading her novel on the way over. Several memorable characters and strong sense of community dynamics. Paris is lovely. Staying just across the river from the Louvre. Veterans in the park are a reminder of the price for such a beautiful civilization. Willa Cather.

508. **To Helen McNeny [in Red Cloud]**, June 15, [1920], from Paris, postcard; WCPM.

It's cold and wet. Has a head cold, but enjoys Paris anyway. Willa Cather.

509. **To Ferris Greenslet**, June 20, [1920], from Paris; Harvard.

Enjoying the food, though prices are high. Not shopping except for necessities. Will spend a few weeks with the Hambourgs and go with them to the south of France and to Sorrento. Edith Lewis going to Italy next week. Has not gone on with "Claude" since arriving, but has planned some cuts, so the money she has spent on drinks has not gone for nothing. French wine is really the essence of the culture. Willa Cather.

510. **To Mrs. George P. Cather [Aunt Franc]**, July 4, [1920], from Paris; Weddle, copy at UNL.

A huge procession of war orphans marched in a parade today to celebrate America. The stars and stripes flying above public buildings. The French like American soldiers, but not Wilson. Hopes to go to Cantigny next week, though trains still disrupted. Feeling good after the voyage. Almost dreads trip to Naples, with travel so difficult now. Willa.

511. **To Charles F. Cather [father]**, July 7, [1920], from Paris; Weddle, copy at UNL.

Has found out the location of Grosvenor's grave. Please let Aunt Franc know. It is registered by the Society for the Care of the American Dead. He is buried in Grave No. 2, Plot B, in the American Cemetery at Villiers Tournelle. From all reports of how the dead at Cantigny were handled, there can be no uncertainty that it is G. P. Will go there next week and take a picture. Isabelle and Jan will go along. Will stay overnight in a home, as there are no hotels. Feeling a little homesick and eager to return to her own country and her own people, although this country and people are wonderful. Willie.

512. **To Mary Rice Jewett**, July 26, 1920, from Paris, postcard; Harvard.

Paris as beautiful as always. Will go to Sorrento for the fall. Willa Cather.

513. **To Ferris Greenslet**, Sept. 1, 1920, from La Côte d'Azur, France, postcard; Harvard.

Has enjoyed traveling through Provence with the Hambourgs. Did not go to Italy because Edith warned her of food shortages. Will return to Paris for a while before sailing from Marseilles. Willa Cather.

514. **To Ferris Greenslet,** Saturday [Nov. 13 1920?]; Harvard.
Arrived yesterday after rough crossing. Has sprained her ankle. Would be glad to see him at Bank Street. W. S. C.

515. **To Elizabeth Shepley Sergeant,** Nov. 19, 1920, from New York; PM.
Just back from France after a stormy crossing. Has a sprained ankle, and the apartment is a mess. Edith sick in bed. Trying to manage everything with one helper. Envies her being in New Mexico. Has seen Amy Lowell's good review of her book. W. S. C.

516. **To Elizabeth Shepley Sergeant,** n.d. [Nov. 21, 1920], from New York; PM.
Enclosing an editorial for her to read, plus a return envelope.

517. **To Mary Austin,** n.d. [late 1920?]; Huntington.
Is very pleased with her article in El *Palacio.* Please drop in Friday afternoon. William Archer will be there. Willa Cather.

518. **To Ferris Greenslet,** Dec. 2, [1920]; Harvard.
Thanks for Elsie Sergeant's book. Overwhelmed with things to do. Will write to him soon about Mr. Llona, who wants to do a translation. W. S. C.

519. **To Fanny Butcher,** Dec. 2, [1920]; Newberry.
What does she think of Mr. Llona? Is recently back from summer abroad and hopes to see her. Willa Cather.

520. **To Ferris Greenslet,** Dec. 14, [1920]; Harvard.
Has received several assurances that Llona is reliable. Please write and say he may do the translation for $50 advance and the rest after publication. Please ask Mr. Linscott to return the photograph she sent some time ago. W. S. C.

521. **To Ferris Greenslet,** Dec. 23, [1920?]; Harvard.
The photo appeared in the *Wanamaker Book News* shortly after the publication of *The Song of the Lark.* First edition of *Bright Medusa* is sold out (3,500 copies) and second edition coming out today. W. S. C.

522. To Fanny Butcher, Jan. 1, [1921?], from New York; Newberry.
Will not be able to visit in Chicago. Is taking her mother to Mayo Clinic for surgery. Willa Cather.

523. To Mrs. Charlotte Stanfield, n.d. [pm. Jan. 6, 1921], from New York; UVA.
Appreciates her note about *Youth and the Bright Medusa*. Willa Cather.

524. To Mary Austin, Jan. 8, [1921]; Huntington.
Appreciated her remembrance at Christmas. Please drop in on a Friday afternoon. Feels proud that she liked *Ántonia*. Willa Cather.

525. To Carrie Miner Sherwood, Jan. 8, [1921?]; WCPM.
Has met [Sinclair] Lewis only twice, the last time a decade ago. Appreciates his always saying such nice things. Please excuse his having written *Main Street* [1920]. Willie.

526. To Mary Austin, Jan. 11, 1921, from no. 5 Bank Street; Huntington.
Will not be able to visit this afternoon. Having to stay in again due to sprained ankle. Willa Cather.

527. To Zoë Akins, n.d. [Jan. 1921?], calling card printed: At home on Friday afternoon, January 14th to March 26; Huntington.
Please drop by on a Friday afternoon. Recently back from long trip to France. W. S. C.

528. To Ferris Greenslet, Jan. 12, 1921, from New York; Harvard.
Has not seen Knopf for a while but has watched his advertising and decided to sign with him for "Claude." Decision based solely on publicity. Not a permanent commitment. Has not yet told Knopf. Greenslet seemed reluctant for her to write about the war or to write again about the West, and this book is primarily war and West. P.S.: Wants to write him personally before he leaves for Europe.

529. To Ferris Greenslet, Jan. 21, [1921]; Harvard.
Greatly indebted to him for his kind letter. *Youth and the Bright Medusa* had sold 3,385 copies as of Dec. 31 – very good for a book of short stories many of which were previously published in book form. Hambourg Trio has been concertizing in New York. No telephone, but let her know when she can phone him. W. S. C.

530. **To Mr. Carroll,** Ash Wednesday [Feb. 9, 1921]; Wellesley.
Please be her valentine and come to tea on Monday the 14th at four. Willa
Cather.

531. **To Mary Miner Creighton,** Thursday [Feb. 10, 1921], on Waldorf-Astoria
stationery; Newberry.
Please drop by for tea tomorrow. Willie.

532. **To H. L. Mencken,** Feb. 20, [1921]; NYPL.
Please let her know when he is going to be in town. Especially wants to
see him. Willa Cather.

533. **To Mary Miner Creighton,** n.d. [Feb. 24, 1921]; Newberry.
Please come to lunch on Saturday. Willa S. C.

534. **To Dorothy Canfield Fisher,** Mar. 21, [1921]; UVt.
She was generous in the *Yale Review* [review of *Youth and the Bright Medusa*].
Nobody else's praise could mean so much in Red Cloud. No one else knows
so well what hard struggles there were in the early years. Now can write
calmly and with pleasure. Is a much tamer person now. Willa.

535. **To Dorothy Canfield Fisher,** Mar. 24, [1921], from New York; UVt.
New novel is well over half done. Feels apprehensive about the part still
ahead. Wishes she could talk with her about it. No one else could help as
Dorothy could. Going to Toronto in two weeks. Willa.

536. **To Fanny Butcher,** Apr. 8, [1921]; Newberry.
Leaving for Toronto and won't be back before the end of summer. May
be able to see Miss Burdette then. Hopes to see Fanny in Chicago. Willa
Cather.

537. **To Dorothy Canfield Fisher,** Friday [Apr. 9, 1921]; UVt.
Believes they can be friends again. Regrets being so stubborn about a bad
story. Dorothy's letters about her books have meant a great deal. Looks forward to sharing their lives again. Willa. P.S.: Leaving tonight for Toronto.

538. **To Dorothy Canfield Fisher,** Apr. 10, [1921]; UVt.
Please look at some of Mr. Victor Llona's French translation and see if it is
really as bad as it seems. Isabelle says hello. Willa.

539. To Sinclair Lewis, Apr. 14, [1921], from Toronto; Beinecke.
Thanks for the kind things he said about her in his Omaha lecture. He is the kind of person whose respect matters. Willa Cather.

540. To R. L. Scaife, Apr. 14, [1921], from Toronto; Harvard.
Understands Sinclair Lewis is saying the kinds of things that may increase sales. Are her books available in the cities where he is lecturing? Willa Cather.

541. To Paul Reynolds, Apr. 27, [1921], from Toronto; Columbia.
Novel still not finished. Knopf may already have promised another magazine first look at the galleys. Which one is Reynolds talking to? Willa Cather.

542. To Ferris Greenslet, Apr. 27, [1921], from Toronto; Harvard.
Sorry he hurt his shoulder. Her sprained ankle still bandaged. Please give Mr. Llona additional time on the translation. Some of what he has done seems worthwhile. Sinclair Lewis and Floyd Dell have been saying nice things about her. Sorry she couldn't go hear Lewis when he was in Toronto. W. S. C.

543. To Laura Hills, May Day [1921], from 38 St. Vincent Street, Toronto; PM.
Enjoyed her letter; opened it when she and Isabelle were having tea and has tacked it up in her studio up under the eaves. Is working on a translation of *Ántonia* into French that will be published in *La Nouvell Revue Francaise*. Feels proud of that. Willa S. C. P.S.: Has met a woman from Boston whose cousin is married to Ms. Hill's cousin – a very nice person.

544. To Mrs. Charlotte Stanfield, June 12, [1921], from Toronto; UVa.
Sorry to have left town without seeing her and Mrs. Boas. Sinclair Lewis said such nice things in his Toronto lecture that she had to beg people to leave her alone so she could work. Health is better than when she left. Novel progressing. Sending a snapshot taken when she was in the Mediterranean. Willa Cather.

545. To Ferris Greenslet, June 17, 1921, from Toronto; Harvard.
Edwin Winter writes that he can't find a copy of *My Ántonia*. Where has he sold second serial rights to *O Pioneers!*? Willa Cather.

546. **To Mr. and Mrs. Partington [?]**, June 23, [1921?], from Toronto; Newberry.
Doesn't believe the story [possibly "Coming, Eden Bower!" *Smart Set* August 1920] reflects anything in Ethelbert Nevin's life, though it's true, she knew him briefly and was impressed by him. Willa Cather.

547. **To Elizabeth Shepley Sergeant**, July 6, [1921], from Toronto; UVa.
How nice, that she is in New Mexico! Having to work on botanical details of a French translation of *My Ántonia*, not a very good one. Probably won't go to Nebraska until September; instead, going to Grand Manan for August. Did she know about Greenslet's broken shoulder? Now that the demand for *Ántonia* is increasing, Houghton Mifflin is out of stock because of a printers' strike. What impossible people! W. S. C.

548. **To Ferris Greenslet**, July 30, [1921], from Toronto; Harvard.
Hopes there will be copies of her books available when she lectures in Chicago, Omaha, and Lincoln in September. Has he seen the current *Nation*? W. S. C.

549. **To Carl Van Doren**, July 30, [1921], from Toronto; Princeton.
Has been noticing his writing on authors in their own styles, and likes what he did with her. Believes her new novel will be her best yet, but he will still probably think it formless. He can return her copy of *The Troll Garden* when she gets back to New York. Willa Cather.

550. **To Ferris Greenslet**, Aug. 26, [1921], from Toronto; Harvard.
Will lecture in Omaha October 29. Has cancelled Chicago lecture. "Claude" won't be out until this time next year. W. S. C.

551. **To Mrs. Babcock**, Thursday [Sept. 1921?]; WCPM.
Looks forward to their sharing a cause. Can't write a statement to be read at the club federation meeting, because has been sick in bed, but please challenge the prejudice against cottonwood trees. Trees are precious on the prairie. Willa Cather.

552. **To Ferris Greenslet**, Sept. 20, [1921], from Red Cloud, Nebr.; Harvard.
Will lecture in Chicago the first week in November. W. S. C.

553. **To Dr. Julius Tyndale**, Sept. 21, [1921], from Red Cloud, Nebr.; UVa.
He may find this telegram from her publisher interesting. It's about the

new novel. [Encloses copy of telegram from Alfred Knopf praising *One of Ours*, still in typescript.] Willa Cather.

554. **To Fanny Butcher,** Sept. 23, [1921], from Red Cloud, Nebr.; Newberry.
Enclosing copy of Knopf's telegram praising the novel [*One of Ours*]. Willa Cather.

555. **To Will Owen Jones,** Oct. 1, [1921], from Red Cloud, Nebr.; UVa, transcription at UNL in Bernice Slote papers, bearing a file date of Oct. 1, 1915.
Probably will have only one day in Lincoln after speaking in Omaha, then on to Chicago. Has enjoyed being at home, where old friends are so supportive. Willa Cather.

556. **To Ferris Greenslet,** Oct. 10, [1921]; Harvard.
Please don't send any more mail to Hambourgs' address in Toronto. They have closed the house and are moving to Paris. Willa Cather.

557. **To Irene Miner Weisz,** Monday [Oct. 31, 1921], from Lincoln; Newberry.
Heard that some people in the audience thought she used the word "smart" to mean "shrewd." She meant it in the sense of style. Glad she came, because Dr. Tyndale enjoyed it. Willa.

558. **To Dorothy Canfield Fisher,** Nov. 5, [1921], written on train crossing New York state; UVt.
Has heard she has been ill. Should rest for a while and enjoy the proceeds from *The Brimming Cup* [1921], maybe go to the Southwest for the winter. Enjoyed visiting in Red Cloud and Omaha but is very tired. Willa.

559. **To Fanny Butcher,** Nov. 5, [1921], written on train; Newberry.
Enjoyed her stay in Chicago, but regrets they only had a half-hour to visit. W. S. C.

560. **To Irene Miner Weisz,** Nov. 10, [1921?], from New York; Newberry.
Still doesn't know the amount of the hotel bill Irene paid, and would like to pay her debt. Isabelle sends thanks for the pleasant stay in Omaha. In Chicago, after her [Cather's] speech at the College Club, there was a dinner given by university classmates. Then went with Fanny Butcher to visit major book businesses, very tiring. Will send some good photos taken in Omaha. Willie.

561. To Ferris Greenslet, Nov. 10, [1921], from New York; Harvard.
Glad *Ántonia* is selling well. Can talk about *Alexander's Bridge* when he is in town. Thanks for the good display of books in Omaha. Sending some clippings for him to show his publicity department. Willa Cather. P.S.: Made calls on major book stores in Chicago, besides lecturing.

562. To Carrie Miner Sherwood, Nov. 10, [1921], from New York; WCPM.
Please send enclosed letter to Irene. Tired out from Lincoln and Chicago. Isabelle leaving Saturday. Willie.

563. To Mrs. Charles Cather [mother], Nov. 26, [1921]; TWU.
Hopes they had a nice Thanksgiving. Had hers at home. Please tell Margie the French woman, Josephine, is back working for her part-time; she is an artist of housekeeping. Cook their own breakfast and have to carry in the ice to the icebox, which is pretty heavy. Would appreciate a couple of aprons for Christmas. Hasn't heard from Isabelle yet. Sorry to have been so testy this summer. Willie.

564. To Mary Miner Creighton, Dec. 1, [1921], from New York; Newberry.
Enclosing a clipping from the *Boston Evening Transcript* about the painter Mary met when she was here. Willie.

565. To Irene Miner Weisz, Dec. 10, [1921?]; Newberry.
Doesn't remember giving her money for ticket to Lincoln. Is sure she owes more of the hotel bill. Has ordered photos from Omaha. Josephine is back for half days; cooks a French dinner every night and will soon have her ailing stomach better. New doctor admires *Ántonia* but would rather he paid attention to her intestines. Willa.

566. To Mary Austin, Dec. 27, 1921, postcard; Huntington.
Only a few people coming to tea this Friday. Do come. Willa Cather.

567. To Blanche Knopf, Dec. 27, [1921], from no. 5 Bank Street; HRC.
Thanks for the Italian cruets and for the book Mr. Knopf sent. Will be in on Fridays again. Willa Cather.

568. To Carrie Miner Sherwood, Dec. 27, [1921], from New York; WCPM.
Thanks for the Christmas box. Especially enjoyed the steamed pudding. Mother sent aprons and other kitchen things. This brings Merry Christmas. Willie. P.S.: Publisher sent two Venetian glass bottles.

569. To Edith Abbott, Wednesday [pm. Dec. 28, 1921]; Chicago.
Will be at her hotel tomorrow at tea time. W. S. C.

570. To Carl Van Doren, Jan. 2, [1922]; Princeton.
Is back at home and hopes he can come for tea on a Friday. Would like to discuss his chapter on Henry James in *The American Novel* [1921]. Willa Cather.

571. To Ferris Greenslet, Jan. 10, [1922?]; Harvard.
Has heard from Omaha that *My Ántonia* is not available. Can get tincture of sweet orange peel these days only with a prescription! W. S. C.

572. To Wilbur Cross, Jan. 10, 1922; Beinecke.
Understood from the Canbys that she would see him before now, so didn't write. Has articles due to the *New Republic* and the *Nation* in February, so can't get one done for the *Yale Review* right away. Willa Cather.

573. To Ferris Greenslet, n.d. [c. Jan. 19, 1922], written at bottom of a note to her dated January 19; Harvard.
Please send copy to this person as she asked before. W. S. C.

574. To Dorothy Canfield Fisher, Jan. 26, [1922?]; UVt.
A great pleasure to be back in touch. Might give a few lectures at the school in Middlebury [the Bread Loaf School]. Is reading proofs of the novel. It was a hard project. Relaxed by writing "Aphrodite" ["Coming, Aphrodite!," *Youth and the Bright Medusa*, 1920; as "Coming, Eden Bower!," *Smart Set* August 1920]. Admires newly translated Turgenev stories, especially "A Quiet Backwater." In seclusion now after having attended several miserable public dinners. Willa.

575. To Mary Miner Creighton, Feb. 4, [1922]; Newberry.
Enclosing a letter from Mrs. Floyd Dell that will amuse her with its revelation of the maternal impulses of even a habituée of Greenwich Village. Willie.

576. To Irene Miner Weisz, Feb. 4, [1922]; Newberry.
Thanks for the comfortable silk undervests. Health is better. Willie.

577. To H. L. Mencken, Feb. 6, [1922?]; Baltimore.
Pleased by his article on "Our National Letters." Earlier in career tried to

counter the influence of foreign writers by following Henry James and Edith Wharton; now realizes their conventions took her further into artifice, away from authenticity. Would like to send him an advance copy of new novel when it becomes available. Does not believe it is a sentimental book. Willa Cather.

578. To Dorothy Canfield Fisher, Feb. 6, [1922], from New York; UVt.
Negotiating with Mr. Davidson at Bread Loaf, but he is awfully vague about details. Would she be willing to read the proofs of the new novel, to watch for anything false or misleading? Willa.

579. To Dorothy Canfield Fisher, Saturday [Feb. 11, 1922?]; UVt.
Thanks for the suggestion on negotiating with Mr. Davison. Will send page proofs when they come. Willa.

580. To Wilfred Davison, Feb. 15, [1922]; Middlebury.
Summer plans still not clear, but believes she could come to Bread Loaf for part of July, for expenses plus $200 for a series of five lectures. Usually gets $200 per lecture or more. Willa Sibert Cather.

581. To Thomas A. Boyd, Mar. 5, 1922; pub. *St. Paul Daily News,* quoted in Bohlke.
Ideas in Boyd's editorial "A Revaluation," which proposed definitions of the novel, need to be stated more clearly. A true artist of literature knows his or her material sufficiently well to write literally, but does not write literally because art is metaphorical or suggestive. Details in writing are there to create effects and serve the end of the literary structure.

582. To Mary Austin, Mar. 18, 1922, from no. 5 Bank Street, New York; Huntington.
Has been ill with the flu, but would like her to come to tea on the 27th. Willa Cather.

583. To Mary Austin, Mar. 25, 1922, from no. 5 Bank Street, New York; Huntington.
Sorry, but can't come to lunch with the Query Club [made up of some of members of the Heterodoxy Club] on Tuesday [the 28th]. Still hopes she can come to tea on the 27th. Willa Cather.

584. To Zoë Akins, Friday [pm. Mar. 31, 1922]; Huntington.
Wishing her bon voyage. Has enjoyed being with her during the winter and seeing her enjoy herself. Willa.

585. To Dorothy Canfield Fisher, Monday [Apr. 17, 1922?] from Galen Hall, Wernersville, Pa.; UVt.
Has received the proofs. Feels confident in Enid, but knows most readers will feel as Dorothy does. Has come to a sanitarium for her health and to work in quiet. Will return to New York the next week. Willa.

586. To Zoë Akins, Apr. 20, [1922?], from Galen Hall, Wernersville, Pa.; Huntington.
Doctor sent her to this sanitorium after she left the hospital. Luxurious surroundings but terrible food. Lost a lot of weight in the hospital; couldn't swallow anything solid for over a week. Working on her proofs. Willa.

587. To Mary Austin, Apr. 21, 1922, from Galen Hall, Wernersville, Pa.; Huntington.
Was sent to this sanitorium after leaving the hospital. Is getting better. Willa Cather.

588. To Dorothy Canfield Fisher, n.d. [Apr. 1922?], apparently a fragment; UVt.
Proofs have arrived, and Dorothy's questions will help her make improvements. Is certain, though, about the independent or traveling guns of the British. Incident of the killing of the German with the locket was from something a young officer told her; she used it because he didn't seem to understand and she liked that. The little girl and the terrible baby also from something told her by a soldier. Used the diary of a physician [Dr. Frederic Sweeney, Jaffrey, N.H.] for the flu epidemic on the transport ship. Is sure of the date U.S. troops went into battle at Chateau Thierry. Claude's feeling about David's violin was from her own feeling of inferiority when they were in France in 1903. Knows readers won't give the book a chance because it is a war novel.

589. To Dorothy Canfield Fisher, Wednesday [Apr. 26, 1922?]; UVt.
New book will be called a war novel. Would never have written such a thing if she hadn't simply had to before she could go on to anything else. Sprang from her cousin Grosvenor, who wanted to escape the farm and

fulfilled his wish by enlisting, only to die at Cantigny on May 27, 1918. Has eliminated her usual pictorial mode in order to approximate the central character's way of looking at the world. He didn't see things as clear pictures. Willa.

590. To Dorothy Canfield Fisher, Friday [Apr. 28, 1922?]; UVt.
Pleased she has offered to review the book. Will want it to be well placed for impact. The fact that Claude was modeled on her cousin is not for general information. Glad to have managed to convey the feeling of the uncultivated person who wants culture. A kind of revenge for the way Dorothy made her feel in France, though a revenge without anger attached. Was with her cousin in Nebraska at the start of the war and felt a strong tie. Feels drained by the effort of writing the book and the closeness to Claude's mind, now lost to her since it is finished. An ordeal but a joyful one. Willa.

591. To George N. Whipple, May 2, 1922, from New York; UNH.
Not interested in public lecturing, in general. Also, is going abroad. Willa Sibert Cather.

592. To R. L. Scaife, May 2, [1922?], from New York; Harvard.
Just found his letter about Mr. Peallie's book. Will read it immediately and write something if they still want it. Got very behind in her work while in the hospital. Willa S. Cather.

593. To Ferris Greenslet, May 2, 1922; Harvard.
Pleased with the royalty statement. When does he need introduction for *Alexander's Bridge?* Would appreciate an advance on amount due in September. Willa Cather.

594. To Carl Van Doren, Monday [c. May 8, 1922?], from no. 5 Bank Street, New York; Princeton.
Thanks for the book, which was waiting when she returned from sanitorium. Glad he likes *Ántonia,* but believes new book is better. Three years of hard work. Willa Cather.

595. To Dorothy Canfield Fisher, Monday [May 8, 1922?]; UVt.
Yes, the story Dorothy sent about the university roughneck has the same idea as her book. Maybe future readers will think it is more true than

Three Soldiers [Dos Passos]. Knopf hopes to see Dorothy in June. Glad Claude can help her understand how she was feeling in that long-past time. Will finish page proofs soon, but doesn't know if she can ever leave this book behind her. Willa.

596. **To Dorothy Canfield Fisher,** Tuesday [May 16, 1922?]; UVt.
Thanks for her sympathetic reading of the novel and especially of Claude himself. Book is shaped by his sense of things. New book now starting on is more outward. Has cut out big chunks of it [*One of Ours*] and probably should cut out the chapter with the shell exploding under him. Willa.

597. **To Dorothy Canfield Fisher,** Monday [May 22, 1922?]; UVt.
Knopf will expect to see her between June 14 and 17. His view of the novel shows the preconceptions she mentioned. Willa.

598. **To Dorothy Canfield Fisher,** Thursday [June 1, 1922?]; UVt.
Congratulations on her article ["Vermont: Our Rich Little Poor State"] in the *Nation*. Hopes they can visit in private before or after they call on Knopf. Willa.

599. **To Dorothy Canfield Fisher,** prob. June 8, 1922; UVt.
Alfred Knopf has jury duty. If he can't be excused, they will have to see him over lunch. W.

600. **To Mrs. Charlotte Stanfield,** n.d. [pm. June 10, 1922], from New York; UVa.
Has been in the country with friends. Just found her note today. Has not been well. Only saw Mrs. Boas once all winter. Tonsillectomy was difficult, and she felt worse after she returned from the sanitorium. Also occupied with proofs. Sorry not to be available to visit. Willa Cather.

601. **To Dorothy Canfield Fisher,** Saturday [June 17, 1922?]; UVt.
Hopes they can have a good talk when Dorothy comes back from Italy. They seem to be living in a different world than the one they used to know. Has sent the proofs to her home for use in writing the review. Enjoyed last night's party. Likes [Donald] Harcourt. Willa.

602. **To Dorothy Canfield Fisher,** Wednesday [June 21, 1922?]; UVt.
Hopes Knopf will reduce the anticipated price of the book. Sorry Dorothy will be having to write a review while she is at sea, when she should be resting. Already looking forward to her return. Memory helps one see who

were the really important people in one's life. Thanks for her help with *One of Ours*. It looked like a failure for a while. She rescued the boy. Willa.

603. **To William Allen White,** June 22, 1922, from New York; Emporia, copy at UNL.

Dorothy Canfield leaving for Italy on Saturday [24th]. She has done so much for the book, including arrange to review it for the *New York Times*. Sinclair Lewis to review it for the *New York Evening Post*. Might he consider doing so? Knopf will send an advance copy in August. Willa Sibert Cather.

604. **To Houghton Mifflin Co.,** n.d. [June 1922, per office notation], from New York; Harvard.

Please send gift books to organization in Italy. Willa S. Cather.

605. **To Helen McAfee** [of *Yale Review*], June 22, 1922, from New York; Beinecke.

Will write them an article when she can. Going to Vermont next week. Willa Cather.

606. **To Henry Chester Tracy** [**Hollywood, Calif.**], June 22, 1922, from New York; UVa.

Can't give him advice on how to write a story except to wait until he feels compelled by his material. Willa Sibert Cather.

607. **To Sinclair Lewis,** June 27, [1922], from New York; Beinecke.

Glad to hear he is reviewing *One of Ours*. It will be either a failure or a triumph, and she is glad friends will be deciding which. Hopes to see him next winter. Willa Cather.

608. **To Wilfred Davison,** July 2, [1922?], from New York; Middlebury.

Sorry to be late getting to Bread Loaf, but expects to be there by mid-month. A friend, Miss Edith Lewis, will probably come, too. Could she get space at the inn? Willa Cather.

609. **To Wilfred Davison,** Sunday [July 9, 1922?]; Middlebury.

Glad Miss Lewis can come. The cottage suite sounds good. Will arrive the 12th. Willa Cather.

610. **To Blanche Knopf,** July 28, [1922], from Bread Loaf Inn; HRC.

Thanks for the check. Will go to Grand Manan by way of Montreal next week. Willa Cather.

611. **To Mr. Maurice,** July 30, [1922], from Bread Loaf Inn; UVA.
    Sorry she is not at home and can't provide letters from ordinary readers.
    Willa Cather.

612. **To Miss Bates,** n.d. [Aug. 1922?], from Grand Manan; Columbia.
    Thanks for looking up quotation. Hopes she will like *My Ántonia*. Willa
    Cather. P.S.: People at Bread Loaf were very friendly.

613. **To Mr. Rugg,** Aug. 10, [1922], from Grand Manan; Dartmouth.
    Sorry to be so slow to return his copy of *Youth and the Bright Medusa*. No,
    seldom gives lectures. Willa Cather.

614. **To Carrie Miner Sherwood,** Sept. 1, [1922], from Grand Manan; WCPM.
    Very touched by her letter about "Claude." Used to fear that her own
    people would never care about her writing. Claude and his mother are her
    tribute to Nebraska. Is sending her letter to Isabelle. Willa.

615. **To Dorothy Canfield Fisher,** n.d. [c. Sept. 1, 1922], from Grand Manan; UVt.
    Enjoyed her three weeks at Bread Loaf except for possible attack of appen-
    dicitis, but is tired and glad to get to Grand Manan. Has written a longish
    short story [perhaps "Uncle Valentine"]. May have to have an appendec-
    tomy soon. Must get to Nebraska in late fall. Willa.

616. **To Ferris Greenslet,** Sept. 1, [1922], from Grand Manan; Harvard.
    Many thanks for his letter about *One of Ours* and corrections in the text,
    which will be made in the third printing. Has finished her preface for
    Alexander's Bridge. Is feeling quite well and has finished a long short story
    she thought had faltered. W. S. C.

617. **To Mrs. Charlotte Stanfield,** Sept. 4, [1922?; UVa. notation guesses 1925],
    from Grand Manan, transcription by Bernice Slote; UVa.
    Has been busy with publication details of new book, but enjoying sum-
    mer trip. Will stay here until about October 1. Is enjoying the quiet and
    hiking along the cliffs. Willa Cather.

618. **To Ferris Greenslet,** Sunday [Sept. 17, 1922?]; Harvard.
    Enclosing preface. W. S. C. P.S.: Has escaped surgery for the present.

619. **To Elizabeth Moorhead Vermorcken,** Monday [prob. Sept. 18, 1922]; PM.
    Has just returned from New Brunswick. Very glad she likes "Claude."

People seem not to read it as a story but only as a statement about war. Pacifists keep writing her accusing letters. People don't seem able to separate political issues from art. Willa. P.S. [written at top left corner]: Just found this note written yesterday, after having written another today, so will send both. W —.

620. **To Elizabeth Moorhead Vermorcken,** Tuesday [Sept. 19, 1922] [attached to no. 619]; PM.

Returned from New Brunswick yesterday. Sorry to have missed her. Glad she likes "Claude." It was exhausting to do, simply took over her life, but she now feels lonely for its company. Keeps getting accusing letters from pacifists who think the book extols war. Actually her only concern was its impact on her character. If she had titled it simply "Claude," as she wanted to, the point would be clearer. But does feel proud of it as a work of fiction. W. S. C.

621. **To Dorothy Canfield Fisher,** Friday [Sept. 22, 1922?], from New York; UVt.

Returned home yesterday to find expressions of sympathy for bad reviews and regret that she tried to write a war novel. Only Dorothy's review shows understanding of the book. Knopf reports good sales, however – already 16,000 out of 37,000 printed. Won't Dorothy's own new book be published soon? [*Rough Hewn*, released October 20, 1922.] Eager to see her. Willa.

622. **To Henry Seidel Canby,** Sunday night [Sept. 1922?]; Beinecke.

Sending thanks to Mrs. Canby, if the wonderful review was written by her. Willa Cather.

623. **To Elizabeth Shepley Sergeant,** Thursday [Sept. 28, 1922?], on stationery of Hotel Irwin, 26 Gramercy Park, New York; Beinecke.

Returned from New Hampshire because of appendicitis. Better now, but is still under doctor's care. W. S. C.

624. **To Dorothy Canfield Fisher,** Tuesday [Oct. 3, 1922?], from Central Park, New York; UVt.

Controversy about the book ought to boost sales, at any rate. Receives letters equally absolute on both sides. Had tea yesterday with William Allen White – such a pleasant person. He kept trying to encourage her and joked that her elite literary set had abandoned her. Sinclair Lewis there also. Glad

she didn't feel irritated with him, because she can never hide it. Willa. P.S.:
Would like to meet Robert Frost.

625. **To Elizabeth Shepley Sergeant,** Oct. 4, [1922]; PM.

Sorry Elsie had to order a copy of the novel; should have remembered to
send one. Enjoyed a recent visit with the William Allen Whites; he teased
her about being abandoned by the more literary reviewers. Debate about
the book in magazines and newspapers very lively. Nothing interesting
in New York on the literary scene except John Galsworthy's new play,
Loyalties, on a Jewish theme. After seeing him at the theater jammed between two Jewish matrons on a hot evening, wonders if he's having second
thoughts. Beyond the royalties it will bring, feels *One of Ours* advanced
her in her writing. W. S. C.

626. **To Wilbur Cross,** Oct. 11, 1922, from New York; Beinecke.

People seem to have strong feelings about *One of Ours*, pro or con. Has
been thinking he might like a memoir about Mrs. James T. Fields [for *Yale
Review*], but through a misunderstanding Henry Seidel Canby is expecting such a piece from her [for *Literary Review, New York Evening Post*]. No
longer interested in doing the article she discussed with Miss McAfee a
year ago. Wants to keep working on a new novelette [*A Lost Lady*]. Willa
Sibert Cather.

627. **To George Seibel,** Oct. 12, 1922, from New York; WCPM.

Appreciates his gracious letter. The book is attracting extreme comments
on both sides. Mr. Knopf very glad. Thanks for catching errors, which will
be corrected in the next printing. Some Germans have expressed anger.
Will be sure to let him know if she is in Pittsburgh. Willa Cather.

628. **To George Seibel,** Oct. 19 1922, from New York; WCPM.

Appreciates his comments on the book in *Issues of To-Day* [?]. Would like
to send a copy to Isabelle McClung. Glad he perceived her effort to present
Claude equitably. Willa Cather.

629. **To William Allen White,** Oct. 19, 1922, from New York; LC.

Appreciates his good words, though they may make the highbrow critics all the more hostile. Is certain the novel is her best technically, and is
certain she knew Claude through and through. Hopes he and Mrs. White
will visit again when they are in New York. Willa Cather.

630. **To Ruth [no last name given],** Oct. 20, 1922, from New York; Middlebury.
Nice of her to write and say she liked the book. Remembers her well, as does Miss Lewis, and hopes to see her again. Willa Cather.

631. **To Duncan M. Vinsonhaler,** Oct. 20, 1922, from New York; UVa.
Appreciates his writing about the book. Can't remember ever wanting so much to get a character across as this one. Will hope to see him if she is in Omaha. Willa Cather.

632. **To Arthur B. Maurice,** Saturday [Oct. 1922?], from New York; Princeton.
Would like to review Dorothy Canfield's next book, not this one. Too soon after she reviewed *One of Ours*. Willa Sibert Cather.

633. **To Mrs. Shotwell,** Oct. 20, 1922, from New York; WCPM.
Many thanks for her good word. Will hope to meet Mr. McNeny in Red Cloud. Willa Cather.

634. **To Zoë Akins,** Oct. 22, 1922, from Chicago, telegram; Huntington.
Congratulations. Please send interesting reviews.

635. **To Dorothy Canfield Fisher,** Monday [Oct. 23, 1922?]; UVt.
Has read her thick book [*Rough Hewn*]. Liked the French part best. Family very well done; the shameful mother accurate of a national type but original in fiction. Marise very well done without excess, but Neale would have been better with less said. He's too familiar, whereas the father is strongly felt but still a puzzle. Is planning to visit Dorothy's mother. Willa.

636. **To Ned Abbott,** Oct. 25, [1922?], from New York; WCPM.
If he weren't a friend from school, would refuse his request for biographical information. Suggests he talk with Mrs. Alice E. D. Goudy in Auburn, Nebraska, who was her high school teacher and knew her all through college. Willa Cather. P.S.: Very proud of Newbranch's editorial. Prefers he not mention the McClure autobiography.

637. **To Irene Miner Weisz,** Oct. 26, [1922], from New York; Newberry.
If it's true that Irene is going to Red Cloud, might they travel together from Chicago? Will speak in Omaha November 27. They could have a good visit. Hopes to stay through Christmas. Is enjoying Claude's success, though appendicitis attacks have dragged her down. Willa.

638. **To Dorothy Canfield Fisher,** Thursday [Oct. 26, 1922?]; UVt.
Enjoyed seeing her mother's oil sketch of her [of Cather]. Book selling well, about 17,000 now, though advertising claims 35,000. Will be going to Nebraska in mid-November. Appendix is all right for now. Willa.

639. **To Irene Miner Weisz,** Tuesday [Nov. 7, 1922], from New York; Newberry.
Has cancelled the lecture in Omaha, but still hopes to get to Red Cloud by Thanksgiving. Still hopes they can travel from Chicago together. Appreciated her letter. Willa.

640. **To Lorna Birtwell,** Nov. 10, 1922; Columbia.
Sorry she could not accept her invitation. Days very full. Leaves for Nebraska in ten days for a long visit. Will have Friday afternoons as usual in February. Willa Cather.

641. **To Irene Miner Weisz,** Tuesday [Nov. 14, 1922], from New York; Newberry.
Will leave New York Sunday the 26th, arriving Chicago the next morning. Could spend Monday night with her. Still not well from pleurisy. So glad Irene will be in Red Cloud and hopes they can travel together. Willie.

642. **To Mr. Charles Towne,** Nov. 17, [1922]; Notre Dame.
Appreciates the regard conveyed in his telegram but cannot undertake what he asks. Willa Cather.

643. **To Ferris Greenslet,** Nov. 17, 1922, from New York; Harvard.
Pleased with the sales report, but the copy of *Alexander's Bridge* hasn't arrived. Did he see her article on Mrs. Fields? ["148 Charles Street," a review of De Wolfe Howe's *Memoirs of a Hostess*, 1922, drawn mainly from Annie Adams Fields's diaries] Is going to Red Cloud next week to spend Thanksgiving and Christmas. Willa Cather.

644. **To Mr. Johns,** Nov. 17, 1922, from New York; UVa.
Appreciates his wonderful letter. No one else has recognized the Parsifal parallels in *One of Ours*. Considered using "The Blameless Fool, by Pity Enlightened" on the title page, but finally decided on the line from Vachel Lindsay. He saw it in spite of her reticence. Hopes to see him and Mrs. Johns on a Friday after the first of the year. Willa Cather.

645. To Ida Tarbell, Sunday [Nov. 19, 1922?], from New York; Allegheny.
Must refuse the Pen and Brush Club's invitation as she will be in Nebraska. Willa Cather.

646. To Mrs. George Seibel, Tuesday [Nov. 21, 1922?; details do not all fit with this date, but she may have been wishing to avoid seeing Mrs. Seibel], from New York; WCPM.
Returned from Boston last night [?] for the opening of a friend's play at the Empire [Zoë Akins's *The Texas Nightingale*]. Leaves Friday [?] for Nebraska to stay through Christmas. Sorry to miss her, but must get ready for the trip. Would like a chance to talk with her about Mr. Seibel's review of *One of Ours*. Willa Cather. P.S.: Do go see *The World We Live In*.

647. To Zoë Akins, Tuesday [Nov. 21, 1922?]; Huntington.
Play is wonderful and a fine production. Jobyna [Howland] wonderful in the lead role – as powerful as a fine car. Great looking, too. Didn't go to her house after the play because has been ill and is in bed as she writes. Willa.

648. To Ida Tarbell, Tuesday [Nov. 21, 1922?]; Allegheny.
Will plan on the first Sunday in February, but please send a reminder. Willa Cather.

649. To E. H. Anderson, Nov. 24, 1922; NYPL.
Hurrying to leave for Nebraska but will answer briefly. Georgine Milmine, now Mrs. Benjamin Wells, of Aubrey, N.Y., gathered material on Mrs. Eddy. McClure bought the material, subsequently lost (along with a first edition of *Science and Health*) when the magazine was sold. Milmine couldn't do the writing, and after sampling short segments of it done by several other people he chose her [Cather]. This was shortly after she came to New York. Carefully checked the material and believes it is all accurate except the first chapter, written by Burton Hendrick, now with Doubleday. His resentment at being removed from the project may be part of the reason Doubleday does not bring it back into print. Please keep confidential. Willa Cather.

650. To Lorna Birtwell, Nov. 27, [1922]; Columbia.
Appreciated her interesting comments on *One of Ours*. Most critics wanted her to repeat *Ántonia*, though only two reviewers had liked it [*Ántonia*] when it was new. Has been delayed by work on proofs of new edition

of *April Twilights*, so won't have Thanksgiving at home after all. Leaves tomorrow. Willa Cather.

651. **To Dorothy Canfield Fisher,** Tuesday [Nov. 28, 1922], from New York; UVt.
Has been ill and won't be able to visit. Leaves tomorrow for Nebraska, too late to reach home for Thanksgiving. Annie Fields was even better than she said in her article. Claude has sold over 30,000. Willa.

652. **To Zoë Akins,** Wednesday [Nov. 29, 1922?]; Huntington.
Does not want to do business with Charley Towne. The Knopfs will try to serialize her story [*A Lost Lady?*]. Appreciates Zoë's helpfulness, but Towne has no credibility. Must go – taxi at the door. Willa.

653. **To Blanche Knopf,** Dec. 4, [1922; stamped into Knopf office Feb. 2, 1923]; HRC.
Enjoyed the basket of fruit they sent for her trip. Happy to be at home. Tomorrow is parents' fiftieth wedding anniversary. Nebraska gives her more joy than any other place. Willa Cather.

654. **To Will Owen Jones,** Dec. 6, [1922], from Red Cloud, Nebr.; UVa.
Strangers are asking for news of her parents' anniversary [humorously said], so she has promised to send information to the newspaper. Willa Cather.

655. **To Zoë Akins,** Dec. 6, [1922], from Red Cloud, Nebr.; UVa.
Wasn't necessary to send telegram to say she understood about Towne. Prairie is beautiful in winter. Father drives her around to the Scandinavian and Bohemian communities in his car. A pleasure to watch the unfolding of the human stories. Willa.

656. **To Paul Reynolds,** Dec. 10, [1922], from Red Cloud, Nebr.; Columbia.
Can't produce to order. If she does any short stories during the winter she will let him show his client. Willa Cather.

657. **To Ida Tarbell,** [c. Dec. 10, 1922], from Red Cloud, Nebr.; Allegheny.
Won't be back for at least a month. Enjoying the winter weather. Greetings to Mary Austin. Willa Cather.

658. **To E. H. Anderson [from Ellen Burns, secretary],** Dec. 11, 1922; NYPL.
Yes, write to Mrs. Wells [Georgine Milmine] but do not mention Cather's

name. Might also write to S. S. McClure for an account of how the material was collected.

659. To Alfred A. Knopf, Dec. 15, 1922, telegram; HRC.
Approves showing manuscript to Hearst.

660. To Blanche Knopf, Dec. 29, [1922], from Red Cloud, Nebr.; HRC.
Everyone is admiring the beautiful tortoise-shell fan. Is pleased with the *Century* offer [to serialize *A Lost Lady* in April, May, and June]. Miss Lewis will have the manuscript ready for them to pick up so they can get it to the printer in time for her to read the book proofs before leaving for Europe on April 1. Willa Cather.

661. To Blanche Knopf, Dec. 30, 1922, from Red Cloud, Nebr., telegram; HRC.
Accepts *Century* offer.

662. To Zoë Akins, n.d. [Jan. 1923, before the 12th], from Red Cloud, Nebr., fragment; Huntington.
. . . Now just parents and one nephew. It has been a wonderful Christmas. May go to Tucson, back to New York by March. Probably will not live there again. Going skating on the river. Willa.

663. To Irene Miner Weisz, Saturday [Jan. 13, 1923], from New York; Newberry.
Arrived last night feeling somewhat better. Appreciates Irene's taking her in to recover. Edith says otherwise she would have been in the hospital. Willa.

664. To Blanche Knopf, Monday [Jan. 15, 1923]; HRC.
Can't go out until she gets over her cold, so won't dine with them tomorrow. Please send manuscript of *A Lost Lady* back for a few corrections. W. S. C.

665. To Blanche Knopf, Thursday afternoon [Jan. 18, 1923]; HRC.
Has seen doctor she recommended and likes him. Manuscript is ready to pick up. Please send proofs of *April Twilights* as soon as possible. W. S. C.

666. To Blanche Knopf, Saturday noon [Jan. 20, 1923]; HRC.
Will have to miss the party. Face still swollen and eye red. W. S. C.

667. To Grace Abbott, Jan. 24, 1923; Chicago.
Received the book she sent right after getting back from Nebraska, when

trying to recover from a cold and needing something good to read. Enjoyed visiting with her sister in Chicago. Has had a good report [about her mother?] from the Mayo Clinic. Willa Cather.

668. **To Irene Miner Weisz,** Jan. 24, [1923], from New York; Newberry.
Enclosing ridiculous letter from Hettie Skeen [Yeiser], trying to fake literary awareness. Is almost well from her cold. Will dine at the Knopfs' on Monday with Myra Hess, pianist. "Claude" still selling well. New edition of *April Twilights* beautifully and expensively done. Willie.

669. **To George T. Keating,** n.d. [Jan. 31, 1923?]; Beinecke.
Will be out of town this Friday but home on the 9th. Hopes he will come to tea. Willa Cather.

670. **To Dorothy Canfield Fisher,** Monday [Feb. 5, 1923?]; UVt.
When will she come visit? New book is almost done. Willa.

671. **To Irene Miner Weisz,** Sunday [Feb. 11, 1923], from New York; Newberry.
Check is to repay her for the bag purchased at Marshall Fields. Josephine is ill; dining at the Wolcott tonight [reason this is on Wolcott stationery]. Knopfs both ill with influenza and had to delay sailing until next Saturday. Please send recipe for Charlotte Russe. Still has a cough. Willie.

672. **To Blanche Knopf,** n.d. [c. Feb. 14, 1923?]; HRC.
Bon voyage. Very happy with their work on *One of Ours* and the recent story. Likes their work in general. Willa.

673. **To Dorothy Canfield Fisher,** Sunday [Feb. 18, 1923?]; UVt.
Disappointed to have missed her. Josephine ill, so she was out doing chores. Won't give any lectures until after her trip to France. Has hired a secretary who says she has declined almost a hundred lectures. Willa.

674. **To H. L. Mencken,** Feb. 27, 1923, from New York; NYPL.
Apparently caught the flu from the Knopfs and is in hospital. Suggests "Paul's Case" for the German translation he spoke of. [Signed for her by M. P. Spaw(?)]

675. **To Dorothy Canfield Fisher,** Friday [Mar. 2, 1923?]; UVt.
Had influenza and spent several days in a hospital; came home yesterday and is still in bed. Josephine very ill. Hopes to sail March 24. Wishes *One of Ours* could have been published anonymously. Willa.

676. **To Zoë Akins,** n.d. [early Mar. 1923?], from no. 5 Bank Street, New York; Huntington.
Just out of the hospital and still weak. New maid coming to interview at four.

677. **To Norman Foerster,** Mar. 8, 1923, from New York; UNL.
Received a copy of his book [*Nature in American Literature*] from Macmillan. Sailing the 17th and will take it with her. Willa Cather.

678. **To H. L. Mencken,** Monday [Mar. 10, 1923?]; NYPL.
Ancestors were Virginians, one great-great-grandfather from Alsace. Otherwise from Ireland, but came to America before the Revolution. Expects to see the Knopfs in Paris. Very pleased with them and likes them personally. Willa Cather.

679. **To George T. Keating,** Mar. 11, [1923], from Lakehurst, N.J.; Beinecke.
Appreciated the roses he sent. Sailing March 24 but will plan to autograph his book when she returns. Hopes he likes the new one, to be out in the fall. Willa Cather.

680. **To Pitts Sanborn,** Mar. [12?], 1923, from Lakehurst, N.J.; UVa.
Has been in this sanitorium since hospital. Sailing March 24. Willa Cather.

681. **To Lorna Birtwell,** Mar. 12, [1923]; Columbia.
Hopes she has not called on a Friday; has not been there. Was in hospital with influenza, then to sanitorium. Plans to sail the 24th. Goodbye until next winter. Willa Cather.

682. **To Elmer Adler,** Tuesday [Mar. 20, 1923], New York; Princeton.
Had to postpone sailing until April, so will be here when *April Twilights* comes out. Looking forward to seeing it. Willa Cather.

683. **To Elmer Adler,** Thursday [Mar. 29, 1923]; Princeton.
Regrets she can't come to tea on the 31st. May stop by his office next week. Willa Cather.

684. **To Elmer Adler,** Sunday [prob. Apr. 8, 1923]; Princeton.
What a beautiful book and beautiful roses with it! Shows what an art printing can be. Looking forward to seeing him on Wednesday. Willa Cather.

685. **To Ferris Greenslet**, May 18, [1923?], from Ville d'Avray, Seine et Oise, France, c/o Jan Hambourg; Harvard.

Sailed April 1 and hopes to be with the Hambourgs until next winter. Is he going to have her select Miss Guiney's poems for the volume or not? Very pleased about the Pulitzer Prize. Willa Cather.

686. **To Judge Duncan M. Vinsonhaler**, May 23, [1923], from Paris; UVA.

Will sit for a portrait in Paris if the people of Omaha want her to. Is being hounded by reporters since the Pulitzer announced. Sends greetings to the Newbranches. Willa Cather.

687. **To Blanche Knopf**, June 12, [1923], from Hotel du Quai Voltaire, Paris; HRC.

Enjoyed the fruit basket during her crossing. Hotel is just across from the Louvre. Enjoying theatre and music inexpensively, though merchandise in shops is high. Will go to the South with the Hambourgs in two weeks. Willa Cather.

688. **To William Allen White**, July 8, [1923]; LC.

Glad he likes *A Lost Lady*. Especially pleases her when midwestern people like her books. Going to Aix-les-Bains soon. Willa Cather. P.S.: Saw Mr. McClure two weeks ago.

689. **To Mrs. George Whicher**, July 18, [1923], from Paris, postcard; PM.

Hopes she enjoys her summer at the Bread Loaf Inn. There are too many people she [Cather] knows in Paris just now; is going away to Aix and Switzerland. Willa Cather.

690. **To Duncan M. Vinsonhaler**, July 28, [1923], from Ville d'Avray; UVA.

Has decided on Leon Bakst for the portrait. He believes he can do it, though he is busy designing sets for Paris Opera. Not sure he will do a good likeness, but it will be an interesting picture. Has agreed to $1,000, the amount Vinsonhaler suggested. Please keep confidential. This has been a difficult matter. Willa Cather.

691. **To Duncan M. Vinsonhaler**, Aug. 1, [1923], from Ville d'Avray; UVA.

Bakst wants to begin the sittings on August 6. Expects it to take two to three weeks. Please keep price confidential, as he usually charges twice that much. Willa Cather.

692. To Irene Miner Weisz, Aug. 11, [1923], from Ville d'Avray; Newberry.
Has been very busy this summer. Had to choose a painter for the portrait commissioned by the people of Omaha. Expects to be at home for Christmas. Looks forward to telling her about Isabelle's house and friends. Bakst paints in a modern style that may not produce a perfect likeness. Fears people in Omaha won't be pleased. Willie.

693. To Duncan M. Vinsonhaler, Aug. [17?, 1923], from Ville d'Avray; UVa.
Has received check for $1000 to pay Bakst. Work has been slow. Her health has not been good, and she is very tired; going to Aix-les-Bains to rest. Not sure her parents will want to go to Omaha to unveil the portrait. Would prefer this to be quiet. May Bakst exhibit the portrait in Philadelphia and Boston before sending it to Omaha? Will probably sail for the U.S. in late October and is not eager to get to Omaha, where the aggressive Mrs. Shotwell lurks. The questions she wrote to Bakst are entirely too personal and intrusive! Willa Cather.

694. To [Sylvia] Beach, n.d. [mid-Aug. 1923?], written on Shakespeare and Co. letterhead; Princeton.
Came by hoping they could go see M. Bient, but found that she was asleep. Went on to see him and he was asleep too! Willa Cather.

695. To Sylvia Beach, n.d. [prob. Aug. 1923]; Princeton.
Hopes to see her when she returns from Aix-les-Bains. Willa Cather.

696. To Zoë Akins, Aug. 22, [1923], from Aix-les-Bains; UVa.
Is spending a month here in quiet after traveling about a lot. Food very good — is gaining weight. Willa Cather.

697. To Mrs. George Whicher, Aug. 23, [prob. 1923], from Grand Hotel, Aix-les-Bains; PM.
Glad she is getting to have the year in Europe she was wanting when they talked in Jaffrey, but regrets they won't be able to see each other. Will be in Aix until early September and plans to sail for Quebec on September 20. Expects to be in Jaffrey again in October. Willa Cather. P.S.: Hambourgs are in Austria.

698. To H. L. Mencken, n.d. [Aug. or Sept. 1923], from Aix-les-Bains; Baltimore.
Sorry, can't commit anything for the first issue of the *Mercury*. Being

treated for neuritis in right arm and has hardly written a thing all summer. Has three new stories planned. Too beautiful here to stay indoors and write anyway. Willa Cather.

699. **To Mrs. George Whicher,** Sept. 5, [prob. 1923], from Aix-les-Bains; PM.
Sorry to have missed her in Paris. Is at Aix for a cure until about October 1. Will hope to see her when she returns to town. Weather is beautiful. Willa Cather.

700. **To Duncan M. Vinsonhaler,** Sept. 6, [1923], from Aix-les-Bains; UVa.
Is resting here for a month. Sixteen sittings for the portrait, rather than the ten anticipated. Has the check in a safe deposit box until the painting is finished. Are they willing for Bakst to exhibit it? Not sure she can bring it with her. Are they willing for a photograph of it to be in the *New York Times*? Mrs. Shotwell's rude letter enclosed. Willa Cather.

701. **To Zoë Akins,** Sept. 14, [1923], from Aix-les-Bains; UVa.
Is spending a month here getting treatment for neuritis on right arm. Will sail as soon as Bakst finishes portrait, paid for by the city of Omaha. Willa.

702. **To Duncan M. Vinsonhaler,** Sept. 21, [1923], from Aix-les-Bains; UVa.
Glad to have his confirmation that people in Omaha pay no attention to Mrs. Shotwell. Touched by Harvey Newbranch's column. Glad people of Nebraska are pleased with her article in the *Nation*. Not sure if she can get painting to Omaha by December 10. Glad to report that *A Lost Lady* is going into a third printing after only a week. Willa Cather.

703. **To Mrs. George F. Whicher,** Tuesday [pm. Nov. 6, 1923], from Ville d'Avray, Seine et Oise; PM.
Has been at Ville d'Avray two days. Could she and the boys come to tea Sunday? And could she and Mr. Whicher come to an art opening tomorrow to meet the artists? Willa Cather.

704. **To Duncan M. Vinsonhaler,** Nov. 9, [1923], from France; UVa.
After a month in Paris is back in the country. Hasn't been writing letters. Sails on the *Berengaria* Nov. 17. Will send painting directly to him when she gets to New York. Seems to be a fine painting, though not a particularly good likeness. Willa Cather.

705. To Mrs. George Whicher, Tuesday [pm. Nov. 14, 1923], from Ville d'Avray, France; PM.

If she can come alone for tea tomorrow, please do. Would hate not to see her. Willa Cather.

706. To Dorothy Canfield Fisher, Nov. 29, [1923]; UVt.

Was delightful of Dorothy to come to the station when she was leaving for France. Had a lovely summery crossing. Now that she's back, has been in bed with a cold and back problems, but also to keep people away. Hopes to start some work next week. Best wishes for a lovely winter. Willa. P.S.: Likes Dorothy's yellow and white cat.

707. [To Thomas Masaryk, Dec. 1, 1923. See no. 1334, Dec. 1, 1936.]

708. To Sister [unidentified], Saturday [Dec. 1923?]; TWU.

Saw Dr. Fordyce, the skin specialist, yesterday, and he diagnosed problem as ringworm; said she must have been in contact with an animal that had it. Cut ten pieces of skin away and sent to a laboratory, and they found ringworm fungus in every piece. First noticed the blisters about two months ago when she was in France. Dog there had seemed to have mange but had recovered several weeks before she noticed the places. Doctor said it takes six weeks to two months to incubate. Has had x-ray treatments and will probably have three more; using iodine and a zinc lotion. Was able to go to the theatre last night wearing long sleeves and gloves. Colored maid is working out well; cooks lunch, does all the cleaning and washing, and manages well with all the shopping and errands; is happy to do that for $20 a week. Happy holidays to everyone. [unsigned; possibly a last page missing]

709. To Duncan M. Vinsonhaler, Monday [Dec. 10, 1923], from New York; UVa.

Sorry she hadn't understood he expected her to be in Omaha for the unveiling of the portrait. No longer plans to be in Nebraska for Christmas; is working on a new book. Would much rather visit when there is no ceremony going on. Has also declined to give William Vaughn Moody lectures in Chicago. People seem bent on keeping her from writing! Picture will be shipped tomorrow. Willa Cather.

710. To O. K. Liveright, Dec. 18, [1923]; UVa.

Glad he is interested in her work, but already has an agent. Willa Cather.

711. **To Duncan M. Vinsonhaler,** Dec. 19, 1923; uva.

Glad the portrait has arrived and they like it fairly well. Doesn't know if Bakst can carry on conversation in English. They spoke in French last summer. Has enjoyed their correspondence. W. S. C.

712. **To Charles F. Cather [father],** n.d. [but with a newspaper clipping from the *Sydney Mail,* Sydney, Australia, stamped July 11, 1923]; UNL.

How did her face get to Australia? Merry Christmas. Willie.

713. **To the City Editor** [*Omaha Daily News*], Jan. 12, 1924, telegram; uva.

Declines to make public statement about portrait. Willa Cather.

714. **To Duncan M. Vinsonhaler,** Sunday [Jan. 13, 1924]; uva.

Enclosing a telegram from newspaper and copy of her answer. Is not pleased with the portrait, but other painters advised it could not be refused. Bakst worked hard on it, and she worked hard sitting. Is sorry if the committee is displeased. Entire matter has been stressful. Willa Cather.

715. **To Miss McAfee [of the** *Yale Review***],** Feb. 7, 1924; Beinecke.

Hasn't been able to do anything for them. Please drop in some Friday in February. Willa Cather.

716. **To Fanny Butcher,** Feb. 7, 1924; Newberry.

Thanks for the art books at Christmas. Is it true she is to be married? Hopes to see her in Chicago in April. Willa Cather.

717. **To Mary Miner Creighton,** Feb. 17, 1924, from New York, telegram [published in the *Webster County Argus* on the occasion of the unveiling of a photograph of her in the Auld Library in Red Cloud], transcription by Bernice Slote; UNL.

"My love and greetings to the old friends of my own home town who are remembering me today. I think they know I would rather have their friendship than any other reward. When I was a child I loved my own town more than most children do, but I could not show it. I used to hope that some day I could make my town pleased with me. If I have succeeded it makes me very happy." Willa Cather.

718. **To Ferris Greenslet,** Feb. 17, [1924]; Harvard.

Is pleased with the idea of doing an edition of Jewett. Will add "The Queen's Twin," "A Dunnet Shepherdess," and "William's Wedding" to the

Pointed Firs sketches. Hears from her local librarian that younger readers sometimes think Jewett's books look like children's books. Type and size of volumes should look more modern. Willa Cather. P.S.: Movie rights of *A Lost Lady* have sold for $12,000.

719. **To Dorothy Canfield Fisher,** Feb. 27, [1924]; UVt.

Letter came at a good time, when she was in bed partly to avoid social obligations, partly because of a stiff neck. Pleased to report people of Red Cloud crowned her picture with a laurel wreath. Has enjoyed reading *The Doctor Looks at Literature* [by Joseph Collins, 1923]. Recommends Mme Curie's book about her husband. Mother is still vexed by Sinclair Lewis's *Babbitt.* Unfortunately for Alfred Knopf, just when readers are prepared to buy books by her about the West she starts writing things where setting doesn't matter. Willa. P.S.: Is the yellow cat male or female?

720. **To Christopher Morley,** Feb. 28, 1924; HRC.

Pleased to accept check in payment for the essay [reprinting of "The Novel Démeublé"]. Willa Cather.

721. **To Wilfred E. Davison,** Feb. 28, 1924; Middlebury.

Would like to come to Bread Loaf again, but is going to Nebraska in April and will not return until fall. Enjoyed seeing the Whichers and Dorothy Canfield while in Paris. Willa Cather.

722. **To Mrs. Charlotte Stanfield,** Mar. 3, 1924, from New York; UVa.

Has had trouble with a stiff neck and is out today for the first time. Hopes to see her soon. Willa Cather.

723. **To Ferris Greenslet,** Thursday [Mar. 6, 1924?]; Harvard.

Has a problem with the Jewett book. Please come Tuesday. Telephone Watkins 7736. W. S. C.

724. **To Zoë Akins,** Saturday [Mar. 8, 1924?]; Huntington.

Many thanks for the roses. Willa.

725. **To Ferris Greenslet,** n.d. [c. Mar. 20, 1924?]; Harvard.

Gossip he heard was wrong. Will write a preface. Is in the country recuperating from influenza. W. S. C.

726. **To Ferris Greenslet,** Sunday [Mar. 23, 1924?], from Pocono Manor Inn, Pa.; Harvard.

Thanks for his good offices [in writing to Mary Jewett]. Came here on Thursday all worn out. Is surprised Mary Jewett would believe someone she didn't know. Will write to her next week. Willa Cather.

727. **To Elizabeth Moorhead Vermorcken**, Mar. 23, [1924], from Pocono Manor Inn, Pa.; PM.

Can hardly do any writing for fending off people inviting her to speak. Has been here to rest in a lovely setting. D. H. Lawrence and wife have been there, marvelous company. Expects to go home in a few days. So few people at the inn, hasn't been bothered by them at all. Appreciates invitation to visit, but that is something she just doesn't do. Willa Cather. P.S.: Ethel Litchfield can tell her why. Does visit Mary Jewett in Maine occasionally, but that's really the only person.

728. **To Ferris Greenslet**, Tuesday [c. Apr. 1, 1924?]; Harvard.

Just back from the country. Can meet him for tea on Thursday. W. S. C.

729. **To Ferris Greenslet**, Apr. 15, [1924]; Harvard.

Between a friend's illness and Josephine's, is driven to distraction, but has started the introduction and will send it to Miss Jewett to see if she accepts. Burton Rascoe caused a lot of mischief. Wants to place "The Queen's Twin" between "A Dunnet Shepherdess" and "William's Wedding." Enclosing a list of stories for second volume. Willa Cather.

List: (1) "A White Heron" (2) "The Flight of Betsey Lane" (3) "The Dunham Ladies" (4) "Going to Shrewsbury" (5) "The Only Rose" (6) "Miss Tempy's Watchers" (7) "Martha's Lady" (8) "The Guests of Mrs. Timms" (9) "The Town Poor" (10) "The Hiltons' Holiday" (or "Decoration Day"?) (11) "Aunt Cynthia Dallet"

730. **To Ferris Greenslet**, Apr. 26, 1924; Harvard.

Prefers to call it a preface, not an introduction. Bostonians would feel they didn't need to be introduced to Jewett. Hopes the tone is right. W. S. C. P.S.: Going to Cos Cob for the weekend.

731. **To Ferris Greenslet**, Apr. 29, [1924]; Harvard.

Glad he likes the preface. Can he send proofs before she leaves for Nebraska May 15? W. S. C.

732. To Ferris Greenslet, May 10, [1924]; Harvard.

Please don't put the Fairchild sonnet as a dedication. It's third-rate and trite. Reluctant to include "Decoration Day" unless Mary Jewett is determined. Be sure to keep "The Hiltons' Holiday," which Jewett believed in (though she thought "Decoration Day" had not aged well). Will withdraw preface if he uses the sonnet. Willa Cather.

733. To Frank Egleston Robbins, May 21, 1924; Michigan.

Is satisfied with arrangements for stay in Ann Arbor. Will attend luncheon, and will appreciate his providing her a cap and gown. Rather short gown, fairly large head size. Willa Cather.

734. To Frank Egleston Robbins, June 8, [1924]; Michigan.

Arriving in Ann Arbor via the "Wolverine" on Sunday morning, June 15. Hopes to be met at the station. Willa Cather.

735. To Irene Miner Weisz, June 10, [1924]; Newberry.

Will reach Chicago the afternoon of June 17 after receiving honorary degree at the University of Michigan the previous day. Would like to spend the night with her. Willie.

736. To Edith Abbott, n.d. [prob. June 20, 1924], from Red Cloud, Nebr.; Chicago.

Has been thinking about her; hopes she will drop everything and get away to England. Mustn't get weighed down by routine, but leave the day-to-day chores in the hands of others and get away while she can, before she is utterly exhausted. Please reply she has bought her ticket. W. S. C.

737. To Dorothy Canfield Fisher, June 27, [1924], from Red Cloud, Nebr.; UVt.

Enjoyed Michigan after all. A dreadful place but interesting people. Enjoying nieces and nephews. Parents amazingly vigorous. Willa.

738. To Irene Miner Weisz, [July 30, 1924], from Hastings, Nebr.; Newberry.

Arriving in Chicago Sunday, August 3. Will leave for New York the next morning. Willa.

739. To Irene Miner Weisz, Tuesday [Aug. 5, 1924], from New York; Newberry.

Had a good trip from Chicago. Is leaving Friday for Grand Manan. Willa.

740. To Miss Chapin, n.d. [prob. Aug. 1924], from Grand Manan; UVa.

Does not review books. Please congratulate Dr. Leach on the revived *Forum*.

Glad he could get the fine story by Miss [Anne Douglas] Sedgwick. Willa Cather.

741. **To Ferris Greenslet**, n.d. [c. Aug. 20, 1924], from Grand Manan; Harvard.
Hasn't received Anne Douglas Sedgwick's *The Little French Girl*, as he promised in letter. Please hold September check until further notice, as she will be there and in Jaffrey. Would he have a pound of caramels sent from Mary Elizabeth's [shop]? Isn't he planning a volume of Miss Guiney's poetry? [*Happy Ending: The Collected Lyrics of Louise Imogen Guiney*, edited by Greenslet, was published in 1927.] Could be working on it while lounging on the cliffs. Willa Cather.

742. **To Ferris Greenslet**, Aug. 28, [1924], from Grand Manan; Harvard.
The two pounds of caramels arrived C.O.D., though she feels sure he paid for it. Has begun Sedgwick's book and likes it so far. W. S. C.

743. **To Zoë Akins**, Sept. 7, [1924], from Grand Manan; Huntington.
Tried to write her a letter on birch bark, but it didn't work well. Has enjoyed recent stormy weather; is working and hiking. Has enjoyed the khaki suit she gave her. W. S. C. [Accompanied by note on birch bark:] Out here in the woods has been working on a new novel, not a pleasant one, rather sour, but interesting in form.

744. **To Henry Seidel Canby**, Sept. 11, [1924?], prob. from Grand Manan; Beinecke.
Will not be back to New York for some time. How is Mrs. Canby? Please reply to Shattuck Inn, Jaffrey, N.H. Willa Cather.

745. **To [Frank Arthur] Swinnerton**, Sept. 18, [1924], from Grand Manan; Arkansas.
Appreciated his sending her the Proust *Within a Budding Grove*. Glad he has had a good trip to Rome. Received an honorary doctorate from University of Michigan in June, then went to Red Cloud. Here on the island since early August, writing. Impossible to tell when a good work period will come. Leaving in three days for Boston and back to New York. Willa Cather.

746. **To Zoë Akins**, Oct. 4, [1924], from Jaffrey, N.H.; Huntington.
Sorry to hear of her father's death. Personal reality lies in families. Sorry to hear she is having to move. Willa.

747. **To Marion [Mrs. Henry Seidel] Canby**, Oct. 5, [1924?], from Jaffrey, N.H.; Beinecke.

Was glad to see her handwriting on the envelope, because it said, even without the letter itself, that she was better. Will see her this winter if she is in New York. Willa Cather.

748. **To Ferris Greenslet**, Oct. 8, [1924], from Jaffrey, N.H.; Harvard.

Was in Boston while he was in Virginia. Enjoyed *The Little French Girl*, though it is overly long. Glad he got money back from the candy shop. Will go on to New York next week. Hoping to finish the new novel this winter. Ready to receive her September royalty check. Telephone number on Bank Street is Watkins 7736, but not to be given out. Willa Cather.

749. **To Ferris Greenslet**, Saturday [prob. Oct. 11, 1924], from Jaffrey, N.H.; Harvard.

Suggests as title for the Jewett volumes:

The Mayflower Edition

of

Sarah Orne Jewett's Best Stories

W. S. C.

750. **To Mr. Miller**, Oct. 24, 1924; Newberry.

Sorry he is irritated by her writing, but he will go on being irritated. Does not agree with his standard of judgment. Writes to suit herself. Reason she took the male point of view in *Ántonia* was certainly not to try to sound like a man. Narrator doesn't really matter anyway, but is only an angle of vision. A story of action doesn't need a clearly defined narrator, but a story of feeling, designed to create a mood, does. Two greatest modern writers were Tolstoi and Turgenev, and they are utterly dissimilar. Willa Cather.

751. **To Mr. [Groff] Conklin**, n.d. [prob. Oct. 1924], from the Shattuck Inn, Jaffrey, N.H.; UVa.

Refuses permission for him to use "Coming, Eden Bower" or "Her Boss." Willa Cather.

752. **To Miss Lathrop**, Nov. 7, [1924?], from New York; Colby.

Appreciates invitation for Thanksgiving. Will hope to be there. Willa Cather.

753. **To Irene Miner Weisz,** Saturday [Nov. 15, 1924], from New York; Newberry.
When is she sending the nice bookends? Will spend Thanksgiving in Boston with Mary Virginia. Willa.

754. **To Carrie Miner Sherwood,** Nov. 16, [1924?]; WCPM.
Appreciates her kindness to mother and to Margie. Loved Margie with the special love one reserves for children or those whose minds never grow up. Enjoyed cooking for her and caring for her a little when she went home. They understood each other. Is fairly well; writing on *The Professor's House,* which should be out next fall. Funny to think of Jessie going around with the movie people on *A Lost Lady!* Willie.

755. **To Miss Lathrop,** Saturday [prob. Nov. 22, 1924]; Colby.
Has had an attack of neuritis and will have to cancel Thanksgiving plans. Unfortunately, active writing brings on these attacks. Does hope to come see Mary Virginia [at Smith College] some time this winter. Willa Cather.

756. **To Eugene Sawyer,** Dec. 3, 1924; Stanford.
Appreciated his letter. Glad he likes her books. Willa Cather.

757. **To Mrs. Elmer Adler,** Dec. 3, 1924; Princeton.
Sorry not to be able to accept her invitations to tea. So busy on her novel she is hardly going out. Willa Cather.

758. **To Blanche Knopf,** Monday [Dec. 8, 1924?]; HRC.
Just getting into some new work and is staying in hiding until it gets further along. Not accepting invitations until after January 1. Please send last part of manuscript and she will get it ready for typesetting. Willa Cather.

759. **To DeWolfe Howe,** Dec. 16, [1924?]; Harvard.
Enjoyed hearing from him. Doubts the young admirers of the New England writers even understand them. Willa Cather.

760. **To Irene Miner Weisz,** n.d. [pm. Dec. 17, 1924], from New York; Newberry.
Can she spend Sunday afternoon on her way to Red Cloud if she is in town? Has a five-hour layover. If not, will ask Edith Abbott to meet her train. Likes the bookends. Willa.

761. **To Fred Otte, Jr.,** Dec. 17, 1924, postcard; WCPM.
Christmas greetings. Willa Cather.

762. **To George F. Whicher,** Dec. 19, 1924; PM.

Sorry she won't be able to see him in New York after Christmas; will be in Red Cloud. Sorry to hear about Mrs. Whicher's problem. Appreciates his asking her to come up for [to give?] the Clyde Fitch lectures, but can't do so this year. Maybe in a year or two. Willa Cather.

763. **To Irene Miner Weisz,** Saturday [pm. Jan. 3, 1925], from Red Cloud, Nebr.; Newberry.

Arriving in Chicago Friday the 9th. Could she meet the train? They could have lunch at Marshall Fields. Leaves at 1:40. Willie.

764. **To Blanche Knopf,** Jan. 4, [1925], note on a torn scrap of paper; HRC.

Carnelians are beautiful. Had a lovely Christmas. Willa Cather.

765. **To Mr. Gluck,** Jan. 21, 1925, transcription by E. K. Brown; Beinecke.

Glad he is using *My Ántonia* in his course on contemporary fiction. First book in which she discarded conventional elements of a novel. Story of a man and woman who are friends, never lovers. Story not made up of the things that usually make up novels. Like the back side of the carpet. Willa Cather.

766. **To Miss Teller,** Jan. 21, 1925; Bryn Mawr.

Miss Feld distorted what she said in interview. Doesn't object to all social workers but to those who take it up only to gather material for fiction. Willa Cather.

767. **To Blanche Knopf,** Friday [Jan. 30, 1925?; stamped into office Feb. 1]; HRC.

Thanks for returning her overshoes and umbrella. W. S. C.

768. **To Thomas Masaryk [president of the Czechoslovak Republic],** Feb. 2, 1925, from no. 5 Bank Street, New York; Berkeley.

Feels honored to receive his letter and glad to have introduced to him the Bohemian people she knew in Nebraska. While in Red Cloud for Christmas took the original Ántonia and six of her children to see the movie of *A Lost Lady*. Usually remains friendly with her characters. Wishes she could introduce to him the real Ántonia and her children. The Midwest is such a combination of contradictories that she can only write about what she lived. Has no biographical material to send him except a publicity brochure from Knopf. Is still only beginning to find her proper voice in fiction. Willa Cather.

769. **To Alice Hunt Bartlett,** 1925; pub. in part in *Poetry Review* of London, quoted in Bohlke.
Does not regard herself as an "effective force in American poetry," as Bartlett said. Of her own poetry, believes "A Likeness," "A Silver Cup," "Going Home," and "Macon Prairie" are the best. The most popular is probably "Spanish Johnny."

770. **To Irene Miner Weisz,** Tuesday [Feb. 17, 1925], from New York; Newberry.
Thanks for the spectacular roses, which have an impact like that of strong personalities. Edith has enjoyed them, too, and Mattie liked them so much, gave her one to wear to a dance for the colored people. Glad she understood the emotions inside the story [*The Professor's House*]. Willie.

771. **To Mary Virginia Cather [mother],** Mar. 2, [1925?]; TWU.
What has she done to upset her so? Hasn't sent anything to Bess [prob. Elizabeth Seymour] or Auntie [Sarah Andrews] since she returned to New York. Hasn't written because she knew Douglass was there. Certainly did not mean to cause discord between her and father about the newspaper story about Margie [*Argus*, October 30, 1924; apparently following a story in one of the city newspapers in Nebraska]. It caused gossip, but isn't angry about it. Hasn't felt really angry toward her since they quarreled about Mrs. Garber. They've been growing closer and mustn't ruin that now. Hopes she and father will let her buy the house so they can pay Elsie to come live with them and look after them. Willa.

772. **To George Whicher,** Mar. 3, [1925], from no. 5 Bank Street, New York; PM.
Misunderstood his previous note about the Clyde Fitch lecture for next year. Please count on her for 1927. Hopes to see him at the birthday celebration for Robert Frost. Willa Cather.

773. **To Irene Miner Weisz,** n.d. [Mar. 16, 1925?]; Newberry.
Has sold the serial rights to *The Professor's House* for $10,000, but don't tell family because they will expect things. Could she please send tablets for washing ecru curtains? Is cleaning house for Virginia's Easter visit. Willie.

774. To Zona Gale, Mar. 20, 1925; HSW.

Person Gale introduced by letter has written, but the name is indecipherable. Maybe it's in Hebrew and a rabbi could make it out! Willa Cather. [Zona Gale note at bottom: Margery Latimer.]

775. To Josephine K. Piercy [from Ellen Burns, secretary], Mar. 20, 1925; Indiana.

Cather has gone to the country to get away from distractions and work on her new novel. Would surely answer her questions if she were there. Ellen Burns, Sec'y.

776. To Mr. Gluck, Mar. 20, 1925; UVa.

Enjoyed reading his students' themes. They all seem to have problems with the terms "romantic" and "realistic." Must learn that "romantic novel" does not mean a love story, but is a two-word noun for a novel with a definite plot. Couldn't write such a novel if she tried. Willa Cather.

777. To Mr. Hunt, Mar. 20, 1925; Harvard.

Very pleased with the volumes of Jewett stories. Please also have a copy of *My Ántonia* sent. Willa Cather.

778. To Mary Austin, Mar. 20, 1925; Huntington.

Hopes to see her house some time. Sorry she couldn't contribute something for the volume on people's "mental processes," but was in Nebraska. Willa Cather.

779. To Irene Miner Weisz, Tuesday [prob. Mar. 24, 1925]; Newberry.

Laundry tablets arrived Saturday, and curtains have been washed and are back up. Enclosing an article by Professor [E. K.] Brown of Bowdoin College. Please share with Carrie. Some time please return the letter from *Collier's* sent earlier; would like to keep it. Willie.

780. To Pat [Knopf], n.d. [spring 1925?]; UVa.

Appreciated his Easter greeting and candy. Glad he likes the new story ["Uncle Valentine"?, Feb., March 1925] and *Ántonia*. Some day he will realize *A Lost Lady* is a better book than *O Pioneers!*. Willa Cather.

781. To F. Scott Fitzgerald, Apr. 28, 1925; Princeton.

Enjoyed his book [*The Great Gatsby*] and never even supposed the passage he points out was derived from *A Lost Lady*. Inevitable that in describing beauty one could only write about the feelings it evoked in oneself. Willa Cather.

782. **To Zoë Akins,** May 9, [1925], from New York; UVa.

Appreciated message from the ship and hopes she is enjoying Paris. Leaves for Bowdoin College tomorrow to give an address, then on to Mary Jewett's house in South Berwick, Maine. Then to Wellesley College to visit Mary Virginia. Leaves for Arizona May 30. Is about halfway through proofs. Willa.

783. **To Mabel Dodge Luhan,** May 23, 1925; Beinecke.

Has just returned from Maine and found her letter waiting. Going to Grand Canyon, then to ranch at Española. May not get to Taos at all, but if it appears she can, will check and see whether there is a house available. Would like to see her house there. Saw Elsie Sergeant yesterday. Sorry to hear Amy Lowell died. Willa.

784. **To Blanche Knopf,** n.d. [c. May 23, 1925]; HRC.

What she is sending is late but was carefully done and seems to be good [essay "Katherine Mansfield"]. Please send proofs. W. S. C.

785. **To Mrs. James Mitchell** [Buffalo, N.Y.], June [?], 1925, postcard; WCPM.

Traveling and can't answer letters. Won't give lectures next winter. Willa Cather.

786. **To Mabel Dodge Luhan,** June 12, [1925?], from Lamy, N.M.; Beinecke.

She and friend are just drifting from place to place. Will read proofs [of *The Professor's House*] at the San Gabriel Ranch near Española. Won't be able to take a house at Taos. Willa Cather.

787. **To Elizabeth Shepley Sergeant,** June 23, [1925], from Santa Fe; PM.

Review was a hard job well done. Is enjoying Santa Fe. Mary Austin is in town and making pronouncements on any subject. Going to San Gabriel tomorrow. W. S. C.

788. **To Mabel Dodge Luhan,** Friday [June 26, 1925?], from Alcalde, N.M.; Beinecke.

Sorry to have missed her. Expects to finish proofs Sunday and leave Monday or Tuesday. Might they rent a guest house after all? Doubts advice on manuscript would be worth board for two. If they don't hear from her by phone, will return to Santa Fe. Willa Cather.

789. To Paul Reynolds, June 28, [1925], from Alcalde, N.M.; Columbia.
Send mail to the Hotel La Fonda, Santa Fe, N.M. Enjoying her trip. W. C.

790. To Mabel Dodge Luhan, Monday [July 6, 1925?], from Santa Fe; Beinecke.
The disagreeable Meyerses, whom they met at Taos, turned up at La Fonda! Is sending some cigarettes. Not very good quality, but no good ones available. These are at any rate fresh. Is receiving letters from people who liked "Tom Outland" in *Collier's*. Still tracking down old priests. Going to Laguna on Wednesday. Willa Cather.

791. To Wilton Graff, July 19, [1925], from Santa Fe; WCPM. [First name of Mr. Graff provided in Bernice Slote papers at UNL.]
Has just returned from a long horseback ride in the Sangre de Cristo Mountains. Appreciates his comments on the book. Will drink his health when she is in Paris next spring. Sorry for having to use hotel stationery. Willa Cather.

792. To Mabel Dodge Luhan, Aug. 7, [1925], from Denver; Beinecke.
Were delayed at Lamy for three days because of flooding at Trinidad. Delayed at New Laguna [the new pueblo of Laguna was built by religious traditionalists after the original Laguna was successfully evangelized by Christians] for three days before a driver would take them to Acoma. Raining every afternoon. Have been in Denver since July 31. Mother is there and going to theater and for rides. Going to Red Cloud August 12, then to Grand Manan. [Continuation Aug. 8] Letter sent to New York has been forwarded. Liked the quotation from Plotinus [Roman comic playwright] but doesn't know who he is. Likes how first volume of memoir is developing. Weeks at Taos were memorable. Brother and family have arrived. Willa Cather. P.S.: Edith Lewis went back to New York on Monday the 3rd.

793. To Mr. [Malcolm] Wyer, Aug. 29, [prob. 1925], from Red Cloud, Nebr.; BYU.
Is pleased to have the book by Father Saljointi [?] and appreciates his bothering to send it. He and the staff at the Denver Library were most kind. Willa Cather.

794. **To Mr. [Malcolm] Wyer,** Sept. 6, [1925], from Red Cloud, Nebr.; BYU.
Appreciates the book he and Mr. Howlett sent. Hopes to see him at the
Denver Library again next summer. Leaves for New York tomorrow. Willa
Cather.

795. **To Fred Otte,** n.d. [Sept. 1925?]; WCPM.
Enclosing photo. Willa Cather.

796. **To Blanche Knopf,** Saturday [Sept. 19, 1925?], from the Shattuck Inn, Jaffrey,
N.H.; HRC.
Spent three days in Boston and talked with Greenslet about selling her
books to Knopf. Please send a copy of the limited edition to her mother
and send her [Cather] their fall list. Needs reading material. W. S. C.

797. **To Mrs. George Whicher,** Oct. 16, [1925], from Shattuck Inn, Jaffrey, N.H.;
PM.
Niece Mary Virginia Auld is a freshman at Smith. Could Mrs. Whicher get
in touch with her some time? The boys would enjoy her. Came here to
work after a wonderful summer in New Mexico living like a Zane Grey
character. Wishes Mrs. Whicher could have attended the birthday dinner
for Robert Frost. Willa Cather.

798. **To Dorothy Canfield Fisher,** Oct. 22, [1925], from Jaffrey, N.H.; UVt.
Has been in New York only three days since the first of June. Enjoys being
here for fall. Walks a lot. Is going back to New York in a week but expects
to leave it permanently before long. Is surprised at how well *The Professor's
House* is selling, considering how gloomy it is. Not her favorite. Wishes
she could see the Frosts again, but never seems to have time. Has been
wanting to work on a story but keeps getting interrupted. Willa.

799. **To Blanche Knopf,** Saturday [Oct. 25, 1925?], from Jaffrey, N.H.; HRC.
Is giving lectures at University of Chicago November 17 through 19, so
can't accept the University Club in New York. Will be back to Bank Street
in a week. "Archbishop" doing well. W. S. C.

800. **To unnamed sister,** Oct. 27, [1925?], from Jaffrey, N.H.; TWU.
Coat left behind was Edith Lewis's. Please send on to New York. Bishops
are going along, but historical facts cramp the writing. Was invited to lecture at Smith College this winter but declined. Would like to buy baby a

coat. Enclosing review. People saying *The Professor's House* is her best book. Can't understand it. W—.

801. **To Mr. Griffith**, n.d. [Oct. 29, 1925?]; UVa.
Thanks for invitation from Authors Club for November 10, but has a commitment in Chicago that week. [Gave the William Vaughn Moody Lecture at the Univ. of Chicago on Nov. 17, 1925 and same lecture at the Women's City Club in Cleveland on November 20.] Willa Cather.

802. **To Irene Miner Weisz**, Nov. 4, [1925], from New York; Newberry.
Just back from New Hampshire. Will speak the night of the 17th. Please reserve hotel room for the 15th through 17th. Could stay the night of the 18th with her. Hopes to have lunch together the day of the lecture and wants her support. Willa.

803. **To Irene Miner Weisz**, n.d. [pm. Nov. 10, 1925], from New York; Newberry.
Arrives Sunday [Nov. 15] at the South Side station. Willa.

804. **To Dr. Stacy and Dr. Moench** [?], [Nov. 1925?], on stationery of the Kahler Hotel, Rochester, Minn.; UVa.
Appreciated the flowers when she left. Enjoyed meeting them. Willa Cather.

805. **To Irene Miner Weisz**, Friday [Nov. 20, 1925], on stationery of the Hotel Statler, Cleveland; Newberry.
Had a good audience in a fine hall, so enjoyed giving the lecture, which went well. Enjoyed visit. Willie.

806. **To Alfred W. Lubin**, Dec. 3, 1925, from New York; UNC.
Is sorry for the delay [?], but has been out of town. Willa Cather.

807. **To Dorothy Canfield Fisher**, Thursday [Dec. 3, 1925?], from New York; UVt.
Returned from Chicago and Cleveland on Saturday and found in accumulated mail a copy of her *Made-to-Order Stories*. Will send it to twin nieces [Roscoe's daughters] in their Christmas package. Visited niece Mary Virginia at Smith College on the way home. Sorry such an unworthy person [?] is settling near Dorothy. Willa.

808. **To Mr. Chambers**, Dec. 4, 1925, from New York; Penn. State.
Hadn't been in town since June until last week, so reply to his letter de-

layed. Rarely lectures, and will be away in Europe during the summer. Willa Cather.

809. To Blanche Knopf, Saturday [Dec. 12, 1925]; HRC.
Gladly accepts invitation to Myra Hess recital in February. Thanks for the gift of a credit at Altman's. W. S. C.

810. To Margaret Crofts, Dec. 13, [1925?]; LC.
Can't make any engagements during the Christmas season as three family members will be with her. To be honest, will not make any engagements until March. Was lazy during the summer but is working well now and must avoid interruptions. Spontaneous things are all right, but planned engagements clutter her calendar and her mind. Maybe they can meet for tea when she is out for a walk in Central Park? Willa Cather.

811. To Blanche Knopf, Dec. 18, [1925]; HRC.
Thanks for remembering her birthday. Has finally finished dental surgery. Willa Cather.

812. To Wilfred Edward Davison, Dec. 21, 1925; Middlebury.
Will be in Mexico and New Mexico all next summer, so can't accept invitation to Bread Loaf. Probably won't ever have time to do it again. Willa Cather.

813. To Miss Lane, Dec. 21, 1925; UVa.
Sorry she can't send a short story, but hasn't written one since "Uncle Valentine." Prefers working in the novel form, and has now begun a new one. Willa Cather.

814. To Mrs. George Whicher, Dec. 21, 1925; PM.
Enjoyed visit. So happy she has extended hospitality to Mary Virginia. Is enclosing an irritating letter from an English teacher. Merry Christmas. Willa Cather.

815. To Mrs. George Whicher, Sunday [pm. Dec. 28, 1925]; PM.
What wonderful cakes she sent! Has enjoyed them with tea. But has enjoyed even more the picture of the children. W. S. C.

816. To William Allen White, Jan. 8, 1926; LC.
Miss Owen ought to be able to get started in magazines. But sketch genre too easy, and she hasn't disciplined her writing. Willa Cather.

817. **To Miss Van Dyne [librarian],** Jan. 8, 1926; Newark.
Glad to be included in their list of best novels. Willa Cather.

818. **To Lillian D. Wald,** Jan. 8, 1926; Columbia.
Will have to miss going to the theater with her. Is going to the country on
Monday [the 11th] to work. Willa Cather.

819. **To Irene Miner Weisz,** Monday [Jan. 11, 1926], from New York; Newberry.
Has a new mink coat purchased by Professor St. Peter [of *The Professor's
House*]. Please ask someone from Mr. Weisz's insurance company to come
by and write a policy on it on Friday or Saturday at noon. Is working hard
and loving her bishop. Willa.

820. **To Carrie Miner Sherwood,** n.d. [prob. Jan. 1926]; WCPM.
[name blotted out; possibly Thomas Masaryk] has just sent some nice
pictures of Bohemia. Is sending some for her and Irene and several to
be framed for Annie Pavelka. Enclosing a check to buy some tulips for
mother. Enjoyed Mary Virginia's visit. Willie.

821. **To Mr. Wyer,** Feb. 15, 1926; BYU.
Appreciates receiving the bibliography about cliff dwellers done by Miss
Gerber and has enjoyed seeing her in New York. Willa Cather.

822. **To Irene Miner Weisz,** Thursday [Jan. 21, 1926], from New York; Newberry.
Glad she shares her pleasure in the mink. Insurance appraiser has been
there. Do read Anatole France's *Thaïs*. Willie.

823. **To E. H. Anderson,** Feb. 15, 1926; NYPL.
Has found someone to do the translations from Swedish she spoke to
him about. Did not mind the philatelist in the private working room; has
probably finished the research she needed to do. Willa Cather.

824. **To Ferris Greenslet,** Feb. 15, 1926, from New York; Harvard.
Mr. Knopf says Houghton Mifflin not willing to sell rights to her books.
Please, then, try to sell copies. Not fair for him to imply that *A Lost Lady*
was only a reprise of *My Ántonia*. True, the original of Ántonia did work for
the original of Mrs. Forrester. Both books consider the same society but
different elements of it and in very different ways. Yes, will try to shorten
the preface [to *My Ántonia*], which is quite necessary to a reader's understanding of the ending. Wants to wait, though, to avoid interrupting the

work in progress. When is the new edition to appear? Must keep Benda illustrations. Willa Cather.

825. **To Blanche Knopf,** Easter Sunday [Apr. 4, 1926]; HRC.
Has enjoyed the rose tree. Is spending Easter in bed. Enclosing some catalog text for *My Mortal Enemy*. W. S. C.

826. **To Paul Reynolds,** n.d. [c. Apr. 25, 1926]; Columbia.
Not writing a love story, but a story of the Southwest at the time New Mexico was seized from Mexico, centering on two Catholic missionaries. Hero is Father Latour, modeled on Bishop Lamy of N.M., who became archbishop and died in Santa Fe in 1886. Lamy saw the transition of N.M. from a wild country to a civilized one. Has been working from a large collection of letters written by Lamy and his vicar to their families. Some incidents invented, some given almost exactly as they occurred. All of part I now written, though not all typed. Part II will not be as long but more solemn in tone. Willa Cather.

827. **To Ferris Greenslet,** n.d. [early May 1926]; Harvard.
Enclosing revised introduction [to *My Ántonia*]. Please send proofs before May 15; will be leaving for New Mexico. W. S. C. P.S.: Please send a copy of *My Ántonia*; had to cut pages out of hers to make the cuts on the introduction.

828. **To Marion [Mrs. Henry Seidel] Canby,** n.d. [c. May 10, 1926]; Beinecke.
Sorry to hear about her tonsils. Off to Arizona soon. Hopes she will like the new book to be published in September [*My Mortal Enemy*]. An experimental form. Willa Cather.

829. **To Ferris Greenslet,** n.d. [May 1926]; Harvard.
Please make a correction on p. 156 in the new edition, to make the phrase about the ripening of the corn more botanically correct. W. S. C. P.S.: Be sure to retain the dedication page.

830. **To Ferris Greenslet,** n.d. [May 1926]; Harvard.
Has received the proofs and will mail them somewhere along the way to New Mexico. W. S. C.

831. **To Blanche Knopf,** May 21, [1926]; HRC.
Sorry not to have seen her before she left. Father telegraphed that she

should stop in Red Cloud. Now on the way to Gallup, N.M.; will read proofs [of *My Mortal Enemy*] there. W.

832. **To Mabel Dodge Luhan,** May 26, [1926], from Gallup, N.M.; Beinecke.
After stopping for a couple of days with her parents and one day at Lamy, reached Gallup very tired. Had the pleasure of sharing that last part of the train trip with Rin Tin Tin [movie star dog] and made his acquaintance during a stop in Albuquerque. Gallup is an awful place. Going to Zuni tomorrow and to Canyon de Chelly later, if Edith recovers from her cold. Brother and family will meet her at Santa Fe June 14. Will get back to work July 1, but not sure where. W. S. C.

833. **To Mr. Sedgwick** [Ellery Sedgwick at *Atlantic Monthly?*], May 28, 1926, from Gallup, N.M.; Columbia.
Will leave it up to Mr. Reynolds whether to serialize the book. Off soon on a long pack trip by horse. Willa Cather.

834. **To Blanche Knopf,** May 28, [1926], from Gallup, N.M.; HRC.
Proofs still haven't arrived. When weather improves will start long horseback trip through Canyon de Chelly. So glad cars can't get there. If they prepare a publicity booklet using the *London Mercury* article, be sure to let her see proof. So easy to get incorrect biographical information into circulation. Please greet Hambourgs while in Paris. Is feeling fine except eyes hurt from the glare of sunshine. Willa Cather. P.S.: After June 1 address will be Hotel La Fonda, Santa Fe.

835. **To Alfred A. Knopf,** June 3, 1926, from Gallup, N.M., telegram; HRC.
Proofs have come. Going to Santa Fe tomorrow. W. S. Cather.

836. **To Mabel Dodge Luhan,** Saturday [prob. June 5, 1926], from Santa Fe; Beinecke.
Would like to rent the pink house for two weeks. Might stay through July if work went well. Edith leaving June 23. Could they have a flat rate for board, as they are used to doing at Grand Manan? Not staying long enough to set up own kitchen. Very comfortable where they are, but too many tourists. W. S. C.

837. **To Mr. Bridges** [of *Scribner's?*], June 10, [1926?], from Santa Fe; Princeton.
Can't reply adequately; on her way to Mexico, won't return to New York until October. Willa Cather.

838. **To Paul Reynolds,** n.d. [c. June 9, 1926], from Santa Fe; Columbia.
Address her at the La Fonda until July 1. W. C.

839. **To Francis O. Matthiessen,** June 10, [1926?], from Santa Fe; Beinecke.
Always glad to help make Sarah Orne Jewett's work better known. Won't
be back to New York until December. Review Mr. [DeWolfe] Howe spoke
about was in *Literary Review* of the *New York Evening Post*. Willa Cather.

840. **To Mary Austin,** June 26, 1926, from Santa Fe; Huntington.
Went to her house a week ago to see if she could work there and has gone
back every day since then. Very quiet and congenial. Sits in blue chair with
big window open and writes on knee. Likes the big room, breeze coming
in at the window. Very generous of her to offer the use of it. Meant to be
at Taos, but Tony Luhan has been in hospital in Albuquerque and Mabel
with him. Will go in early July, when Miss Foote [?] will be there. Hopes
her operation is done soon. Waiting is bad. Willa Cather.

841. **To Zoë Akins,** July 4, [1926?], from Denver; Huntington.
Sorry to have missed her; certainly did not mind visit by Jobyna [How-
land]. Has enjoyed time in New Mexico. Is going to Red Cloud now because
of her mother's health. Glad the two plays are working out well. W. S. C.

842. **To Irene Miner Weisz,** Sunday [Sept. 5, 1926?], from Red Cloud, Nebr.;
Newberry.
Arriving Chicago Wednesday morning. Glad to escape the hot weather.
Willie.

843. **To Ferris Greenslet,** Monday [Sept. 13, 1926?], from no. 5 Bank Street, New
York; Harvard.
Please send three copies of the new edition of *My Ántonia*. Is pleased with
his ad. W. S. C.

844. **To Blanche Knopf,** n.d. [Sept. 22, 1926?], from Jaffrey, N.H.; HRC.
Is delighted with the beautiful Chinese blouse she sent. It fits well, and
everyone admires it. Is feeling very good about *Archbishop*. Will have copy
ready for the printer in November. Please send three copies of *My Mortal
Enemy* and two of *A Lost Lady*.

845. **To Mabel Dodge Luhan,** Sept. 26, [1926], from Jaffrey, N.H.; Beinecke.
Plans for new house are wonderful; view will be splendid. May buy or

build in Taos herself, but if so, much simpler, more of a hut, with a bare interior like rooms at Isleta [pueblo]. Is staying at Jaffrey until October 20. Serialization of *Archbishop* in the *Forum* begins in January. Willa.

846. **To Mary Virginia Auld,** Friday [Oct. 1, 1926], from Jaffrey, N.H.; UNL, copy, not original.

Sorry not to have been in New York when she came by. Has thought of asking her here for a week, but May Willard is coming in. W. S. C.

847. **To Blanche Knopf,** n.d. [c. Oct. 6, 1926], from Jaffrey, N.H.; HRC.

Please tell this person she can't print *My Mortal Enemy* in a collection of short stories. Copies have arrived. Printing is good. Rest of *Archbishop* manuscript will be there about October 29. Please send Virginia Woolf's *The Voyage Out.* W. S. C.

848. **To Mary Virginia Auld,** Thursday noon [Oct. 7, 1926], from Jaffrey, N.H.; UNL, copy, not original.

Please tell May Willard she should have stayed and protected her from phone calls from women's clubs. Word has gotten out that she is there. W.

849. **To Dorothy Canfield Fisher,** Oct. 14, [1926], from Jaffrey, N.H.; UVt.

Just received copy of *Her Son's Wife* that she sent to the apartment. What a somber book; has the middle-aged quality Dorothy saw in *The Professor's House.* Harsh but true that problems are perpetuated in successive generations. Has seen it in action herself. Admires the book but can't enjoy such unrelieved somberness. Mood overwhelms her, much as in *Ethan Frome* [Wharton]. After all, it is possible for a person to emerge from a squalid home and see beauty – like that of Jaffrey. Willa.

850. **To Blanche Knopf,** n.d. [c. Oct. 14, 1926], from Jaffrey, N.H.; HRC.

Is *My Mortal Enemy* out yet? People are asking. Will be back in New York the first week in November. Wonderful weather here. W. S. C.

851. **To Edward Wagenknecht,** Oct. 15, [1926], from Jaffrey, N.H.; PM.

"The Bohemian Girl" was never published as a book; withdrew it from book publication because judged it unworthy. The only copy of *The Troll Garden* she has belonged to Sarah Orne Jewett, with Jewett's marginal notes. Never lends it. Unreprinted stories are without merit – such as "A

Death in the Desert," such a weak story! Willa Cather. P.S.: Will be interested in seeing his book. Doesn't agree this is a great period in literature in English.

852. **To Mrs. Charlotte Stanfield,** Oct. 16, [1926], from Jaffrey, N.H.; UVA.
Glad to hear from her and get her correct address. Glad her health holds up. Please pass along greetings to Mrs. [Franz?] Boas. Hopes she will like the remembrance of a pleasanter New York, about 1904, in the new book. Can't stand New York now unless she gets away most of the year. Willa Cather.

853. **To Blanche Knopf,** Friday [Oct 22, 1926], from Jaffrey, N.H.; HRC.
Woolf book arrived today. Splendid weather, and work going well. W. S. C.

854. **To Blanche Knopf,** Sunday [Oct. 24, 1926], from Jaffrey, N.H.; HRC.
Hasn't seen the *New York Times* review [of *My Mortal Enemy*] and will avoid it. Maybe the advertising should not call it a novel but just a story. Returning soon. W. S. C.

855. **To Elizabeth Moorhead Vermorcken,** Oct. 27, [1926], from Jaffrey, N.H.; PM.
Appreciates her letter about the new story [*My Mortal Enemy*], which she has been trying to work out for years. Review in the *Chicago Tribune* gets the point very accurately. Most people say things like, we're all our own worst enemy. Maybe so, but that wasn't the point. Hopes to have some free time this winter. Please call if she is in town. Has had a good time here in Jaffrey, doing some mountain climbing. Likes being away from New York. W. S. C.

856. **To Harriet Monroe,** Oct. 27, 1926, from Jaffrey, N.H.; Chicago.
Appreciates her sending [Fanny] Butcher's review, which shows a grasp of what the book means. It's true, as other reviewers have said, that we are our own worst enemies, but that isn't what the book is saying. Eyes are better. Willa Cather.

857. **To Fanny Butcher,** Oct. 27, [1926], from Jaffrey, N.H.; Newberry.
She is probably the only person who has perfectly understood the book. Meant to be showing the basic attraction/repulsion of being in a marriage.

Henshawes are intense lovers. Please send another copy of the review. Has enjoyed her stay in Jaffrey and feels proud of the mountain climbing she has done. *Archbishop* begins in the *Forum* in January. A completely new form for her. Willa Cather.

858. **To Ferris Greenslet,** Saturday [Nov. 6, 1926?], from New York; Harvard.
Just back from Jaffrey. Enjoyed meeting the calculating Mrs. Brown at Peterboro'. Willa Cather.

859. **To Harry Brent Mackoy** [attorney in Kenton County, Ky.], Nov. 11, 1926, from New York; Kentucky.
Is not related to Catherine D. Cather. Please inform the editor of *Onward* that she should not make such an assertion again. Willa Cather.

860. **To John Meloy Stahl,** Nov. 11, 1926, from New York; Colby.
Has just returned, having been away since May. Cannot accept his invitation. Must finish new novel; serialization begins in December [*sic*]. Can't take time to come to Chicago. Willa Cather.

861. **To Miss [Marion Edwards] Park,** Dec. 1, [1926], from New York; Bryn Mawr.
Steadfastly refuses to speak at colleges, but nevertheless feels inclined to accept her invitation. Evening of December 16 possible. Please, no public reception before the lecture. Willa Cather.

862. **To Fred Lewis Pattee,** Dec. 2, [1926?], from New York; Penn. State.
Can't agree to reprint of "The Willing Muse." Not a good story. Doesn't want to be represented by it. Willa Cather.

863. **To Fanny Butcher,** n.d. [Dec. 1926]; Newberry.
Yes, send it along and she'll be glad to do that favor [sign a copy?]. Not going home for Christmas. W. S. C.

864. **To Miss [Marion] Park,** Dec. 7, [1926]; Bryn Mawr.
Will plan for January for the lecture. Willa Cather. P.S.: Please don't spread it to other college presidents that she will speak at Bryn Mawr.

865. **To Dorothy Canfield Fisher,** Wednesday [Dec. 15, 1926?], from New York; UVt.
Will write for as long as it takes to smoke a cigarette. Has been busy send-

ing off Christmas presents. Niece Mary Virginia is coming to visit soon, no doubt traveling in something like the style of Queen Marie [of Romania, who traveled from Seattle to New York by train in November 1926 with great publicity]. The queen stopped off in Red Cloud [on Nov. 11], by the way, and was presented a copy of *One of Ours*. New book [*Archbishop*] will be serialized starting in January. Writing it gave her a feeling of great happiness. Willa.

866. **To Will Owen Jones**, Dec. 31, [1926?]; UVa.
Sorry to have been unable to contribute to the collection of letters, but didn't receive request until return from Jaffrey. Willa Cather.

867. **To Francis O. Matthiessen**, Jan. 3, 1927; Beinecke.
Plans to write a short critical study of Jewett in the next year or so, but that won't prevent his doing so. Suggests he approach Mary Jewett and Dr. Eastman, as well as Ferris Greenslet. Only letters to her from Jewett that she wishes to make public are in the Fields edition. Willa Cather.

868. **To Fred Lewis Pattee**, Jan. 3, 1927; Penn. State.
Suggests he use "Paul's Case" or "The Sculptor's Funeral." Willa Cather.

869. **To Ferris Greenslet**, Jan. 3, 1927; Harvard.
Sylvia Bates wants to use about 10,000 words of *My Ántonia* for a textbook. Gives permission, but it is up to him regarding Houghton Mifflin policies. Willa Cather.

870. **To Mary Virginia Auld**, Monday [Jan. 24, 1927], from New York; UNL.
Spoke at Bryn Mawr on Thursday evening. [Error for Tuesday, January 18? College newspaper printed a report on her talk on January 19.] Enjoyed it, but has subsequently had a lumbago attack. Is in bed today and will probably miss the American Society of Civil Engineering dinner on Wednesday. Was invited by the President of the Great Northern Railroad and has looked forward to meeting men who would be attending. W. S. C.

871. **To George Seibel**, Jan. 24, [1927?]; WCPM.
Sorry she was away in Philadelphia when he was in New York. Please send his address. Wanted to send him a copy of *My Mortal Enemy* in the fall, but didn't have address. Willa Cather.

872. **To Miss [Marion] Park,** Tuesday [Jan. 25 or Feb. 1, 1927?], from New York; Bryn Mawr.

Is sorry to have waited so long to write and say that she enjoyed her visit to Bryn Mawr. Willa Cather.

873. **To George Seibel,** n.d. [early February 1927?]; WCPM.

He is correct about the point of the story [*My Mortal Enemy*]. If readers don't get that point, there's nothing to it. W. S. C.

874. **To Mary Austin,** Feb. 10, 1927, from New York; Huntington.

Enjoyed her letter. She shouldn't regret being away from New York; terrible weather and no good plays. Is sending *The Time of Man* [Roberts], which is being much talked of. Doesn't find it interesting herself. Willa Cather.

875. **To Mary Virginia Auld,** Saturday [Feb. 19, 1927]; UNL, copy, not original.

Appreciated the valentine treat, which helped cheer her up from a period of feeling down, mainly because she can't look forward to another writing project as rewarding as *Archbishop*. Has been to a Rin Tin Tin movie. [Edward] Steichen is coming to dinner; will wear her beautiful new dress. Is reading proofs with Edith. W. S. C.

876. **To Allan Nevins,** Feb. 20, 1927; Columbia.

Can't take on a review of [Sinclair?] Lewis's book. Has a pressing commitment. Willa Cather.

877. **To George Seibel,** Feb. 22, 1927; WCPM.

Has no address in New York just now, but stays at hotels when in town. Now on her way to visit her brother in Wyoming. Glad to hear he and Mrs. Seibel are well. Is well herself, when not in the city. Willa Cather.

878. **To Blanche Knopf,** Monday [Feb. 28, 1927]; HRC.

Thanks for the flowers. Will plan to go to the Boston Symphony with her on March 10. W. S. C.

879. **To Solton Engel,** Mar. 15, 1927 [note found in his copy of *April Twilights*]; Columbia.

Interesting that he has found this copy of her first book, apparently a copy presented by a friend to the friend's aunt, now deceased. Will be glad to autograph it. Willa Cather.

880. To Dorothy Canfield Fisher, n.d. [c. Mar. 19, 1927]; UVt.
Hopes they can see each other in April. Willa.

881. To Will Owen Jones, Mar. 22, 1927; UVa, quoted in Bohlke, dated June 2, 1927.
Congratulations to the *Nebraska State Journal* on its sixtieth anniversary. First saw herself in print in the *Journal*, when her essay on Thomas Carlyle was printed at the initiative of Professor Hunt. That changed her from the study of science to literature. A flowery piece of writing, but honest about her feelings of juvenile bitterness. When she began to write for the *Journal* was paid a dollar a column – about what they were worth! Mr. Gere never repressed her excesses, but his facial expression often led her to be more self-critical as she worked her way through to better ways of writing. Willa Cather.

882. To Dorothy Canfield Fisher, n.d. [late Mar., 1927?]; UVt.
Will look forward to seeing her on April 17. Recommends she read J. W. N. Sullivan's *Beethoven*. Willa.

883. To Stephen Tennant, Mar. 28, [1927], from no. 5 Bank Street, New York; Yongue.
Anne Douglas Sedgwick has sent a note written by him praising *My Mortal Enemy*. Appreciates his favor. Most of her books made out of old memories from which the extraneous has dropped away. Now reading proofs of a book that gave her joy to write, *Death Comes for the Archbishop*. Willa Cather.

884. To Mary Virginia Auld, Sunday [Apr. 10, 1927], from Atlantic City, N.J.; UNL.
Town is crowded for Holy Week, but they have a room overlooking the water. Wonderful weather. W. S. C. P.S.: She and Edith both like her new bob.

885. To Irene Miner Weisz, Apr. 23, [1927]; Newberry.
Enclosing a letter about *My Mortal Enemy*; please pass it on to Carrie. Has had a number of letters from priests who've read *Archbishop*. Willie. [Letter enclosed from Charles Phillips, professor of English at Notre Dame.]

886. To Blanche Knopf, Saturday [May 21, 1927], from Shepherdstown, W.Va.; HRC.

Enjoying this beautiful place after festive visit to Washington. Will be back about middle of the week. W. S. C.

887. **To Mary Virginia Auld,** Wednesday [June 8, 1927]; UNL, copy, not original.
Leaving Sunday for Wyoming. Noise of the subway is a torture. They are emptying the apartment. Suggests she stay at the New Willard when in Washington. Didn't go to Winchester; to get out of attending a banquet there, told people she would be in Wyoming on May 31. Will probably be in Red Cloud in about a month. Can all meet there and dance the Charleston on the new rug. Willa. P.S.: Sending address of Howard Gore.

888. **To Blanche Knopf,** n.d. [c. June 12, 1927]; HRC.
For next three weeks send mail care of brother Roscoe in Casper, Wyo. W. S. C.

889. **To Will Owen Jones,** June 26, [1927], from Casper, Wyo.; UVa.
Glad he likes the sketch of Mr. Gere in her public letter. Willa Cather.

890. **To Dorothy Canfield Fisher,** Aug. 17, [1927?], from New York; UVt.
Letter reached her in Wyoming, and she meant to answer it from Red Cloud but father had a heart attack. Better now. Came back to New York day before yesterday to vacate apartment. Putting things in storage. Has cancelled trip to France. Brother Douglass plans to take parents to California this winter. Doesn't suppose people who are used to movies will care for *Death Comes for the Archbishop,* a book without women. Sorry moviemakers will soon be at Acoma. Willa.

891. **To Carrie Miner Sherwood,** Monday [late August 1927?], from New York; WCPM.
Has no home address, a bad feeling. Please send mail care of Knopf. *Archbishop* will be out in a few days. Willie.

892. **To Fanny Butcher,** Thursday [Sept. 1, 1927], from the Hotel Webster, New York; Newberry.
Has moved out of her apartment and put everything in storage. Neighborhood ruined by subway construction. What does she think of *Archbishop*? Review in *New York World* calls it weak as a novel. What is a novel? This is more like a legend. No women but the Virgin Mary. Took joy in doing it. She and Grant Overton were the only two reviewers who liked *My Ántonia,*

and this is even less like a conventional novel. A narrative; something like a folk song. Was to have sailed on the *Berengaria* yesterday, but cancelled because of her father's illness. Willa Cather.

893. **To Zoë Akins,** Sept. 13, 1927, from the Shattuck Inn, Jaffrey, N.H.; UVa.
Came here Tuesday [Sept. 6] with Edith. Both worn out. Hasn't seen copies of *Archbishop* yet. Willa S. C.

894. **To Carl Van Vechten,** Sept. 16, [1927], from Jaffrey, N.H.; Richmond.
Pleased he likes the book. Tried to make it a selfless, impersonal sort of book. Willa Cather.

895. **To Frank Asker,** Sept. 17, [1927], from Jaffrey, N.H.; Newberry.
Story closely follows history. Review in the *Boston Transcript* about a week ago put it well. Willa Cather.

896. **To Fanny Butcher,** Sept. 17, [1927], from Jaffrey, N.H.; Newberry.
Thought she said legend, not folklore. A very different thing. The two priests' lives were like works of art. Hopes to go out to Arizona soon. Glad to autograph copy. A very gracious review. Willa Cather.

897. **To George Seibel,** Sept. 17, [1927], from Jaffrey, N.H.; WCPM.
Would be glad to send a picture but everything is in storage. Now resting up after the move. Glad he's going back into newspaper work. Willa Cather.

898. **To William Allen White,** Sept. 17, [1927], from Jaffrey, N.H.; LC.
Is glad he liked *Archbishop*. Most of it quite true. Gathered stories from Mexicans and priests and from Lamy's and Machebeuf's letters home. The letters gave her their personalities. Willa Cather.

899. **To Mary Miner Creighton,** Sept. 17, [1927], from Jaffrey, N.H.; Newberry. Pub. in *Red Cloud Chief* Oct. 20, 1927; quoted in Bohlke.
Will be glad to write the inscription for the memorial to Mrs. Brodstone [mother of Evelyn Brodstone] at the hospital. Remembers her well. Glad to hear she saw father and mother out driving.

900. **To Mabel Dodge Luhan,** Sept. 17, [1927], from Jaffrey, N.H.; Beinecke.
Are there instead of in Rome because of father's illness and the effort of moving out of the apartment. Also, Edith's mother had a stroke. What a year! Book seems to be going well. Willa.

901. **To Miss Chapin [with Knopf],** Sept. 24, [1927?], from Jaffrey, N.H.; Harvard.
Doesn't want to emphasize landscape; that sounds like descriptive ornamentation and implies there is action in it. Willa Cather.

902. **To Miss Chapin,** Sept. 24, [1927?], from Jaffrey, N.H.; Harvard.
Sending suggested advertising copy, which emphasizes turbulence of the period immediately after the Mexican War. Willa Cather.

903. **To Elizabeth Moorhead Vermorcken,** Sept. 27, [1927], from Jaffrey, N.H.; PM.
Friends must get tired of her writing book after book. Fortunately, they aren't all alike. Was in Wyoming this summer, unable to go abroad because of father's illness. Has moved out of Bank Street. Is enjoying being in Jaffrey, but wishes she still had the pleasure of working on something like *Archbishop,* which she finished there last year. It's hard, losing that pleasure and losing Bank Street at the same time. Willa Cather.

904. **To Francis W. Talbot, S. J.,** Oct. 8, 1927, from Shattuck Inn, Jaffrey, N.H.; GU.
Has received a copy of *America* with his review of *Archbishop;* is pleased by his understanding of what she was doing. Prefers to call it a "historical narrative," though publisher refers to it as a novel because the public understands that term. Glad he realizes purpose was to celebrate the lives of two men of real nobility and their relationship with a place. The story really lay in their engagement with that place. Willa Cather. P.S.: Would appreciate his sending her another copy of the journal, to send to her father.

905. **To Ida Tarbell,** Friday [Oct. 7 or 14, 1927?], from Jaffrey, N.H.; Allegheny.
Letter gave her great pleasure. Writing [*Archbishop*] was the greatest pleasure she ever had. Is receiving and treasuring many letters from missionary priests. Rector in Denver says he is still using Joseph Machebeuf's chalice and vestments. Misses the book now that it has gone from her. Also, is homeless at present. Will probably spend winter in Arizona. Willa Cather.

906. **To Miss Rubin [at Alfred A. Knopf],** Oct. 12, [prob. 1927]; HRC.
Prefers for the office to give the usual permission and keep the fee as low

as possible, or none. This woman can give good publicity for *Archbishop*. Willa Cather.

907. To Blanche Knopf, Thursday [Oct. 20, 1927], from Jaffrey, N.H.; HRC.
Thanks for the scarf. Will be back to New York next week. Feels sure *Archbishop* will go well in spite of slow start. Willa Cather.

908. To Mrs. [Alice Corbin] Henderson, Nov. 8, 1927; LincCity.
Gives permission to use "Spanish Johnny" but only as printed in *April Twilights*, not the garbled version in the anthology edited by Harriet Monroe. Is glad she likes *Archbishop*. Many people don't because they find it defies classification. Willa Cather.

909. To Ferris Greenslet, Nov. 8, 1927; Harvard.
Has neither a phone number nor an address. Is staying at the Hotel Grosvenor. Willa Cather.

910. To Mrs. George Whicher, Tuesday [pm. Nov. 8, 1927], from Grosvenor Hotel, New York; PM.
Appreciates the invitation to visit, but cannot. Is going to Nebraska soon. Also, Edith Lewis's mother ill. Enjoyed being in Jaffrey during the fall but has not been well lately. Needs to get away from New York. Enjoyed writing *Archbishop*, but now that it is out there are too many events and letters. Enjoys letters from Catholics, however. Nephew is enjoying Amherst. Willa Cather.

911. To Fanny Butcher, Nov. 8, 1927; Newberry.
Sorry to hear Fanny has sold her bookshop. Has been back from Jaffrey two weeks, staying at Hotel Grosvenor. Seeing a doctor about her appendix. Hates being homeless. Willa Cather.

912. To Mary Austin, Nov. 9, 1927; Huntington.
Is homeless and staying at the Grosvenor. Planning to spend Thanksgiving with parents. Reviewers debating whether *Archbishop* ought to be called a novel. Hopes a few months in New York will help Mary through trying period. Willa Cather.

913. To Blanche Knopf, n.d. [c. Nov. 12, 1927]; HRC.
[Two quotations from Robert M. Lovett review in *The New Republic*.] Either of above quotations will make a good ad. W. S. C.

914. To Fanny Butcher, Nov. 21, [1927], from New York; Newberry.
Appreciates her concern, but won't have to have appendectomy. Probably it's living in a hotel that is making her sick. Has written an open letter to *Commonweal* about the novel and her sources. Is looking forward to starting west. W. S. C.

915. To Dorothy Canfield Fisher, Nov. 27, [1927]; UVt.
Leaving December 1. Happy Christmas. Willa.

916. To Blanche Knopf, Dec. 31, [1927], from Red Cloud, Nebr.; HRC.
What a splendid Christmas box! Children delighted by everything. Brothers Roscoe and Douglass there for a few days. Lovely snowy weather. Parents well. Feels like a farm person at heart. Will probably leave New York for good. Will go on to Arizona in a couple of weeks. Going skating on the river this afternoon. Happy New Year. W. S. C.

917. To Mrs. Field, Jan. 3, [1928], from Red Cloud, Nebr.; UVa.
Glad she likes *Archbishop*. Willa Cather.

918. To Francis Biddle, Jan. 4, 1928 [note accompanying a book given to Biddle]; GU.
The book cannot make sense to a reader who does not know the area. Willa Cather.

919. Zoë Akins, [Jan. 1928?], from Red Cloud, Nebr., fragment; Huntington.
Alone with parents and one nephew. Has enjoyed Christmas. Going to Arizona for a little quiet. Will be in New York in March, but may never live there again. Going skating this afternoon. Willa.

920. To Father Malone, n.d. [prob. Jan. 1928; replying to letter from Malone dated Dec. 1, 1927], from Red Cloud, Nebr.; UVa.
Thanks for his note about the book. Got a sense of the two priests from Howlett's book on Machebeuf. May be in Denver later in the winter. Appreciates the clergy's general willingness to overlook errors in details. Willa Cather.

921. To Blanche Knopf, Monday [Jan. 9, 1928], from Red Cloud, Nebr.; HRC.
Please fend off these correspondents. Give Heinemann permission to use the *Commonweal* letter in pamphlets. Please send biographical pamphlets to give to clubs. W. S. C.

922. **To Carrie Miner Sherwood,** n.d. [shown as 1928 in C. M. S.'s hand], [inscription in copy of O *Pioneers!*]; WCPM, printed in O'Brien.

"For Carrie Sherwood. This was the first time I walked off on my own feet—everything before was half read and half an immitation [sic] of writers whom I admired. In this one I hit the home pasture and found that I was Yance Sorgeson [Sorgenson; Webster County farmer] and not Henry James. Willa Cather."

923. **To Dorothy Canfield Fisher,** Jan. 18, [1928], from Red Cloud, Nebr.; UVt.
A Cather family Christmas is epical. A happy time, but she is spent. Willa.

924. **To Ferris Greenslet,** Jan. 21, [1928], from Red Cloud, Nebr.; Harvard.
Has been here since early December and is off to Arizona. Miss Lewis not along. Refuses to praise any book for print. W. S. C.

925. **To Paul Reynolds,** Jan. 23, [1928], from Red Cloud, Nebr.; Columbia.
Doing some repairs on parents' house. May have a two-part story finished by spring. Willa Cather.

926. **To Blanche Knopf,** Feb. 14, 1928, telegram; HRC.
Sorry to have been so demanding at a time when Blanche was ill. Father is improving. Will be in New York next week. Willa Cather.

927. **To Miss Rubin** [with Alfred A. Knopf], Sunday [early 1928?]; HRC.
Please ask Mr. Knopf to write about the French rights. Relatives of her dead French missionaries keep after her. Willa Cather.

928. **To Dorothy Canfield Fisher,** Apr. 3, [1928], from Red Cloud, Nebr.; UVt.
Father died March 3, a week after she left for New York. Kept his boyishness to the end. Got back to Red Cloud just at dawn when he was laid out at the house, everyone else asleep, so had some time alone with him. So glad to have had long, happy winter visit with them. Mother has gone to California with Douglass. Is staying to get some repairs done on the house. Willa.

929. **To Mrs. Stowell,** Apr. 11, [1928], from Red Cloud, Nebr.; WCPM.
Hasn't answered her letter because so much has happened. Father died March 3, a quick, gentle death. Is staying on to get some repairs done on the house for when her mother comes back from California. Will hope to see her next time she is in Boston. Willa Cather.

930. To Blanche Knopf, Apr. 13, 1928, telegram; HRC.
Has been detained by need to have repairs done and to rest. Will be back
about May 1. Willa Cather.

931. To Ferris Greenslet, May 4, 1928, from New York, telegram; Harvard.
Is just back from Nebraska and needs to know total royalties for 1927, for
income tax return. Will appreciate his help. Willa Cather.

932. To Ferris Greenslet, May 5, 1928, telegram; Harvard.
No, can't undertake biography of Amy Lowell. Willa Cather.

933. To Burges Johnson, [1928?], excerpt made by E. K. Brown; Beinecke.
Most English teachers have never actually written a thing and think being
scholarly means avoiding any taint of common sense. One critic makes a
big point of broad *a* sounds in female names in her books. Could quote
others equally foolish. One says title *Death Comes for the Archbishop* shows
she is now willing to acknowledge death. What it shows is that [Hans]
Holbein used the title in his woodcut and she saw Latour's death as a
victorious one, a kind of riding away with death.

934. To Mary Austin, May 9, 1928, from New York; Huntington.
Could as soon think of writing a history of China as to write the biography
of Amy Lowell that Greenslet was trying to get her to do. Might consider
taking up Austin's suggestion [?] but is not writing now. Father died in
March. Has been to Mayo Clinic on the way back to New York. May go to
California, where mother is visiting Douglass. Troubles almost too much
just now. Willa Cather.

935. To Marion [Mrs. Henry Seidel] Canby, May 29, [prob. 1928], from the Grosvenor Hotel, New York; Beinecke.
Should never look for a subject but let the subject find her. Imagination
merely sets free one's memories and feelings. Going north soon. Enjoyed
seeing her. Willa Cather.

936. To Mary Jewett, May 30, 1928, from New York; Harvard.
So appreciated Dr. Eastman's letter. Stopped by Mayo Clinic on the way
home, but the problem proved insignificant. Hotel maid promptly fell ill
with influenza, and she caught it from her. Was in bed two weeks. Is still
quite weak. Will go accept an honorary degree from Columbia June 5, then

to Grand Manan with a friend to recuperate. Doesn't feel well enough to stop by Boston. Keeps thinking of her and is glad her nephew wrote. Willa Cather.

937. **To Carrie Miner Sherwood,** n.d. [June 7, 1928?], from New York; WCPM.
Just over a bad case of influenza. Edith was gone to her mother's funeral. Please send the measurements for father's window [at the church]. Willie.

938. **To Carrie Miner Sherwood,** June 13, [1928]; WCPM.
Awarding of honorary degree at Columbia was an occasion of dignity; glad Carrie and Mary persuaded her to accept. Hard to shop for stained glass window, so will let it wait until fall. Going to Grand Manan next week. Sending some books for the library. Also sending the Columbia diploma. Willie.

939. **To Colonel Butler,** June 14, 1928; Colby.
Yes, is a woman; can't explain name. In the South, however, it was common to feminize the name of a male relative. Wish they had just left it William. Glad he likes the book. It stays very close to fact. Willa Cather.

940. **To Mr. Johnson [from Sarah J. Bloom, secretary],** June 18, 1928; AAAL.
Is attending to Cather's mail while she is at Grand Manan. Is not forwarding letters except from family and close friends, so that she can be free to work. Will show her the letter when she returns. Sarah J. Bloom, Secretary.

941. **To Carlton Wells,** n.d. [c. July 10, 1928], on his letter to her dated July 3, 1928; Newberry.
Gives permission for him to use essay "Nebraska" in a textbook. Willa Cather.

942. **To Alfred Knopf,** July 11, [1928], from Grand Manan; HRC.
Getting settled after a week in Quebec. Ocean in front and pine woods in back. Please send a catalog and let her know sales of *Archbishop*. Willa Cather.

943. **To Josephine Piercy,** Aug. 8, [1928]; Indiana.
May quote from the essay she referred to. Believes sketch of Nat Wheeler in *One of Ours* better than the one of Godfrey St. Peter in *The Professor's House*. The right readers understand her books instinctually. The wrong ones never understand, but that's all right. Willa Cather.

944. To Elizabeth Moorhead Vermorcken, Sept. 19, [1928]; PM.

Can't remember if she ever wrote about Elizabeth's mother's surgery. Life has been very disordered. Has been at Grand Manan, off the coast of New Brunswick, at the house she and Miss Lewis have there. Expects to go to Quebec in a few weeks. It has been a hard year. Likes the essay on herself in Whipple's book *Spokesmen* [R. K. Whipple, *Spokesmen: Modern Writers and American Life,* 1928], which has a fine essay on Henry Adams. Greetings to her mother. Willa Cather. P.S.: Likes Thornton Wilder's new book [*The Bridge of San Luis Rey,* 1927?].

945. To Mr. Goodman, Sept. 26, 1928, from New York; UVa.

Seldom writes short stories and does not like writing essays about her own writing, so will not contribute to the volume he is editing. Willa Cather.

946. To Zoë Akins, Oct. 1, [1928], from New York; Huntington.

Would like to see her, but doesn't know where she is. W. S. C.

947. To Professor Goodman, Oct. 9, [1928?]; UNL.

Was in Boston when he was on the radio, so didn't hear. Appreciates his interest in her work. Willa Cather.

948. To Professor Goodman, Oct. 13, 1928; UNL, copy, not original.

Friend who heard his radio talk liked what he had to say, but regretted he pronounced her name as if it were Kayther. Should rhyme with "gather" or "rather." Willa Cather.

949. To Zona Gale, Oct. 23, 1928, from New York; HSW.

What she says of life in Portage is very appealing. Has been living in hotels since no. 5 Bank Street was demolished. Willa Cather.

950. To Professor Goodman, Sunday [Oct. 28, 1928], from Grosvenor Hotel, New York; UNL.

Accepts his apology. Could see him on Wednesday the 31st. Willa Cather.

951. To Ferris Greenslet, Nov. 11, [1928], from Chateau Frontenac, Quebec; Harvard.

No, will not authorize a Book League edition of *Ántonia.* Didn't like the cheap edition of *The Professor's House* that Knopf tried. Doesn't think approaches like the Book-of-the-Month Club will prove lasting. *Ántonia* will maintain its market as long as she keeps producing. Willa Cather.

952. **To Irene Miner Weisz,** n.d. [c. Nov. 20, 1928?]; Newberry.
On the 29th, will be remembering their trip to Red Cloud for her parents' anniversary and what a happy time it was. Willie.

953. **To Ferris Greenslet,** Dec. 5, 1928, from New York; Harvard.
Pleased with German edition of *Ántonia*. Sorry to have missed him when he called. Will go to Red Cloud for Christmas. Willa Cather.

954. **To Mary Virginia Auld,** n.d. [Dec. 14, 1928?], from New York; UNL, copy, not original.
Grandmother [Mary Virginia Cather] is better. Douglass suggests they not come, because it will agitate her. W. S. C. P.S.: Going to a performance of *Norma* today.

955. **To Blanche Knopf,** n.d. [Dec. 26, 1928?]; HRC.
Thanks for satin quilt she sent for Christmas. Willa Cather.

956. **To Mr. and Mrs. George Whicher,** Jan. 1, [1929], from New York; PM.
Meant to spend a few weeks at the Lord Jeffrey after the holidays, but mother has suffered a stroke. Will have to go to California soon, which means abandoning work on which she had enjoyed making a start. Even worse, has to go to Long Beach. San Francisco would be all right. It will be another bad year. Has a little gift for them. Willa Cather.

957. **To Carrie Miner Sherwood,** Jan. 21, [1929?], from Hotel Grosvenor, New York; WCPM.
Has had bronchitis. Sorry not to have come for Christmas. Likes design for stained glass window, but with mother's illness can't deal with it. How is Dr. Creighton? Willie. P.S.: Enclosing check for church.

958. **To Mr. Lohmann,** Feb. 1, [1929], from New York; Yale.
Recovering from bronchitis, but will be happy to accept an honorary degree on June 19. Leaving for California in a few days. Mail can be sent to Knopf. Willa Cather.

959. **To Blanche Knopf,** Saturday [Feb. 2, 1929], from Atlantic City, N.J.; HRC.
Weather delightful. Is relaxing, being wheeled along the boardwalk. W. S. C.

960. To Ferris Greenslet, Feb. 3, [1929]; Harvard.

Does not want a dollar edition of *My Ántonia*, but will agree to a dollar edition of *O Pioneers!* provided they keep it in stock in the regular edition also. After the 12th write care of Knopf. Willa Cather.

961. To Thomas Masaryk, Feb. 12, [1929?], from New York; Berkeley.

Is very pleased and grateful for his letter; especially glad he liked *Death Comes for the Archbishop*. Based on lives of actual first French missionaries who came into the formerly Spanish territory in the southwestern U.S. Sketch on the cover was taken from an old picture of Archbishop Lamy on horseback. Since publication, has received letters from many Catholics, traders, and Army men who were in the old West. Is sending him her published account of how she became interested in the story and gleaned material for it ["On *Death Comes for the Archbishop*," *Commonweal*, November 23, 1927]. Finds it gratifying that he takes an interest in her books. Willa Cather.

962. To Josephine K. Piercy, Feb. 19, [1929?]; Indiana.

No, Piercy must not state that the passage about Nat Wheeler is Cather's favorite passage from her own writing, because that is not true. Meant only to suggest that it would be better than the passage she was proposing to quote. No, she may not quote any part of the letter. Apparently was not guarded enough when she wrote it. If she needs to address her in future, it should be in care of A. A. Knopf. Willa Cather.

963. To Carrie Miner Sherwood, n.d. [late Feb., 1929?], from New York; WCPM.

Enclosing something [what?] to be placed in her copy of *My Ántonia*. Leaving for California March 4. Willie. [Note: Edith Lewis had wired Helen McAfee on January 16, 1929, that she was on her way to California.]

964. To Josephine K. Piercy [of New Haven, Conn.] [from Ellen Burns, secretary], Feb. 28, 1929; Indiana.

Cather has gone to California and will not return for some time. Piercy may quote from "The Novel Démeublé" and (if Knopf gives permission) from *The Professor's House* but not from her letter. Should remind her, quoting from a letter without permission is illegal. Ellen Burns, Sec'y.

965. To Blanche Knopf, Mar. 15, [1929], from Long Beach, Calif.; HRC.

Was too upset to write at first. Mother can't speak and has to be fed, yet her mind seems sound. Is staying at hotel near nursing facility. Can be reached care of Douglass. Willa Cather.

966. **To Mary Jewett,** Apr. 7, [1929], from Long Beach, Calif.; Harvard.
Was happy to receive her Christmas card. Mother had a stroke in December and is in serious condition. Many things to struggle with in arranging for her care. Willa Cather.

967. **To Zoë Akins,** Saturday [Apr. 1929?], from Long Beach, Calif.; Huntington.
Has been there two weeks. Mother's condition very sad. Wants to see Zöe, but no one else. Willa.

968. **To Miss Pirrell,** May 13, [1929], from Pasadena, Calif.; WCPM.
Has been traveling. Thanks for letter. Willa Cather.

969. **To Carrie Miner Sherwood,** May 14, [1929], from Pasadena, Calif.; WCPM.
Please forward her thanks to Lizzie, who sent a greeting to mother on Mother's Day. Is staying at the sanitarium. Very sad to watch mother failing. Must get back to New York by mid-June to receive honorary doctorate at Yale. The last she will accept. Only other woman writer honored by Yale in that way was Edith Wharton. Willie.

970. **To Carrie Miner Sherwood [?],** n.d. [prob. May 21, 1929]; WCPM.
Wants inscription on window to read simply "In memory of Charles F. Cather, who loved this church."

971. **To Mr. Lohmann,** May 24, [1929], from Pasadena, Calif.; Yale.
Is still with her mother, but will return to New York first week of June. Please send tickets for commencement to 35 Fifth Avenue. Willa Cather.

972. **To Dorothy Canfield Fisher,** n.d. [late May or early June 1929?], from Long Beach, Calif.; UVt.
Had bronchitis in January, after mother suffered stroke in December. Has been here since February. Found a house and moved her mother, who is entirely paralyzed on right side. Elsie [sister] there with her. Hates California; it seems like a place removed from God. How much better if this had happened to her mother at home! Feels disoriented and despairing. Willa.

973. **To Wilbur Cross,** n.d. [early June 1929?], from Long Beach, Calif.; Beinecke.
Looking forward to seeing him and to the dinner. Mother in very sad con-

dition. Hard to get good care for someone in a situation like this, in such a place as California. Willa Cather.

974. **To Zoë Akins,** July 8, [1929], from Quebec; UVa.
Received Yale degree and came here to escape summer heat. Going to Grand Manan tomorrow. Willa.

975. **To Carrie Miner Sherwood,** July 25, [1929?], from Grand Manan; WCPM.
Please send recipe for cottage cheese and a container of furniture wax. Island is beautiful, all trees and wildflowers. House very peaceful with a view of sea from cliffs. But all security in life has collapsed since father died. Willie.

976. **To Blanche Knopf,** Aug. 16, [1929], from Grand Manan; HRC.
Sorry to hear she broke her collarbone. Has been working well, also walking and taking boat rides and enjoying the case of champagne she bought in Canada. W. S. C.

977. **To Mariel Gere,** Aug. 21, [1929?], from Grand Manan; WCPM.
Wanted to let her know about Professor Bates. Saw him very little after he left the university. He remained boyish and yet matured, a very gentle person and quite individual. Willa.

978. **To Zoë Akins,** Sept. 7, 1929, from Grand Manan, telegram; Huntington.
Not possible [to see her?] because of previous plans.

979. **To Miss Aaron [at Knopf],** Sept. 10, [1929], from Grand Manan; HRC.
Going on to Boston, then to Jaffrey, N.H. Probably not back to New York before mid-October. Willa Cather.

980. **To Blanche Knopf,** Sept. 21, [1929], from Jaffrey, N.H.; HRC.
Arrived last night. Will probably be back before Blanche sails. Please say no to enclosed inquiry about reprinting her work. Does not like illustrated *Archbishop,* but since it has been done please urge Mr. Stimson [in production dept. at Knopf] to get it out in time for Christmas trade. W. S. C.

981. **To Elizabeth Shepley Sergeant,** Oct. 2, [1929], from Jaffrey, N.H.; PM.
Likes her book [*Short As Any Dream*]. Likes its treatment of blood inheritance much better than *Orlando* [Woolf]. Likes its balance between somber facts and positive mood. One weakness is introducing the writer herself.

They must talk about this. But she really captured the way life rushes by with no regard for persons. Willa. P.S.: Appreciated her letter from California. Has considered moving to San Francisco, but is fearful of doing so.

982. **To Zona Gale,** Oct. 16, [1929?], from Jaffrey, N.H.; HSW.
Glad to get her letter and to hear that she would like them to be neighbors in Portage. Since mother's stroke, has practically lived on trains. Will have to go back west after a few more weeks. So a winter of quiet work in Wisconsin is impossible. Sorry to hear of her father's death. A fast death is a blessing. Is feeling low, but her letter helped. When in New York will be at the Grosvenor. Willa Cather.

983. **To Blanche Knopf,** Oct. 17, [1929], from Jaffrey, N.H.; HRC.
Will stay three more weeks, so won't see Blanche before she sails. Book going well. A quiet book, mostly Quebec; wants it to be good. Is enjoying the out-of-doors, and her quiet room at the Grosvenor not available for a while yet. Best wishes for the trip. Please see Isabelle and send a report on how she is. Willa Cather. P.S.: Please send a copy of Zona Gale's new book.

984. **To Carrie Miner Sherwood,** Oct. 25, [1929?], from Jaffrey, N.H.; WCPM.
Enclosing a letter from an admirer that pleases her a great deal. Leaving for New York tomorrow. Willie.

985. **To Harvey Newbranch,** Oct. 27, 1929; pub. *Omaha World-Herald*, quoted in Bohlke.
Regrets the disappearance of local opera houses in small towns of Nebraska. Remembers the excitement when touring companies came to Red Cloud. With her friends, would go watch the train arrive and the theatrical company get off. Is not sorry there are now motion pictures, but wishes they had not brought demise of live performances. Does not believe movies touch emotions of audience as live performances did, though they are fine entertainment. Willa Cather.

986. **To Blanche Knopf,** Sunday [Oct. 27, 1929? Note: Oct. 29, perhaps date of receipt, written at top by B. K., but year is uncertain. Reference to Quebec would seem to place it in 1928, but reference to Gale's book would seem to link it to Oct. 17, 1929 letter, datable as to year by the location in Jaffrey]; HRC. Expects to be in town November 22 but will be in Quebec between

this date and then. Please keep the ticket so it won't get lost. Likes Zona Gale's book. W. S. C.

987. To Fanny Butcher, Nov. 2, [1929], from Grosvenor Hotel, New York; Newberry.

Had a hard winter in California but a wonderful, restful summer on Grand Manan. Willa Cather.

988. To Albert G. Feuillerat, Nov. 6, 1929; Yale.

Sending her publisher's pamphlet with biographical information and a list of books with information about her and her work. Has marked the two best. Hard to answer his question about French influence. From adolescence and for many years thereafter read and liked French prose writers from Hugo to Maupassant. Read all of Balzac more than once before the age of twenty, though not much now. Doesn't believe she ever imitated any French writer, but did admire them more than their English contemporaries because of freer experimentation and greater thematic range. Tone of British writers of that period, including Hardy, sometimes mechanical or patronizing, though it doesn't really bother her. Believes French language itself more exciting to her than English when she was younger. Now prefers Prosper Merimée to the others. Likes his reserve, as well as other qualities. Willa Cather. P.S.: Suggests he read "The Novel Démeublé."

989. To Mr. Vance, Nov. 14, 1929, from the Grosvenor, New York; UVa.

Would be glad to autograph the picture he sent, but prefers to replace it with one of the originals when she can get it out of storage. Willa Cather.

990. To Burton J. Hendrick [National Institute of Arts and Letters], Nov. 21, 1929; AAAL.

Is pleased to learn she has been elected to the Institute. Letter was slow reaching her because of incorrect address; also, has been in Canada. Is mostly in California, due to mother's illness. Very pleased to accept membership. Will hope to see him again soon. Willa Cather.

991. To Zona Gale, Nov. 25, 1929; HSW.

Won't be able to get to Portage; must go to Pasadena soon after Christmas. Keeps wanting to quote Kent in *King Lear*: "Fortune, turn thy wheel." Read Gale's book with grim humor. Impossible to live in isolation but impossible to avoid harming others if one isn't isolated. Has been wanting to talk with her about a particular matter. Will she be in New York before Christmas?

992. **To Carrie Miner Sherwood,** n.d. [December 1929?], from New York; WCPM. Glad to hear Dr. Creighton and Mary are accompanying her on her trip. Willie.

993. **To Elmer Adler,** Dec. 3, [1929], from Grosvenor Hotel, New York; Princeton. Can't have tea with him until after Christmas. Willa Cather.

994. **To Zona Gale,** Dec. 3, [1929]; HSW.
Sorry to have missed her when she was in town. Must have been at the dentist when she phoned. Can only say again what Kent said in *Lear*. Christmas shopping for old German and Bohemian friends on Nebraska farms. Would feel guilty if she skipped them and they died before next Christmas. Willa S. C.

995. **To Albert G. Feuillerat,** Dec. 16, 1929, from the Grosvenor Hotel, New York; Yale.
Is pleased with his article on her books. Interesting that the first he read was *Death Comes for the Archbishop*. Would like to read the article he mentioned on Mérimée, who was also a fine critic, especially his essay on Gogol. Willa Cather.

996. **To Mary Miner Creighton,** [1929], Christmas card; Newberry.
With love, Willa.

997. **To Dorothy Canfield Fisher,** Dec. 20, [1929], from Grosvenor Hotel, New York; UVt.
Commercial stationery reflects her life just now, very unsettled. Going to California again in January. Appreciated letter from Spain; received it at Grand Manan. Had a good rest, both there and in New Hampshire. New York has worn her out again. Yes, remembers Lizzie Hudson Collins, cousin of Wilkie Collins; an actress in Pittsburgh. Would like to have kept in touch with her. Has sent off eight Christmas boxes to farm women in Nebraska. Has loved them, and they her, for many years. Hears mother has improved a little. Still, a quick death would be much better. Sorry the letter seems blue, but is feeling homesick. Willa.

998. **To Zoë Akins,** Dec. 31, [1929?]; UVa.
What a beautiful crucifix she sent! It speaks of the Southwest. Will be in California in February. Leaving now for Quebec for a week and will toast her with champagne. Willa.

999. **To Fanny Butcher,** Jan. 2, [1930], from Quebec; Newberry.
Sorry to hear her father died. A hard loss, she knows from experience. Looks forward to the day when she can be with her friends again. Willa Cather.

1000. **To Irene Miner Weisz,** Jan. 16, 1930; Newberry.
Hasn't heard from her in a long time. Mary Virginia is proving her mettle and says Irene is a good driver of a car. Willie.

1001. **To Carrie Miner Sherwood,** Jan. 16, 1930, from the Grosvenor, New York; WCPM.
Appreciated her nice letter but can't answer at length now, because a friend in Philadelphia is dying. Willie.

1002. **To Ferris Greenslet,** n.d. [early 1930], from Grosvenor Hotel, New York; Harvard.
Please send a statement of royalties paid in 1929. Will leave for California soon and needs to do income tax early. Willa Cather. P.S.: Likes *Laughing Boy* [LaFarge] a great deal.

1003. **To Ferris Greenslet,** Feb. 6, 1930, from New York; Harvard.
Not fair of him to have used her praise of *Laughing Boy* in an ad. Has steadfastly refused to give commendations of books even by old friends, and now he has publicized what she said in private without authorization. Please send a copy of new edition of *Ántonia* so she can mark some corrections for the English edition. Since she will be leaving about the 20th, could he send March royalty check early? Willa Cather.

1004. **To Irene Miner Weisz,** Feb. 6, 1930, from New York; Newberry.
Appreciates her telegram. So glad Carrie is going to Europe. Expects to sail May 14 on the *Berengaria*, but needs to get to California first. Probably will take route through Chicago so she can see Roscoe in Wyoming. Mary Virginia working hard and getting by on little money. Sends her groceries now and then. Can't go to Red Cloud; too hard emotionally. Willie. P.S.: Please keep information about Mary Virginia secret.

1005. To Wilbur Cross, Feb. 11, [1930]; Beinecke.

Is glad to answer his questions, but has very little time to see friends. Yes, is working on another book, but unsettlement of present life is impeding it. Willa Cather. P.S.: Recommends he read *Laughing Boy* [LaFarge].

1006. To Irene Miner Weisz, [Feb. 16, 1930], from New York; Newberry.

Expects to get to Chicago the morning of Feb. 26 and would like to spend a night with her. Let her know if it isn't convenient. Willa.

1007. To Ferris Greenslet, Feb. 20, 1930, from New York; Harvard.

Has deposited the check. Is sending Heinemann several corrections, which she hopes he will also make. On p. 121, "Austrians" should be changed to "Prussians." Leaving Monday for California. Willa Cather.

1008. To Dorothy Canfield Fisher, Mar. 10, [1930], from Pasadena, Calif.; UVt.

Mother had a laugh from the picture of Mark Twain dinner. Seems a little better than last year, but still terrible condition. Sister away for a little rest. English nurse has been caring for her for a year and is very good. Has a cottage [at Las Encinas Sanitarium] of her own and is comfortable physically, but life looks bleak. Willa.

1009. To Carrie Miner Sherwood, n.d. [c. Mar. 15, 1930], from Las Encinas Sanitarium, Pasadena, Calif.; WCPM.

Mother about the same. Enjoyed visit with Irene on the way. So glad to hear about their trip plans. Willa.

1010. To Paul Reynolds, Mar. 25, [1930], from Calif.; Columbia.

Yes, please sell British serial rights to "Neighbor Rosicky." That is, assuming she still owns the rights. Willa Cather.

1011. To Carrie Miner Sherwood, Apr. 21, 1930, from New York; WCPM.

Not going to Oberammergau after all, but may see her in Paris. Doesn't know what her banker will be, to receive mail. Will have to wait for consecration of father's window at the church. Maybe at Christmas, when Elsie will be there. Paying for it herself, as care of mother is a strain for everyone. Sanitarium is best possible, but can't make paralysis anything but miserable. Comes away feeling very low every time she is there. Willie. P.S.: Hopes Evelyn Brodstone is better.

1012. To Ferris Greenslet, May 5, 1930; Harvard.

Sailing May 14 and will not return until October. Can always reach her care of Morgan & Co., 14 Place Vendome, Paris. If he uses "Double Birthday" in the volume he is planning, should not say she chose it because she thinks it is very good, because she doesn't. Willa Cather.

1013. To Ferris Greenslet, May 5, [1930?], from Grosvenor Hotel, New York; Harvard.

Not true she is leaving Knopf. Will tell him first if she ever does. Willa Cather.

1014. To Mabel Dodge Luhan, July 1, [1930], from Paris; Beinecke.

Her article on Lawrence captures him better than anyone else has done. So glad to hear that [Robinson] Jeffers liked *Archbishop*. Admires [Jeffers's] "Roan Stallion" and "Night." Paris has deteriorated, more like New York now. Wouldn't have come except to see a seriously ill friend. Misses New Mexico and is tired of festivities. Willa.

1015. To Carrie Miner Sherwood, [July 17, 1930?], from Paris; WCPM.

Won't be there when Carrie arrives, but with friends near Marseilles. Can't rearrange schedule. Will probably sail for home September 20. Shouldn't try to see everything in the Louvre but stay with the Grand Gallerie, which has the most worthwhile things. Should see Notre Dame more than once. Hopes all three will enjoy the week in Paris. Willa Cather.

1016. To Mrs. C. F. Lambrecht, Aug. 21, [1930?], from Italy, postcard; WCPM.

Is in the Italian Alps, on the Austrian border. Sends love to her, Lydia, and Pauline. Willa Cather.

1017. To George Austerman, Sept. 14, [1930], from Paris; UVa.

She and Edith sailing for Quebec September 27 on the *Empress of France*. Will arrive in Jaffrey about October 5. Hope to have same rooms as before, 324 and 328 with shared bath, and hope to stay through November. Willa Cather.

1018. To Dorothy Canfield Fisher, Sept. 30, [1930], from aboard the SS *Empress of France*; UVt.

Sorry to hear her mother died but glad she did not have to linger. Deaths of those close to one leave the world seeming shrunken. Hopes to visit her in Vermont during time in Jaffrey. Her own mother still suffering the punishment of lingering illness. Willa.

1019. **To Wilbur Cross,** Oct. 5 [pm. Nov. 7, 1930], from Jaffrey, N.H.; Beinecke.
Hopes to see him on the 14th. Came here directly by way of Quebec. Willa Cather.

1020. **To Elizabeth Shepley Sergeant,** Thursday [Oct. 19, 1930?], from Hotel Irvin, New York; Beinecke.
Had to come back from Jaffrey with appendix problem. No address but Knopf at the moment. W. S. C.

1021. **To Ferris Greenslet,** Oct. 20, [1930], from Jaffrey, N.H.; Harvard.
Please send royalty check. Appreciates his sending Chief Justice Holmes's letter about *My Ántonia*. Enjoyed summer in France, but always prefers to spend fall in New England. Willa Cather. P.S.: Please send copy of *Laughing Boy* to Jan Hambourg. W. S. C.

1022. **To Mrs. William Vanamee** [Asst. to the President, American Academy of Arts and Letters], Oct. 31, 1930, telegram; AAAL.
Is delighted to accept the Howells Medal of the Academy, but would prefer not to make a speech. Willa Cather.

1023. **To Robert U. Johnson,** October 31, [1930]; AAAL.
Will be pleased to be present for the presentation of the Howells Medal, but hopes not to make an acceptance speech. Is grateful for this honor. Willa Cather.

1024. **To Robert U. Johnson,** Nov. 12, [1930], from New York; Harvard.
Thanks for letter with instructions. Glad to make a few remarks upon receiving the medal [Howells Medal of the American Academy of Arts and Letters]. Will be there tomorrow (Thursday), but leaving Saturday. Willa Cather.

1025. **To Dorothy Canfield Fisher,** Nov. 18, [1930], from New York; UVt.
Enclosed photo explains why she had to return to New York. Medals are not something she enjoys, but the people who award them mean well. Didn't come to visit before she left because work was going well and she was afraid to disrupt it. Glad to receive a copy of *Deepening Stream*. Will

read it as soon as doctors have finished checking out her appendix. Except for that has been feeling well. Willa.

1026. To George F. Whicher, Friday [prob. Nov. 21, 1930]; PM.
Had to leave Jaffrey to receive a medal as one of this good-looking group. Probably won't be able to get back this year. Enjoyed his note and hopes they can have a brief visit in New York before he sails. Willa Cather.

1027. To Dorothy Canfield Fisher, Dec. 1, [1930]; UVt.
Likes her book [The Deepening Stream] very much, especially Morris and his wife. He is entirely real. Likes Adrian, too. All the Paris part quite wonderful, and Matey very good in that section. Earlier she is too fully specified. A mistake to try to tell all, as she did herself in The Song of the Lark. Proust succeeds in it, of course, but that's in the first person. Writers ought to keep the third person more distanced than most do; it shouldn't resemble first person. Looks forward to telling her about someone she met at Aix-les-Bains this summer [Mme Franklin Grout, niece of Flaubert]. Willa.

1028. To Ferris Greenslet, Dec. 4, 1930, from Grosvenor Hotel, New York; Harvard.
Why have the Benda drawings been dropped from My Ántonia? At least they could drop the line on the title page referring to the drawings, if they're going to do that. Would like them to be restored and once she can get her possessions out of storage, can provide the originals if the plates are too worn. Willa Cather.

1029. To Ferris Greenslet, Dec. 26, [1930], from Grosvenor Hotel, New York; Harvard.
Please send a copy of The Song of the Lark, and please don't destroy plates of the Benda drawings. Wants to discuss possibility of restoring them. Willa Cather.

1030. To Eleanore Austerman, Dec. 28, [1930], from Grosvenor Hotel, New York; UVa.
Thanks for the picture of her sons. Willa Cather.

1031. To Margaret Crofts, Jan. 2, [1931?], from the Grosvenor Hotel, New York; LC.
Appreciates the green tomato condiment. Willa Cather.

1032. **To Dorothy Canfield Fisher,** Jan. 13, [1931], from Grosvenor Hotel, New York; UVt.

Will look forward to seeing her on the 20th. Willa.

1033. **To Read Bain,** Jan. 14, 1931; Michigan.

Out of many fan letters, it is easy to recognize one of substance. Yes, it is disadvantageous for a writer to be female. Suggests Virginia Woolf for an accurate statement. Often returns to early memories, because young children are virtually without sex. Interesting to hear which books he prefers, but believes *A Lost Lady* is better than either of the two he named. Willa Cather.

1034. **To Zoë Akins,** Jan. 15, [1931?]; Huntington.

Mary Virginia kept trying to take over the green jacket Zoë sent for Christmas, but can't have it. Wore it the day she finished the last chapter of new novel. No, doesn't like the new play much [*The Greeks Had a Word for It*, running since Sept. 25, 1930], mainly because of the lead actress but also because it shuts one into a dreary world with no way out. Will go back to California about the end of March. So tired of being unsettled! Willa.

1035. **To Carrie Miner Sherwood,** Jan. 16, [1931?], from Grosvenor Hotel, New York; WCPM.

Enjoyed her long letter, but can't write back at length because leaving for Philadelphia, where an old friend is dying. Willie. P.S.: Jan. 17. Having to go to the funeral – Dr. Lawrence Litchfield, whom she knew in Pittsburgh.

1036. **To Mabel Dodge Luhan,** Jan. 17, [1931?], from New York; Beinecke.

Very much admires *Lorenzo in Taos* [published in 1932; she must have seen manuscript or proof]. It equals the Buffalo section of *Intimate Memories*. Whether one agrees or not with the views of the people, they are well presented. [D. H.] Lawrence himself is caught better than anyone else has ever caught him, down to his giggle, or snicker. Country itself has its own life, and Tony's car takes on real significance. Edith away for a week, but read it, too. Is leaving for California before long. Mother about the same. Hopes to go to Mexico City before long. Willa Cather.

1037. **To Ferris Greenslet,** Jan. 26, [1931], from the Grosvenor, New York; Harvard.

Please send a statement of royalties paid during 1930. Will be in New York until latter part of February, and will hope for a chance to see him. Willa Cather.

1038. To Ferris Greenslet, n.d. [late Jan. or early Feb. 1931?]; Harvard.
Plan on February 19. Willa Cather.

1039. To Ferris Greenslet, n.d. [c. Feb. 15, 1931], from the Grosvenor Hotel, New York; Harvard.
Sending address of Deidrich Navall. Knopf sending Greenslet a copy of *Archbishop*, which she hopes he will send to Justice Holmes. Willa Cather.

1040. To James Southall Wilson, Mar. 3, 1931; UVa.
Is leaving soon for California, where her mother is an invalid. Cannot serve on organizing committee on southern writers. Use of her name in such a way would bring other demands on her time. Willa Cather.

1041. To Irene Miner Weisz, Mar. 3, 1931, from New York, telegram; WCPM.
Would like to spend the night with her on March 10. Willa Cather.

1042. To Irene Miner Weisz, Mar. 3, [1931], from New York; Newberry.
Arriving the morning of March 10 and hopes to spend the night with her. If not convenient, will go straight through. Willie. P.S.: Has already telegraphed.

1043. To Josephine Goldmark, Mar. 3, 1931; PM.
Had hoped to have a talk with her, but must rush off to California. Liked her book [*Pilgrims of '48: One Man's Part in the Austrian Revolution of 1848, and a Family Migration to America*, 1930]. Enjoyed the presentation of the Brandeis family as well as the Goldmarks. Has enjoyed knowing immigrant families in Nebraska and seeing how their lives flowered. Willa Cather.

1044. To Irene Miner Weisz, n.d. [Mar. 12, 1931], from train crossing Kansas; Newberry.
Dreamed last night they were traveling together to Red Cloud for her parents' 50th anniversary. Hadn't been a considerate daughter, so didn't deserve the happiness that trip gave her. Irene the only friend who is an active part of both her Red Cloud life and her life since then. Probably why she tells her so much about the Menuhins, so she will go on being a part of it. Hopes to go to Red Cloud for a long visit some time, and hopes she will come. Willie.

1045. To Zoë Akins, Sunday [Mar. 22, 1931], from San Francisco; Huntington.
Is there to receive honorary doctorate. Will be back in Pasadena in about ten days. Mother's condition worse. W. S. C.

1046. To Blanche Knopf, n.d. [c. Mar. 27, 1931], from San Francisco; HRC.
Awarding of honorary degree was quite festive. Is having a fine time, but getting tired. Will be back in Pasadena April 1. W. S. C.

1047. To Carrie Miner Sherwood, Apr. 7, [1931], from Pasadena; WCPM.
Thanks for the Easter lilies sent to mother, who is weaker than last year but still in good spirits. Will send the Doctor of Laws hood. Willie.

1048. To Zoë Akins, n.d. [c. Apr. 21, 1931]; Huntington.
Mrs. McEnerny [a cousin of Zoë's] has found some errors in the novel with respect to Catholic observances. Will correct them even though it is in page proofs. Willa.

1049. To Blanche Knopf, Apr. 28, [1931]; HRC.
Please relay her thanks to Van Loon. Suggests she see May issue of *Atlantic Monthly* for something by her drawn from Virginia [poem "Poor Marty"]. So glad to have caught the errors in *Shadows*. W. S. C.

1050. To Dorothy Canfield Fisher, May 1, [1931], from Pasadena, Calif.; UVt.
Mother was worse when she arrived, but somewhat better now. Speech completely gone. Brother Douglass still very devoted. Has finished page proofs of *Shadows on the Rock*. Working on it held her [Cather] together for five years. Will go away to Canada for hot part of summer. Willa.

1051. To Blanche Knopf, May 2, [1931], from Pasadena, Calif.; HRC.
Please send *Jenny* by Sigrid Undset. Willa Cather.

1052. To Sara Teasdale, May 10, [1931], from Pasadena, Calif.; Wellesley, typed transcription at NYPL.
Brought her letter along to California, where mother has been in sanitarium almost three years. Has been with her a lot of the time and has lost track of friends. Book just finished helped her hold together. Zoë has been a good friend. Please send a collection of selected poems. New poets don't let emotion blossom in their poems. Willa Cather.

1053. To Mrs. C. S. Hunter [in Washington, Pa.], June 6, 1931; UNL, copy, not original.

Yes, is the daughter of Jennie Boak Cather. Mother had stroke and is in sanitarium. Father died four [sic] years ago. Remembers Aunt Susan Hackney and cousin Katy Gamble. Appreciates invitation to visit. Willa Cather.

1054. To Dorothy Canfield Fisher, Sunday [June 7 or 14, 1931], from New York; uvt.

Will go to Princeton tonight to receive honorary degree. Only feeling toward *Shadows on the Rock* is appreciation that it carried her through difficult time. Tried to capture reality of old life in Quebec. Jacques modeled on a nephew who still remembers how she pulled him uphill on his sled during the winter before father died, when he was five. Willa.

1055. To Carrie Miner Sherwood, n.d. [June 19, 1931]; wcpm.

Sending press clippings about honorary degree at Princeton. Sat beside Charles Lindbergh at the formal dinner and had lunch with him and his wife. Hated not to stop in Red Cloud, but will come some day. Willie.

1056. To Carrie Miner Sherwood, n.d. [June 1931], from Grosvenor Hotel, New York; wcpm.

As she can see by newspaper photos, was the only woman to receive an honorary degree. Is sending hoods. W. P.S.: Edith says she got double the applause of the men. Sending a check for Mr. Bates's window [Rev. John Mallory Bates].

1057. To Zoë Akins, n.d. [pm. June 21, 1931], from Grosvenor Hotel, New York; uva.

Princeton festivities went fine. Enjoyed meeting the Lindberghs, especially Mrs. Willa.

1058. To unnamed "boys" [sons of Annie Pavelka?], June 26, 1931, from Grosvenor Hotel, New York; wcpm.

Did not forget their commencement. Has shown their pictures to friends in Pasadena and New York as examples of the fine Bohemian boys in Nebraska. Has had a commencement of her own – honorary degree at Princeton. Met the Lindberghs. Sorry not to stop when she came through, but will be there before another year goes by. Willa Cather.

1059. To Father Talbot, June 26, 1931, from Grosvenor Hotel, New York; gu.

Was pleased by his letter about *Shadows on the Rock*. Found it difficult to get a balanced view of the early historical figures of Quebec. Has long admired the quality of loyalty to a tradition and religion that she found there. Believes the France of two hundred years ago was a nobler place than the France or the United States of the present. Tried to be as accurate as possible, though did make some deliberate changes, such as the placement of the King's warehouse at that time. Appreciates his interest. Willa Cather. P.S.: Some serious errors in Catholic observance in the first draft were corrected by Mrs. Garret MacEnerney, of San Francisco.

1060. **To Henry Seidel Canby,** June 26, 1931, from Grosvenor Hotel, New York; Beinecke.

Hoped to see him, but understands he is away. Leaving for Canada in a few days. He understood what she was doing in the new book quite precisely. Interesting that he liked Bishop Laval best, as she does also, for his loyalty to French ways. Left it up to Knopf to decide about Book-of-the-Month Club, but he would not have allowed it if she had opposed. Wants to know when Mrs. Canby's book of verse is published. Since in California so much with her mother, loses touch with things in New York. Willa Cather.

1061. **To Blanche Knopf,** Wednesday [July 1, 1931]; HRC.

Please answer crazy writer of enclosed letter. W. S. C.

1062. **To Blanche Knopf,** July 10, [1931], from Grand Manan; HRC.

Still getting settled and tidying up the house. Some things rusty and moldy, as house is near edge of cliff overlooking the water. Don't telegraph about negotiations with London agent on *Shadows*; not convenient to receive telegrams here. Please have grocer send Italian tomato paste, garlic, and wild rice, also caviar; show prices lower than actual, to minimize high import duty. Willa Cather.

1063. **To Edward Wagenknecht,** n.d. [pm. July 23, 1931], from Grand Manan; PM.

No, does not give permission to use her name in the announcement. Would subject her to endless approaches from periodicals. Willa Cather.

1064. **To Marion [Mrs. Henry Seidel] Canby,** n.d. [c. Aug. 1, 1931?], from Grand Manan; Beinecke.

Was disappointed to miss her in New Haven. Seems to have been living on trains, rushing to family crises; never sees anyone. Has built a house here in a quiet place near the sea, and is again feeling happy to wake up in the morning. Willa Cather.

1065. **To Irene Miner Weisz,** n.d. [pm. Aug. 6, 1931], from Grand Manan; Newberry.

Please see August *Atlantic Monthly* and keep clipping. Glad to have pleased this reviewer [Ethel Wallace Hawkins]. Enjoying quiet of the island. Willie.

1066. **To Mary Virginia Cather [mother],** Aug. 10, [1931]; WCPM.

Is enjoying beautiful weather and long walks on the cliffs. Receiving many letters about new book, though secretary handles most of them in New York. Sorry about bad picture on the cover of *Time*. Interesting that the same reviewers who panned *Archbishop* now call it a classic. Willie. P.S. to Elsie and Douglass: Please read her the review.

1067. **To Charles McAllister Wilcox [in Denver, Colo.],** Aug. 10, [1931], from Grand Manan; UVa.

Glad secretary sent his letter on to her. Quite willing for him to see her letter to Father Malone. Please give him her regards. Historians of Quebec say new book is accurate. Willa Cather.

1068. **To Carrie Miner Sherwood,** n.d. [August 1931?], from Grand Manan; WCPM.

Please let her know whether she likes the new book and whether she received the degree hoods. Book selling well, though some critics quite negative. Enclosing review from *Atlantic*. Willie.

1069. **To Dorothy Canfield Fisher,** Aug. 14, [1931], from Grand Manan; UVt.

Need to prevent outrageous project, even if it means their publishers have to buy off this Mr. Allan. Enjoying cool and quiet. Island very isolated. Carpenter who built their cottage thinks she is a newspaper writer. Mother weakening. Willa.

1070. **To Elizabeth Moorhead Vermorcken,** Aug. 24, [1931], from Grand Manan; PM.

Glad she likes the new book; many do not. The word "shadows" in the title should have given them some indication of the intent. Has enjoyed summer at Grand Manan. Will leave toward the end of September and go to California to see her mother. Isabelle and Jan have been to Brussels. Has lost track of Ethel Litchfield. Willa Cather.

1071. To Wilbur Cross, Aug. 25, [1931], from Grand Manan; Beinecke.

Many thanks for insightful review. First reviewer to understand how *Shadows* differs from *Archbishop*. Title indicates mood – how a particular culture has endured while individual lives have passed over it. Thinks of the spirit of the place more as a song than a legend. Life of an ordinary household more interesting to her than exciting things like Indian wars. Salad dressing the true beginning of a society. Hard for an American to capture the sense of that culture, but enjoyed trying. Wishes American writers did more experimenting. Willa Cather.

1072. To Dorothy Canfield Fisher, n.d. [Sept. 1931], from Grand Manan; UVt.

Mother died August 31. Could not get to the funeral. Staying here through September and then will go to be with Douglass. A strange feeling, being the "older generation." Willa.

1073. To Blanche Knopf, Sept. 20, [1931], from Grand Manan; HRC.

Thanks for letter of condolence. Feels strange having no parent to be accountable to, but is glad mother's illness is over. Will probably go to Jaffrey October 1, but maybe to Virginia instead. Willa Cather.

1074. To Dorothy Canfield Fisher, Oct. 2, [1931], from Grand Manan; UVt.

Has lingered here, but will leave for Jaffrey or for New York next week. Will probably go west in November and spend Christmas in Red Cloud. Interested in Dorothy's comments on Ruth Suckow. Disliked her early work intensely, but will read the new book. Thanks for letter of condolence. Feeling displaced and lacking in purpose. Willa.

1075. To Mr. Meromichey [?], Oct. 5, 1931; UVa.

Prefers young people to read her books voluntarily, not on assignment. But if he is going to assign one, suggests *Death Comes for the Archbishop*. Or young people might be interested in *One of Ours* or *The Professor's House*. Willa Cather.

1076. To Fanny Butcher, Oct. 14, [1931], from New York; Newberry.

Glad to receive her card from Aix-les-Bains. Mother died August 31. Surprisingly, even a long illness does not prepare one for the end. Please send several copies of her review. Most reviewers have complained of what is missing from *Shadows on the Rock*. Sales strong, however. Willa Cather.

1077. To Alexander Woollcott, Oct. 15, [1931]; Harvard.

Just back from Canada and finds his discerning review. Realizes that the deep meaning of both of last two books is moral character of the French. Appreciates his sending her the telegram from Edward Sheldon; glad he finds the book rings true. Willa Cather.

1078. To George Austerman, Oct. 20, 1931, from Grosvenor Hotel, New York; UVa.

Had hoped to spend all of October in Jaffrey but will not be able to come at all. Please let friends there know about mother's death. Hopes they are well. Willa Cather.

1079. To Read Bain, Oct. 22, 1931; Michigan.

Has been back in New York only a few days. Please either discontinue use of middle name or spell it right. Yes, most reviewers criticize her for not writing a typical historical novel with lots of action. No, is not Catholic but respects the Catholic Church as the religion most dear to humanity and for the longest time. Willa Cather.

1080. To Mary Austin, Oct. 22, 1931; Huntington.

Little wonder Austin has lost track of her. Hopes to be in New Mexico within the next year; they have much to talk about. Will consider donating for preservation of Spanish crafts when economy improves, but just now is helping two brothers plus others who are hard hit. Is sorry to hear her eyes are troubling her. Willa Cather.

1081. To Paul Reynolds, Oct. 22, 1931; Columbia.

Doesn't have an appropriate story on hand at the moment. Knopf placed one for her recently, but that doesn't mean she won't use his services in future. May come back to New York to live since mother's death. Willa Cather.

1082. To Marion [Mrs. Henry Seidel] Canby, Oct. 30, [1931]; Beinecke.

Was pleased to receive her poems. They carry the voice of friendship. Feels very displaced and lacking in purpose. Willa Cather.

1083. To Carrie Miner Sherwood, Nov. 10, [1931], from Grosvenor Hotel, New York; WCPM.

Sending a box of clothes to have when she is there. Will be in Red Cloud about December 1. Willie.

1084. To [DeWolfe] Howe, Nov. 11, 1931; Harvard.

Please destroy her letters to Annie Fields. They are not genuinely charac-
teristic in tone, since she was never comfortable with Mrs. Fields on paper,
though she was in person. Willa Cather. P.S.: No, please send the letters;
will decide whether to return any to him to retain.

1085. To Thomas S. Jones, Jr., Nov. 11, 1931; Columbia.

Sorry her letter seemed curt. Has learned to be suspicious of approaches
by strangers. Glad to see he shares her appreciation for that period of
Canadian history. Does he know the *Jesuit Relations* and Abbé Scott's *Life
of Bishop Laval*? Willa Cather.

1086. To [DeWolfe] Howe, n.d. [but prob. in response to his of Nov. 16, 1931],
from Grosvenor Hotel, New York; Harvard.

Appreciates receiving the packet of letters. Will look them over after first
of year. Willa Cather.

1087. To Ferris Greenslet, Nov. 26, [1931]; Harvard.

Yes, would like new edition of *The Song of the Lark* without Breton picture
on jacket. Can't write preface now; indeed, doesn't want to write any more
prefaces, prefers to maintain some mystery. Would not want *Commonweal*
letter about *Archbishop* to be used as a preface. Please eliminate the verse
that follows dedication to Isabelle McClung. *Shadows on the Rock* doing
splendidly. Willa Cather.

1088. To Blanche Knopf, Sunday [prob. Dec. 1931]; HRC.

Enjoyed birthday and appreciated beautiful gladioli she sent. W. S. C.

1089. To Blanche Knopf, Dec. 16, [1931], from Red Cloud, Nebr.; HRC.

Has gotten the house cleaned and a new roof on. Former maid now living
in Colorado has come to help. Please send two copies of *Shadows on the
Rock*, one of the Modern Library *Archbishop*, and one of *Red Bread*, book
about Russia, to give for Christmas presents. Brothers and sisters arriving
next week. Willa Cather.

1090. To Zoë Akins, Dec. 18, [1931], from Red Cloud, Nebr.; Huntington.

Understood why she did not send condolences right away. Glad the lingering has ended. Has the house ready for sisters and brothers. Glad she
liked the book despite its lack of drive. Some readers find it sanctimo-
nious. Willa.

1091. To Blanche Knopf, Dec. 26, [1931], from Red Cloud, Nebr.; HRC.
Thanks for beautiful green dressing gown. It's been a wonderful Christmas. Is planning a children's party. Willa Cather.

1092. To Mariel Gere, Monday [Dec. 28, 1931], from Red Cloud, Nebr.; WCPM.
Thanks for pudding she sent for Christmas. Saving it for New Year's, when Douglass will be there. Cherishes many beautiful memories of good cheer in the Geres' home. Has had a Christmas both joyful and sad. Willa.

1093. To Ferris Greenslet, Jan. 5, [1932], from Red Cloud, Nebr.; Harvard.
Who is in charge of the Jewett estate? Having a wonderful time. Willa Cather.

1094. To Cyril Clemens, Jan. 12, [1932?]; WCPM.
Will be going abroad soon, so can't judge contest. Willa Cather.

1095. To Carrie Miner Sherwood, Feb. 9, [1932], from Grosvenor Hotel, New York; WCPM.
Thanks for checking on the mortgage. Is recovering from influenza. English reviews of *Shadows* all very positive. Is sorrowing over the Lindbergh baby. Willie.

1096. To Ferris Greenslet, Feb. 15, [1932], from Grosvenor Hotel, New York; Harvard.
Please avoid adding credence to the rumor that she modeled Thea Kronborg on Olive Fremstad. Story does not resemble her life at all. Simply remain silent on the matter. Please send report of royalties paid in 1931. Willa Cather.

1097. To Carrie Miner Sherwood, Feb. 19, [1932]; WCPM.
Has not written sooner because of influenza soon after getting back. Went to a concert given by Yehudi Menuhin and out to supper with him and has felt unwell ever since. And secretary went away on vacation! Keeps thinking about happy weeks in Red Cloud and visits with Carrie and Mary. Probably it was run-in with Will Auld that has unsettled her. Isn't even sleeping well. He still won't give her the facts on whether the mortgage in question has been recorded. Willie.

1098. To Elmer Adler, Mar. 5, [1932]; Princeton.
Sorry she will miss his tea on Thursday. Willa Cather.

1099. To Zoë Akins, Mar. 11, 1932, from New York, telegram; Huntington.

Delighted with the news her telegram brought [that Zoë was getting married].

1100. To Ferris Greenslet, Mar. 13, 1932; Harvard.

Will agree to selling film rights to *The Song of the Lark* if they will commit in writing not to ask her to consider film of *My Ántonia*. Doubts a film would increase sales of *Lark*. Film of *A Lost Lady* brought her letters from obviously uncultured people, confirming her view of the low class of movie audiences. Willa Cather.

1101. To Carrie Miner Sherwood, Mar. 15, [1932], from Grosvenor Hotel, New York; WCPM.

The young man's [?] business proposal has destroyed her concentration on a day when she was beginning a new story. Please keep an eye out; will get her lawyer onto it if he makes another move. Why can't people leave her alone? [Several words blotted out.] Willie. P.S.: So terrible about the Lindberghs.

1102. To Helen Sprague, Mar. 20, [1932?]; WCPM.

Weather has been cold since she got back, but once she got over the flu has been going to concerts and operas. Sees Virginia about once a week. Despairing about the Lindberghs' baby! Police don't seem to be doing anything, and no one respects their privacy. When her child arrives, don't smother him with motherly doting. That ruins children. Willa Cather.

1103. To Zoë Akins, Mar. 20, [1932]; Huntington.

Still amazed by her wonderful news. Sorry she won't be in California this year to see her new home. How did all this come about? What nerve she has always had – and now the nerve to do this! But if marriage can ever be made to work, it will be Zoë who can do it. Feels happy just thinking about what a good friend she is and how happy her life is going to be. Willa.

1104. To Mrs. Williams, Apr. 19, 1932; Colby.

Has been called out of town and therefore slow to answer her letter. Appreciated it and sends condolences. Willa Cather.

1105. To Carrie Miner Sherwood, n.d. [prob. late Apr. 1932; ref. to letter from Borneo is to a letter from George W. Bullock, a District Officer in British North Borneo, dated Jan. 6, 1932]; WCPM.

Finds she failed to send check for maintenance on the house and yard. Enclosing a letter from Alfred Knopf about Sigrid Undset, whose books she probably knows; also letter from someone in Borneo. Please return them. Sorry to hear she has had shingles. Appreciates all her kind deeds, seeing that the yard is kept up and so forth. Hopes Helen Mac's delivery will be easy. Willie. P.S.: Take a few dollars out of the check for flowers on parents' graves, please.

1106. **To Marion [Mrs. Henry Seidel] Canby,** Apr. 21, [1932?]; Beinecke.
Has just found her book of verses [*High Mowing*, 1932] among a great many books that have come by mail. Likes them very much. Will be in town at the Grosvenor for about two weeks. Hopes they can talk. Willa Cather. P.S.: Especially likes "Timid One" [a poem that expresses a wish for escape from being one's self].

1107. **To Mabel Dodge Luhan,** Apr. 28, [1932?], from Grosvenor Hotel, New York; Beinecke.
Will write a proper letter after Yehudi Menuhin sails next week. Was sick with influenza all of February and since then trying to catch up on all sorts of things. Has a copy of *Lorenzo* and will write about it soon. Willa.

1108. **To Carrie Miner Sherwood,** May 2, [1932?], from Grosvenor Hotel, New York; WCPM.
Letters seem to have crossed. Edith sent Traveler's Aid booklet so Carrie could see pictures of real people the Society has assisted, not as an appeal for donation. Glad to get good news about Helen Mac [baby?]. Had a nice visit with Yehudi Menuhin day before he left for France. What a lovely person! Willie.

1109. **To Ferris Greenslet,** May 2, 1932; Harvard.
Only reason she authorized a cheap edition of *O Pioneers!* was to save *Ántonia* from the same. But even though he says it is doing well, it is not benefiting her, because sales of the regular edition have disappeared. He ought to adjust her rate of royalties to make up for it. Willa Cather.

1110. **To Walter Newman Flower [director of Cassell & Company, London],** May 25, 1932; UVa.
Appreciates his sending English reviews of *Shadows on the Rock*. Hopes he

will give more care to physical aspects of the next volume, *Obscure Destinies*. Did not like the dust jacket of *Shadows*. Willa Cather.

1111. To Ferris Greenslet, May 31, 1932; Harvard.
Has studied history of royalty payments on *O Pioneers!* that he sent. Would still like to discontinue the cheap edition. Success of *Archbishop* and *Shadows* ought to shore up sales of regular edition of *O Pioneers!*. Willa Cather.

1112. To Ferris Greenslet, Monday [May or June 1932?]; Harvard.
Can meet him for tea at 4:15 at Longchamp, 12th and Fifth Avenue. W. S. C.

1113. To Mrs. William Vanamee [National Institute of Arts and Letters] [from Sarah J. Bloom, secretary], June 15, 1932; AAAL.
Cather is out of the country and not expected back until fall. Rarely forwards mail. Sarah J. Bloom, Secretary.

1114. To Helen [Sprague?], June 24, [1932?], from Grand Manan; WCPM.
Please write and tell her all about the baby. Lindberghs' ordeal only seems to get worse. What disgusting deception of them! Has been enjoying their quiet cabin and the cool, foggy weather. [signature illegible]

1115. To Carrie Miner Sherwood, July 4, [1932], from Grand Manan; WCPM.
Read proofs of "Two Friends" [*Woman's Home Companion* July 1932] before she left New York. Sorry about the terrible illustrations, done by a ninny who knows nothing about the West. Hates publishing in magazines, but they pay well. Elsie reports house and yard look good. Cabin here very pleasant, even without indoor plumbing. Everything such a nice green this year. Mary Virginia coming to spend a month; will stay at inn where they take their meals. Please tell Helen Mac how she enjoyed the letter about the baby, Bernard. Hopes she and Mary weren't bothered by anything in "Two Friends." Willie.

1116. To Ferris Greenslet, July 17, [1932], from Grand Manan; Harvard.
Here she is trying to eliminate cheap editions and Cape gets one out. But Murray must have had authority to sell British paperback rights. Is sending Cape a preface just to make sure it won't look like a new book. Houghton Mifflin may use it in future if they wish. Staying until September. Willa Cather.

1117. To Ferris Greenslet, July 29, [1932?]; Harvard.
Hasn't answered his letter because it is obvious he won't be persuaded. Willa Cather.

1118. To Carrie and Mary Miner, Aug. 4, [1932?], from Grand Manan; WCPM.
Mary Virginia there vacationing. Wonderful weather. Worries Elsie won't keep up the yard at home. Some time wants to tell them about D. H. Lawrence, whom she knew well. Very fine writer, but full of extreme views. Willie.

1119. To William Lyon Phelps, Aug. 16, [1932?], from Grand Manan; Beinecke.
Appreciates his calling her attention to the astronomical error in *Obscure Destinies*. Has changed "transit" to "occultation" in the second printing and cabled Cassell to catch it in the English edition. Willa Cather.

1120. To George Seibel, Aug. 21, [1932?], from Grand Manan; WCPM.
Appreciates receiving his radio talk. Glad he likes "Old Mrs. Harris," which she believes better achieved than most of her works. Glad to hear about the Seibels' grandchild. Would enjoy corresponding with him again if he won't publish her letters. Sorry to have become so untrusting. Willa Cather. P.S.: Saw May Willard in San Francisco last year. Would like to see anything he has written about Thomas Mann, especially *The Magic Mountain*.

1121. To George Austerman, Sept. 2, [1932], from Grand Manan; UVa.
Expects to arrive [at the Shattuck Inn] on Monday, September 12. Please have rooms 324 and 328 ready, with the bath between, as usual. Will be alone this time and can stay only a few weeks. Willa Cather.

1122. To Zoë Akins, Sept. 16, [1932], from Jaffrey, N.H.; Huntington.
Glad she has married an interesting person, so marriage won't become boredom. Enjoyed seeing pictures of their house. Very glad she likes "Old Mrs. Harris," which is the best story in the volume. People may not understand it if they don't know the beautiful but deceitful South. Returning to New York soon; will stay at the Grosvenor again while looking for an apartment. Is ready for some adventures or surprises in her life – and would like to be more adventurous in her writing as well. Willa.

1123. To Thomas Masaryk, Sept. 23, [prob. 1932], from Jaffrey, N.H.; Berkeley.

Hopes he has received a copy of her new book [*Obscure Destinies*, pub. August 1932] and agrees that "Old Mrs. Harris" rings true, more true than the book about Quebec last year. Books drawn from early memories are always truest. Even so, likes to try different things. Being true is her greatest wish. No, is not becoming a Catholic, though greatly admires Catholic missionaries. Enclosing her letter to Gov. Cross ["On *Shadows on the Rock*," *Saturday Review of Literature*, Oct. 17, 1931]. Willa Cather.

1124. To Carl Van Vechten, Friday [Oct. 14, 1932], from Grosvenor Hotel, New York; Beinecke.

Going to Chicago Tuesday to receive a gold medal. Will be back about Nov. 1 and may let him photograph her then. Wants to talk with him about opera. Willa Cather.

1125. To Irene Miner Weisz, Friday [Oct. 14, 1932], from Grosvenor; Newberry.

Will get to Central Station in Chicago at 8:30 Wednesday morning. Really doesn't want a gold medal, but Knopf says it would be unacceptable to refuse it. Willie.

1126. To Ferris Greenslet, Oct. 20, [1932], from the Grosvenor, New York; Harvard.

Will be at this address until late November. Hopes they can have tea together some time soon. Willa Cather.

1127. To Irene Miner Weisz, Monday [Oct. 24, 1932], from New York; Newberry.

Trip to Chicago was a lucky charm, bringing nice letters from Douglass and Elsie. Is feeling better about things and willing to go more than half way with them if only they will be honest with her. Also had some cheering news from [Bernard] McNeny [about being able to save Pavelka farm from foreclosure]. Has ordered Irene a dress like the one she admired. It will be $69.50. Enjoyed their visit. Appreciates Irene's tolerance of her failings and still being her friend. Willie.

1128. To Irene Miner Weisz, n.d. [Oct. 27, 1932]; Newberry.

While in Red Cloud, please verify that the mortgage is registered in her name. [With a slip of paper bearing legal description in Cather's hand, with date, book, and page of recording in Irene's hand.]

1129. To Irene Miner Weisz, Saturday [Oct. 29, 1932], from Grosvenor Hotel, New
York; Newberry.

Appreciates the candy. Is sending Hugo's latest letter. He seems in a little
better spirits. Willie. [With letter from Hugo Pavelka dated October 24,
thanking her for referring him to Bernard McNeny for advice.]

1130. To Ferris Greenslet, Oct. 31, 1932; Harvard.

Emphatically wants to keep her books out of cheap editions. Is sorry she
allowed the Modern Library *Death Comes for the Archbishop*. Prefers to sell
fewer copies with better royalty on each. Will explain more when she sees
him. Willa Cather.

1131. To Ferris Greenslet, Nov. 2, [1932], from the Grosvenor Hotel, New York;
Harvard.

Has received the royalty report. All books doing well except *O Pioneers!*.
How soon will copies of the cheap edition be exhausted, so they can get
back to the regular edition? W. S. C. P.S.: Glad to see the Benda pictures
have been restored to *Ántonia*. Hopes he will like *Obscure Destinies*.

1132. To Zoë Akins [Mrs. Hugo Rumbold], Nov. 21, [1932]; Huntington.

Shocked to hear of Hugo's death. At least they had a little time. After one
is forty-five death seems to rain down, and after fifty it becomes a storm.
Should let her daily routine carry her along, and avoid alcohol for now.
Would like to come to California to be with her, but has an eye infection.
Also, has just signed a lease on an apartment — 570 Park Avenue. Hang on,
and time will restore her. Willa.

1133. To Mrs. Alfred Carstens [of Fremont, Nebr.], Nov. 21, 1932; WCPM.

Doesn't answer all the letters she gets, but enjoyed Mrs. Carstens's; almost
like a visit home. Surprised at the question of why she hasn't written
about religion, since so many people find two of her books steeped in it.
Hopes that doesn't mean she doesn't recognize Catholicism as religion.
Is a Protestant herself, but it was Catholicism that preserved Christianity
between 300 A.D. and Martin Luther. Wishes Christians would be better
informed about history and more broad-minded. Willa Cather.

1134. To Grace Lockwood Roosevelt, Nov. 21, 1932; Harvard.

Sorry to have received her letter too late to accept invitation, but probably couldn't have accepted anyway. Will be in New Hampshire in December. Willa Cather.

1135. **To Mabel Dodge Luhan,** Nov. 22, [1932], from Grosvenor Hotel, New York; Beinecke.

She and Edith have leased an apartment and are decorating it. Almost ready to move in. Edith very busy at work; hopes she will resign soon. What about Mary Austin's book [*Earth Horizon*]? So full of special pleading and self-pity. Not true *Archbishop* was written in Austin's house – didn't even want to go to the house, but had to, to be polite. Couldn't help it the archbishop was French. Houghton Mifflin had to make deletions [from *Earth Horizon*] after some 30,000 copies were sold, under threat of lawsuit by H. G. Wells. Has she read Hemingway's fine new book [*Death in the Afternoon*]? Would like to go to Mexico this winter, but must get settled first. Has heard lots of people talking about *Lorenzo in Taos*. Willa.

1136. **To Zoë Akins,** Thursday [late Nov. 1932?]; Huntington.

Thanks for the beautiful mimosa tree. Has bought a red coat. Going to Boston Symphony with Alfred Knopf Saturday night. Almost finished fixing up apartment. Willa.

1137. **To Carrie Miner Sherwood,** Sunday [Dec. 11, 1932?]; WCPM.

Thanks for packet of reviews. Isn't the Bladen [Nebr.] bank going to pay off its depositors? Or the Inavale bank? Please use enclosed check to buy Christmas fruits and vegetables for the Lambrechts and some good coffee. Is in the middle of moving. Willie. P.S.: Roscoe's daughter, Virginia, coming for holidays.

1138. **To [Helen Sprague?],** [prob. December 1932], fragment; WCPM.

P.S.: *Obscure Destinies* selling well in England. The pianist Myra Hess came by and said her friends were praising it, and reported good words John Galsworthy had asked her to convey. W. P.S.: Sorry little Bernard is ill, making Christmas sad.

1139. **To Mary Miner Creighton,** Dec. 20, 1932, Christmas card; WCPM.

Remembering her friendship last Christmas. Willie.

1140. **To Carrie Miner Sherwood,** Dec. 20, 1932, Christmas card; WCPM.

Thinking of her. Willie.

1141. To Zoë Akins, 1932, Christmas card; Huntington.
Willa.

1142. To Zoë Akins, Dec. 22, [1932], from 570 Park Avenue, New York; Huntington.
She and Edith have had one problem after another since moving in, including broken water pipe. Visiting niece is staying in hotel. Her last letter talks about Hugo's good points and her own faults. He must have been very good for her, helping her suppress her southern vagaries and try to be accurate and honest. Glad she married him, even though it was brief. Willa.

1143. To Irene Miner Weisz, Thursday [Dec. 22 or 29, 1932?]; Newberry.
Keep this a secret – is being awarded the Prix Fémina Americain for *Shadows on the Rock*. French ambassador will host a luncheon in her honor. Just when she wants to stay busy on the apartment! W.

1144. To Ferris Greenslet, n.d. [c. Dec. 29, 1932]; Harvard.
Is horrified by the chopped-up version of *Ántonia* done by this Miss Hahn. Will still allow him to use first 30 pages after introduction, but with no cuts and with Miss Hahn to have nothing to do with it. Would prefer to drop it altogether. Are they trying to turn it into Zane Grey? He's never treated *Ántonia* well; has treated her like a cheap strumpet, tried to ruin her character. Doesn't want to be represented in a volume for children that gives them chopped-up versions of things. Even so, is still his friend and sends New Year's wishes. But not to Miss Hahn! Willa Cather.

1145. To Ferris Greenslet, Dec. 30, [1932]; Harvard.
Sorry her letter so messy, but typewriter isn't unpacked. W. S. C.

1146. To Zoë Akins, Dec. 31, 1932; Huntington.
Beautiful potted apple tree arrived Christmas Eve and is still blooming. The wonderful Josephine is back! Still a wonderful cook. Has decided many of the details in *Shadows on the Rock* came from Josephine. Wishes Zoë were beginning the new year with Hugo, but remember, our personal lives aren't measured by time. Willa.

1147. To Fanny Butcher, n.d. [early 1933?], from 570 Park Avenue, New York; Newberry.

Disappointed to miss her. Just settling into the apartment. Willa Cather.

1148. To Dorothy Canfield Fisher, Jan. 11, [1933], from 570 Park Avenue, New York; UVt.

So much to catch up on. Has taken an apartment with Edith. Hopes Dorothy will come to tea. Please see February *Atlantic* ["A Chance Meeting"]. Still remembers when she first read Flaubert in Red Cloud, and later with George Seibel in Pittsburgh. Has been able to save three farms in Nebraska by catching up their interest payments. So glad Dorothy likes "Old Mrs. Harris," a story that almost does what she set out to do in it. Willa.

1149. To Mr. Cashiell, Jan. 16, 1933; Princeton.

Appreciates his letter, but rarely writes short stories, and when she does Knopf places them. Willa Cather.

1150. To Dr. Merores [?], Jan. 16, 1933; UVa.

Sorry to hear he began a German translation of *Death Comes for the Archbishop* without her agreement or a publisher. Arranging for translations is very complicated and time-consuming. Mr. Knopf handles it all for her. Interesting that he knows Mrs. Brandeis. Once knew Judge Brandeis fairly well, and his sisters Pauline and Josephine Goldmark are dear friends. Can't help find a publisher for his translation. Willa Cather.

1151. To Sinclair Lewis, n.d. [Jan. 1933?], from New York; Beinecke.

Telephone number is Regent 4-8354. Hopes they can get together. Willa Cather.

1152. To Paul R. Reynolds, Jan. 16, 1933; Columbia.

Has been busy moving into the new apartment. Here is new address, which she will share with very few. Please keep it to himself! Willa Cather.

1153. To Mr. [Carlton F.] Wells, Jan. 16, 1933; Newberry.

Glad he sent the English reviews of *Obscure Destinies*, especially the one from *Manchester Guardian*. Interesting that he was a professor at Michigan when she received honorary degree there. The first university to give a person an honorary degree is brave. Princeton was brave in giving her its first to a woman. Best wishes with his work at the British Museum. Willa Cather.

1154. To Harvey Taylor, Jan. 16, 1933; UVa.

Is not interested in a bibliography of her work and does not care to help. People doing research projects keep her from her work. Willa Cather.

1155. To Irene Miner Weisz, n.d. [Jan. 19, 1933], from 570 Park Avenue, New York; Newberry.

Has taken on so many social engagements, doesn't have time to write letters. Both Myra Hess and the Menuhins are in town. Is glad to have a home again and to have Josephine back, cooking better food than ever! Edith so busy she can't do much about getting settled. How is Helen Mac's baby? Willie.

1156. To Whitney Darrow, Jan. 24, [1933]; Princeton.

Accepts invitation to Friends of the Princeton Library dinner on May 4. Willa Cather. [Others who accepted were Wilbur Cross, Robert Frost, Mr. and Mrs. Ira Gershwin, Ellen Glasgow, and Mr. and Mrs. Oliver LaFarge.]

1157. To Zoë Akins, Wednesday [prob. Jan. or Feb. 1933]; Huntington.

Enjoying the apple tree she sent [Dec. 24, 1932], which turns winter into spring. Won't be able to visit her tomorrow, due to a business appointment. W. S. C.

1158. To Dorothy Canfield Fisher, n.d. [Jan. or Feb. 1933]; UVt.

Would rather Dorothy write an article on her than anyone else [resulting in "Daughter of the Frontier," *New York Herald Tribune*, May 1933]. Tired of hearing she has sacrificed to art. Has always indulged herself by following likes and avoiding dislikes. Has luxuriated in a great deal of music. Has shut out people in general in order to devote herself to real friends. Willa.

1159. To Carrie and Mary Miner, Jan. 31 [1933?]; WCPM.

Enjoyed their Christmas letters and rereads them when feeling down. Wishes they could come see her and Edith's apartment. Furniture prices low these days, so they have added some good new pieces to go with the old. Enjoying it very much. Went to celebration for Yehudi Menuhin's sixteenth birthday last week. Must stop and go help Josephine defrost the refrigerator. Willa.

1160. **To Dorothy Canfield Fisher,** n.d. [Feb. 1933]; UVt.
Will see her Thursday the 16th at four. Willa.

1161. **To Dorothy Canfield Fisher,** n.d. [Feb. 16, 1933]; UVt.
Is pleased with the article. Has corrected her birth date – December 7, 1876
[sic]. Seems strange to read a summation of her books. Yes, the common
thread is escape. Still has that feeling of spaciousness and possibility when
she takes a train west across the country. Unfortunately, just when she is
enjoying that feeling the most she always feels the most homesick. Willa.

1162. **To Dorothy Canfield Fisher,** Feb. 17, 1933, telegram; UVt.
Please leave out some of the dates, especially graduation from college. They
make her feel old. Willa.

1163. **To Zoë Akins,** Feb. 19, [1933]; Huntington.
Many thanks for the pictures of her home and of herself and of Hugo.
Many people in town now, no chance of working. Regrets the news about
Sara Teasdale. Why didn't she find anything to live for? Off to a concert
with the Menuhins! Willa.

1164. **To Dorothy Canfield Fisher,** n.d. [Feb. 1933?]; UVt.
No, please do not use the pictures. Such bad ones she's surprised Dorothy
has kept them all this time. W.

1165. **To Dorothy Canfield Fisher,** n.d. except Monday [Feb. 20, 1933?]; UVt.
Thanks for being so tolerant about the dates. It wasn't reasonable, but felt
devastated about them. Hopes she will come see the apartment. Willa.

1166. **To Cyril Clemens,** Feb. 27, 1933; WCPM.
Sorry not to have replied sooner to thank him for sending Miss Hazen's
letter about *My Ántonia.* She is a keen analyst. Willa Cather.

1167. **To Gertrude Battle Lane** [of *Woman's Home Companion*], Feb. 28, 1933; LC.
Doesn't have anything to offer. Has done little except get settled in new
apartment. Will hope to get back to a long story she was working on [prob.
Lucy Gayheart], and if so will ask Mr. Knopf to send it to her. Willa Cather.

1168. **To S. S. McClure,** Mar. 15, [1933], from 570 Park Avenue, New York; Indiana.
Has had bronchitis, but is getting better. Can he come to dinner on Saturday? Willa Cather.

1169. To S. S. McClure, Mar. 17, 1933, telegram; Indiana.
Did he receive her note inviting him to dinner? Willa Cather.

1170. To Blanche Knopf, Monday [Mar. 20, 1933]; HRC.
Just opened the package with homemade jam. Has had some with her tea.
W. S. C.

1171. To Mrs. George Whicher, Apr. 1, [1933], from 570 Park Avenue, New York;
PM.
Sorry to have missed her. Was away in Atlantic City recovering from bron-
chitis. Returned just today. Has been busy getting settled in the new
apartment. Is confiding her address, which she gives out to very few. Willa
Cather.

1172. To Pauline Goldmark, Apr. 18, [1933], from 570 Park Avenue; WCPM.
Could she and Josephine [Goldmark] come to tea on Saturday the 22nd at
five? Willa Cather.

1173. To Argus Book Shop, Inc. [Chicago], Apr. 24, 1933; Beinecke.
Sorry to have been slow answering, but has been away. Biography of Mary
Baker Eddy was the product of a group of four or five staffers at *McClure's*.
Merely brought together parts written by others. Was only an editor, not
a writer. Willa Cather. P.S.: Must not use her words in catalogs, and so on,
which would be illegal.

1174. To Irene Miner Weisz, Apr. 26, 1933; Newberry.
Is making a talk at the Friends of Princeton Library dinner on May 4. She
might want to listen on the radio. Willie. P.S. Why doesn't she write?

1175. To Carrie Miner Sherwood, Apr. 26, 1933; WCPM.
She may want to listen to talk on the radio May 4. Willie. P.S.: Please thank
Helen Mac for the picture of the baby. [Cather's speech at the Friends of
Princeton University Library dinner, May 4, 1933, honoring Pulitzer Prize
winners, is at Princeton.]

1176. To George Whicher, Apr. 8, 1933 [error?; pm. May 8, 1933], from New York;
PM.
Could he exert his influence to help her get two rooms at the Lord Jeffrey
in Amherst for June 17, 18, and 19? Will be there to accept an honorary degree from Smith at the commencement when Virginia graduates. Realizes

they would invite her to stay with them, but she doesn't visit friends —
especially when receiving honorary degrees! Also, Miss Lewis will be with
her. If the Lord Jeffrey is impossible, a room in Springfield would be all
right. Hopes to see them. Willa Cather.

1177. To George and Harriet Whicher, May 12, [1933], telegram; PM.
Appreciates their efforts to find her a hotel. Please book the two rooms
at South Hadley. Will probably arrive the Friday before commencement.
Willa Cather.

1178. To Mrs. Zimbalist, May 16, [1933?]; LC.
Just finished reading Marcia Davenport's book on Mozart [pub. 1932] and
liked it very much. It evoked his music as she read. Willa Cather.

1179. To Mr. Mason, May 21, 1933; UVa.
Already told Mr. Taylor she was not interested in a bibliography and declined to help. People should not be urged to give up their work to do
things that don't interest them. Willa Cather.

1180. To Mrs. George Whicher, May 22, 1933; PM.
Appreciates her kindness in searching for hotel accommodations, and also
her thoughtfulness to have made the reservation in Miss Lewis's name.
It's obvious that Smith College is not going to be so thoughtful. The tone
of their letters is truly condescending. Perhaps they should plan to have
dinner together on Saturday rather than Friday. Maybe West Virginia [the
niece] could come, too. Has lived in such a rush lately, hasn't even written
to her. Looks forward to seeing the Frosts as well. Willa Cather.

1181. To Norman Foerster, May 22, 1933; UNL, copy, not original.
Gives permission for him to use pp. 14–51 of *Death Comes for the Archbishop*,
provided Knopf agrees. Usually an extract from a novel is unsatisfying,
but this can hardly be called a novel anyway. Please address mail care of
Knopf. Willa Cather.

1182. To S. S. McClure, May 26, [1933?]; Indiana.
Was hoping to see him before summer, but since it has turned hot is
leaving town. Will hope to see him again in the fall. Recalls that he worked
well with young people, back in the magazine days, because he had such
a spark of youth himself. Willa Cather.

1183. To Mrs. George Whicher, Sunday [pm. June 5, 1933], from New York; PM.
Yes, the Faculty House sounds even nicer than the inn. Many thanks. Will let her know their train schedule. Willa Cather.

1184. To Helen McAfee, n.d. [pm. June 7, 1933]; Beinecke.
Hopes a woman named Kraruth is not doing an article for the Review. Has received a letter from her asking impertinent questions. Willa Cather.

1185. To Mrs. George Whicher, June 15, [1933], telegram; PM.
Will take the noon train to Springfield tomorrow [Friday]. Will look forward to their joining her and Miss Lewis for dinner. Willa Cather.

1186. To Dorothy Canfield Fisher, June 22, [1933]; UVt.
Has received a copy of the *Herald Tribune* article and sent it to Isabelle. Is grateful Dorothy wrote about her so nicely. Nowadays is happiest if she can forget the past, or at any rate her own place in past scenes. Has always been trying to escape herself and has been happiest when she was best escaping. Where have the years gone? Is happy when she can avoid thinking. Going to Grand Manan next week. Dorothy won't be going to Germany this year, will she? Willa.

1187. To Blanche Knopf, July 20, [1933], from Grand Manan; HRC.
Has had a wonderful two weeks watching the wild flowers bloom. Received a note from Pat yesterday. Niece is here, as well as Edith, but usually she takes her walks alone. May get to work soon. Willa Cather.

1188. To Pat Knopf, Aug. 15, [1933], from Grand Manan; Wellesley.
Sorry to hear his vacation was spent having his appendix out. But he will enjoy New Mexico more without one, when he gets to go. Walking a lot here on trails along the cliffs. Saw the Italian air fleet pass over this afternoon – hated their looks. Willa Cather.

1189. To Zoë Akins, Aug. 26, [1933], from Grand Manan; Huntington.
Bookends arrived after she left, but secretary is keeping them safe in New York. Has enjoyed the knit jackets. Working on a new book about a giddy young girl, but not enjoying the work as much as she has some books. Island very pretty now with wild flowers. Hated seeing the Italian air fleet pass over earlier. Willa.

1190. To George Austerman, Aug. 26, [1933], from Grand Manan; UVa.

Expects to arrive around September 15, along with Miss Lewis, and will hope to have the two rooms with bath that she had last year and Miss Lewis the nearest room with bath on same side of hall. Will wire him from Boston exact arrival information. Willa Cather.

1191. To Mrs. Alfred Carstens, n.d. [c. Sept. 1, 1933]; WCPM.

Appreciated the nice letter. Willa Cather.

1192. To Sinclair Lewis, Sept. 2, [1933?], from Grand Manan; Beinecke.

Hopes to see him in New York this winter. Now has an apartment – 570 Park Avenue, though that is a secret she guards carefully. Spent four years in Pasadena, California, with her mother and is now getting back to her friends. Odd, critics carp at her for not writing like a man and at him for not writing like a woman! Going to Quebec soon, before returning to New York. Willa Cather.

1193. To George Austerman, Sept. 19,[1933], from Grand Manan; UVa.

Expects to arrive Monday, October 2, along with Miss Lewis. Please have their old rooms, 324 and 328. Will be there for the month of October. Willa Cather.

1194. To Alfred Knopf, Sept. 24, [1933], from Grand Manan; HRC.

Will be leaving the 30th and arriving at Jaffrey October 3. Beginning to like the idea of an illustrated *Archbishop*. Willa Cather.

1195. To Miss Vanamee [National Institute of Arts and Letters] [from Sarah J. Bloom, secretary], Oct. 4, 1933; AAAL.

Cather is away from New York and not expected back for some time. May return in time to decide whether to attend the Institute dinner on November 8. Sarah J. Bloom, Secretary.

1196. To Mrs. George Whicher, Wednesday [Oct. 11, 1933], from Jaffrey, N.H.; PM.

The cushions fit perfectly. Will leave one at the Shattuck Inn to use next year and take one to New York. Glad to have good foot rests at such a bargain. Enjoyed seeing her Sunday. Willa Cather. P.S.: Are the mountains in Austria really more beautiful than Monadnock?

1197. To Elmer Adler, Saturday [Oct. 21, 1933, replying to his of Oct. 19, 1933]; Princeton.

Resolving some details of the printing of "December Night." Is pleased with his conception and confident the result will be fine. Willa Cather.

1198. To Carrie Miner Sherwood, Oct. 22, [1933?], from Jaffrey, N.H.; WCPM.
Treasures her letter. No, won't get to Red Cloud this year. Is working happily on a new book. This is where she finished *Ántonia*, began *Archbishop*, and wrote most of *Shadows*. Always has the same rooms high up under the roof. Is enjoying long walks in the woods. Willie.

1199. To Blanche and Alfred Knopf, Oct. 26, [1933?], from Jaffrey, N.H.; HRC.
Regrets her tardiness in thanking them for the books they sent, but between working and good weather for walks has not been taking time to write letters. Today, completed the first draft of *Lucy Gayheart*. There is much more to be done to pull it up, but if they will protect her privacy over the winter she can get it done, if not in the new apartment, where she has not yet become accustomed to working, then back here at the Shattuck Inn. Ankle holding up well. Mount Monadnock beautiful, with a dusting of snow and roiling clouds above it. Sorry for the ornate writing. Willa Cather.

1200. To National Institute of Arts and Letters [from Sarah J. Bloom, secretary], Nov. 2, 1933; AAAL.
Cather is away and not expected back for several weeks, so will be unable to attend the luncheon on Nov. 9 [?]. Sarah J. Bloom, Secretary.

1201. To Mrs. Genevieve Richmond, Dec. 8, 1933; First Church.
Did not write Georgine Milmine's biography of Mary Baker Eddy, only did some editorial work on it, including a few paragraphs of rewrite. It was done only for the magazine articles. Doesn't believe she ever even saw the book. Indeed, Milmine may have put back in some of the material she cut out. Wishes certain people wouldn't go about saying she wrote it. Willa Cather.

1202. To Ida Tarbell, Dec. 13, [1933], from New York; Allegheny.
Enclosing a check to assist S. S. McClure. Willa Cather.

1203. To Fanny Butcher, Dec. 13, [pm. 1933]; Newberry.
Appreciates her sending the clippings of her review. Feeling better than when she was in town. Had dinner with the Knopfs last night – such fine people. Willa Cather.

1204. **To Mabel Dodge Luhan,** Dec. 14, [1933?], from 570 Park Avenue, New York; Beinecke.

Found her letter waiting when she returned from New Hampshire. Glad she is having her portrait done. Enjoyed being lazy all summer, but worked hard during the fall. Anticipates a good musical season in New York and is looking forward to the Menuhins' arrival in January. Does she know where Elsie Sergeant is? Willa.

1205. **To Carrie Miner Sherwood,** Dec. 14, [1933?]; wcpm.

Please have Mrs. Burden [storekeeper] pack up a box of Christmas groceries for Mrs. Lambrecht and purchase some good coffee for Annie Pavelka. Has sent Annie a check and some discarded clothes. Is sending a check to [name blocked out]. But the spectacle of poverty may be even harsher in the city. Willie.

1206. **To George and Eleanore Austerman,** Dec. 1933, [copy of "December Night" with autograph]; uva.

1207. **To Zoë Akins,** n.d. [Dec. 1933], [copy of "December Night" with autograph note]; uva.

Believes she will enjoy the pictures. Willa.

1208. **To Cyril Clemens,** Dec. 28, [1933?], from 570 Park Avenue, New York; wcpm.

Glad to accept the medal of the International Mark Twain Society. Is proud to think, as Albert Bigelow Paine reports in his biography, that Mark Twain expressed admiration of one of her poems [later letter says "The Palatine"]. Willa Cather. P.S.: Sorry to be slow responding, but is just back from northern Canada [?].

1209. **To Zoë Akins,** Jan. 2, [1934], from New York; Huntington.

Thanks for plants she sent for Christmas and for copy of "Little Willie," which is very funny. How did she know about the family nickname? Does not care to see [Maxwell] Anderson's rendition of Mary Stuart [*Mary of Scotland, 1933*]. Is trying hard to complete work on *Lucy Gayheart*, but people won't leave her alone. Hates meeting with financial advisors who tell her she is losing money. W.

1210. **To Ida Tarbell,** Jan. 7, [1934?]; Allegheny.

Sending another check for Mr. McClure. Why do they never see each other? Willa Cather.

1211. To Cyril Clemens, Jan. 10, 1934; WCPM.

Doesn't know when she will be in the West, probably not until next winter. Has lost her copy of article about *My Ántonia* written for Mark Twain Society. Could he provide the name of the woman who wrote it? Willa Cather.

1212. To Cyril Clemens, Jan. 27, 1934; Virginia.

Thanks for the copy of Miss Hazen's article. No, has not become a Catholic, though admires the Church and contrary to her Episcopal bishop, believes it the source of all Christian churches. Glad to hear of the postage stamp honoring Mark Twain. Willa Cather.

1213. To Cyril Clemens, n.d., typed commentary about Mark Twain with hand corrections [possibly the material referred to in no. 1214]; WCPM.

Once met a Russian violinist who said he would greatly like to see the Mississippi River. He grew up near the Volga and had read *Huckleberry Finn* in translation as a boy and wondered if the Mississippi was like the Volga. Hard to imagine how the regional colloquialism of the book could be translated into Russian. But the book has enough vitality to shine through even botched language.

1214. To Carrie Miner Sherwood, Jan. 27, 1934; WCPM.

International Mark Twain Society has voted *My Ántonia* a silver medal, but must go to St. Louis to receive it. She might enjoy reading enclosed report done for the Society. Please don't show people in Red Cloud who are spiteful or would gape at Annie Pavelka to see how dissimilar Ántonia is. Why won't people believe fiction is *not* a direct portrait of real people? "Two Friends" not about Mr. Miner and Mr. Richardson, but the emotional response to them felt by a child. It recreates a memory. Similarly, Ántonia sums up emotions about immigrant people she knew there. Mr. Sadilek's suicide was the first thing she heard about upon arriving in Nebraska. Her fiction has always been a precise representation of her feelings, never faked or exaggerated feeling. Willie. P.S.: Enjoyed seeing Irene when she was in New York.

1215. To Carrie Miner Sherwood, Feb. 12, [1934?]; WCPM.

Often wishes she had time to write her a long letter. Business matters wear her out. Has been struggling to prevent radio broadcasts of her books.

Also letters about translations. Would prefer to spend her time producing new work. Knopf indulges her determination to avoid commitments. Happiest part of the season has been the presence of the Menuhin family. Enjoyed reading Shakespeare with the children and sledding with Yehudi on his birthday, followed by a small party with champagne smuggled in by his mother. Enclosing letters from Hephzibah and Yaltah, but she must not show them to anyone. Willie.

1216. To Bishop George Allen Beecher, Feb. 13, [1934?]; HSNeb.
Can he come to dinner with one of his parishioners [herself] on Wednesday, the 14th? Please telegraph response, as she shuts off the phone while working. Willa Cather.

1217. To Carl Van Doren, Mar. 7, 1934; Princeton.
Sorry to refuse him but does not want parts of *My Ántonia* or *A Lost Lady* excerpted for an anthology. Willa Cather.

1218. To Carl Van Doren, Mar. 22, 1934; Princeton.
Yes, glad for him to use the chapter he mentions from *The Song of the Lark.* Willa Cather.

1219. To Dorothy Canfield Fisher, Mar. 29, 1934; UVt.
Has to dictate this letter because of a sprain to the tendon in her left wrist, now inflamed. Is in splints and a sling, and surprisingly enough, can't write with right hand. Please visit next time she is in town. Willa.

1220. To Mary Miner Creighton, Thursday [Mar. 29, 1934], from New York; Newberry.
Has been in splints for four weeks, left hand useless, right hand overworked so can't write. Menuhins have been distracting her. Enclosing check to the church guild. Willie.

1221. To Margaret Crofts, Saturday [Mar. 31, 1934?]; LC.
Sorry to hear of her father's death. Has been in splints for torn tendon that became inflamed. Has to see doctors twice a day. Will hope to talk with her soon. Willa Cather.

1222. To H. L. Mencken, Apr. 20, 1934; NYPL.
Thanks for his advice about encyclopedias. Will try to find a used set of the

ninth edition, as she has heard newer ones not so good. Having a tiresome time with this sprained tendon, which is slow to heal. Willa Cather.

1223. **To Dorothy Canfield Fisher,** Saturday [Apr. 21, 1934?]; UVt.
Thanks for the flowers she sent. Hopes to see her in May. Left hand still in splints. Willa.

1224. **To Mabel Dodge Luhan,** May 1, [1934]; Beinecke.
Sorry to have missed her. Wish she had stayed at the Grosvenor while she was in town. Hand out of splints but not useful yet. Enjoyed *Four Saints* [*in Three Acts*; New York premiere on February 20, 1934]. Willa.

1225. **To Yaltah and Hephzibah Menuhin,** May 3, [1934?]; Princeton.
Wishes she could have accompanied them to Marseilles; has always liked it. Isabelle wrote that Yehudi's concert in Paris was a great success. Expects to finish new book before leaving in July for Grand Manan. Hoping hand will be well enough to let her enjoy the rougher life there. Will use splint if it hurts. As Shakespeare writes, "My very chains and I grow friends . . ." Hopes they can read Shakespeare together again some day. Greetings to all. Aunt Willa.

1226. **To Allan Nevins,** n.d. [c. May 5, 1934]; Columbia.
Enjoyed reading his book *Fremont*. Caught the spirit of that thrilling time in America. Hand out of splints about a week ago. Willa Cather.

1227. **To Zona Gale,** May 23, 1934; HSW.
Sorry to have missed her when she was in town. Was in Atlantic City. Has had an arduous time with the left wrist. New book about a month from finishing. Willa Cather. P.S.: Has been telling people she was away. Keeps it a secret when she is in town so people won't bother her.

1228. **To Carrie Miner Sherwood,** July 3, [1934?]; WCPM.
Please pick out some good canned fruit for Mrs. Lambrecht's birthday. It's terribly hot in New York, but has stayed in town to finish *Lucy Gayheart*. To be serialized in *Woman's Home Companion* starting in April 1935, preceding book publication. Magazine's offer was too good to refuse. Sorry they are having such a drought. Expects to leave for Grand Manan mid-month. Willie.

1229. To Alfred A. Knopf, July 25, 1934, from Grand Manan, telegram; HRC.
Does not like type font, too large and unromantic. Please use font like *A Lost Lady*. Getting settled. Willa Cather.

1230. To Blanche Knopf, July 26, [1934]; HRC.
Appreciates their indulging her on type size. Is enjoying the silver candlesticks they gave her, which are on their second stay in Grand Manan. Flowers and spruce trees beautiful. W. S. C.

1231. To Mary Miner Creighton, Aug. 9, 1934, from Grand Manan, telegram; Newberry.
Sorry to hear of the death of Dr. Creighton. Willa Cather. [followed by note:] Sending roses with her love. Willie.

1232. To Mary Miner Creighton, n.d. [c. Aug. 15, 1934], from Grand Manan; UVa.
Grieving the loss of Dr. Creighton a week ago. Theirs was a rare marriage, with more happiness than most. Always appreciated his care of mother. Remembers his asking once that she show kindness toward a patient who was going through a difficult time. Showed so much delicacy in thinking about the patient's need for friendship and in the way he made the request. Willie.

1233. To Marie M. Meloney, Aug. 26, [1934?], from Grand Manan; Columbia.
Just received her letter written a month ago. Sorry she didn't get to inscribe the book for J. M. Barrie. Willa Cather.

1234. To Zoë Akins, Sept. 9, [1934?], from Grand Manan; Huntington.
Has enjoyed her summer here, after the bad winter with her injured tendon. Has read galley proofs of *Lucy Gayheart* and thinks it is pretty good after all. Serializing it first to maximize income during these hard times. Economic troubles in the Midwest have been compounded by unbearable heat and drought. Looking forward to seeing *The Old Maid*. Prefers not to read the [Wharton] novel from which it was adapted. Someday hopes to see her home. Has just been watching a pod of whales in the water just in front of her house. Does so enjoy the North Atlantic; has less and less interest in the South, though she used to yearn for it so much. Willa. P.S.: Leaving for Jaffrey, N.H., September 15.

1235. **To Blanche Knopf,** Sept. 10, [1934]; HRC.

Enjoyed her letter from Nevada. People Blanche mentioned have the expansiveness and generosity of the *Lost Lady* period, like the old railroad aristocracy. W. C.

1236. **To Joseph Remenyi,** Oct. 10, [1934?], from Jaffrey, N.H.; WRHS.

Has just returned from Canada and begun to answer letters. Gives permission to make a Hungarian translation of either "Paul's Case" or "The Sculptor's Funeral." Secretary will send one of the pamphlets Knopf puts out giving biographical information. Can't send a photograph just now. Willa Cather.

1237. **To Joseph Remenyi,** Oct. 12, [1934?], from Jaffrey, N.H.; WRHS.

Can send a passport photograph taken some years ago, the only one she has with her to send. Requests like this take so much of her time she can hardly write! Willa Cather.

1238. **To Mrs. Vanamee [American Institute of Arts and Letters] [from Sarah J. Bloom, secretary],** Oct. 29, 1934; AAAL.

Cather is away; does not know when she will be back. Therefore cannot accept the invitation to the Academy luncheon on November 8. Sarah J. Bloom, Secretary.

1239. **To Harold Goddard Rugg,** Nov. 10, 1934; Dartmouth, copy at UNL.

Not true that the biography of Mary Baker Eddy is an "unknown Cather." Only did some editing on it. Willa Cather.

1240. **To Cyril Clemens,** Nov. 21, [1934], from New York; WCPM.

Will not be able to go to St. Louis for the dinner. Still loves *Huckleberry Finn* as much as ever. Medal can safely be sent to her. Willa Cather.

1241. **To Edward Wagenknecht,** Nov. 22, 1934; Beinecke, copy at WCPM.

Cannot read his last name. His friend's book about Sarah Orne Jewett is very poor, and manners offensive. Appreciates his telling her the incident about Mary Jewett. Dr. Eastman, Jewett's nephew, kept her posted after Mary Jewett's stroke. Willa Cather.

1242. **To Carl Van Vechten,** Sunday [Dec. 9, 1934], from 570 Park Avenue, New York; Beinecke.

Appreciated hearing from him on her birthday and enjoyed the roses. Willa Cather.

1243. **To [Egbert Samuel] Oliver**, Dec. 13, 1934; PM.

Too tired of answering questions from men writing books on creative writing to answer his. Silly to try to teach it anyway. People should be taught to write clear, correct English and let creative writing take care of itself. Willa Cather.

1244. **To Zoë Akins**, Saturday [Dec. 15, 1934]; Huntington.

She always sends the best flowers! These Roman hyacinths remind her of original of the *Lost Lady* [Mrs. Garber]. Can she come to dinner on Friday the 21st? Willa.

1245. **To Henry Seidel Canby**, Dec. 18, [1934?]; Beinecke.

Do come for tea on Christmas afternoon. Willa Cather.

1246. **To Mr. and Mrs. C. W. Weisz**, n.d. [pm. Dec. 22, 1934], Christmas card, Newberry.

With love. Willa Cather.

1247. **To Ferris Greenslet**, Jan. 4, [1935?], from New York; Harvard.

Is free on the 17th and will expect to see him then. Yes, willing for Tauchnitz to have *My Ántonia*. Willa Cather.

1248. **To Cyril Clemens**, Jan. 10, 1935; UVa.

Very glad to receive the Mark Twain medal and his account of the dinner. Willa Cather.

1249. **To Mrs. C. F. Lambrecht, Lydia, and Pauline**, Jan. 19, [1935?]; WCPM.

Appreciates the quilt they made her. Recognizes many of the flowers on it. Among them, lilies-of-the-valley, crocuses, and peonies are her favorites. But almost likes the solid squares better, because of the quilting. Willie Cather.

1250. **To Alexander Woollcott**, Feb. 8, 1935, [excerpt]; Harvard.

No, cannot agree to radio or phonograph renditions of her books. Hates the exaggerated manner of many readers in such recordings, how they turn the works into sentimental nonsense. [unsigned].

1251. To Thomas Masaryk, Feb. 14, [1935?], from 570 Park Ave., New York; Berkeley.

It is nearing his birthday. Extends good wishes and praise for his achievements. Values his regard. It is a puzzling and disordered time. Public opinion in a state of confusion, moral values being overthrown without the creation of new ones. The regard of people one esteems is the only source of satisfaction in today's world. He is the only public figure with whom she has corresponded who is not exiled. Many scholars have been driven out of their homelands and taken refuge in America. Willa Cather.

1252. To Fanny Butcher, n.d. [c. Feb. 1935], from New York; Newberry.

So she is about to be married to a Mr. Bokum! Best wishes. Don't read new story in *Woman's Home Companion*; wait for the book. Willa Cather.

1253. To Carrie Miner Sherwood, Mar. 15, [1935]; WCPM.

Is recovering from attack of appendicitis. Willie.

1254. To Joseph Remenyi, Mar. 19, 1935; WRHS.

Appreciates the book but can't read a word of Hungarian. Willa Cather.

1255. To Carrie Miner Sherwood, n.d. [1935?]; WCPM.

Hopes to write a long letter in a few days. Enclosing a check for church guild and sending Sigrid Undset's newest book. Willie.

1256. To Ferris Greenslet, Apr. 11, [1935]; Harvard.

Appreciates his understanding letter. Isabelle McClung Hambourg has arrived from Europe, very ill. Will stay nearby under doctor's care while Jan Hambourg goes on tour for six weeks. Willa Cather.

1257. To Zoë Akins, Good Friday [Apr. 19, 1935]; Huntington.

Has had various problems since she was there – appendicitis in mid-March, Mary Virginia's operation soon afterward, and Isabelle McClung Hambourg's arrival on March 27, very ill. Isabelle now in a hospital. Jan and his brothers away on concert tour to raise money. Has full responsibility for Isabelle. Also, Josephine Bourda and family returning to France in May to stay. (Josephine never received the dog she [Zoë] was sending her.) Another bout of appendicitis April 7. Sent her proofs of *Lucy Gayheart* last week; please read to see what the book is like, don't just go by the serial version. Glad to see splendid success of *The Old Maid*. Was progressing well on new work when all this trouble hit. So glad to have Alfred Knopf as a supportive friend. Willa. P.S.: Yes, early part of *Lucy Gayheart* resembles the mood of *The Master Builder* [Ibsen], but hopes she will agree the last part, which is the best, is very much in her own manner.

1258. **To Zoë Akins,** n.d. [pm. May 10 or 20, 1935 (not clear)]; Huntington.
People are very pleased about Zoë's Pulitzer Prize. Is still very stressed by daily attendance at hospital. Couldn't give any help in preparing for Mary Virginia's wedding except to write checks. Willa. P.S.: Try to read *Lucy Gayheart* in one sitting.

1259. **To Irene Miner Weisz,** May 14, [1935], from New York; Newberry.
Thanks for roses. Isabelle has enjoyed them. What does her doctor say? [signature illegible]

1260. **To Zoë Akins,** n.d. [May 27, 1935]; Huntington.
How nice of her to send Josephine a present! W. S. C.

1261. **To Marie M. Meloney,** May 29, 1935; Columbia.
Has intended for some time to write and thank her for relaying James M. Barrie's message about *My Ántonia*. Cannot try to write a story using the idea she suggested. Ideas for stories must be her own. Willa Cather.

1262. **To Mr. C. W. Weisz,** June 5, [1935]; Newberry.
Is worried about Irene. Please let her know how she is. Willa Cather. P.S.: Is the Hotel Sissons still in operation?

1263. **To Roscoe Cather,** June 12, 1935 [note at end says this is a carbon copy made for Carrie Miner Sherwood]; WCPM.
Returning Virginia's letter. Mary Virginia's wedding was beautiful. Was at the Little Church Around the Corner, which their father used to like so much when he came to New York. Isabelle insisted on attending. Likes the groom, Dick Mellen, a new M.D. from Harvard beginning internship at Bellevue Hospital. Mary Virginia will continue working at the library. Own plans not clear. P.S. to Carrie: Has the Miner farm been damaged by flooding of the Republican River?

1264. **To Mrs. C. F. Lambrecht,** n.d. [June 1935], on printed announcement of the marriage of Mary Virginia Auld to Dr. Richard Hager Mellen on Saturday, June 1, 1935; WCPM.

Knew she would be interested in this. Likes the young man very much. Willa Cather.

1265. To Cyril Clemens, June 15, [1935]; UVa.

Sorry to have been unable to write sooner. Willa Cather.

1266. To Ferris Greenslet, June 29, 1935; Harvard.

Going to Chicago with Isabelle while Jan Hambourg gives master classes there. Expects to sail on the *Berengaria* on July 26 if Isabelle is no worse. To Venice, then to Paris to join the Hambourgs, who will have returned by then. Willa Cather.

1267. To Irene Miner Weisz, July 13, 1935, from New York; Newberry.

Sorry about forgetting to sign check for the second time. A signed one enclosed. Was able to get a compartment on train by telling the man who had it – who turned out to be an officer of the Pullman Company – that her friend was ill. Red cap [train station attendant] got a wheelchair for Isabelle, and she was taken straight to her hotel across the street from Cather's apartment. No use sending flowers for Isabelle's voyage home, as they don't yet know which sailing they will be able to take. Appreciates Irene's kindness while they were in Chicago. Willie.

1268. To Irene Miner Weisz, Friday [pm. July 19, 1935], from New York; Newberry.

No, not leaving on the *Berengaria*, but on an Italian ship a week later, to Genoa. *Lucy Gayheart* having good early sales. Willie.

1269. To Carrie Miner Sherwood, July 26, [1935], from New York; WCPM.

Sending a check for the Red Cross and $10 to buy a few things for Mrs. Welch. Isn't very well, but will leave for Italy next week. Hambourgs left today. Feeling very down in spirits. Willie.

1270. To Mary Miner Creighton, Aug. 8, [1935?]; Newberry.

Has passed the Azores. Will send this letter off at Gibraltar. Flowers she and Irene sent for the voyage are still beautiful. Having a rough passage, but beginning to get her energy back. The thought of their long friendship is restorative in itself. Willie.

1271. To Carrie Miner Sherwood, Aug. 22, [1935?], from Italy; WCPM.

Woke up this morning thinking of her and enjoying the sight of the dawn light on the snow peaks of the Dolomites. Flowers stayed nice all the way to Gibraltar. Expects to feel up to going to Venice soon. Willie.

1272. **To Irene Miner Weisz,** Aug. 26, 1935, from Cortina, Italy, postcard; Newberry.

A lovely village. Going to Venice by automobile tomorrow for about three weeks. Hears that Isabelle is about the same. W.

1273. **To Irene Miner Weisz,** Sept. 8, 1935, from Venice; Newberry.

Having a good holiday. Venice the most beautiful she has ever seen it. Going to Paris in two weeks to be close to Isabelle. [signature blurred]

1274. **To Zoë Akins,** Sept. 16, [1935?], from Venice, postcard; Huntington.

Has enjoyed a month in this wonderful city. Was ill when she left New York, but rested up in the Dolomites. Willa.

1275. **To Zoë Akins,** Oct. 22, [1935], from Paris; UVa.

Sailing tomorrow. Has been here over a month with a sick friend. Willa.

1276. **To Yaltah Menuhin,** Oct. 23, [1935], from Paris; Princeton.

With Edith Lewis, is sailing in a few days. Glad to receive her letter from South Africa. Her visit to the cave interesting. As for herself, prefers to stay on the surface. Surprising that she found *Lucy Gayheart* so far from New York. Isabelle asked that they leave Paris without saying goodbye, and will do so. She is very ill. Must get home and get back to work, to keep a sense of reality. Sorry not to be in Paris for Yehudi's first European recital. Willa Cather.

1277. **To the Very Rev. Francis R. Lee** [Dean of St. Mark's Pro-Cathedral], n.d. [Nov. 1935?]; pub. *Hastings* [Nebr.] *Daily Tribune* Dec. 2, 1935, quoted in full in Bohlke.

Please convey greetings to Bishop and Mrs. George Beecher on the occasion of the twenty-fifth anniversary of his consecration as bishop. Wishes she could be there on November 30. He has affected the lives of many people.

1278. **To Ferris Greenslet,** Nov. 30, 1935, from New York; Harvard.

Arrived last week after a rough voyage that she enjoyed. Isabelle will never improve, but was feeling somewhat better than in the summer. Likes Anne Morrow Lindbergh's book [*North to the Orient*, 1935]. Willa Cather. P.S.: Please send a copy of the Cape edition of *The Song of the Lark*.

1279. To George Austerman, Dec. 3, [1935]; UVa.

Please do all he can to help Stephen Tennant enjoy Jaffrey. Willa Cather.

1280. To Henry Seidel Canby, Dec. 6, [1935]; Beinecke.

Leaving town until after Christmas. Hopes he will come to tea when she gets back. Willa Cather.

1281. To Carrie Miner Sherwood, Dec. 9, [1935]; WCPM.

Doesn't believe *Lucy Gayheart* is one of her best, though the Hambourgs and Myra Hess do. Glad Carrie likes it. Selling well comparatively speaking, but book sales are all slow. Health not very good, probably due to nervous strain during spring and summer. No, can't come home for Christmas. Maybe Carrie would send reviews on to Roscoe? No one else in the family would care. Willie.

1282. To William Connely, Dec. 10, 1935; HRC.

Did not receive his letter about the two professors from England coming to the U.S. until some months later, when she was in Venice. Did not answer the accumulation of letters that came then. Yes, their lives have changed a lot since Bank Street. Would never have thought he would become a professor. Willa Cather.

1283. To Dorothy Canfield Fisher, n.d. [December 1935], Christmas card; UVt.

Got back in late November after August and September in Italy and a month or so with Isabelle in Paris. Willa.

1284. To Irene Miner Weisz, n.d. [pm. Dec. 18, 1935], Christmas card; Newberry.

Drawing on front [of New York skyscrapers] was done by the artist who did the dust jacket of *Lucy Gayheart.*

1285. To Carrie Miner Sherwood, n.d. [Dec. 1935?]; WCPM.

Likes *North to the Orient*. Pass enclosed clipping along to Helen Mac; shows bad effects of a quarter century of movies and shabby publicity. Please get a side of bacon or a ham sent to Mrs. Lambrecht. W.

1286. To Walter Sherwood [husband of Carrie Miner Sherwood], [Dec. 19, 1935?]; WCPM.

Enclosing clipping about some bonds that sound like a crooked deal. Willa S. C.

1287. **To Mrs. Mellen** [prob. mother-in-law of Mary Virginia Auld Mellen, who married Richard Mellen in 1935], n.d. [Dec. 1935?]; UVa.
Seldom gives people her own books, but may send one to Dick's mother. Exceptionally satisfied with the second story in the new book ["Old Mrs. Harris"]. Willa Cather.

1288. **To Dr. Leech,** Dec. [2]7, 1935; UVa.
Returned to town just before Christmas and hopes to see him and Mrs. Leech soon. Willa Cather. P.S.: Happy New Year!

1289. **To Zoë Akins,** Dec. 27, 1935, from New York, telegram; Huntington.
Glad to read good news about the play. Congratulations to her and to Jobyna [Howland].

1290. **To Carlton F. Wells,** Jan. 7, 1936; Newberry.
Has had a mountain of mail to get through since returning from Europe. Glad to find his letter. He is the only person who has noticed her alteration of the text of the aria from *Elijah* [Mendelssohn's]. Even baritones who have sung it don't seem to have noticed. Of course, the change [from "If with all your heart you truly seek me" to "If with all your heart you truly seek him"] is all-important. Willa Cather.

1291. **To Pat Knopf,** Jan. 19, 1936; UVa.
Typescript of *A Lost Lady* was surely forged. Burned the only one she had before moving from Bank Street. Hopes he will be able to see *Libel*, current play. Her English friend who is staying at Jaffrey [Stephen Tennant] is enjoying the snow there. Glad to autograph books for him whenever he sends them. Going for a walk in the park in a little while. Willa Cather.

1292. **To Mrs. Sidney Mattison** [Great Neck, Long Island; who had written asking for a souvenir letter for the little girl she named after Cather], Jan. 21, 1936; WCPM.
Doesn't like her first name well enough to be glad to hear that babies are named after her, but does send best wishes to the little girl. Maybe she will like the name. Willa Cather.

1293. **To namesake** [accompanying no. 1292].
Likes the picture her mother sent. Seven is a nice age. Enjoyed being seven herself. Please always be sincere, and if she doesn't like her books, say so.

Couldn't be proud of a namesake who didn't speak her own mind. Willa Cather.

1294. To Carlton F. Wells, Jan. 23, 1936; Newberry.

No, can't allow him to publish quotations from her earlier letter. Assumed the writer of such an intelligent letter as the one he wrote would know better than to try to use it for publicity. Willa Cather. P.S.: Had not realized she was writing to an English teacher who meant to read her letter to his class. Is usually cautious, but apparently not cautious enough.

1295. To Mabel Dodge Luhan, Feb. 5, 1936; Beinecke.

Enjoyed her Christmas card, with its sprig of sage. Spent a very pleasant time in Italy latter part of summer after wearing herself out caring for a sick friend. Returned shortly before Christmas. Enjoyed the rough passage, but Edith so sick she had to be carried off the boat. Still hasn't caught up on her letters. Doesn't she like the Anne Lindbergh book! Willa.

1296. To Miss Walker [for Margaret Cousins], Feb. 17, 1936; HRC.

Appreciates the invitation, but doesn't write many short stories and gives [Gertrude] Lane [of *Woman's Home Companion*] the first chance at them. Willa Cather.

1297. To Brother Barron, Feb. 17, 1936; WCPM, transcription, not original.

Just back from the North and understands his letter and manuscript came while she was away. Never reads manuscripts because at least half a million aspiring writers would be sending them if she did. Willa Cather.

1298. To William Lyon Phelps, Feb. 17, 1936; Beinecke.

Has read his article on Mark Twain in the *Yale Review*. Knew Mark Twain in his last years. Has always found the Van Wyck Brooks book about him grossly inaccurate. Glad to hear Phelps thinks so, too. If Brooks had been able to spend five minutes talking with the grand old man in his bed, he would have written differently. Willa Cather.

1299. To Carlton F. Wells, Feb. 27, 1936; Newberry.

Appreciates his assurance of his good intentions. Willa Cather.

1300. To Ferris Greenslet, Mar. 2, 1936; Harvard.

Is he in Boston at present? Wants to write a personal letter and needs to know where to send it. Willa S. Cather. Signed by S. J. Bloom.

1301. To Ferris Greenslet, Mar. 8, 1936; Harvard.

Sorry to hear he has had influenza. Has three questions: (1) Is he still interested in doing a subscription edition? Appreciates his not persisting about it during the past year when she was so weighed down by other cares. (2) Is it true a garage now stands on the site of Annie Fields's house at 148 Charles Street? (3) Is he willing to grant permission to reprint the preface she wrote for Mayflower edition of Jewett? Wonders if it is even wise to try to talk about Jewett these days; her language and sensibility almost archaic. Nervy young people of Jewish and Greek extraction associated with New York University have imposed their language instead. But gets letters now and then from people who are interested in Jewett. Willa Cather.

1302. To [Alfred] Dashiell, Mar. 9, 1936; UVa.

Is leaving New York soon and won't be back for two years, so can't accept his invitation. Hasn't attended PEN meetings in some time, though she once enjoyed them. Lost touch with many of her friends during her mother's long illness. Willa Cather.

1303. To Ferris Greenslet, Monday [after his Mar. 11, 1936, letter answering her three questions of Mar. 8 in the positive]; Harvard.

Will have her secretary begin counting words in her various books. Willa Cather.

1304. To Carrie Miner Sherwood, n.d. [Mar. 1936?]; WCPM.

Might want to listen to broadcast of Yehudi Menuhin on Sunday, March 29. Please let Irene know, too. W.

1305. To Cyril Clemens, Mar. 15, [1936?, prob. written before no. 1336]; WCPM.

Has just returned from West Coast and found his letter. Would be glad to have the booklet on Housman dedicated to her, but imagines it has already been published by now. Enjoyed reading the Housman issue of the *Quarterly*. Has he seen the drawing of Housman in William Archer's *Modern English Poets*? [Probably Archer's *Poets of the Younger Generation*, 1902.] Willa Cather.

1306. To Chilson Leonard, Mar. 19, 1936; Phil-Ex.

Has no photographs of Nebraska in 1885 or 1895. Understands from Professor Pupin [?] of Columbia that it resembled the plains of Russia. Otto Fuchs not a representation of a specific person but a composite of many, as are most minor characters. Blind d'Arnault modeled on Blind Boone. Has also heard of a similar Blind Tom and Blind Noah. Actress Jim sees in *Camille* based on Clara Morris. Many relics such as the Spanish sword have been found in southwest Kansas. Good reading does not come from factual information, however, but from cultivated taste. Does not approve of required reading of contemporary writers in English courses, which should center on great English writers of the past and on Latin writers. Wishes his students were reading *Kidnapped* [Stevenson] or *Vanity Fair* [Thackeray] rather than *My Ántonia*. Willa Cather.

1307. To Helen [Sprague?], Mar. 22, 1936; WCPM.
Is writing to let her know about Menuhin broadcast on March 29, but has wanted to write for some time. Doesn't take very seriously the authorial ambitions of so many young people. What they really want is the glamour they associate with being a writer or being in the movies or some other publicized activity. It's a fad. Likes Mary Virginia's husband. What did she name the little girl? Willa Cather. Signed by S. J. Bloom.

1308. To Irene Miner Weisz, n.d. [pm. Mar. 25, 1936], from New York; Newberry.
How is she? Please write. Willie.

1309. To Carl Van Vechten, Apr. 3, [1936]; Beinecke.
Photos won't do. Please destroy the negatives, and they'll try again some time. Willa Cather.

1310. To [Mr. and Mrs. George Whicher?], n.d. [prob. 1936], Easter card with note; PM.
Were abroad all fall, got home shortly before Christmas. A very trying time, with many friends ill. Hopes for better things in the spring. Willa Cather.

1311. To Carl Van Vechten, Wednesday [Apr. 8, 1936]; Beinecke.
Glad he wasn't offended by her note of the 3rd. Appreciates his generosity about it. Willa Cather.

1312. To Miss Rubin [with Alfred A. Knopf], n.d. [but stamped in at Knopf office Apr. 13, 1936]; HRC.
Please get copyright of *Atlantic* article transferred to her so it can be used in book of essays. Willa Cather.

1313. To Blanche Knopf, Wednesday [Apr. 15, 1936?]; HRC.

Sorry, but can't have dinner with them tonight. Got chilled in the park yesterday and has lost her voice. Did she see the letter in the *Saturday Review* about her and [Sinclair] Lewis? Has liked their advertising recently. Willa Cather.

1314. To Norman Foerster, Apr. 16, 1936;. UNL, copy, not original.

Glad he feels like recommending her for honorary degree, but would rather not. Has another one to accept the same week as Rockford College commencement. Early June will be a busy time. Glad to hear from him again. Willa Cather.

1315. To Zoë Akins, Apr. 19, [1936]; Huntington.

Has been sick in bed for three days. Never got her telegrams. Was in New Hampshire March 14 through 25 [with Stephen Tennant?], but Edith would have received them. Except for these last few days, has been quite well all winter. Glad she is back from Europe. Willa

1316. To Zoë Akins, Monday [Apr. 27, 1936], from New York; Huntington.

Is quite well now. Many thanks for the rose tree. Has been reading *The Last Puritan* [Santayana]. Can't read his technical books, of course. Still misses Josephine, whose letters are as pleasant as she was herself. Had a Swedish maid for three months but let her go, so plodding and unimaginative. Appreciates the invitation to Green Fountains [Zoë's house in California], but doesn't feel she is very good company these days. W.

1317. To Cyril Clemens, Apr. 30, 1936; UVa.

Not sure why *The Song of the Lark* has not been translated into Spanish. Glad he likes her article in *Commonweal* enough to republish it as a pamphlet, but it belongs to Knopf and he will use it in a small volume of essays soon. Leaving soon to spend all of May in New England botanizing with friends. Willa Cather.

1318. To Annie Pavelka, May 19, 1936; WCPM.

Has not been well the past few months, but has appreciated her letters. Glad she could get a washing machine with the $55 sent at Christmas, but wants to pay the other $10 it cost. Please call it "Willie's Washer." Always liked Willie better than Willa. Sending a box of clothes, some worn very little, for herself or her daughters. Willa Cather.

1319. To [Bruce] Bliven, June 13, 1936; Newberry.

Can't let him use the essay he wants ["The Novel Démeublé"] because it will be in volume being published by Knopf that same month. Willa Cather.

1320. To Ferris Greenslet, July 24, [1936], from Grand Manan; Harvard.

Sorry to hear of his accident while fishing. No, won't have another book for a while. Has another partly done, but since Isabelle's illness broke in on it hasn't been able to take it back up. Please send a book the size he plans for the collected edition. Surely he doesn't expect her to autograph every volume in 12,000 sets! Willa Cather.

1321. To Lydia [Lambrecht], Aug. 10, [1936], from Grand Manan; WCPM.

Did not forget her mother's birthday, but had twin nieces visiting and was busy with them. Has had with her at Grand Manan the quilt they made her. Willa Cather.

1322. To Zoë Akins, n.d. [Aug. 1936?], from Grand Manan; Huntington.

Enjoying this cool, green island, the most restful place in the world even without amenities. Nineteen-year-old nieces there with her and love it. Their first time to see the ocean. Feels sure Zoë's house would be too organized for her. Prefers a couch of junipers at the edge of a cliff. Willa.

1323. To Cyril Clemens, Aug. 15, [1936?]; WCPM. Probably written before no. 1336.

Appreciates his offering her the vice-presidency of the Mark Twain Society. Willa Cather.

1324. To Zoë Akins, Aug. 30, [1936]; Huntington.

Thanks for writing to her about Jobyna [Howland's] death. Wishes they had lived in an earlier time, when people stayed put and didn't lose track of their friends. Never sees friends in Nebraska, can only send a few comforts to try to help them through the Depression and heat waves and drought. Glad Jobyna did not go all to pieces with alcohol before she died. Why do people overdrink, when a little wine in moderation is so good? Willa.

1325. To Carrie Miner Sherwood, Sept. 7, [1936], from Grand Manan; WCPM.

Sorry to hear of Margie [Miner] Gund's illness. Has worried a lot about Irene this year. Weather has been nice at Grand Manan, but hasn't enjoyed time there very much. So many deaths and illnesses among people they know there. Did enjoy the twins. Loves Carrie more all the time. Willie. P.S.: Going back to New York next week.

1326. **To Ferris Greenslet,** Sept. 8, [1936], from Grand Manan; Harvard.
Sending three of the Knopf-published books with hand corrections. Please keep for use for the collected edition. Will probably write a preface for *One of Ours*. Willa Cather.

1327. **To Irene Miner Weisz,** n.d. [pm. Sept. 24, 1936], from New York; Newberry.
Heard from Elsie that Margie is in a hospital in Chicago. Please send some flowers from her. Leaving for New Hampshire in a few days. Willie.

1328. **To Edith [Lewis],** Sunday [Oct. 4, 1936], from Jaffrey, N.H.; WCPM.
Is looking out the window of Edith's room at the woods. Feeling fine, with an embarrassingly hearty appetite, and sleeping soundly. Wakes up during the night long enough to enjoy the mountain air and the moonlight. In an hour will see a confluence of Jupiter and Venus. Last night it lasted about an hour before the lady [Venus] dropped over the horizon leaving him [Jupiter] alone. They were splendid. Can't believe all this beauty and order is only a matter of physics. Has been wearing her white silk suit. All the things Edith packed came through without wrinkling. Now will dress for dinner, so as not to miss a minute of the planets. With love, W.

1329. **To Henry Seidel Canby,** Oct. 7, [1936], from Jaffrey, N.H.; Beinecke.
Just arrived from three months in Canada and found his letter in accumulated mail. Has just learned of Mary Austin's death. Has he begun his work as executor? Willa Cather.

1330. **To Ferris Greenslet,** Oct. 13, [1936], from Jaffrey, N.H.; Harvard.
Please send copies of *My Ántonia* and *The Song of the Lark* so she can begin to make corrections. Will send the Knopf-published books soon. Willa Cather.

1331. **To Fanny Butcher,** Oct. 16, [1936], from Jaffrey, N.H.; Newberry.
Enjoyed receiving her card from Quebec. When book of essays comes out, please don't think praise of Thomas Mann is due to Knopf's publishing him. Agreed with Fanny that *The Magic Mountain* was dull, but likes the Biblical trilogy very much. Willa Cather.

1332. To Ferris Greenslet, Oct. 30, [1936], from Jaffrey, N.H.; Harvard.

Is returning *My Ántonia* with only a few corrections. Has marked some broken letters; type needs to be fixed. Mr. Rollo Ogden wants her to substitute his translation of a Spanish song in *The Song of the Lark*; better than the translation she used before. Returning to New York November 6. W. S. C.

1333. To Ferris Greenslet, Nov. 14, 1936, from New York; Harvard.

Is leaving Monday [16th] to go to Washington, D.C., where a relative is ill. Probably will not be back by Wednesday when he is there. Willa S. Cather. Signed by S. J. Bloom, Secretary.

1334. To Thomas Masaryk, Dec. 1, 1923 [error for 1936?]; Berkeley.

Is sending him a book of essays including one he may especially enjoy about Boston before World War I, "148 Charles Street," which begins on page 52. Thinks of the years before 1914 as a pleasant time in Europe and America when one could travel without passport to so many wonderful places that it was hard to choose. Always remembers his good words to her. Willa Cather.

[The dating of this letter is a puzzle. It seems to refer to *Not Under Forty*, in which "148 Charles Street" (which first appeared in the *New York Evening Post Literary Review*, Nov. 4, 1922, pp. 173–74, under the title "The House on Charles Street") does begin on page 52. Yet the book was not published until November 1936. The letter is unmistakably dated in Cather's handwriting. A reply from Masyryk's secretary dated January 16, 1937, thanks her for a copy of *Not Under Forty*. Dennis Halac, who studied the original letters in Prague, states that the letter refers to *Not Under Forty*, yet accepts the 1923 date; "Ever so true: Willa Cather and T. G. Masaryk," *The New Criterion*, November 1993, 36–40. My guess is that Cather made a slip of the pen – though how a person could make a slip of 1923 rather than 1936 is unaccountable. It remains a great mystery.]

1335. To Mary Miner Creighton, Dec. 6, [1936]; Newberry.

Sorry not to have written in so long. Just back from Washington, where an old friend died. Did not know about Margie's death until later. How is Irene? She never answers letters. May have said or done something that offended her. Still gets the Red Cloud newspaper. Heard Evelene Vestey was there for Louie's funeral. He was one of those who never grow up.

Maybe that's the way to be happy. Glad her father did not live to see these hard times. Had hoped to be in Red Cloud for Christmas, but will not be able to get away. Has just received a huge gardenia bush from the Menuhins for her birthday. Would like to go see the Menuhins, but can't rest when she is with them, they are too exciting and she enjoys them too much. Did enjoy the twins' visit this summer. Sorry to be so gloomy, but is feeling tired. Always so much pointless activity when something new is published. Willie.

1336. To Cyril Clemens, Dec. 11, 1936; UVa.

Sorry not to have replied to his letter in the summer, but received it only recently. Doesn't understand his reference to a "pilgrimage" to see A. E. Housman. Why would he presume to describe an incident he knew nothing about? Has never given out information about the occasion except to private friends. Hopes he won't put anything about it into his biography of Housman. Considers his request for information rude. Willa Cather.

1337. To Zoë Akins, Dec. 15, [1936], from New York; Huntington.

Please tell Mr. Totheroh that she does not authorize his dramatization of *A Lost Lady.* He should have asked her before he worked on it. Her sale of screen rights does not imply that anyone can use the book who wants to. Will keep the manuscript until she sees her. Has already marked it up some. This may seem curt, but it's a business letter, not a personal one. Has many demands on her time. W. S. C.

1338. To Jean Louise Williams, Dec. 16, [1936], from New York; Sweet Briar.

Thanks for her note. Willa Cather.

1339. To Ferris Greenslet, Dec. 18, 1936; Harvard.

Appreciates his note about the book. Hopes the type in the collected edition will look somewhat like that in the Thistle Edition of Stevenson. Will see him in January if it is after the 12th, as she will be in Washington again with her uncle [?]. Willa Cather.

1340. To Mabel Dodge Luhan, Dec. 18, 1936; Beinecke.

Was glad to receive her letter, but it creates a problem. Would be glad to contribute to the hospital, but is already contributing heavily to old friends in Nebraska who are in absolute penury from drought. Is cutting back on Christmas presents to do all she can for these people. Government relief seems to go only to those who won't work, and the New Deal has cut into her income from investments. Hope things not as bad in New Mexico as in Nebraska. Willa.

1341. **To Fanny Butcher,** Dec. 18, 1936; Newberry.
Please don't use a quotation from her letter in review. Sorry to hear she has been ill. Is she working too hard or having too hectic a social life? Solitude would be the most restorative thing, about two years of it! Willa Cather.

1342. **To Zoë Akins,** Sunday [Dec. 20, 1936], from New York; Huntington.
Needs to follow-up that business letter with a personal one. No, isn't angry. Play manuscript butchered her book, showed no understanding of Mrs. Forrester. Doesn't hold that against her. Sorry to be in such a rush. Life very hectic now, but will cheer up again soon. W.

1343. **To Mary Miner Creighton,** Dec. 22, 1936, Christmas card; Newberry.
What a wonderful letter she wrote! Cried over it, but it helped. Has been so worried about Irene. Willie.

1344. **To unknown person,** [1936], Christmas card; wcpm.
Mary Virginia and her husband will be there for Christmas Eve dinner. Will be thinking about friends in Red Cloud. Willa Cather.

1345. **To Irene Miner Weisz,** Dec. 24, 1936, Christmas card; Newberry.
Picture shows her own Quebec. With love. Willie.

1346. **To Mrs. [Margaret?] Crofts,** [1936?], Christmas card with picture of four cowboys or farmers, some sheep, and angels overhead; UNL.
Doesn't like pictures like this, in the Grant Wood style, on Christmas cards, but bought them to help someone. Might think of the cowboy-looking shepherds as C.C.C. fellows [Civilian Conservation Corps, a New Deal initiative] and one of the angels above as President Roosevelt. W. S. C.

1347. **To unknown person [possibly Mr. and Mrs. George Whicher],** n.d. [1936?], Christmas card; PM.
Doesn't really care for Christmas cards in the Grant Wood style. Maybe they are C.C.C. boys with Roosevelt trumpeting in the sky. Such bad times! Willa Cather.

1348. **To Carrie Miner Sherwood**, [1936?], Christmas card; WCPM.

Can't honestly say she likes these cowboy-looking shepherds. W. C.

1349. **To [Helen Sprague?]**, Dec. 26, [1936]; WCPM.

This Miss Mary Kiley is a doll! Such an appealing child! Wish the picture had come before Mary Virginia and her husband were there, so they could see it. Has a week of teas and dinners ahead, but will then go into seclusion for a while. W. S. C.

1350. **To Stephen Tennant**, Jan. 6, [1937]; Yongue.

The debate over Joseph Conrad is endless. Prefers a more direct, unadorned sentence style. Few writers can give themselves up to baroque emotionalism and succeed. Turgenev could. Conrad becomes artificial or decadent. Listened to the king's abdication speech on the radio [Edward VIII abdicated on December 11, 1936] and found it plausible and distinguished. An example of rhetorical control. What does he think of the people close to the king? [letter breaks off]

1351. **To Carrie Miner Sherwood**, Jan. 7, 1937; WCPM.

Is grieving for Margie and for Cornelia Otis Skinner, who lived only a few blocks away. Didn't see her very often and now regrets not making the effort these last few weeks. Enclosing a birthday gift a week late. Mary Virginia's husband has had a sinus operation and been very ill. Their apartment was burglarized, but Mary Virginia never complains. Finds her such a cheering presence. Willie.

1352. **To Zoë Akins**, Jan. 18, [1937], from New York; Huntington.

Loves the Chinese nightingale! But don't order from Thorley's florist shop again; quality has deteriorated. Will try before long to explain why she so dislikes Dan Totheroh's dramatization of *A Lost Lady* and send it back. How could Zoë have liked it? Dialogue doesn't fit the characters. Maybe she thinks it doesn't matter how a book is butchered so long as it becomes a play. However bad [Eugene] O'Neill is, at least he makes up his own drivel. Is always struggling to protect books from stage and radio. But as to radio, hopes she listened to king's speech. Sorry to be so cross. Please don't hold it against her. W.

1353. **To Carrie Miner Sherwood**, Jan. 20, [1937]; WCPM.

Enclosing a letter from Cornelia Otis Skinner's daughter. Please return it after Mary sees it. Menuhins coming in tomorrow. Willie. P.S.: English reviews all good.

1354. To Carl Van Vechten, Jan. 30, 1937; Richmond.

Has made a note of his new address. Please don't describe her new book as nostalgic! People say that about all her books. Isn't homesick all the time. Willa Cather.

1355. To Cyril Clemens, Jan. 30, 1937; UVa.

Believes the article he mentioned was published in the *Saturday Review* and written by that inveterate liar Ford Madox Ford. Certainly never led any group of ladies to go see A. E. Housman. Did meet him, but not at Cambridge. Did not talk about his poetry. This has been very annoying. Alfred Knopf has suggested she write her recollection of the meeting, to silence questions. Will probably do so some time, in the plain style of her recollections of meetings in *Not under Forty*. Willa Cather.

1356. To Mrs. George Whicher, Feb. 13, 1937; PM.

Sorry not to have seen her while she was in New York. Was in Washington when she arrived, and then Mary Virginia's husband hospitalized with pneumonia. Then had to do all her work on corrections and design elements for Houghton Mifflin subscription edition on such a tight schedule she could not see anyone except Mary Virginia until finished. Alfred Knopf in Europe, so couldn't be there to help. Please send Stephen's address at Columbia; hopes to see him. Willa Cather.

1357. To Bernard DeVoto, Mar. 10, 1937; Stanford.

Appreciated his published letter to Edmund Wilson. Has wanted to say something along those lines herself – that economic conditions are a very small part of human life. Theorists the only ones interested in theories. Social crusaders seem to lose sight of individual human beings. Leo Tolstoi decided, in the end, that it was a mistake to try to reform society. Glad he stepped up to say the world is made up of persons, not masses, and that history, not theories, is our best guide to understanding humanity. Willa Cather.

1358. To Mrs. Henri Raffy [Katherine Foote], n.d. [pm. Mar. 10, 1937], from 570 Park Avenue, New York; PM.

So glad to hear from her. World seems to be going down a whirlpool. Hopes they can meet again before it drops to destruction. Remembers the past as being much happier. Willa Cather. P.S.: Usually keeps her address secret, but is sending it to her.

1359. **To Zoë Akins,** Mar. 16, [1937], from New York; Huntington.

Is in bed with lumbago and also is not writing letters because starting a new book. In spite of both of those things, wanted to write and say how much she liked her poems. Keep sending those, not plays written by idiots [ref. to Totheroh]. Hope it's nicer in California than in New York, where it's very cold for March. Willa. P.S.: Likes *Tovarich* [a play by Jacques Deval] very much.

1360. **To E. K. Brown,** Apr. 9, 1937; Beinecke.

Found his essay when she returned. Likes the way he presented his opinions of her books. Very fair, though too much emphasis on geographic surroundings. Not true the Southwest is not her own country in the way Nebraska is. On the contrary, knew it well. Please read her comments on *Death Comes for the Archbishop*. Believes it is quite possible to admire Latour and Vaillant equally, though they are so different. Willa Cather.

1361. **To Mrs. Vanamee [American Institute of Arts and Letters],** Apr. 9, 1937; AAAL.

Notices her address is listed in the Institute directory as 570 Park Avenue. Is giving up her lease next month. Address should be shown as care of Alfred A. Knopf. Willa Cather.

1362. **To Cyril Clemens,** Apr. 9, 1937; UVa.

Hopes it is all right, autographed book to him rather than to Mark Twain Society. Cannot write even a short piece about G. K. Chesterton for their quarterly. Has promised Knopf not to do any incidental writing. Maintaining this as a general rule saves many problems. Willa Cather.

1363. **To Mr. [Sydney] Jacobs [production manager at Knopf],** Sunday [Apr. 18, 1937?]; HRC.

Proofs look all right. Willa Cather.

1364. **To Zoë Akins,** Apr. 19, 1937; Huntington.

Here are comments on Mr. Totheroh's play. When Mrs. Forrester enters the judge's office she says, "My, your stairs are steep!" – very low class usage, makes her look common. Then he has her refer to her age; she would never have done so. She tells a Swede his son's eyes are as blue as mountain lakes – language of a pretentious social climber. Same when she says she would die to have eyes like that – makes her seem low class. Repeatedly so. On p. 13 he has the judge imply that Captain Forrester has behaved unethically – contrary to the whole ethical foundation of the book! Couldn't read beyond the first act. It was like a betrayal of the person she knew after whom Mrs. Forrester was modeled. Once again, thanks for sending the verses. Is not irritated with her any longer and is sorry this incident has caused disharmony between them. Willa.

1365. To Brother Emil Mohr, May 7, 1937; Notre Dame.

He made a good choice of vocation. So important to try to convince young people that the world doesn't have to be as it is, that it was peaceful and orderly and happy before 1914 [the year World War I began]. Envies him the pleasure of teaching Latin. Such a clean and austere language; so cleansing to read Virgil at the end of a cluttered day. Willa Cather.

1366. To Sister Lecrois, June 12, 1937; Manhat.

Is very pleased by her letter. Is glad when French people find an authentic note in her two priests [in *Death Comes for the Archbishop*]. They were modeled on real figures from history whom she studied so closely she felt she knew them. Unfortunately, her student cannot hope to publish a translation of the book into French, as that has already been done and by now has been published. Will have Miss Bloom enclose a copy of the short essay about the writing of the book done for a Catholic publication [*Commonweal*]. Willa Cather.

1367. To Stephen Tennant, June 26, [1937?]; Yongue.

Is not writing many letters but devoting time to work. At tea time, often thinks of *Lascar* [his book-in-progress]. Looks forward to reading a book about that place [Marseilles]. Conrad gives a glimpse of it in *The Arrow of Gold* before the book goes off in other directions. How is he? and where is he? W. S. C. P.S.: Will probably leave for the Canadian Rockies about July 15.

1368. To Zoë Akins, June 30, 1937; Huntington.

Will explain at another time what has been driving her and wearing her out this year. Leaving for Grand Manan in a few days, to stay two months.

Nieces will be there. Many thanks for wanting to dedicate book of poems to her, but if so, please do it simply, without extra words. Taking extra shoes with her for walking at the island, and packing is a chore. Willa.

1369. To Ferris Greenslet, July 3, 1937; Harvard.
Agrees to revisions in the plan for the Autograph Edition, as outlined in his letter of yesterday, provided they are agreed to by Knopf. Is very pleased with Mr. Evans's work (in production department) and his sound suggestions, but less pleased with editorial department. They made unnecessary trouble for her by sending incorrect proofs, made suggestions that had already been disapproved by Mr. Rogers, and have now made nonsensical suggestions about the captions for the photographs. Will not sign anything until he sends her proofs of the engravings with captions in place. Actually, is sorry she ever got into this project. Willa Cather.

1370. To Alexander Woollcott, n.d. [written at the bottom of his letter dated July 18, (1937?)], from Grand Manan; Harvard.
No, does not give permission to use "Old Mrs. Harris" in anthology. Willa Cather.

1371. To Mr. Perkins [with Charles Scribner's Sons], n.d. [replying to his of Aug. 25, 1937], from Grand Manan; Princeton.
Would like to agree [to his request for an introduction to new edition of Edith Wharton's *Ethan Frome*] but is just starting on a trip with brother's family into far northern Canada. The subject deserves more time and effort than she could give it just now. Willa Cather.

1372. To Stephen Tennant, Aug. 29, [1937]; Yongue, copy, not original.
Sent him a letter at Aix-les-Bains, but he may not receive it, so sending this to his home address. Please send an advance copy of his book and she will take it up with Knopf. Hand is better. Is enjoying the weather. Geologists tell her the rock that makes up their island is thirty-six million years old but has not been above water all that time. Lovely spruce trees keep it cool and shady. W. S. C.

1373. To Cyril Clemens, Sept. 27, 1937; UVa.
Does not recognize initials F. S. and does not remember visiting anyone in Bronx Park. Neither she nor Ida Tarbell makes it a practice to go to literary

teas. Whoever told him that was not truthful. Willa S. Cather, signed by
Sarah J. Bloom with note "dictated by Miss Cather."

1374. **To [Stephen Tennant]**, n.d. [1937?], fragment, possibly continuation of
Jan. 6, 1937; Yongue.
… concerning translations and editions. Has learned to gain happiness by
replicating the Miracle of Loretto, which she once thought the most pre-
posterous of all religious tales. Will tell him some time. It's not a matter
of religion. W.

1375. **To Carrie Miner Sherwood**, Oct. 20, 1937; Newberry.
Sending two copies of prospectus about autograph edition. Ridiculously
expensive, but wanted Carrie to see it. Enclosing letters from Roscoe
and twins. They met Yehudi Menuhin and both parties liked each other.
Yehudi always likes genuine people. Has started a new book. Willie.

1376. **To Norman Holmes Pearson**, Oct. 23, 1937; Beinecke.
Cannot agree to send him copies of revised edition of *Death Comes for the
Archbishop* for the section he is using in his anthology, but he may be able
to get them from Ferris Greenslet. Not many changes. Likes his selections
of poetry. In the prose, wonders why he didn't represent Poe with "The
Cask of Amontillado," a better story than "The Fall of the House of Usher."
Likes Poe's poetry better than his stories. Willa Cather.

1377. **To Zoë Akins**, Oct. 28, [1937?]; Huntington.
Appreciates the generous inscription in her book of poems. Likes them,
though not so well as her earlier ones. Beware of New York theatre critics. They have it in for her. Better not have a new play this year. Knows
from experience how spiteful they can be. N.Y.U. graduates with foreign-
sounding names are writing all sorts of shabby things about sex-starved
spinstress writers from New England. If they attacked her plays in this
way it would affect their reception in the whole country. A book's reception not determined by reviews to the same extent. Shouldn't have been
so unguarded as to say all this, so destroy the letter. W. S. C.

1378. **To Zoë Akins**, Friday [Oct. 29, 1937?], from Jaffrey, N.H.; Huntington.
Doesn't care for the manuscript; naturalism not Zoë's style. Recommends
Anne Parrish's new novel [*Golden Wedding*, 1936]. Is working well and feel-
ing good. Edith Lewis coming tonight for a week. W. S. C.

1379. To Fanny Butcher, Nov. 4, 1937; Newberry.

Extends sympathy for painful sore. Remembers the infected place on back of her head when she was working on *The Song of the Lark*. Kept putting off going to the hospital; took codeine for the pain and kept writing; was finally put into the hospital after she went into delirium. Didn't write sooner because uncle was ill in Maryland and niece [Mary Virginia] has been distraught with husband's pneumonia. In addition, has been preparing for a subscription edition from Houghton Mifflin. Willa Cather.

1380. To Zoë Akins, Nov. 8, [1937?]; Huntington.

Received flowers and hopes they indicate she is forgiven. Knows she wrote too severely, in a crabby tone. The ones who have it in for her are a New Deal crowd. Everything keeps breaking in on work on new novel. Wishes she hadn't gotten into dealings with Houghton Mifflin again. Hopes they won't betray her and sell movie rights to *Ántonia*. W.

1381. To Yaltah Menuhin, Tuesday [Nov. 23, 1937]; Princeton.

Will meet her at noon at the 58th Street door of her hotel for a walk in the park. If she can't go, don't worry, will go on alone. Aunt Willa.

1382. To Irene Miner Weisz, Dec. 21, 1937, Christmas card; Newberry.

Hopes she will write. Willa Cather.

1383. To Carrie Miner Sherwood, [1937?], Christmas card; WCPM.

Hopes it will be a good year for her and that they may meet again during it. Willie.

1384. To Yaltah Menuhin, Dec. 27, [1937]; Princeton.

Will stop by hotel at noon for a walk. Aunt Willa.

1385. To Ferris Greenslet, Jan. 29, 1937 [actually Dec. 29, 1937]; Harvard.

Thanks for Christmas greeting. Sends New Year's wishes. Does not want an edition of *My Ántonia* illustrated by Grant Wood. Iowa, his home, is really very different from Nebraska. Please leave *Ántonia* as is and give assurance that Benda illustrations will be kept. Has read one of Houghton Mifflin's recently published books and likes it, but doesn't dare name it for fear his publicity department will advertise the fact. Willa Cather.

1386. To Zoë Akins, Dec. 30, [1937]; Huntington.
Chrysanthemums arrived looking freshly cut. Reminded her of *Remembrance of Things Past* [Proust], always the smell of chrysanthemums in the drawing room of Odette. Loves the orange marmalade, too. Had a delightful Christmas, with Menuhin children in town. Their presence reassures her that youth can still be wonderful. W.

1387. To Yaltah Menuhin, Wednesday [Jan. 5 or 12, 1938]; Princeton.
Tried to describe to Isabelle how beautiful a bride she was. Wishes she could have made a quick sketch, as Stephen [Tennant] could have. Has enjoyed knowing her since she was six. Aunt Willa.

1388. To Ferris Greenslet, n.d. [c. Jan. 10, 1938]; Harvard.
Does not belong to any club except the Episcopal Church Guild in Red Cloud. W. S. C.

1389. Notes on backs of photographs [prob. in connection with work on Autograph Edition, so 1937 or 1938]; Harvard.
Approves photo in striped front with open collar and hat with flowers, though it makes her complexion look like a Negro's. May approve 1920 passport photo and snapshot made in Ville d'Avray with dog or cat, but they aren't good prints so can't tell. Doesn't like reduction of photo made by Nicholas Murray in 1924, in ornate jacket, because all shadows are bleached out. Doesn't like print from photo by Ensminger in 1937 because contrasts of blacks and whites are too severe. Does not approve the Steichen photo in middy blouse.

1390. To Yaltah Menuhin, Jan. 11, 1938; Princeton.
Will come by hotel a little before noon and they can go see Lady Hamilton [painting at Frick Museum]. Aunt Willa.

1391. To Hephzibah Menuhin, Thursday [Jan. 13, 1938]; Princeton.
Thanks for protecting her from the reporter. Weather too damp to go out, but evening will probably be fine. W. S. C.

1392. To Sinclair Lewis, Jan. 14, 1938; Beinecke.
Enjoyed reading *The Prodigal Parents*, reminded her so of home. Americans are so naïve! Don't seem to realize there is such a thing as evil in the world. But American kindness shines through, too. America has let

in too many immigrants who proved to be crooks and do-nothings, and their grandchildren are ruining the country. The U.S. is in trouble! Willa Cather.

1393. **To Ferris Greenslet,** Jan. 24, 1938; Harvard.
Is sending Stephen Tennant's book of drawings. Publishers in England would like to export unbound sheets to an American publisher. Promised to show it to Houghton Mifflin and Knopf without having seen it. Now realizes Americans would find it offensive. It bears the traces of his rebellion against strict upbringing. Please send a letter she can pass on to Tennant. W. S. C.

1394. **To Mrs. George Whicher,** n.d. [pm. Jan. 26, 1938], from New York; PM.
Where will she be staying while in New York? Will hope to see her after February 15. A great deal of good theater and music this winter. Willa Cather.

1395. **To Cyril Clemens,** Jan. 28, 1938; UVa.
The Mr. Lamy who has written him is a great nephew of Archbishop Lamy, on whom she based Latour in *Death Comes for the Archbishop.* Has never met him. Willa Cather.

1396. **To George Austerman** [from Sarah J. Bloom, secretary], Jan. 31, 1938; UVa.
Letting him know not to worry about Mrs. Osborne [?]. If she makes an approach, will simply recommend the Shattuck Inn as a quiet place for writing.

1397. **To Ferris Greenslet,** Feb. 2, [1938?]; Harvard.
Has a sore throat, but will answer his letter about Stephen Tennant soon. Tennant might develop a real style if he would concentrate more on his art. W. S. C.

1398. **To Mr. and Mrs. George Whicher,** Feb. 14, 1938; PM.
Can they come to dinner at seven on Saturday? Willa Cather.

1399. **To Yaltah Menuhin,** Sunday, Feb. 20, [1938?]; Princeton.
Thoughts went with her out to sea. Enjoyed the verses she sent. Weather terrible, so has stayed at desk working on new story. Ate a little orange from Yehudi's orange tree yesterday. Very juicy but sour! Aunt Willa.

1400. To Henry Seidel Canby, Mar. 2, 1938, from New York; Beinecke.

Yes, may keep her name on the roll of PEN, but does not care to meet visiting dignitaries or go to meetings. Writers should spend their time writing instead of talking about it. Was pleased by his review of Katherine Anthony's book on Louisa May Alcott. Glad to know he is as tired of Freudian extremes as she is. Annie Fields once asked her to destroy some letters that included some from Alcott. They seemed cheerful, friendly, and practical, with no trace of trauma from having dealt with naked men as a nurse. Wishes now the letters were still in existence to refute the likes of Anthony. Willa Cather.

1401. To Ferris Greenslet, Mar. 2, 1938; Harvard.

Is recovering from influenza. Enjoyed reading about his meeting with Stephen Tennant and mother and stepfather, Sir Edward Grey. Didn't mean Grey was stern, but his interests and Stephen's utterly dissimilar. Very pleased with *O Pioneers!* in autograph edition. Did he hear the recital Hephzibah and Yehudi Menuhin gave in Boston? Such a joy to know them! Willa Cather.

1402. To Marutha Menuhin, n.d. [Mar. 1938?]; Princeton.

Meant to send enclosed clipping sooner, but was ill with influenza. There must not be an appendix left in the whole Menuhin family. Now Hephzibah! [signed:] Vassinka.

1403. To Allan Nevins, Mar. 22, [1938]; Columbia.

Sorry he did not receive her letter written four years ago. Secretary found the draft and is enclosing it. Glad to have heard from him. Would like to see a new edition of his book on Fremont. Willa Cather.

1404. To Ferris Greenslet, Mar. 22, 1938; Harvard.

Appreciates the copy of *Grey of Fallodon* [Trevelyan], which she enjoyed reading. Did not like May Sarton's *The Single Hound*; didn't resemble real people. Very different from *The Enemy Gods* [LaFarge, 1937], which she liked very much. Usually does not care for novels about writers, a genre Robert Louis Stevenson referred to as cannibalism. George Gissing's *Grub Street* an exception. Doesn't care for very fanciful fiction either, including Walter de la Mare. The fanciful works well in poetry, but not in prose. Willa Cather.

1405. To George Austerman, Mar. 31, 1938; UVa.

Sorry not to have gotten to Jaffrey this winter, due to influenza. Glad he sold the McCoy farm to people of the right sort. Wishes undesirables weren't buying houses in the village. Hopes to spend the summer working; not sure where will be the right place. Willa Cather.

1406. To Mary Miner Creighton, n.d. [Apr. 16, 1938?]; Newberry.

Wishing her a good voyage. Willie.

1407. To Zoë Akins, June 4, 1938; Huntington.

Right hand was smashed in a drug store door in May. Can't write. Appreciated the orange blossoms, which came while she was in Atlantic City but were still fragrant when she returned. Orange marmalade a treasure. Is feeling reconciled to Hephzibah's and Yehudi's marriages. Isabelle wrote from Sorrento that the entire family, including the new husband and the new wife, visited her there. Though usually so critical of people's shortcomings, Isabelle likes them in spite of theirs. Is herself somewhat like a porcupine when meeting people, so is glad Isabelle reassured her about these new members of the Menuhin family. Thinks Thornton Wilder's new play [Our Town] quite good, authentically in the spirit of New England. Has felt that the dead remain part of people's lives there, as in the play. Willa.

1408. To Mrs. William Stix [Yaltah Menuhin], June 5, [1938]; Princeton.

Enclosing the book she asked for. Sorry the ink ran on the inscription. Willa Cather.

1409. To Mrs. Aley, June 8, 1938; LincCity.

Is soon to leave for Canada, but appreciates hearing from her after so long. Hasn't seen her since they met in Altman's; was shopping in preparation for trip to California during mother's illness. Willa Cather.

1410. To Mr. Dooher, June 29, [1938?]; HRC.

Leaving for Canada, so can't write at length. Does not sell her manuscripts. However, has an unpublished poem by Housman that he gave her when she met him. [Not clear if she means she would sell it.] Willa Cather.

1411. To Mabel Dodge Luhan, June 30, 1938; Beinecke.

Brother Douglass died of a heart attack in early June. He had spent her birthday with her last December in New York. Is having trouble getting over it. Willa Cather. P.S.: Got a laugh for the first time in a long while from *The Laughing Horse* [satirical literary magazine published in Taos, N.M., by Witter Bynner's secretary and friend Spud Johnson]. It caught Mary Austin and Mabel herself quite well.

1412. **To Houghton Mifflin Company** [from Sarah J. Bloom, secretary], July 14, 1938; Harvard.
Please advise whether final corrected proofs of *The Song of the Lark* have been sent to Cassell & Company.

1413. **To Margaret Moody** [secretary to Ferris Greenslet] [from Sarah J. Bloom, secretary], July 18, 1938; Harvard.
Have final corrected proofs of *The Song of the Lark* been sent to Cassell? Have no way of knowing whether the galleys they say they have received are the final corrected ones. Please check.

1414. **To Margaret Moody** [from Sarah J. Bloom, secretary], July 26, 1938; Harvard.
Appreciates the information.

1415. **To A. Artinian** [from Sarah J. Bloom, secretary], Aug. 5, 1938; HRC.
Cather is in Europe, and letters are not being forwarded. Sarah J. Bloom, Secretary.

1416. **To Yaltah Menuhin**, Sept. 3 [1938?], from Grand Manan; Princeton.
Thinks of her often. Believes California must be making her homesick for Paris. Failures from all over America drift to the west coast, making it a dismal place. Is returning to New York next week. Isabelle still doing well. Aunt Willa. P.S.: Miss Lewis sends love.

1417. **To Miss McKinder**, n.d. [c. Sept. 19, 1938], from New York; HRC.
Has found her letter and does not recall whether she answered. Douglass, the brother to whom she was closest, died suddenly – such a shock. Went to Grand Manan for a few weeks, but that time is a blur. Willa Cather.

1418. **To George Austerman**, Oct. 9, [1938?]; UVa.
Would like to come for three or four weeks to work and believes the room at the end of the hall that Mrs. Buck used to have would be best at this time of year, if it is available. Expects to arrive the 14th at 4:48. Please ask a reliable driver to meet her train. Willa Cather.

1419. To Ferris Greenslet, Oct. 12, [1938]; Harvard.

No, does not want a radio adaptation of *My Ántonia.* Isabelle McClung died two days ago in Sorrento. Now the two people she loved best are gone. Willa Cather.

1420. To Irene Miner Weisz, Oct. 14, [1938]; Newberry.

Isabelle has died. Can't imagine how she can go on, with both Isabelle and Douglass gone. Willie.

1421. To Mr. Baxter [from Sarah J. Bloom, secretary], Oct. 24, 1938; HRC.

Writing for Cather, who is in Europe [not true]. Does not autograph books except for people she knows. Enclosing a slip with a signature that he may paste into his book.

1422. To Ferris Greenslet, Oct. 27, [1938]; Harvard.

Had planned to go to Naples this week to see Isabelle. Appreciated his letter about the set of her books in Quebec, a place she is fond of. Going to Jaffrey next Monday, again working on the interrupted manuscript. Willa Cather. P.S.: Writing will steady her.

1423. To Zoë Akins, Nov. 13, [1938], from Jaffrey, N.H.; Huntington.

Douglass, the brother she most loved, died in June of a sudden heart attack. He had spent her birthday with her last December. Only four months later, on October 10, Isabelle died. Wrote many letters to inform people — the only service she could give Isabelle. Feels emotionally numb. Regrets Yehudi's wife takes such bad pictures. She is Scotch, not Jewish. Feels confident it is a good marriage. Was happy to see them. Then Douglass died the next week. Willa. P.S.: No, does not like Hephzibah's mother-in-law.

1424. To Mrs. Vanamee, Nov. 15, [1938], from Jaffrey, N.H.; AAAL.

Because of the hurricane and flooding in Jaffrey, was unavailable by telephone when Miss Bloom received the telegram announcing election to the American Academy of Arts and Letters. Appreciates the honor and is pleased to accept. Still best to address her care of Alfred A. Knopf. Willa Cather.

1425. To President Butler [American Academy of Arts and Letters], Nov. 16, [1938]; AAAL.

Regrets having received his letter only today. Is grateful to accept election to the Academy. Has heard many of his public statements, with which she agrees. Senses the country is drifting toward dreadful events contrary to its traditional values and daily experience. Willa Cather.

1426. **To President Butler,** Nov. 25, 1938, from Jaffrey, N.H.; AAAL.
In accordance with Mrs. Vanamee's request, is sending this formal acceptance of membership in the Academy. Willa Cather.

1427. **To Mrs. Vanamee,** Nov. 28, [1938]; AAAL.
The enclosed formal acceptance is sent for their files. Willa Cather.

1428. **To Lydia [Lambrecht],** Dec. 14, 1938; WCPM, transcription.
Sending a Christmas box to her mother tomorrow. Douglass's death left her ill for quite a while, but can now do Christmas shopping. Sending some wool cloth to be made up into a dress for mother. Sending hoods for her and Pauline, very stylish; also some wool gloves and scarves. Hopes they won't mind making up the dress. Willa Cather.

1429. **To Mr. and Mrs. C. W. Weisz [Irene Miner Weisz],** 1938, Christmas card; UNL.
Picture on the card is like Quebec, as on p. 133 of *Shadows on the Rock.* Willie.

1430. **To Carrie Miner Sherwood,** [1938?], Christmas card; WCPM.
Maybe picture on card is like Red Cloud. Willie. [On adjoining page:] Wishes Isabelle could have lived a little longer.

1431. **To [Carrie Miner Sherwood?],** [prob. Dec. 1938]; WCPM.
Yehudi has come to console her. He cared about Isabelle, too. It was she who introduced them. Willie.

1432. **To Edward Wagenknecht,** Dec. 31, 1938; PM.
Appreciates his comments on the Autograph Edition. Never saw his article in *Sewanee Review.* Six of the early stories he lists are not really hers. "On the Divide" a college theme that the young professor greatly revised on his own before sending it to *Overland Monthly* without her knowledge. Some of the things he added – for example, all of the wood-carving parts – were not very credible. "El Dorado" also extensively revised by the same professor; she never intended to publish it. [But see letter no. 70.] Others the collaborative work of a group of young newspaper people, including herself, in Pittsburgh; should not be considered her work. Her name used only

because she had published stories before. Since no money involved, didn't seem to matter; were just having fun. First published story really hers was "Death in the Desert." Does not want these early stories reprinted; keeps them protected by copyright for that reason. Has even been able to stop circulation in mimeograph copies. Would prefer not to have to consult her attorney on this. No commercial or scholarly interest justifying republication. Does not consider it friendly of him to wish to do so. Like a fruit grower, a writer has the right to cull the crop. Willa Cather.

1433. **To [Burges] Johnson,** Jan. 12, 1939; Amherst.
Gives permission to quote from anything in *Not Under Forty* and conditional permission to quote from letter to Pat Knopf explaining reasons for structure of *The Professor's House.* Prefers the distinct separations of that form to the mixture of unexpressed feelings typical of modern fiction, though it could have been done that way. Outland's life had become as real to the professor as his own; he became part of the old house. Glad Pat is studying with him. Willa Cather.

1434. **To Edward Wagenknecht,** Jan. 23, 1939; PM.
Appreciates his agreeing not to publish commentary on uncollected stories. His inquiry reminds her to indicate her wishes about them in her will. Regrets acerbic tone of her letter, but was afraid he meant to reprint the stories. Has had to stop some impositions of this sort over the years, for example when a magazine printed "Her Boss" without permission. Such matters take up time that could be spent in new writing. Wishes he had explained his intentions more clearly in his first letter. Willa Cather.

1435. **To Mrs. William Stix [Yaltah Menuhin],** Monday [Jan. 23, 1939], from New York; Princeton.
Weather very cold, but still walks around the reservoir [in Central Park]. Misses her. Is dealing with a great deal of business, particularly the effort to prevent publication of a poor translation of *Death Comes for the Archbishop* into French. Is sending James M. Barrie's *The Boy David* but suggests she first read First and Second Samuel in the Bible. One needs to know the Biblical story in order to enjoy the play. Is glad Barrie liked *Archbishop.* Aunt Willa. P.S.: Has just reread First and Second Samuel and the young David is delightful. Psalms of David are splendid poetry, too.

1436. To Norman Foerster, Feb. 13, 1939; UNL, copy, not original.

No, cannot accept his invitation. Rarely has uninterrupted time to work and would have none if she attended conferences or gave lecturers. Glad he wrote a book about the faults of state universities [*The American State University, Its Relation to Democracy*, 1937], a threat to public life. Willa Cather.

1437. To Bishop George Allen Beecher, Ash Wednesday, 1939 [Feb. 22]; HSNeb.

Thanks for his letter at Christmas. Still remembers the time he came to her apartment for dinner on Ash Wednesday. He has meant a great deal to her family. Sorry to hear about the injury to his eye. Always wishes the best to him and Mrs. Beecher. Willa Cather.

1438. To Yaltah Menuhin, Feb. 28, [1939?; prob. Feb. 27]; Princeton.

Wishes she were there to cheer a rainy day. Enclosing a letter from Stephen Tennant. At times he lets emotions run away with him. Prefers simple, direct language. English poetry has greater riches and variety than French, but English prose is better plain, with strong emotion kept firmly controlled. Glad to hear she likes Barrie. He can get away with sentiment because he always does it with a hint of a laugh. Was glad to hear from her father and Yehudi on Saturday before they sailed. Sorry she is having respiratory trouble. Suggests she read at night when she is having trouble, to try to take her mind off it. Myra Hess came to tea yesterday and sent her greetings. Aunt Willa. P.S.: Good that Stephen went to Egypt even if it did cause him to rhapsodize; he needs it for his health. [Tennant was in Egypt in early 1939. That fact, together with the reference to Yaltah's illness, seems to confirm the dating of this letter. On the other hand, the reference to Yehudi's sailing conflicts with the statement that he is in Jaffrey. I conjecture no. 1439 was written later in the day. However, inconsistencies make it unclear.]

1439. To Yaltah Menuhin, Monday night [Feb. 27, 1939, pm. Feb. 28, 1939], from New York; Princeton.

Has heard from her mother that she has bronchitis. Is enjoying the miniature orange tree she sent. Yehudi is in Jaffrey enjoying the snow and the mountains [? – see no. 1438]. Mozart once wrote, "Happiness? That is in the imagination" – may mean that happiness is not real or may mean that only people with imagination can be happy. Real seeing, like real happiness, is inward. Now will use imagination and think of Yaltah as being well. Aunt Willa.

1440. To Dorothy Canfield Fisher, Mar. 5, [1939]; UVt.

Has not been writing many letters recently, except to family and to friends of Isabelle. In December 1937 brother Douglass came to New York to spend her birthday with her. He died on June 13, 1938, age fifty-two, the only joyful and attractive member of the family. On October 10 Isabelle died in Sorrento of nephritis after four-year illness, during which her loving though unreliable husband cared for her. This has been the hardest year of her life. Is enclosing a letter from Jan Hambourg. Please return it, but don't write back. Is worn out with letters about Isabelle. Enjoyed [the picture of?] Dorothy's two granddaughters. Enjoyed having her two nieces with her at Grand Manan in the summers of 1936 and 1937. Both married this year – as well as three Menuhins! Likes Yehudi's wife. Appreciates receiving Dorothy's new book and will read it soon. Eyes giving her trouble, but what is worse is the trouble of keeping people away who want to come and comfort her. Doesn't want them; wants quiet for reflection. Willa.

1441. To [Josephine Frisbie?], Mar. 16, [1939?]; WCPM.

Glad to hear the Amboy mill is still running. A reassurance that reality persists. Willa Cather.

1442. To Dayton M. Kohler, Mar. 16, 1939; VTech.

Feels hopeless with the news that Hitler has gone into Prague. Is thinking about her friend President Masaryk and the Czech people she knew years ago. Britain seems to have lost its sense of honor, which she always thought was so strong. Hardly feels like going on living in this deteriorated world. Appreciates his letter, however. Willa Cather.

1443. To Allan Nevins, Mar. 18, 1939; Columbia.

Doesn't care to join clubs. Has lived in eight different states, each with its own writers' club, state historical society, and so on. Has friends in each. Only way not to offend is to keep from joining any. Did weaken and join the Mark Twain Society on the understanding that her name would not be on the letterhead, and it was put there anyway. Willa Cather.

1444. To Yaltah Menuhin, Sunday [mid-Mar. 1939?]; Princeton.

Enclosing an interesting story she found about a cat. Has had influenza and been keep in by bad weather. Hasn't been to the theater or to hear any music all month. Has tried to spend her time remembering happy things, like their presence last year. The last time she, Hephzibah, and Yehudi would ever be so free of adult cares. Suggests she try to vegetate and not think too much for a while. Aunt Willa.

1445. **To Ferris Greenslet,** Sunday [Mar. 1939?]; Harvard.
Recommends he read *The Sword in the Stone* [White, 1939]. W. S. C. P.S.: Concedes that it's fanciful, but not sentimental.

1446. **To Dorothy Canfield Fisher,** Monday [Mar. 1939?], from Mohonk Lake, New York; UVt.
By speaking of the two people themselves, she wrote the only comforting words possible. Douglass remained unmarried, was always available and always a lover of life. Isabelle grew more spiritually beautiful with every year. Has been here a week for rest. Glad Dorothy has been to Santa Fe. Would like to go back if it weren't for writers' colonies. Willa.

1447. **To Carrie Miner Sherwood,** Mar. 28, [1939?]; WCPM.
Enclosing donation for tree-planting fund. Receives Red Cloud newspaper only sporadically. Could Carrie speak to them about showing the address more clearly? Willie.

1448. **To Bishop George Allen Beecher,** Monday [Apr. 1939?]; UNL, copy, not original.
Sorry she sent an unsigned check when she was ill. Glad to hear he is going to Japan. Weather in New York so damp she is confined to home. Willa Cather.

1449. **To Mrs. William Stix [Yaltah Menuhin],** Apr. 11, [1939]; Princeton.
Yehudi surprised her for Easter with some recordings made in England not released in the U.S. One was their recording of Mozart's Sonata in B-flat. Has enjoyed it. Glad she is living where the weather is sunny. Very cold in New York. Aunt Willa. P.S.: Stephen is at Rhodes.

1450. **To Ferris Greenslet,** May 8, 1939; Harvard.
Hears that people are complaining of cuts in *The Song of the Lark*. Made these for the Autograph Edition and wanted them made in future editions, but it might be good to show on the title page that it is a revised

edition. Willa Cather. P.S.: Is enclosing a letter from the Works Progress Administration, which she hates, asking permission to have *The Best Stories of Sarah Orne Jewett* Brailled. All right with her, if he thinks so. W. S. C.

1451. To Allan Nevins, May 10, [1939?]; Columbia.
Glad to see the new edition of his book. Looking forward to rereading it. Willa Cather.

1452. To Zoë Akins, May 20, [1939?]; Huntington.
Was ill with influenza from February until end of April. Was in Atlantic City in March, but it rained all the time. Only cheerful spot of entire winter was the presence of Yehudi Menuhin and his wife. Can't get over loss of Douglass and Isabelle. Has been too ill and glum to work. Hasn't even been writing letters. Failed to thank her for the nice cutting board; will keep it at Grand Manan. Wishes to be back at Bank Street and Zoë on Fifth Avenue. Willa. P.S.: The current state of the world casts a cloud over everything.

1453. To Sister Mary Agatha, June 23, 1939; UNL, copy, not original.
Failed to answer her letter about *Shadows on the Rock* because of illness. Is glad she likes it better on rereading. True, a lesser book than *Death Comes for the Archbishop*, perhaps because it reflects her depression during her mother's illness. Willa Cather.

1454. To Burges Johnson, n.d. [1939?]; Beinecke. Partial transcription by E. K. Brown. Pub. *CEA Newsletter* Dec. 1939; quoted in Bohlke.
Like Henry Seidel Canby, does not believe in teaching contemporary literature. More important to use limited school time to teach classics of English literature. Essential reading in school includes Shakespeare, Milton, Fielding, Jane Austen, with Thackeray, George Eliot, George Meredith, and Thomas Hardy as the most recent. Young people should read contemporary literature as they want to, not as assignments. True literary taste is as rare as perfect pitch, but students can glean something from exposure to the classics, even if they don't have real aptitude.

1455. To Carrie Miner Sherwood, June 28, 1939; WCPM.
Is sending a book she meant to send at Christmas, about several modern writers [apparently including herself]. Recommends she read chapter in *School of Femininity*, by Margaret Lawrence. Only Carrie and Mary, among

people in Red Cloud, would read it without feeling spiteful. Has heard someone in Red Cloud claims to be the original of *Lucy Gayheart*, but Carrie knows who the skater was. Does she remember for sure the color of Sadie Becker's eyes? Hasn't been writing letters; still can't get over grieving for Douglass. They had such a joyful time when he came for her birthday. Will never be the same since losing both him and Isabelle. Only the affection of the Menuhins cheered her this past year. Enjoys knowing Yehudi's wife. Willie. P.S.: Sorry to have missed seeing Father Fitzgerald; was in New Hampshire. Leaving for Canada soon.

1456. **To Evelyn Scott,** Oct. 5, 1939; HRC.

Has recently come back from a long stay abroad [?] and is trying to catch up on letters. Only agent she knows is Paul Reynolds. Sorry to hear magazines' editorial policies are determined by politics. Doesn't believe it is true in all cases. Willa Cather.

1457. **To Helen McAfee,** Oct. 19, [1939]; Beinecke.

Pleased by A. E.'s remarks quoted on page 81 in *Yale Review*. Willa Cather. [Reference is to Frank O'Connor, "Two Friends: Yeats and A. E. (George Russell)," pp. 60–88 in the fall 1939 issue. Russell comments on the "emptiness" and "dead end" in poetry that he believes T. S. Eliot and Stephen Spender represent.]

1458. **To Ferris Greenslet,** Oct. 19, 1939; Harvard.

Thanks for the books. Notes errors in biographical information on William Archer, whom she knew beginning in 1908. Attended George Meredith's funeral with Archer in London and sat with him in [William Butler] Yeats's box with Lady Gregory at a performance by the Abbey Theatre Company in London. He was one of the first critics to recognize John Millington Synge's work. Was a great enthusiast of Ibsen and translated several of his plays. Hopes this can be corrected. Willa Cather.

1459. **To Dorothy Canfield Fisher,** Nov. 8, [1939?]; UVt.

Read *Seasoned Wood* while at Grand Manan. Especially enjoyed Aunt Lavinia and Miss Peck, who has a great reality about her. Surprised she gave Mr. Hulme her father's middle name, since the character lacks Mr. Canfield's sturdiness and humor. The state of the world is very somber. Wishes people had never learned to refine petroleum. Willa.

1460. **To Julian Street,** Nov. 9, [1939]; Princeton.

Is completing a new book. Shares his love of fine wine and French cooking. Will be glad to autograph his books. Is glad she has not followed trends. Willa Cather.

1461. **To Nell and Helen [?],** Nov. 24, [1939?]; WCPM.

Sorry to hear of their father's death. He was so helpful to her parents. Knows from experience that they will never stop missing him. Willa Cather.

1462. **To Judge [Robert] Grant [American Academy of Arts and Letters],** Nov. 25, [1939]; AAAL.

Is writing to object to the amendment of by-laws recently passed. Willa Cather. [On Oct. 13, 1939, the directors of the Academy passed a resolution to expand eligibility for membership beyond the members of the National Institute of Arts and Letters.]

1463. **To Julian Street,** Dec. 19, 1939; Princeton.

Enjoyed his letter about wines. With a proper cellar, would spend more than she could afford at Bellows. If by Château Cantenac-Brown 1926 he meant Château Brane Cantenac, she likes it better than Mouton-Rothschild. Alfred Knopf gave her six bottles of Brane Cantenac 1900 for Christmas last year. In champagnes, finds Perrier-Jouët too dry; prefers a good year of Louis Roederer. Feels sure he will be horrified by this confession. Looks like a hectic Christmas, with many people in town. Has been rereading Guizot's and Michelet's histories of France. Much better reading than the newspapers. Willa Cather.

1464. **To Yaltah Menuhin,** Dec. 19, [1939]; Princeton.

Enjoyed the birthday letter, but hopes she did it only on impulse, not from duty. As Edith has already written, Yehudi and Nola brought the baby for her to see. Saw the three of them in the park the day of Yehudi's recital at Carnegie Hall. Has sent Yaltah's mother some books. Aunt Willa.

1465. **To Helen Cather Southwick,** Dec. 20, 1939, extract made by E. K. Brown; Beinecke.

Trying to finish her book, on which she left off work when Douglass died and then Isabelle.

1466. To Dr. May, Jan. 4, 1940; UVa.

Appreciates his introduction to the Allens, but has not written because of influenza. Wishing him Happy New Year. Willa Cather.

1467. To Julian Street, Jan. 14, [1940?], a torn scrap; Princeton.

Enjoyed his letter. Does he know a red wine Chateau Berliquet? Alfred Knopf has sent her some from the Bellows stock, as well as four bottles of a white Hermitage 1895! W. S. C.

1468. To Carrie Miner Sherwood, Jan. 29, [1940?]; WCPM.

Showed Dr. Lewis's letter to an orthopedic surgeon, and he understood the nature of Mollie's injury from the description and agreed with the treatment. Is sending a check to help pay for nurse. Would like to cover the cost of the nursing, if Carrie will let her know how much. Very cold here; has had bronchitis. Appreciated her letter and Mary's. Yehudi and wife now gone to California. Willie.

1469. To Pendleton Hogan [in Washington, D.C.], Feb. 5, 1940, from New York; UVa, also copy at WCPM.

His letter came while she was in the West on vacation [?]. Glad he likes *My Mortal Enemy*. Reason Ewan Grey and Esther do not reenter the story is that people dropped out of Myra's life. She had too many friends; that was one of her problems. Couldn't possibly keep up with them all. It was her excessive devotion to people that made her think of Oswald as her enemy at the end, as if he had destroyed her inner peace. But she could never have had inner peace. Knew the original of Myra quite well. She died fifteen years before the book was written. Will stop with that one question. Willa Cather.

1470. To George and Eleanor Austerman, Feb. 7, 1940; UVa.

Thanks for the Christmas card and picture of Kurt. Hopes to see them this year. All the news from England is bad. Willa Cather.

1471. To Head of Department of English, Mount Saint Mary's College, Emmitsburg, Md., Feb. 7, 1940; UVa.

Has received two letters from John J. Walsh about his thesis. Is not a Catholic, though published reports have said so. Please tell this student he can't always believe what he reads in books. Is sorry people write things about her that are not true. Willa Cather.

1472. **To Ferris Greenslet,** Feb. 12, [1940?], extract made by E. K. Brown; Beinecke.
Sorry to see an old friend of his [John Buchan, Lord Tweedsmuir] has died.
Knows by experience how empty one's world begins to look. Realizes she
is often shrewish, but does grieve for her friends' losses. Willa Cather.

1473. **To Julian Street,** Feb. 15, 1940; Princeton, copy, not original. [File includes
note that a handwritten label "Chateau Berliquet 1900" was pasted onto
the original.]
Here is the label; Alfred Knopf had two bottles. A wine different from any
she ever tasted, more herbal than fruity. Wishes she had a stock of it. Willa
Cather.

1474. **To Zoë Akins,** Feb. 15, 1940; Huntington.
Glad she enjoys her home, providing a retreat from the fact that all the
inheritance of history is in peril. Would like to have a similar retreat. Can't
make the cottage on Grand Manan more comfortable without ruining it.
Wishes she had not written *Starvation on Red River*. Too strident, too un-
believable, with none of her own voice in it and not a single character one
can care about. Much like *The Little Foxes* [Hellman] in this respect. Please
go back to her own kind of play. Willa.

1475. **To Frederick Paul Keppel,** Feb. 16, 1940; Columbia.
Doesn't speak to learned organizations; changes her mind too often to
make definitive pronouncements. Willa Cather.

1476. **To H. L. Mencken,** Feb. 21, 1940; NYPL.
Needs to know whether the *Baltimore Sun* was in publication in 1850. Willa
Cather. P.S.: His *Happy Days* makes her wish she had been born sooner and
lived only through that period.

1477. **To Ferris Greenslet,** Feb. 24, [1940]; Harvard.
Yes, will change the name of the bull [in *My Ántonia*] to Andrew Jackson for
this one edition of a thousand copies. Father's bulls were actually named
Gladstone, for a stubborn disposition, and Brigham Young, for breeding
competence. Willa Cather. P.S.: Yes, agrees to donate a set of the autograph
edition to the fundraising for Finland.

1478. **To Carrie Miner Sherwood,** Apr. 2, 1940; WCPM.
Saw in the newspaper that there had been a speech at a club in Red Cloud

about Cornelia Otis Skinner. Sending a sketch of Skinner that was given her by Skinner's daughter. A typical story of that period when young people were escaping from prairie towns to bigger cities to experience more of the world. Willie.

1479. **To Miss Leighton [secretary at Houghton Mifflin],** Apr. 2, 1940; Harvard.
Please inform Miss Howell [who had suggested she write a script for Ingrid Bergman] that she is away, that she has no particular attitude one way or the other about films, and does not write for the stage. Sorry to learn movie rights to *The Song of the Lark* are still with an agent. Would be very disappointed if it were made. Willa Cather.

1480. **To the Board of Directors of the American Academy of Arts and Letters,** May [n.d.] 1940; AAAL.
Is writing to protest the passage of the amendment to by-laws, Article IV, Sections 2 and 10, passed on April 12. Hopes this action can be reversed. Willa Cather.

1481. **To Mrs. Vanamee [American Academy of Arts and Letters],** May 29, 1940; AAAL.
Is honored to have been asked to serve on the nomination committee for the Howells Medal and would enjoy working with the other members of the committee [Ellen Glasgow, Stewart E. White, and Thornton Wilder] but feels too little acquainted with recent fiction to be able to contribute to the task. Has mostly been reading about 13th century France for several years. Willa Cather.

1482. **To Carrie Miner Sherwood,** June 5, [1940?]; WCPM.
Is sending a contribution toward the Red Cross quota for Webster County, which is appropriate since she owns land there. Has been out of the hospital for almost three weeks but still not well. Throat problem similar to the ones her mother used to have. Willie. P.S.: Prefers to write checks on her Chase Bank account because they will be returned for tax records. Glad to give to the Red Cross; one charity that does what it claims to do.

1483. **To Carrie Miner Sherwood,** Thursday [June 6, 1940?]; WCPM.
Forgot to mention, wants her contribution to be anonymous. Mary Virginia reminded her that people there might think she was showing off. She was probably thinking of her father when she said that. Willie.

1484. **To Ferris Greenslet,** June 10, 1940; Harvard.

Very pleased with the autobiography of John Buchan being serialized in the *Atlantic*. Congratulations on securing a book of such good sense that allows one to think about a different life than that in the present troubled state of the world – as different as Virgilian pastoral. Has been accused of escapism, but realizes one can't escape everything. Is utterly unable to escape the sorrow now threatening all that has made life worth living in this world. Her doctor says people in hospitals these days lack the will to get well. He has forbidden her to go to Philadelphia to accept an honorary degree from the University of Pennsylvania this month because her physical resistance is so low. Willa Cather. P.S.: Please check current edition of *My Ántonia* from the Riverside Press and see what poor quality paper they are using. One side of the page bleeds through to the other.

1485. **To Carrie Miner Sherwood,** June 12, [1940]; WCPM. Note: handwriting notably atypical, sprawling and clumsy.

No, is not cross that her name was shown on the list of contributors. Was to have received an honorary degree today, but doctor forbade her to go. Is going to Jaffrey, N.H., tomorrow. Edith will keep strangers away. Sorry to miss Mary's visit. Enclosing Virginia's new address on 77th Street. Willie.

1486. **To Lydia Lambrecht,** n.d. [pm. June 12, 1940], from New York; Newberry.

Is sending a little money to help out. Congratulations to Julius on Super-Anxiety II. [Encloses a letter from a member of the English Department of Hastings College, Frank S. Hewett, to a Mrs. Woodward, identifying Julius as the brother of Lydia Lambrecht and owner of a prize bull named Super-Anxiety.] Willa Cather.

1487. **To Carrie Miner Sherwood,** July 15, [1940]; WCPM.

Sorry to have missed Mary's visit, but the time in New Hampshire helped her feel better. Worry about friends in England keeps her down. Willie.

1488. **To Carrie Miner Sherwood,** Sept. 4, [1940?], from Grand Manan; WCPM.

Will be here two or three more weeks and would appreciate a letter. So glad Carrie went to Europe before all this hatred burst into violence. Has not heard from Irene since last fall. Has enjoyed being outdoors here, but should have worked harder. Virginia was with her and they walked a lot. Virginia upset about disharmony in her family. [two passages blacked out]

We all experience troubles. Keeps having to remind herself that virtues like generosity still exist! Willie.

1489. To Zoë Akins, n.d. [mid-Sept. 1940], from Grand Manan; UVa.
Came to the island in early August to escape heat in New York. Appreciated her letter, but didn't answer it before leaving town because working hard on new book. Did not care for the watercolor she sent. Has finished her book and is now getting proofs. Going back to New York soon but dreads it; isn't up to seeing people. Needs to stay here and rest. Willa.

1490. To [Burges] Johnson, Sept. 21, 1940; Amherst.
Yes, may use the quotation as revised, with an explanatory note that it was sent to a friend's son. Otherwise will be deluged by letters from students wanting her to explain this and that. Mostly sends a form letter to students and to English teachers. Such correspondence has delayed completion of her new book. Willa Cather. [typed name only, no signature]

1491. To Ferris Greenslet, Sept. 21, 1940, from New York; Harvard.
Appreciated his offering her a copy of *Lord Tweedsmuir,* but didn't answer because completing her new book. Knopf pleased with it. Has not yet received *Audubon's America,* and looks forward to it as well as the book on Tweedsmuir. Glad they have both known such fine people. Greatly admires the present conduct of the British. Even Stephen Tennant, as pampered as he has been, says he is proud to be in England now. Finished reading Churchill's *Life of Marlborough* at Grand Manan and considers it a very great work. Willa Cather. P.S.: The books have arrived.

1492. To Josephine Frisbie, Sept. 27, 1940; WCPM.
So glad to receive pictures of the Amboy Mill. Very reassuring to know it is still there. Glad to get her opinion of the park in Red Cloud, which sounded rather awful in the newspaper. Picture of her father just as she remembered him. Mother was very fond of both of Josephine's parents. Often thinks mother would have been happier spending last years in Red Cloud, but Douglass was thankful to have her in California and actually enjoyed her company, even after she could no longer speak. Willa Cather.

1493. To Bishop George Allen Beecher, Sept. 28, 1940; HSNeb.
Appreciated his letter about dedicating the altar rail at Grace Church, a place she loves as she loves few others. Remembers the evening of her and

parents' confirmation, which meant so much to them all. Glad to hear Molly Ferris was able to be there for the dedication. Hopes to visit Red Cloud this winter and talk with him about the things that have kept her away. Willa Cather.

1494. To Carrie Miner Sherwood, n.d. [Sept. 1940], from New York; WCPM.
Is back home and completing the final work for publication of the new book on December 1. Will send an early copy. Willie.

1495. To Sigrid Undset, Monday [prob. Oct. 1940]; Oslo.
So gratified that they share convictions, as her letter shows. War news shows that the mills of the gods are grinding.

1496. To Van Wyck Brooks, Oct. 14, 1940; Penn.
Shares his high opinion of Archibald MacLeish's statement about the war. [MacLeish called on the U.S. to enter the war in order to defend democracy against fascism.] People pay far too little attention to statements by important leaders. No one has made more forceful and important statements than Winston Churchill, but neither he nor MacLeish is likely to be able to wake people up to the dangers. Willa Cather.

1497. To Dorothy Canfield Fisher, Oct. 14, 1940; UVt.
Is unable to write by hand because of sprain. Now they are even on misquoting titles. Has regretted calling her last book "Seasoned Wood" [instead of *Seasoned Timber*]. Now Dorothy has called hers "Sapphira and the Slave Maid," which loses the doubling of the "r" sound. Glad she likes what she has read of it. Galley proofs need a lot of correction. Abandoned it in the middle when Douglass and Isabelle died, but had already written the epilogue, which was the target. Has overridden her reluctance to shift from third person to first because the incident such an important one in her childhood. Grandmother Boak a Confederate and lost two sons in the South's army, but cared about justice and actually did take Nancy across the Potomac. Postmistress was her great aunt, Sidney Cather Gore. Enjoyed hearing the southern speech in her mind as she wrote it, especially the black people's speech. Realizes their speech patterns are not consistent in the book, but house servants varied their speech. Might not have finished the book had it not been for the war, but writing it helped her escape the anxiety. Willa.

1498. To Dr. Damrosch [American Academy of Arts and Letters], Oct. 25, 1940; AAAL.

Has returned her ballot for the Howells Medal. Continues to hope amendment passed last spring, so inconsistent with the goals of the Institute and the Academy, will be reversed. Plans to attend the annual meeting if possible. Willa Cather.

1499. To Van Wyck Brooks, Oct. 26, 1940; Penn.

Writing to call his attention to an error on page 434 of his book on New England. Not true she edited the letters of Sarah Wyman Whitman. Willa Cather.

1500. To Mrs. Vanamee [from Sarah J. Bloom, secretary], Oct. 26, 1940; AAAL.

Verifying the time of the Academy meeting on November 14. Sarah J. Bloom, Secretary.

1501. To Julian Street, Oct. 26, 1940; Princeton.

Returned from Canada only a few days ago [?] to find even the poorest quality wines very expensive. Appreciates his sharing Margaret Kennedy's letter about quality of life in England nowadays. Wants to show it to her niece before returning it. Hopes he will like the new book. Not true it was five years in the writing, since for much of that time she wasn't writing at all. Willa Cather. P.S.: Has received a case of Sancerre Sauvignon 1938, from the Anjou region. Does he know it?

1502. To Viola Roseboro', Nov. 9, 1940; UVa.

Sending her an advance copy of the book, to be released December 7. Realizes she is not so interested in fiction any more, but much of this is not fiction but family stories and local stories, with an absolutely factual epilogue. Sorry not to have written sooner, but has been back from Canada only a few weeks and very occupied with the book. Easy to catch the manners of southern society, but the problem of evil in an intimate domestic setting difficult to catch. Willa Cather. P.S.: House servants spoke one way to them and another way to each other.

1503. To Laura Hills, Nov. 9, 1940; PM.

Has to send a typed letter because right hand is unusable. Damaged it signing five hundred copies of a deluxe edition of *Sapphira and the Slave Girl*. Is sending her one of only two advance copies she has received so far.

Book not officially out until December 7. Epilogue is absolutely true, a very vivid memory from childhood. W. S. C.

1504. To Ferris Greenslet, Nov. 9, 1940; Harvard.
Would Houghton Mifflin be willing to pay the $1,091.63 shown on her last statement now instead of in March, as is the usual practice? Income will be considerably higher next year, and would like to keep her income tax down. Is pleased with the national election because Roosevelt will support England better than Willkie would have. Willa Cather.

1505. To unnamed nun [addressed only as Sister], Nov. 23, 1940; Loyola.
Yes, several of her books show admiration for Catholic missionary priests. Has known and personally admired several – Father Connelly in Winslow, Arizona, Father Haltermann in Santa Cruz, N.M., and a Belgian priest who died in World War I while serving as a chaplain in the Belgian army. Enclosing a reprint of her letter to the *Commonweal* about sources for *Death Comes for the Archbishop.* Willa Cather.

1506. To Ferris Greenslet, Sunday [c. Nov. 24, 1940]; Harvard.
Must scrawl a letter in spite of sprained right thumb because secretary out of town. Very much appreciated his and Mrs. Greenslet's letter. Many memories of Virginia went into the book. Wrote a great deal more, simply for the pleasure of recalling life there, but cut out all that didn't serve the plan for the book. Nancy was real, and her mother really a servant in the family. Books about slavery usually exaggerate one way or the other. Own family found its superficial aspects pleasant and didn't think much about what lay beneath. Material discarded from the book weighed six pounds. W. S. C. P.S.: Yes, may place the note on names [at end of *Sapphira*] where Knopf placed the note on design in the first edition, which will probably shift for the second. How important a thumb is!

1507. To Elizabeth Shepley Sergeant, Nov. 27, 1940; PM.
Sending an advance copy of *Sapphira and the Slave Girl* but can't autograph it because of strained tendon of right thumb. Please give her best wishes to Pauline and Josephine Goldmark. Willa Cather. [signed by Sarah J. Bloom]

1508. To Fred Otte, Nov. 28, 1940; WCPM.
Glad to receive letter and birthday wishes. Was surprised the book was released on her birthday. Can still remember teaching at that grimy school.

Enjoyed teaching and might have continued if S. S. McClure hadn't called her away. Willa Cather.

1509. To Viola Roseboro', Nov. 28, 1940; UVa.

Greatly appreciated her letter about the book. Writing it allowed recovery of early memories and escape from painful events. Glad it rings true to someone born a southerner. Willa Cather.

1510. To Zoë Akins, Dec. 1, [1940]; UVa.

Why she not come in November? Nieces come, Menuhins come, others come, Zoë not come. Is to be in hospital most of December because of tendon damage. Is using this Indian language to write tersely while splint is off for a while. Willa.

1511. To Carrie [Miner Sherwood], Elsie [sister], and Roscoe [?], Dec. 6, 1940; WCPM.

Has to write a shared letter because of inflamed tendon, reason she did not come to Red Cloud for Christmas. Is trying to avoid surgery and trying to avoid hospital until after Christmas by resting the hand as much as possible. Doctors say it is a common problem among people who do repetitive small movements of the hand, and since she writes by hand she is subject to it. Hopes they understand why she can't travel. The last straw, putting the hand completely out of commission, was autographing 520 copies of a special edition. W. S. C.

1512. To Julian Street, Dec. 9, 1940; Princeton.

Will gladly autograph a book for him and Mrs. Street when hand is usable. Getting a copy sent without autograph for now. Willa Cather. [signed by Sarah J. Bloom]

1513. To Dorothy Canfield Fisher, Dec. 13, 1940; UVt.

Can't write, because hand in splints. Please send a copy of her write-up on *Sapphira* for the bulletin of the Book-of-the-Month Club. May have to spend Christmas season in hospital. [signed by Sarah J. Bloom]

1514. To Elizabeth Shepley Sergeant, Dec. 13, 1940; UVa.

Has not written because of thumb problem; hand now in splints. Can't even sign a check. Will soon go into the French Hospital and be pampered by nurses there. [signed by Sarah J. Bloom]

1515. **To Julian Street,** n.d. [perhaps referring to enclosure mentioned in no. 1516]; Princeton.

Thanks for sharing the enclosed letter. It's true, the Germans will never change. W. S. C.

1516. **To Viola Roseboro',** Dec. 13, 1940; UVa.

Enclosing a letter written by Margaret Kennedy that Julian Street shared and did not want returned. Very tedious to have hand in splints here at the holiday season. Miss Lewis sends greeting. Willa Cather. [signed by Sarah J. Bloom]

1517. **To Ferris Greenslet,** Dec. 13, 1940; Harvard.

Trusts Mr. Rogers to place the explanatory note for the Autograph Edition where he thinks best. Right hand in splints, so can't even sign checks for Christmas presents. Willa Cather. [signed by Sarah J. Bloom]

1518. **To Fanny Butcher,** Dec. 21, 1940; Newberry.

Going into the hospital tomorrow. Wishes she could have autographed books for her. [signed by Sarah J. Bloom]

1519. **To Elizabeth Shepley Sergeant,** Dec. 21, 1940; PM.

Certainly not offended by her piece for the Book-of-the-Month Club bulletin. Going to the hospital tomorrow for two weeks. Send no flowers. Always hates to see flowers neglected in a hospital. Do not worry that Christmas will be depressing; will have favorite room and indulgent nurses. Willa Cather. [signed by Sarah J. Bloom]

1520. **To Ferris Greenslet,** Dec. 22, 1940; Harvard.

Enclosing a letter from an attorney in Pittsburgh who asks about a story she had in a Christmas volume a few years ago, called "Double Birthday." Please send a copy of the book if any available, then return letter. Going to hospital tomorrow. Hopes 1941 will be better than expected. Willa Cather. [signed by Sarah J. Bloom]

1521. **To Zoë Akins,** Dec. 30, 1940, from French Hospital, New York; Huntington.

Wishing her a happy new year. Christmas here was very pleasant, and hand improving. Wait until they can visit in person to say what she thinks of *Sapphira*. Willa Cather. [signed by Sarah J. Bloom]

1522. To Fanny Butcher, Jan. 9, [1941?]; Newberry.

In response to her question, would most like to have written *War and Peace*. Doing so would have required having the richness of experience that went into it, and she would have liked that, and then to have achieved such form in the book. *War and Peace* has both abundance of life and structured restraint. Willa Cather.

1523. To Bruce Rogers, Jan. 25, 1941; Newberry.

Sorry not to have seen him when he was in New York, but has been in hospital. Does not mind omitting capitalization of "o" in Moses, which was there to emphasize the way Negros sing the word. "Milldam" was often used instead of "millpond" in Virginia. "Down the millrace" is true to the localized use for going either way, but it might be better to make it "along the millrace." Stairs did creak; house built of unseasoned wood. Realizes excisions of extraneous material may have left some details like these unclear, and appreciates his calling them to her attention. Willa Cather.

1524. To Henry Seidel Canby, Feb. 4, 1941; Beinecke.

Has not replied to the various letters about the Academy [of Arts and Letters] because of incapacity to right hand. But now can sign her name, at least. Is pleased by his review of the new book. Shares his doubt about the epilogue, but it was important to her. Willa Cather.

1525. To Mr. Watson, Feb. 12, 1941; Buffalo.

Delayed answering his good letter because of incapacity to right hand. Always tries to avoid propagandizing in fiction. Doesn't believe even Dickens wrote for that purpose, though social reforms did result. Glad to hear young people like her books. Writes about people or places in which she has strong personal interest. Usually has a book considerably worked out in her mind before she begins to write. Then the writing is an enjoyable experience. Willa Cather.

1526. To Margaret Crofts, Feb. 12, 1941; LC.

Has found her last two years' Christmas cards very interesting, though the one last year was rather dreadful. Keeps it in the Michelet volume on the Dark Ages. Glad that she, a southerner, likes the new book. Spent a pleasant Christmas in the French Hospital, where the director is an old friend. Willa Cather.

1527. To Mr. Gardiner, n.d. [c. Feb. 15, 1941], excerpt made by E. K. Brown; Beinecke.

Liked his magazine article "Modern Authors Can Be Gentlemen" and appreciated his comment on her. [John] Steinbeck and [William] Saroyan do not use the full range of the English language, but only write in monosyllables. Samuel [Eliot] Morison manages to use even ordinary slang in such a way that it fits the need of the moment, without destroying the dignity of his writing. Enjoyed Morison's book about Columbus [1941]; had not known the role of religion in Columbus's life.

1528. To Mr. Gardiner, n.d., excerpt made by E. K. Brown; Beinecke.

He may use what he wants from her letter. Thoughts were stimulated by his statements about the neglect of the language nowadays. Hardly anyone reads Shakespeare for the language any more.

1529. To Viola Roseboro', Feb. 20, 1941; UVa.

Hand in splints again. Appreciates her words of sympathy about the reviews of *Sapphira and the Slave Girl*, but is used to it. New York reviewers say every time that her new book is not as good as the previous one. If that were true, they should have dropped into the abyss by now. There were only two good reviews of *My Ántonia* in the whole country, by Fanny Butcher and by Grant Overton. Is asking Miss Bloom to enclose Henry Seidel Canby's review of *Sapphira*. Actually, the reviews Knopf has sent for her to read have seemed surprisingly good. Willa Cather. [signed by Sarah J. Bloom]

1530. To Bishop George Allen Beecher, Feb. 25, 1941; HSNeb.

He has probably heard about her hand problem. Used it too soon and had a relapse. Please address her by first name, as friends in Red Cloud do. Had a pleasant if not merry Christmas in the hospital. Enjoyed hearing the nurses speak French. Wishes she could have been in Red Cloud for the funeral of Mollie Ferris. One consolation for hand problem is she will be able to get to Lenten services more often than usual. Will be thinking about Grace Church and her Bishop. Willa Cather. [signature very shaky]

1531. To Miss Hoyer, n.d. [1941], excerpt made by E. K. Brown; Beinecke.

Does not believe General Pershing was ever a teacher, but he was military commandant at the University of Nebraska [ROTC] in 1894 and replaced her mathematics instructor for a week when he was ill. Please correct untrue reports. Gets very tired of untruths being published, such as reports that she is a Catholic.

1532. To Mrs. George Whicher, Mar. 5, 1941; PM.

Sorry to have missed her while she was in New York for Yehudi Menuhin's recital, but was in the hospital. Did get to hear the recital, as Yehudi's mother took her and nurse to a private box. Was somewhat disappointed in his playing. Is now at home, but cannot use right hand. Strained the tendon in her thumb. Wants to hear about Stephen's wedding. Willa Cather, by S. J. Bloom, then signed by Willa Cather with left hand.

1533. To Alexander Woollcott, Mar. 17, 1941; Harvard.

Appreciates his kind words in his Second Reader, three years ago now, and appreciates his reprinting of Kenneth Grahame's *Golden Age*, as well as his bringing to her attention the paper on Boswell by Pottle. Recommends *Johnson without Boswell* [Kingsmill], recently published by Knopf. Is it really he who is acting in *The Man Who Came to Dinner*? Such a surprise! Recommends French Hospital, where nurses speak French and even cooks are French. Had very good care and good food. A Catholic hospital, but nurses not nuns, so no black habits about. One accompanied the wife of ex-president of Chile on airplane when President Roosevelt provided her transportation back to Santiago. American airmen so fine – keep up her faith in America in spite of Communists having gotten hold of much of the country. Willa Cather.

1534. To Carrie Miner Sherwood, Mar. 22, 1941; WCPM.

Keeps thinking about her and wishes she could write a real letter, by hand. Was saddened by Mary's telegram telling of Walter's [Carrie's husband's] death, but had heard how ill he was. Also heard how beautifully she was taking care of him. Remembers first seeing his picture in her watch case when she was going away to school at St. Mary's. Has spent a great deal of time alone this winter enjoying precious memories like that. Sees very few people besides Mary Virginia and Yehudi Menuhin and wife. Will write again soon. Hand is improving since going to Dr. Ober, a surgeon from Boston. Enjoys remembering evenings she spent with Carrie and Walter ten years ago, when they both gave her good advice. Willie.

1535. To Langston Hughes, Apr. 15, 1941; Beinecke.

Appreciated his gracious letter and is glad characters in *Sapphira and the Slave girl* seemed real to him. All the colored people in the book were people she knew in Virginia or elsewhere. Willa Cather.

1536. To Stephen Tennant, Apr. 15, 1941; Yongue.

Likes the cover for *Lascar*; it transports her to Marseilles. Likes the way the church towers over all while frivolous and shabby and alluring things wash around it. Sense of crowding and human variety perfectly captures Marseilles. Surprising he never read [Guy de] Maupassant until recently. Glad he is feeling well and enjoying himself. Was sorry to learn that Virginia Woolf had died; knows that was a loss to him. Hand improves very slowly. Willa Cather.

1537. To Ferris Greenslet, Apr. 19, 1941; Harvard.

Everyone she knows who went to Florida for the winter got sick. Survived New York winter with no worse than colds. High spirits impossible these days, with the world as it is. Isabelle McClung's brother was wise to marry a member of the Mellon family – his only wise deed. He was good-looking but otherwise a disappointment. Willa Cather.

1538. To Carrie Miner Sherwood, Apr. 24, [1941?]; WCPM.

Sending a check to help with window for Mollie [Ferris]. Enjoys thinking of Carrie's trip – most cheerful thing she has to think about. Willie.

1539. To Mr. Phillipson, May 4, [1941?]; WCPM.

Is packing to go to California, where her brother is ill. Has always loved Latin and taught it for that reason. Not a disaster to miss out on a college education; he can learn from the legal papers he works with much of the discipline in language that study of Latin would provide. Willa Cather.

1540. To Mary Willard [in San Francisco], May 6, 1941; UVa.

Is grieved to hear of May's death. Knew her even before she knew Isabelle. Edith Lewis phoned Ethel Litchfield, who was so overcome she had to hang up without saying anything. Called back and implored her [i.e., Cather] not to die before she did because couldn't bear another death of a dear friend. Feels that way herself. Such a precious group of friends. Remembers how they enjoyed folk dancing classes. May was the best dancer of the group and the youngest-looking. Hasn't seen Ethel recently. Brother

Roscoe ill in Colusa, California with a heart lesion. Don't answer, just wanted to say she shares her grief. Willa Cather.

1541. To Irene Miner Weisz and Carrie Miner Sherwood, May 16, 1941; WCPM.
Has been under a great deal of stress since mid-March. An old and dear friend died in San Francisco, and Roscoe has been in hospital with heart lesion. Local heart doctor let him go on with high blood pressure several months before calling in a specialist. Attack might have been averted if he had taken action sooner. Is going to California as soon as doctors will let him have a visit, probably June. Not letting Elsie Sergeant know how seriously ill he is. Has thought of them a great deal during these weeks and wishes she could have been with them to see exhibit of French paintings in Chicago. Has had many touching letters since publication of *Sapphira* and felt under emotional strain. Will probably not see them on her way to California, because doctors can make special arrangements for her on train from Montreal. Edith will go. With hand in metal gauntlet cannot even dress herself without help. Still hopes to write again with special brace. Sigrid Undset and the Menuhins have helped cheer her up. Undset a woman of great character and many abilities; knows everything about flowers; is a person cut on a heroic scale and never speaks of her son's death in German concentration camp. Willie. P.S.: What she said about Madame Undset to be kept confidential. Wanted them to know about this wonderful person who could not be broken even by the German Army.

1542. To Mrs. [Rose] Ackroyed [Ackroyd], May 16, 1941; UVa.
Enjoyed her letter. Her grandmother, Mary Ann Anderson, a childhood favorite in Virginia. Used to watch out the window for her to come up the road when in bed sick. Saw her again on visit to Virginia after graduating from college. Walked together up the beautiful Hollow Road to her house on Timber Ridge. Mrs. Anderson always took such a keen interest in people's lives. Mrs. Ackroyed's Aunt Marjorie and Uncle Enoch went to Nebraska with the Cather family. He went to California two years later with two other men from Winchester and only wrote once after that, but Marjorie stayed with the family until she died. Remembers hours spent with Marjorie on the back porch or in the kitchen. Is enclosing a recent picture of Willow Shade, now in bad repair, and has circled the window from which she used to watch for Mrs. Anderson. Willa Cather. P.S.: The woman who wove their rugs was Mrs. Kearns.

1543. To Sigrid Undset, May 18, 1941; Oslo.

The lilies of the valley have been delightful, and her letter as well. So happy that after knowing each other through their books for so long they now know each other personally and realize how many tastes and beliefs they have in common. Scarcely maintains a desire to live, with so much bad news, especially agreement of Hitler with the Vichy French. Hopes she will come to visit again soon.

1544. To Zoë Akins, June 7, 1941; Huntington.

Received her sad note about a week ago and has kept thinking about her. Remembers her own father's death. When she reached Red Cloud everyone in the family was asleep. Had several hours alone with him. When the sun came up it cast a rosy glow over his face so he looked quite like himself, almost cheerful. Imagines death as something happy, whether there is awareness after it or not. Not easy to convey what she means. Maybe one day can help Zoë understand why she kept herself so isolated this past winter. Willa.

1545. To Carrie Miner Sherwood, June 14, 1941; WCPM.

Has read her letter several times. Is glad she and Mary will be together next winter. Will come to Red Cloud in the fall to see them, but wants to keep it a secret from anyone else. Need time together to forget destruction the world is undergoing. Is leaving for California in a few days, Edith going along since she still can't fasten her own corsets etc. Will use this for their summer vacation instead of going to Grand Manan. Doesn't feel up to going to southern California to see brothers Jim and Jack and families. Willie. P.S.: Please tell Mrs. Stockman, appreciated her letter.

1546. To Miss Geffen [American Academy of Arts and Letters] [from Sarah J. Bloom, secretary], Aug. 12, 1941; AAAL.

Cather is in California due to the illness of her brother. Is not forwarding mail. Therefore, it will be some time before she can consider writing for the "Schrift Fest" for Dr. Damrosch. Sarah J. Bloom, Secretary.

1547. To Carrie Miner Sherwood and Mary Miner Creighton, Aug. 24, [1941], from Victoria, Canada; WCPM.

Had a good visit with Roscoe in San Francisco and is enjoying this part of Canada. Didn't see any friends, but kept her strength and attention solely for him. Brace is off most of the time. This is the first letter she has written, besides a short note to Mary Virginia. Willie.

1548. To Zoë Akins, Sept. 17, 1941; Huntington.
Had left New York before the flowers came. Left June 20 via the Santa Fe with stops in Chicago and New Mexico before meeting Roscoe and wife at Fairmont Hotel in San Francisco. Spent a month there, Roscoe coming for long visits every weekend. His condition still very guarded. Returned by way of Vancouver and Canadian Rockies. Stopped using the brace on her hand while in Victoria. Heat in New York now devastating. Willa.

1549. To Zoë Akins, Sept. 22, 1941, from New York, telegram; Huntington.
Sends condolences on the death of her mother.

1550. To Julian Street, Oct. 3, 1941; Princeton.
Appreciates his sending Margaret Kennedy's book [*Where Stands a Winged Sentry*]. Had a tiresome summer. Enjoyed four weeks at the Empress Hotel in Victoria, but travel difficult these days. Willa Cather.

1551. To Ferris Greenslet, Oct. 20, 1941; Harvard.
Glad to receive her royalty notice and to hear he is well. Has just come back from long, tiring trip to California. Six weeks in San Francisco spent with her brother were very happy; was able to take off Dr. Ober's brace during that time. Roscoe will never be his old self, but is adjusting well. Then spent some time in Victoria, Lake Louise, and Montreal. Splendid scenery but still prefers eastern part of Canada and Atlantic Ocean. Willa Cather. P.S.: Please send a copy of latest edition of *My Ántonia*.

1552. To Stephen Tennant, Oct. 20, 1941; Yongue, copy, not original.
Likes the first version of the *Lascar* cover better than the second. Wonders if the British officer Percy Wyndham who fought in the American Revolution in Virginia was related to him. Willa Cather. P.S.: Hand somewhat better but still can't write well.

1553. To Carrie Miner Sherwood, Nov. 3, 1941; WCPM.
Sorry to say, will not be coming to Red Cloud this fall. Had a hard summer and has felt the strain. Edith ill for a week at Lake Louise and travel difficult. Was in hospital with severe anemia after they got back. Still quite weak and becomes faint with any excitement. Very little appetite. Also

some family problems. Family in southern California very hurt by her not letting them know she was in the state. Was able to stop using the brace on her hand while in San Francisco, which pleased Roscoe. Hopes to get really well soon. Mary Virginia cheers her up and does some of her shopping, and niece Margaret, Roscoe's daughter, comes into New York for tea occasionally. Must not take on anything else until she regains some strength. Hand much steadier now. When destroying some old manuscripts yesterday, compared present handwriting to that of years ago and found it more legible now. Willie.

1554. **To Miss Manwaring,** Nov. 14, 1941; Wellesley.
Has decided to allow use of "Paul's Case" because "The Sculptor's Funeral" overused and not a very strong story to represent her. Will let Alfred Knopf decide whether to allow use of one of the stories in *Obscure Destinies.* Willa Cather.

1555. **To Carrie Miner Sherwood,** Saturday [Nov. 15, 1941?]; WCPM.
Understands she is leading the Red Cross drive there and wants to contribute. Hand much better; can write some. Can dictate letters but not new work. Blood count coming up; feels much better. [unsigned].

1556. **To Carl J. Weber,** Nov. 17, 1941; Colby, copy also at WCPM.
Will consider placing Jewett's letters there when ready to place them at all. They are personal letters and mean a great deal to her. Allowed Mrs. Fields to use letters that seemed to have a public interest, because she was convinced they provided good advice to any young writer. Willa Cather.

1557. **To Sigrid Undset,** Nov. 17, [1941]; Oslo.
Please come to dinner at seven Saturday, the 22nd. Wants to hear her opinion of the new Christian brotherhood with Stalin.

1558. **To Felicia Geffen [American Academy of Arts and Letters] [from Sarah J. Bloom, secretary],** Nov. 26, 1941; AAAL.
Cather is sending her contribution to the "Schrift Fest" for Dr. Damrosch today. If too late to include in the volume, please return it so that she can present it personally. Sarah J. Bloom, Secretary.

1559. **To Sigrid Undset,** Tuesday [Nov. 26, 1941]; Oslo.
On p. 366 of Mathews [*Field Book of American Wild Flowers*] she will find

an entry on the swamp milkweed (Asclepias incarnata), which they discussed. Mathews does not note, however, its willow-like and *shiny* leaves. It was a special thrill to have found one once in a desert canyon rather than a swamp. Greatly enjoys her visits.

1560. **To Sigrid Undset**, Dec. 2 [1941]; Oslo.

Feels very happy about her letter. There were not so many serious admirations in one's life, and has long felt such admiration for Undset. Glad she had felt it in return. The fact that they care for the same things is a strong foundation for friendship. Sorry her handwriting is not clear. P.S.: So glad the good news from Russia! [The *New York Times* of Dec. 2, 1941, reports that the German Army had been driven out of Rostov in a "rout."]

1561. **To Zoë Akins**, Dec. 6, [1941?]; UVa.

Glad to receive her card. 1942 promises to be a bad year. Does admire Churchill, though. Suggests she read Gregor Ziemer, *Education for Death* [1941], which was called to her attention by Sigrid Undset. Willa.

1562. **To Lydia [Lambrecht]**, Dec. 8, 1941; WCPM.

Sorry to learn of her mother's death. Could not write at the time because hand still in brace. Was preparing to go to California to be with Roscoe, then in hospital in serious condition. Spent the summer there and did not get back to New York until late fall. Not doing much Christmas shopping this year; is enclosing only a small check. Regrets not seeing her mother in recent years. Has lost many old friends as well as brother Douglass. Life has been difficult. Willa Cather.

1563. **To Fanny Butcher**, n.d. [Dec. 1941?]; Newberry.

Hand somewhat stiff from months in steel brace, but almost well. Wishing her a merry Christmas. Willa Cather. [Note: At top of page appears a list of three books: Arthur Koestler, *Scum of the Earth*; W. L. White, *Journey for Margaret*; William L. Shirer, *Berlin Diary*.]

1564. **To Carrie Miner Sherwood**, Dec. 22, [1941?]; WCPM.

Is sending a book by William Allen White's son about military aircraft and minesweepers and such. Willie.

1565. **To Sister Agatha**, Dec. 23, 1941; UNL, copy, not original.

Yes, remembers *Toby Tyler*, which her grandmother used to read to her and her brothers when they were little. Did she ever read *Talking Leaves?* — a small, square book in similar format from same publisher. Enjoyed her students' newspaper. Wishing her a cheerful and holy Christmas, though it is hard to be cheerful these days. Willa Cather.

1566. **To Sigrid Undset,** Christmas Eve [Dec. 24, 1941]; Oslo.
Flowers she sent brightened the day. Has not felt so excited about Christmas since childhood. Maybe Churchill [who had come to confer with Roosevelt after the recent bombing of Pearl Harbor] traveled by reindeer like Santa Claus. His presence and his shrewd, searching gaze would wither political pettiness. He knows the American idiom from his mother, and American politicians will realize he is sharper than they are. His coming is almost a miracle. Reminds her that the battle cry of the Crusaders was "God with us!"

1567. **To Mary Willard,** Dec. 26, [1941], from New York; Amherst.
Enjoyed the wreath she sent, which brought back many memories. Willa.

1568. **To [Carrie Miner Sherwood],** n.d. [possibly late 1941 or early 1942, when Carrie and Mary were spending the winter together after both widowed], fragment without salutation; WCPM.
Recovering from influenza. Will write soon, but not about the unhappy things. Thinks of her and Mary often. Willie.

1569. **To Mrs. Ackroyd,** Dec. 27, 1941; UVa.
Treasuring the card and photograph [of Mrs. Anderson], taken when she was older, but recognizes her nonetheless. Yes, remembers her Uncle Snowden clearly. Remembers once when she was about five years old, when she and Marjorie had gone to visit at Mrs. Ackroyd's grandmother's house on Timber Ridge, a heavy rainstorm came up and Snowden rode up on his horse and took her home riding in front of him on his cavalry saddle. Willa Cather.

1570. **To Sigrid Undset,** Saturday [Jan. 24, 1942], [with a clipping from the *Commercial Advertiser*, Red Cloud, Nebr., dated Monday Jan. 5, 1942: "'Bob' Smith Shoots Down Four Jap Planes."]; Oslo.
Has been thinking about Undset since reading her *Elleve Aar,* or *The Longest Years.* [*Elleve Aar,* literally "eleven years," was an autobiographical novel about Undset's childhood. It was first published in English translation

in 1935, titled *The Longest Years.*] Was in France in 1937 when the translation appeared, but had not read it until now. Would like to ask about
many things in the book. Can claim that in one way she surpassed Undset
in childhood, in that when she was seven, she could sew quite well! Was
pleased to read that on Christmas Day a Nebraska boy had taken down
four Jap planes—even more pleased to discover he was Bob Smith from
Red Cloud, who had gone to school with her nieces. Liked his cable to
his father [quoted in the clipping: "Just arrived from Kumming. Came
through both battles of Rangoon safely. Knocked down four ships personally. Happy New Year."]. There are millions of American boys like him, but
not from big cities. Please come spend an evening as soon as their siege of
visitors from the West is lifted.

1571. **To Ferris Greenslet,** Feb. 16, 1942; Harvard.

Has received his letter but wants to think about proposal from Reader's
Book Club. Not sure she wants her income increased, with income tax
taking so much of it. Believes this would cut into regular sales. News
from England very bad. Wonders if even Churchill is losing his strength.
Undset's book about escape from Norway and journey through Russia is
extraordinary. Wishes she had titled it more simply. Willa Cather. P.S.: *Has*
thought about it and does not agree.

1572. **To Mary Miner Creighton,** Feb. 19, 1942; WCPM.

Please tell Carrie, will write as soon as possible. Was selecting some books
from her shelf to send to military camps and found the enclosed about
Prague; thought they would enjoy it. Has read Sigrid Undset's book about
escape from Norway and except for the title likes it very much. Undset
found Russia simply filthy but managed to take an interest in it nonetheless. Fears there will be strong public reaction against Undset's admiration
for Japan, but she will not take back what she believes. Willie.

1573. **To Benjamin Hitz,** Feb. 21, 1942; Newberry.

Appreciates his sending Father Petit's letters. Has quite a collection of
letters from missionary priests. Willa Cather.

1574. **To Mrs. Sidney Florance,** Feb. 23, [1942]; Newberry.

Enclosing two form letters regarding the Myra Hess Fund, to which she
is a regular contributor. Willa.

1575. To Irene Miner Weisz, Feb. 27, 1942; Newberry.

Enclosing a letter from Mary Virginia describing her move to Chattanooga. When the only orthopedic surgeon in the city was called away to the Army, the hospital wrote to the orthopedic hospital in New York and they recommended Richard Mellen. Going south seems like regressing to a more primitive place, but physicians have assured her it is a good move. Will miss her dreadfully; often a cheering presence when feeling down. Will miss her help with shopping and scouting out sales. Please share this with Carrie and Mary. Willie.

1576. To Irene Miner Weisz, Apr. 18, 1942; Newberry.

Enjoyed her visit, but next day was found to have 102.8 degree fever and sent straight to the hospital. Had an inflamed gall bladder. Doctor wants to operate, but since fever is gone now prefers to wait. Doesn't see how she can come to Red Cloud as planned. Hates feeling defective. News from Roscoe [who had pneumonia in March, according to letter and telegram from brother Jack] is encouraging. He is able to sit up. Willie.

1577. To Mr. Birnbaum, Apr. 18, 1942; AAAL.

Sorry to be late responding to his request for materials for Academy archive. Is sending the first page of the first draft of *Death Comes for the Archbishop*. Does not have a first edition. Please return the page when he can. Willa Cather.

1578. To Mrs. George Whicher, Apr. 22, 1942; PM.

Was in hospital with a bad throat and high temperature when her letter came. Right hand doing well now, under Dr. Ober's care. Did she get to hear Jack sing at St. Paul's Chapel March 15? Was in the hospital then, so couldn't go. Surprised to hear Jack is studying law, though his innate brightness will surely enliven the level of law practice in this country. Life is so hectic nowadays, with the stressfulness of world events. Willa Cather. P.S.: Understands she met Sigrid Undset at Mount Holyoke. Glad American readers have been willing to read Undset's *Return to the Future* in spite of its praise for Japan. Undset liked the cleanness and elegance of the Japanese, in contrast to the dirtiness of the Russians. *Gunner's Daughter* [*Kristin Lavransdatter*, 1927?] probably her best book. W. S. C.

1579. **To Zoë Akins,** Apr. 28, [1942], from New York; Huntington.

Roses and camellias arrived just as she was giving a dinner party for an old friend and gave a magic touch to the occasion. Roscoe has been ill again, this time with pneumonia, and nearly died. Hasn't been able to go see him because has been in hospital herself. Roscoe really the only family she has left; other two brothers not close. [Doesn't mention sister.] March and April terrible months to live through. Hope she continues enjoying her house and garden. Willa.

1580. **To Martin Birnbaum [American Academy of Arts and Letters] [from Sarah J. Bloom, secretary],** Apr. 20, 1942; AAAL.

Cather could not find a first edition of *Death Comes for the Archbishop*. Instead, is sending a copy of the first printing in Swedish. Sarah J. Bloom, Secretary.

1581. **To Mrs. Arthur J. McElhone [American Academy of Arts and Letters] [from Sarah J. Bloom, secretary],** Apr. 28, 1942; AAAL.

Cather unable to locate an early photograph of herself. Is sending one supplied by her niece, Virginia Auld. Please return it. Sarah J. Bloom, Secretary.

1582. **To Whit Burnett,** Apr. 29, 1942; Princeton.

Sorry not to have replied to his letter, but has been out of town [?]. Does not give permission for her stories to be in collections even when editors are old friends. Willa Cather. [Burnett replied by asking to use "Two Friends" in *This Is My Best* since it had already been anthologized. On July 6, 1942, Alfred Knopf wrote that she would probably prefer to be represented by "Neighbor Rosicky."]

1583. **To Sigrid Undset,** n.d. [May 14, 1942]; Oslo.

Please come to dinner at seven on Saturday. Sorry for the short notice, but is on a tight schedule. Is beginning to feel like herself again, and no longer dismal. Would love to see her.

1584. **To Sigrid Undset,** Wednesday [June 3, 1942]; Oslo.

Please come to dinner at seven on Saturday, June 6, if she is in town. Seeing Undset again would be a great joy. Is not an invalid now!

1585. **To Mabel Dodge Luhan [from Sarah J. Bloom, secretary],** July 28, 1942; Beinecke.

Cather has undergone surgery for removal of gall bladder and appendix. Will be at Presbyterian Hospital until August 15. Registered under Edith Lewis's name, so no letters should be sent there and she does not want flowers, as she finds it distressing to see them neglected.

1586. To Viola Roseboro', Aug. 29, 1942; UVa.

Hopes Miss Bloom let her know about the operation. Did read the manuscript she had sent. In first reading of chapter on Jerry Macauley entirely misread her purpose and wondered why not a clearer picture, with details. Then realized her intention was to give the subjective effect Macauley had on her, a different matter. Reading it that way, enjoyed it a great deal. Hopes her eyes are better and heat not bothersome. Willa Cather.

1587. To Ferris Greenslet, Sept. 7, 1942; Harvard.

Summer was dreary, with surgery for gall bladder and appendix on July 24. Has lost twelve pounds, from 122 to 110. Clothes all useless. Hopes to spend October at Stockbridge, Massachusetts. Until this year, had not been in the hospital since tonsils were removed sixteen years ago [not true]. Please call if he is in town later in the month. Telephone number Regent 4-8354. Greetings to Mrs. Greenslet. Willa Cather.

1588. To Carrie Miner Sherwood [from Sarah J. Bloom, secretary], Sept. 7, 1942; WCPM.

Hoping she received check for the Ladies Guild of Grace Church written shortly before entering the hospital. Cancelled check has not come back.

1589. To Carrie Miner Sherwood, Sept. 9, 1942, on same page as no. 1588; WCPM.

Thinks about her and about Red Cloud but is not able to travel. Surgery went well, but recovery difficult. Very little appetite. Has lost fourteen pounds, from 124 to 110. Doctor sending her to the Berkshires for October, a much shorter train ride from New York than Red Cloud. Edith will go along. Willie.

1590. To Julian Street, Sept. 21, 1942; Princeton.

Has not written because of the war, gall bladder surgery, and difficult recovery. Miserable weather has held her back. Has lost eighteen pounds. Is going to the Berkshires to recover. Willa Cather.

1591. To Carrie Miner Sherwood, Friday [Sept. 1942]; WCPM.

Appreciates her letter. She mustn't worry. Lost fifteen pounds, from 126 to 111, and is still weak but nausea gone. Will surely recover faster now. Willie. P.S.: While in bed, kept thinking about old friends – in the words of the hymn, "whom I have loved long since, and lost awhile."

1592. To Allan Nevins, Sept. 26, [1942]; Columbia.

His letter came while she was in the hospital, but enjoyed reading it afterward. Glad to hear about the Auvergnat priest who liked her book. Willa Cather.

1593. To Julian Street, Oct. 1, 1942; Princeton.

Appreciates his good wishes. It must have been even worse for Mrs. Street, recovering in Tucson in 108 degree weather. Won't be going to the Berkshires after all, but will be at the Williams Inn in Williamstown through November. Will register under the name Winifred Carter. Willa Cather.

1594. To Sigrid Undset, Oct. 23, [1942], from the Williams Inn, Williamstown, Mass.; Oslo.

What a heartwarming little book! [Undset's memoir for children *Happy Times in Norway,* published by Knopf in 1942] It flooded her with memories of days when the world was free, and the beautiful, variegated pattern of different countries lay under a sky undarkened by death. Spent a dreary summer drearily, hospitalized four weeks for removal of gall bladder. Has had a slow recuperation, which has tried her patience. Has been here in the Berkshires a few weeks, and has enjoyed the quiet. Will leave for Boston tomorrow.

1595. To Ferris Greenslet, Nov. 15, 1942, from New York; Harvard.

Has just come back from several weeks in Williamstown, Massachusetts. Would have gone to Jaffrey, but the train ride would have been more tiring. Housekeeper ill; getting along as best they can with only a cleaning woman and man. Curtains all down and furniture in dust covers. Please delay his visit until later in the month. Willa Cather. P.S.: No, met Woodberry only at 148 Charles Street. Once went with him to call on Amy Lowell, who, after having invited him to see some manuscripts by Keats, did not show him a one.

1596. To Carrie Miner Sherwood, Nov. 15, 1942; WCPM.

Thanks for sending the bittersweet [pieces of a vine]. Has just returned from three weeks at Williamstown. Unfortunately, housekeeper is ill; have only a cleaning woman three days a week and a house man to do heavy work. Having to eat all meals out. Is still not gaining weight. Can bear anything if only the Expeditionary Force routs Rommel out of Egypt. Everything will be better once the Mediterranean is liberated. Willie.

1597. To Sigrid Undset, Monday [Nov. 23, 1942]; Oslo.

Received her letter before she left Williamstown. Is amazed she was able to coax the gardenia plant into a second bloom. Has never been able to do so herself. War news is looking hopeful. Looks forward to seeing her. Housekeeper has been ill, but they've had rugs and curtains out for cleaning and the apartment is getting back to normal.

1598. To Alexander Woollcott, Dec. 1, [1942?], from 570 Park Avenue, New York; Harvard.

Will write a proper letter on December 6 and make the suggestions he asks for. Has only recently come home from the hospital. Willa Cather.

1599. To Zoë Akins, Dec. 4, [1942?]; Huntington.

Didn't tell her when they spoke on the telephone last summer that reason for going into the hospital was to have gall bladder and appendix removed. Operation went well, but recovery difficult. Went from 126 pounds to 110. Dreadful heat during August and September made matters worse. Is now feeling better and up to about 115, but still hasn't felt like shopping and dresses all too big. She has surely realized something was wrong for some time; recalls her asking once if she had offended in some way. Of course, they have always had different ideological views, but it's true, was cross and irritable. Hopes to develop greater patience now, maybe even with filmmakers who take advantage of fine old books. [some of letter cut away] Likes a good film, such as Noel Coward's, but absolutely hates filmed versions of classics. Anyway, Happy New Year. Willa.

1600. To Alexander Woollcott, Dec. 5, 1942; PM.

Has also been in the hospital recently, having her gall bladder removed. Wishes the surgeon hadn't insisted on Presbyterian Hospital. Appreciates his sending her the Nolans' letter. Glad to hear Robert located a church and served mass. Isn't a Catholic, but believes spirituality is helpful. Believes the anthology for soldiers should have lively material such as they liked reading themselves when they were eighteen or nineteen. Sarah Orne Jewett too quiet and subtle. Young people want to read something that seems like real life to them. Aren't interested in style and form. Hard to think of what would be good. Classic American literature too far removed from present-day experience, and new books often too preoccupied with social problems. They might like some of the early Robert Frost or even some of Longfellow's poems. Perhaps simply an edition of *Huckleberry Finn* would be best – the most thoroughly American book ever written. Glad he likes *Sapphira and the Slave Girl*, and particularly glad he liked the epilogue, which retells one of her most important actual memories. Still vividly remembers the moment when Nancy entered the room where her mother and Grandmother Boak and she were waiting, and remembers the afternoons she spent in the kitchen with Nancy, her mother, and Grandmother Boak. [Note: No mention of Cather's mother.] Willa Cather.

1601. To Viola Roseboro', Dec. 18, 1942; Amherst.

Has just returned from Williamstown, from an inn she had heard was pleasant. Enjoyed the stay, though weather not very good. Enjoyed the college students and escaped recognition except by a professor from Shepherdstown, Virginia, near Winchester, who wrote that he had recognized her accent. Had thought it was gone long ago. Has gained back from 110 to 115 pounds. Nerves needed a rest, and solitude was good. Willa Cather. P.S.: Christmas will be happy only if there are victories in Africa.

1602. To Elizabeth Shepley Sergeant, Dec. 18, 1942; PM.

Sorry to have been out of touch so long. Had gall bladder and appendix removed in July, and heat of summer made recovery difficult. Lost eighteen pounds, from 128 to 110, then lost more after leaving hospital. Spent October in Williamstown, a nice college town, but weather was wet and couldn't get exercise. Has gained back to 115, but still has no clothes that fit and doesn't feel like shopping. Maid is ill, so no one to answer the phone, but being shut off from the world this way is beneficial. Has been trying to catch up on correspondence. Finds it nerve-wracking to be so behind. Willa S. C.

1603. To [Josephine Frisbie?], 1942, Christmas card; WCPM.

Wishing a happy, though it can't be merry, Christmas to her friends at the mill. Willa Cather.

1604. To Stephen Tennant, Dec. 22, 1942, from New York, telegram; Yongue.

Sending Christmas wishes. Willa Cather.

1605. To Irene Miner Weisz, Dec. 26, [1942]; Newberry.

Homemade jam and marmalade delightful. Lost a great deal of weight in the hospital and cook has been ill since October. Not conducive to regaining her weight. Many thanks. Willie.

1606. To Sigrid Undset, Dec. 27, [1942]; Oslo.

The narcissus she sent for Christmas was like a promise of spring, reminded her of Schubert's "Dream of Spring in Winter" [from Die *Winterreise*, 1827]. Has had a strange Christmas, both secretary and housekeeper ill for weeks and she and Miss Lewis on their own, with just a cleaning woman and a part-time housekeeper. Does not really mind washing dishes, but it keeps her from other things. Has not regained full strength, but has gained five pounds and can at last enjoy eating again, after months of feeling repelled by food even though hungry. This explains her seclusion recently.

1607. To Laura Hills, Dec. 29, [1942]; PM.

Very happy to receive her letter. Dr. Ober's brace cured the damaged tendon in her right thumb, after ten months of having no use of it. Even slept in the brace. Likes her "Hurricane" picture a great deal. Misses niece Mary Virginia, with her husband at an Army camp in Colorado, but enjoys her nice letters. She and Edith Lewis have no maid at present, so she spends most of her working time in the kitchen. Willa Cather.

1608. To Hendrick Van Loon, Jan. 1, 1943; Cornell.

Appreciates his note and accompanying Biblical message. Friendly gestures especially important these days. Enjoys knowing others who refuse to believe the war is putting an end to all the values of the past three thousand years. Feels glad to have lived and learned the little she has about human history. The war has destroyed a great deal, but not everything. Willa Cather.

1609. To Alexander Woollcott, Dec. 4, 1943 [actually Jan. 4, 1943?]; Harvard.
Was away two weeks at Christmas [?]. Wants him to know she had no personal reason for reluctance to approve using an excerpt in his anthology, but prefers to leave such matters to Alfred Knopf, who was out of town when second request, dated December 10, came. Wishing him a happy new year, although it seems unlikely to be possible. Sometimes wonders why human life was put on the planet at all. Willa Cather.

1610. To Mary Willard, Jan. 10, [1943]; Amherst.
So good of her to keep up May's old custom of sending a Christmas wreath. Tried to send a telegram the day after Christmas, but operator would not accept anything not related to war or business. Had four difficult months following surgery and lost sixteen pounds, but is herself again now. Willa.

1611. To Zoë Akins, Friday night [Feb. 5, 1943]; Huntington.
Appreciated the turkey she sent. Tried to send a telegram, but they wouldn't accept it. The night they carved it they had a guest from Pittsburgh and opened some champagne from Alfred Knopf. Enjoyed cold turkey tonight and will have turkey hash tomorrow. The apricot jam looks lovely. Gratefully, Willa.

1612. To Ferris Greenslet, Friday [prob. Feb. 5, 1943]; Harvard.
Dislikes Doubleday ad in the newspaper [not in file]. Willa Cather.

1613. To Ferris Greenslet, Feb. 6, 1943; Harvard.
Enclosing a letter from Curtice Hitchcock. Might he find a copy of the reproduction of Dickens's *A Christmas Carol* published by Atlantic Monthly Press in 1920? Willa Cather. P.S.: Enjoyed his visit.

1614. To Helen [Sprague?], Feb. 20, 1943; WCPM.
Her Christmas card was a reminder to write. Missed her three years ago when in New York at Christmas; was in hospital with damaged right hand. Then Roscoe had heart attack, and went to California to be with him. So time passed. Hopes to go to Red Cloud before long, when fully recovered from surgery. Willa Cather.

1615. To Lydia [Lambrecht], Feb. 20, 1943; WCPM.
Sending a package of Christmas cards that she may be able to reuse or use for scrapbooks. Had a bad year, with gall bladder surgery, but it is behind her. Hopes the war will end soon. Willa Cather.

1616. To Ferris Greenslet, Feb. 24, 1943, telegram; Harvard.

Agrees to Heinemann proposal to release *My Ántonia* in the Oxford University Press series. Willa Cather.

1617. To Ferris Greenslet, Wednesday [Feb. 24, 1943?]; Harvard.

Checked with Alfred Knopf before sending telegram to make sure Heinemann offer did not conflict with a proposal relayed to her by Allan Nevins. W. S. C.

1618. To Carrie Miner Sherwood, n.d. [Mar. 5, 1943?]; WCPM.

Sending some money for the Webster County Red Cross. Feeling better again. Yehudi and Nola and their two children live nearby, and they add to her life. Willie.

1619. To Bishop George Beecher, Mar. 7, 1943; UNL, copy, not original.

Sorry not to have answered his two letters more fully. Recovery from gallbladder surgery has been difficult. Still not strong enough for the long train ride to Red Cloud, but has a little more energy than a few months ago. While in bed spent much of her time thinking about old friends. Willa Cather.

1620. To Mr. Phillipson, Mar. 15, 1943; WCPM.

Was pleased with his letter because he writes in good sentence structure. His high school teacher must have taught him well. As to "Paul's Case," once had a student in Latin class who was nervous and always trying to seem interesting, always hanging around actors in touring companies. The part about New York reflects her own feelings when first there. The part about jumping under the train entirely made up. Understands his desire for beauty, but if he has that desire he will find it in the artistic treasures of the world. Willa Cather.

1621. To Mrs. Flynn, [prob. c. Mar. 1943, following German surrender at Stalingrad], transcription made by E. K. Brown; Beinecke.

Sorry to be late replying to invitation to tea being held in the Jewett garden in May. Has many happy memories of that garden. Was last there three years before Mary Jewett's illness. Would be too painful to go there again. Sorry the village has not kept up the house where Sarah and Mary Jewett gathered such beautiful things. Similarly, Mme Franklin-Grout's estate in France, which was left as a retreat for women writers, was turned to other purposes by the French government right away and her Flaubert collection sent to a museum in Rouen that no longer exists. Tolstoi's estate has been damaged by the Germans. Sarah Orne Jewett still lives in her work.

1622. To Miss Masterson, Mar. 15, 1943; WCPM.

Her letter was marvelous, with a true sense of personality. People have been set traveling to Quebec by *Shadows on the Rock* and to New Mexico by *Death Comes for the Archbishop,* and now she to Virginia by *Sapphira and the Slave Girl.* Hasn't been back since completing it, or to Quebec since *Shadows* or New Mexico since *Archbishop.* Loses a place once she writes about it. Area around Timber Ridge and the Capon River is beautiful. Was very sad to see the double ess curve on the road up from Gore to the top of the ridge. Sorry to have seen Willow Shade in ruins; so pretty forty years ago, but then turned into an apartment house. Still remembers it as it was when Nancy came back. Grandmother really did take Nancy across the Potomac. Willa Cather.

1623. To Ferris Greenslet, Monday [Mar. 29, 1943?]; Harvard.

Appreciates the copy of *A Christmas Carol.* Has never been able to appreciate all of Dickens's books, but always liked this and *Great Expectations.* Has just reread it. Enjoyed retreating to the past. W. S. C.

1624. To Dorothy Canfield Fisher, Mar. 31, [1943]; UVt.

Read her article about France in the *Yale Review.* Meant to write but didn't know what to say and was down from appendix and gallbladder operation. Lost sixteen pounds. Recovering well now but sometimes wonders what is the purpose, when the world is being smashed up. Doesn't care to live to see the new world that is being promised. Willa. P.S.: But England and Churchill are admirable!

1625. To Sigrid Undset, Mar. 31, [1943]; Oslo.

Thanks for sending her retelling of the story of Thorgils and Thorfinn [*Bulletin of St. Ansgar's Scandinavian Catholic League of New York* no. 41, Feb. 1943: 1–6; summarizes the medieval Icelandic *Flóamanna Saga,* about hardships endured by early settlers of Greenland and the hero Thorgils's miraculous suckling of his orphaned infant]. Has read it twice. The courage and trials of the early Norse explorers seemed to exceed anything in human experience. Wonders why God lets the long battle in Africa go on.

1626. To Mrs. Field, Apr. 19, 1943; UVa.

Remembers her well though it was long ago. Sorry to hear Mr. Field has died and she has left Shepherdstown. Met a professor from Shepherdstown last fall. So now she is in Santa Barbara! Remembers that area as being very pleasant. Was there during mother's illness. Sorry not to be able to write by hand, but has sprained the tendon of right hand. Willa Cather.

1627. To Mrs. [Mabel Beeson] Wyeth, Apr. 28, 1943; LincCity.

Appreciates her letter and would agree to receive her books and sign them, but the number of such requests has made this a chore. Hurt tendon of right thumb a few years ago when signing copies of a special edition of *Sapphira and the Slave Girl* and is more careful now. Will sign three loose pages and send them. Willa Cather.

1628. To Ferris Greenslet, May 3, 1943; Harvard.

Sending a request from Burges Johnson, who appears to think he will get anything he asks. He wants to use an entire chapter. Has referred him to Houghton Mifflin, but suggests they refuse. The College English Association has done some good things, but even for them does not care to let down protections around *My Ántonia*. Even this past year, with the war going on, it sold over 2,500 copies. Willa Cather.

1629. To Ferris Greenslet, May 24, [1943]; Harvard.

Please handle the enclosed request for information. W. S. C.

1630. To William Lyon Phelps, May 29, 1943; Beinecke.

Appreciates his telling her J. M. Barrie's comment about *A Lost Lady*. Had little direct contact with Barrie because of his shyness. First heard through another person that he liked *Death Comes for the Archbishop*. Then heard he would like autographed copy of *My Ántonia*. A similar pleasure was hearing through Stephen Tennant that Thomas Hardy's widow said Hardy liked *A Lost Lady*. Willa Cather.

1631. To Carl Van Vechten, June 6, 1943; Beinecke.

Did not receive his letter for a while because the doormen at her apartment house took the stationery to be an advertisement. Thus, missed his tea. Very sorry. Willa Cather.

1632. To Lt. Harrison T. Blaine, June 9, 1943; Jaffrey, copy at WCPM.

Enjoyed his letter and is glad he wrote. Interesting that his mother owns High Mowing. Wrote much of the later part of *My Ántonia* in a tent at the bottom of the hill between there and Stony Brook Farm, when Mrs. Robinson owned the property. Was staying at the Shattuck Inn and would go up the road and through the hedge to the tent. Would go back to the inn at midday through the woods, where there was an abundance of lady's-slipper and Hookers' orchid. [Varieties of both lady's-slipper and wild orchid are marked in Cather's personal copy of Mathews's *Field Book of American Wild Flowers* at the HRC.] Once saw a fox. Glad he loves both High Mowing and the book that was partly written there. Has not gone to the inn much since the woods were damaged by a hurricane. Willa Cather.

1633. To Carrie Miner Sherwood, June 9, 1943; WCPM.

Taking time out from responding to soldiers' letters to indulge in the pleasure of writing to her and Irene. *My Ántonia* is twenty-five years old now. It did not sell many copies at first but kept growing and steadily sells four to six thousand a year (though not this past year). *Archbishop* sells more, but its special appeal to Catholics inflates the market. Moviemakers keep wanting *Ántonia*, but won't sell it. Had to fight Alexander Woollcott when he wanted to put it into an anthology. Allowed the Readers' Union in England, which serves veterans of the First World War who missed out on higher education, to put out a paperback edition of 20,000 a few years ago, now out of print. Doesn't mean to brag, but feels proud and happy that people still care about the book. Hopes it is a satisfaction for her as well. Enclosing a letter from a Lt. Harrison Blaine that she would like to have back. Willie

1634. To Ferris Greenslet, June 9, 1943; Harvard.

Enclosing a letter written many years ago by Mr. W. C. Brownell to Viola Roseboro' in which he commented on *My Ántonia*. It shows his sensitive reading of a book very unlike the eighteenth-century writers he generally cared for. Please return it. Willa Cather.

1635. To Carrie Miner Sherwood, Friday 18 [June 1943]; WCPM.

Very pleased to receive the article about Bishop Beecher. Is leaving next week for Maine, a place on the ocean north of Portland. Needs to escape business details of new editions coming out in England. Can't go to Grand

Manan because food so restricted now. Has lost back to 112 pounds. Wishes Mary Virginia were still here. Willie.

1636. **To Helen Cather Southwick,** July 22, 1943, from Asticou Inn, Northeast Harbor, Maine, extract made by E. K. Brown; Beinecke.
Please do not send any of her letters on to her brothers and sisters, who usually seem to misunderstand her.

1637. **To Bishop George Allen Beecher,** Aug. 13, [1943], from Asticou Inn, Northeast Harbor, Maine; UNL, copy, not original.
Saw the tribute to him in the *World Herald*. Especially enjoyed the photos. Has had a trying summer, with New York heat, but is enjoying the cool weather here. Food scarce. Sorry to write with such a poor pen. Willa Cather.

1638. **To Carrie Miner Sherwood,** Sept. 18, 1943, from New York; WCPM.
Enclosing two letters from Mary Virginia to explain why she cannot come to Red Cloud. Felt energetic while in the cool climate of Maine, but returned to New York to find summer heat lingering on and the apartment a mess. Without a good maid to take over, wore herself out cleaning the place. Has lost five pounds again. Also, found that travel is very difficult these days. Very sorry not to be coming to visit. Did she receive the long letter about *Ántonia*? Sorry to hear about Willard Crowell's accident. Please don't tire herself out with Red Cross work, and maybe they can have some time together before long. Willie.

1639. **To Laura Hills,** Sept. 23, 1943; PM.
Sorry to have to send her a typed letter. Had a wet summer in Maine. Left the New York heat in June for Portland, which she remembered as being very pleasant, but with all the shipbuilding going on it is miserable. So they went to the Asticou Inn in Northeast Harbor, which was cool but rainy. Bar Harbor is practically deserted. Hitler has ruined the New World as well as Europe. Is looking forward to a visit from her niece in October and Yehudi and Nola Menuhin with their two children after that. Will share a letter from them about their recent tour of South America. Yehudi has been to England to entertain soldiers, went over on bomber. Willa Cather.

1640. To Ferris Greenslet, n.d. [prob. Oct. 1943; written at bottom of his letter dated Oct. 5, 1943, mentioning a check enclosed]; Harvard.
Why no check? Will write tomorrow. W. S. C.

1641. To Houghton Mifflin Company, Oct. 14, 1943 [typed form letter supplied by Ferris Greenslet with letter showing the same date; postscript added in Cather's hand]; Harvard.
Gives permission to print copies of her books published by Houghton Mifflin with a second publisher shown as distributor, under War Production Board Order L 245 and Interpretation no. 1 of that order. Other aspects of contract with H.M. to remain the same. Willa Cather. P.S.: Agrees to Literary Classics, Inc. as the least objectionable cooperating "publisher," though dislikes their advertising.

1642. To Patrick Anthony Lawlor, Oct. 20, 1943; Columbia.
Yes, he may use her essay on Katherine Mansfield. Will forward the request to Knopf, since the publisher's consent is also necessary. Willa Cather.

1643. To Ferris Greenslet, Oct. 22, 1943; Harvard.
Has received two letters from him. Since he mentions he has been fishing, assumes he is well. The second [saying that they need to reprint *O Pioneers!* and would like to do so with another company's imprint along with their own on the title page in order to utilize that company's quota of paper, under wartime rationing] is most unwelcome. Why should her books be victimized, since they are not long and do not sell huge numbers? Understands that in England the system is to trim down popular hits in order to protect small-market books. This might mean, for example, trimming part of the margin off *The Robe* [Douglas] to save paper for printing Julian Huxley or T. S. Eliot. Is not signing the consent form he sent. Willa Cather.

1644. To Mary Miner Creighton, Oct. 30, 1943;. UVa.
Sending her annual checks for the guild at the Episcopal church and for the Red Cross. Is it true that the Old Age Pension in Nebraska has been cut? If so, will increase amount to several older people there. Rationing a real bother and the quality of food often poor after one manages to get it. Mary Virginia is in town and a cheering presence, as ever. People do need cheering up these days! Terrible things happening to people she knows in England, and friends in France have been killed or are missing. Willie.

1645. To Ferris Greenslet, Oct. [?], 1943, transcription made by E. K. Brown; Beinecke.

Returned from Philadelphia today and began to read in his book [*Under the Bridge*]. It shows what an interesting and enjoyable life he has had, without being too familiar in tone. Appreciates what he says about her. Agrees with most of his comments about writers, but not about Sydnor Harrison, who always seemed like a shallow journalist to her. Willa Cather. P.S.: Shouldn't spelling of scientist Zinsser be Zinsner?

1646. To Sigrid Undset, Dec. 8, [1943]; Oslo.

Enjoyed her article in the *New York Times Book Review* about the lost books of childhood. Would like to see her. Could she come to dinner at seven on Saturday? If she can, please telephone between one and two o'clock; the number is Regent 4-8354.

1647. To [Carrie Miner Sherwood?], 1943, Christmas card; WCPM.

Only the one shown here gave life any value. Willie.

1648. To Irene Miner Weisz, n.d. [pm. Dec. 19, 1943], Christmas card; Newberry.

Wishes she could go with her to Mexico. Willie.

1649. To Mr. Phillipson, Dec. 23, 1943; WCPM.

No, Thea Kronborg was modeled on a singer; was well acquainted with her. Yes, much of the required reading in schools was dull, such as *Silas Lapham* [Howells] and *The House of the Seven Gables* [Hawthorne]. Doesn't agree that *Silas Marner* [Eliot] is dull, despite slow pace. Conveys much of England itself. Willa Cather.

1650. To Arthur Train [President, National Institute of Arts and Letters], Dec. 23, 1943; AAAL.

Is delighted to accept the Institute's Gold Medal for fiction. Sorry to be late replying, but was away. Willa Cather.

1651. To Bishop George Beecher, Dec. 25, 1943, Christmas card; HSNeb.

[Written beneath the cover picture of Canterbury Cathedral:] A bulwark of civilization for more than thirteen centuries. [Written under printed greeting inside:] He is still her bishop, though retired. Willa Cather. [Written on left side, opposite printed greeting:] Has been rereading the Venerable Bede. Seem to be nearing a world lacking Christianity, which will mean putting out the light, leaving nothing but darkness and misery.

1652. To Sigrid Undset, n.d. [Dec. 25, 1943]; Oslo.

Is delighted with the lovely white calla lilies she sent, but it has been a terrible Christmas; feels impending horrors unparalleled and unknown. For the first time in her life feels afraid of the future – of losing everything she cherished in the world and all the finest youth of the world. The most devilish thing in the world is the cold pride of science, the absolute enemy of happiness. Please forgive such a dreary note for Christmas Day, but it is a dark time. [The horrors referred to are probably the report of the previous day's effort by some 1,300 U.S. bombers to knock out German secret weapons sites.]

1653. To Elizabeth Shepley Sergeant, Dec. 31, 1943; PM.

Hand is in brace again, so can't write. Many things have kept her distracted. Nieces in town looking for places to live while husbands in the military – one of them with a baby; no maid when they got back from Maine; five books out in military editions and a consequent flood of letters from soldiers. Tried to send Christmas notes for the first time in several years, and strain on hand put it back into brace. Feels worried about her since the cold weather set in. Hopes she is in town. Is still eighteen pounds underweight and feels the cold. Is cranky toward her friends sometimes and doesn't deserve the favor of a real letter, but please just drop a note. Willa Cather.

1654. To Irene Miner Weisz, Dec. 31, 1943; Newberry.

Greatly appreciates pudding she sent, which conveys real friendship. Has had a difficult year. Three old friends in Pittsburgh died, and has not heard from Carrie in a long time. Must have hurt her feelings or offended her in some way. Really did mean to go to Red Cloud in the fall, but coming back from Maine to find no household help was daunting. Didn't get anyone until November 1, and then had problems. Mary Virginia's visit helped, but only because she kept her distance, stayed at a hotel and only dropped by for brief visits. Sad, but any kind of pleasure or emotional excitement is exhausting. Nerves seem messed up since the operation. Would be impossible to go to Red Cloud, where there would be such emotional strain, both happy and troubling, not to mention scoffers like Helen Mac. Afraid she would cry all the time. Elsie has made things hard, too. [sentence blacked out] No use saying any more about that. All together, things have been difficult. Has received a nice letter from Mary, who says there are two sides to every story, which is true. Carrie seems to have given up on her. Wishing her a happy winter in Mexico and hopes she will come to New York next spring. Then she can see for herself how things are. Willie.

1655. **To Ferris Greenslet [from Sarah J. Bloom, secretary], Jan. 3, 1944; Harvard.**
Cather having difficulty with her hand. Was working on something she enjoyed and overdid it. Will take up business correspondence again soon.

1656. **To Fred Otte, Jan. 17, 1944; WCPM.**
Appreciated the letter, but he needs to work on writing more clearly. Willa Cather.

1657. **To Mrs. George Whicher, Jan. 24, 1944; PM.**
Sorry not to have written in so long. The world is all in distress, everyone's lives disrupted. All the young people in her family caught up in the war. Mary Virginia and husband, Dick Mellen, at Camp Carson in Colorado, and her brother at a camp in Arizona, one of the least attractive spots in the state. Enjoyed having Mary Virginia in town for a visit recently. Another niece's husband is commander of an aircraft carrier in the Pacific. Everyone lives in suspense. Will paste their Christmas card with picture of Beacon Street into Annie Fields's *Memories of a Hostess*. Doesn't understand why Boston has messed up the area around Trinity Church. Spent last summer in Maine; very comfortable in spite of poor food. Wishing them a happy new year. Willa Cather. P.S.: Has sprained right hand again and is back in Dr. Ober's brace.

1658. **To Helen Cather Southwick, Feb. 12, 1944, extract made by E. K. Brown; Beinecke.**
Recalls meeting Paul Robeson at the Menuhins' apartment when Yehudi was fourteen. Wondered if she was going to feel the effects of her southern heritage [because of race], but once she came into the presence of the man all she thought about was his greatness. Recalls seeing Robeson and Uta Hägen in *Otello*. She conceived and acted the part beautifully.

1659. **To Viola Roseboro', Feb. 12, 1944; UVa.**
Has thought of her often this winter, not just because of Ida Tarbell's death but because of the world's death. So glad Roseboro' was able to travel before this disaster of a war. Why did the world have to come to destruc-

tion in their lifetimes? and after they had already been through one war? Heard Sir James Jeans say humans want to believe the world will live forever, since they know they personally cannot. So why does their generation have to see this? Hasn't written because so many of her younger relatives have had their lives uprooted by the war. Hates to think of Nebraska boys off on Pacific islands, where the suffering is the worst. Human fallibility brought it on – or no, it was scientists who brought it on. Would like to come see her, but has not been well since gallbladder operation. Willa Cather.

1660. **To Elizabeth Shepley Sergeant,** Thursday [Mar. 9, 1944?]; UVa.
Glad she can come to dinner on Saturday March 18. Sorry for the sloppy handwriting, but hand still in the Ober brace. Willa Cather.

1661. **To Sinclair Lewis,** Mar. 22, 1944; WCPM.
Hasn't anything to contribute to Mr. Troxell's collection. Most of her handwritten drafts are destroyed. Has sold three, two to a collector in England, one to France. Has no idea whether they still exist. Asks Knopf to destroy final typed draft from which type is set. Supposes he does. Enjoyed seeing him. Willa Cather.

1662. **To Bishop George Beecher,** Mar. 28, 1944; UNL, copy, not original.
Appreciates his Christmas letter about his missionary travels in western Nebraska. Wonderful to think of this being done when the light is so dimmed in the world. Often thinks about Grace Church and her confirmation there. Hand collapsed shortly after Christmas, when she was happily working on something new. Inflamed sheath of the large tendon of the right thumb. Knows there are rumors in Red Cloud that her entire right arm is paralyzed, but that is not true. When people stop taking pleasure in other people's misfortunes there will not be any more wars. Willa Cather.

1663. **To Annie Pavelka,** Apr. 1, 1944; WCPM.
Sending a money order with best wishes for Easter. Is it possible she has not yet been able to cash the check sent at Christmas? A bad winter in New York. Has been unable to work for two months because of her hand. Misses her work. Willa Cather [typed, not signed].

1664. **To Josephine Frisbie,** Apr. 6, 1944; WCPM.
Sorry to be so slow answering her letter dated December 27. Was reminded

of it by notice of Charlie Platt's death in the Red Cloud newspaper. Glad she was able to visit him last summer. Wonders if the Amboy mill is still in operation. Still treasures the pictures of it she sent four years ago. Has hoped to get back to Red Cloud but doesn't feel up to the emotional jolt. Has she read John Hersey's *A Bell for Adano*? A very good book, shows integrity. Willa Cather.

1665. To Yaltah Menuhin, Apr. 14, 1944; Princeton.

Glad to get her letter and picture of her and Lionel. Will autograph a photo and send to her when hand is better. Glad she is maintaining her music and still doing concerts. Aunt Willa. P.S.: Hard to believe Lionel is seventeen months old!

1666. To Elizabeth Moorhead Vermorcken, May 5, 1944; PM.

Has to dictate this letter because of inflamed tendon in her right thumb; has hand in a brace again. Sorry to hear she had to escape Italy and leave her books behind. So sad to see the world destroyed like this. Glad to hear she thinks her [Cather's] books have stood the test of time. Especially glad to hear she still likes *The Professor's House*, which most people do not. Especially enjoyed writing it because of the structural experiment. Tried to use the Blue Mesa like an open window on the sea in a Dutch interior painting. Still remembers when they met, when she had read "Paul's Case" and came to call. That world is gone. Wishes they had been born in 1850 and missed the disasters of this century. Willa Cather.

1667. To Enit Kaufman, May 15, 1944; HRC.

Appreciates her interest and regards it as a compliment, but does not care to have her portrait painted for *American Portraits* [pub. Henry Holt, 1946]. Realizes Dorothy Canfield is involved in this effort as well, but even so, does not believe she belongs among the list of people it will include. They are much more public people. Learned from having her portrait published in *Good Housekeeping* about fifteen years ago that publicity brings interruptions. Willa Cather.

1668. To Dorothy Canfield Fisher, May 26, 1944; UVt.

So long since she heard from her! Is sending a copy of letter to a Mrs. Kaufman, who wanted her to sit for a portrait. Never again! Many family events have kept her occupied, let alone the war. Has been drawn back in by the family net. Now has three nieces and a nephew living nearby. Has had little energy since the gallbladder operation. Is worn out from constant housekeeping, now that all of New York is burning soft coal. Please help Mrs. Kaufman understand. Willa.

1669. To S. S. McClure, May 26, 1944; Indiana.

Very happy to see him last Friday. Would like to tell him sometime all the things that have kept her so preoccupied these past ten years. Supposes she can't visit him at his club, but he could come to the apartment or they could meet somewhere. Hates for him to think she is neglectful of her Chief. Willa Cather.

1670. To Bishop George Beecher, June 10, 1944; UNL.

How is it that retirement only meant he was taking up new work? Knew he would not be happy without working. He is a soldier for the Lord. Willa Cather.

1671. To Frank H. Woods, June 14, 1944; Beinecke, copy also at WCPM.

Was away in Quebec when his letter arrived. Enjoyed receiving it and re-membering his mother. Glad *My Ántonia* reminds him of Nebraska. Many people did not like it at first, but those who did liked it very much, and it gradually gained momentum. Brought her into correspondence with Thomas Masaryk for eight years. It is rather formless but captures her feeling for the area. Willa Cather.

1672. To Alfred Knopf, June 20, [1944]; HRC.

Shocked to learn of his father's death. Greatly respected him – as she also does Alfred. Thinks of them both as people of quality. Willa Cather.

1673. To Zoë Akins, Aug. 4, [1944], from Maine; Huntington.

Enjoyed receiving her card from the Southwest. They must have left New York about the same time. W. S. C. P.S.: Suggests she read *Army of Shadows* [by Joseph Kessel, published by Knopf in 1944].

1674. To Marie Adelaide Belloc Lowndes, Oct. 4, 1944; HRC.

Regrets her letter has been lying unanswered for two months. Has been in Grand Manan. New York is insupportable, and travel west is difficult because roads [i.e., railroads] almost totally occupied with military transport. Only place she could go for quiet was to the island, and no mail was forwarded. S. S. McClure now lives at the Union League Club in New York. His eruptive energy has dissipated, replaced by an overwhelming gentleness and calm. If the war ever ends, hopes to get back to London and see her. Childhood years in both France and England must have produced an interesting person! Willa Cather.

1675. To Ferris Greenslet, Oct. 13, 1944; Harvard.

Returned a week ago from vacation. Is glad to divide royalty from Armed Services edition of *My Ántonia* evenly. Puzzled by reference to a proposal for Spanish and Portuguese translations for marketing in South America, having heard from a friend that a translation was being made in Spain to be sold there. This proposal Greenslet presents doesn't sound very profitable. Let it go. Willa Cather.

1676. To Zoë Akins, Nov. 2, [prob. 1944]; Huntington.

Believes she shows good judgment in deciding to sell her house. Really too much for her to keep up alone. She and Edith have help only four hours a day and have to seek their dismal dinners out. Food is dreadful. What a war! Willa.

1677. To Irene Miner Weisz, Nov. 4, 1944; Newberry.

Enclosing clippings from the awarding of the Gold Medal of the National Institute of Arts and Letters. Enjoyed seeing some old friends at the ceremony. Imagine – Mr. McClure is eighty-seven! Willie.

1678. To Carrie Miner Sherwood, Nov. 9, 1944; WCPM.

Thanks for the box of bittersweet, which she has in a bowl in her bedroom. [several lines blacked out] Wishes they [?] would use Mari Sandoz's book instead of hers. Sandoz would like the publicity. Just wanted to warn her about these people. Willie. P.S.: Enclosing checks for the Red Cross and for the Ladies Guild of Grace Church.

1679. To Ferris Greenslet, Nov. 20, 1944; Harvard.

In response to proposal for a translation to be published by a house in Barcelona [mentioned by Greenslet in Nov. 17 letter], will think about it after she receives a Dun & Bradstreet report on them. Willa Cather by Sarah J. Bloom. P.S.: Right hand is hurt again.

1680. To Ferris Greenslet [from Sarah J. Bloom, secretary], Nov. 25, 1944; Harvard.
Cather's hand is again a problem, and she is unable to write. Enclosures are self-explanatory.

1681. To Ferris Greenslet [from Sarah J. Bloom, secretary], Dec. 9, 1944; Harvard.
Please return Archibald MacLeish's letter.

1682. To Fred Otte, Dec. 12, 1944; WCPM.
Glad to receive his birthday letter. Must find the steel industry energizing. Knows about dogs! Fanciers seem to take on the personalities of the different breeds. Collie lovers all sociable and sentimental. But beware Norwegian elkhounds! Anyone who stays around them will become snappish. Willa Cather.

1683. To [Lydia Lambrecht?], Dec. 12, 1944; WCPM.
Glad to hear from her. Was worried about the Amboy mill. Glad the Frisbie family is still running it. Willa Cather.

1684. To Professor Carl J. Weber, Dec. 12, 1944; Colby.
What he was told about her visit with Housman was incorrect. Hopes to write her own account of the event, to correct misinformation. Certainly Housman was not rude to her and her friends, though they deserved it for brashly dropping in without notice or invitation. Willa Cather.

1685. To Stephen Tennant, n.d. [late 1944]; Yongue, copy, not original.
Received his letter dated December 8, 1943, but the postmark is October 17, 1944. How can he ask what she thinks of Jane Austen and Emily Brontë? Anyone with good sense knows they are both wonderful, though in very different ways. Believes he would not like George Sand. She was a wordy, moralizing writer and almost never sincere. See "A Chance Meeting" in *Not Under Forty* re. George Sand. How can he say the public is never deceived? They always are! Not humanity in the long run; after two or three centuries the sound writers last, others don't. Those who last comprise the "great tradition." While ill, read Chaucer and he made her want to get well again. That's what a "great tradition" means. Why does he imagine she does not value critical writing? Is now going to talk to him very directly. Why did he begin *Lascar* if he wasn't going to persevere on it simply for the joy of doing so, not for any other reason? It's been ten years now.

Why hasn't he written it? Quit talking about it and just do it! W. S. C. P.S.: When he writes again, please leave a wider margin.

1686. To Irene Miner Weisz, n.d. [pm. Jan. 4, 1945]; Newberry.
Will treasure her letter. Right hand collapsed again, interrupting the writing of a new story. Is trying to rest it. Willie. [Irene's letter in a 1944 Christmas card said Cather's books had meant a great deal to her.]

1687. To Zoë Akins, Jan. 5, 1945; Huntington.
Don't worry that the turkey never came. Did receive the beautiful cyclamen. Would write by hand but it is bad again – just when she was greatly enjoying work on something new. Has plenty of time and has been thinking, has not only gotten a lot of what she wanted in life but has avoided things she mostly did not want: excess money, publicity, having to meet many people. Got plenty of that when she was editor of *McClure's*. Willa Cather.

1688. To Zoë Akins, Tuesday [pm. Jan. 6?, 1945]; Huntington.
Thanks for the beautiful camellias. Together with the cyclamen and a cyclamen from Nola and an orange tree from Yehudi, it has made her a private tropics in spite of winter outside. More snow last night. Hand still bad. Removes the brace two hours a day to work on a story that interests her greatly. Willa.

1689. To Irene Miner Weisz, Jan. 6, 1945; Newberry.
Has kept hoping to write a letter by hand, but has been in brace since December 16. Is afraid of losing the story she was enjoying working on. Cries every time she reads her letter. In the early days, when making her living in newspaper work or teaching and sending money to family, wrote for the joy of it. Over the years has managed to recapture many happy memories by writing. The world has been good to her, but Red Cloud has not. Hard to believe Helen McNeny would lecture on Granville Hicks, who built his career attacking her, in the Auld Library! Naturally, this delights people in Red Cloud who like to spend their time figuring out where she got everything in her books. Truth is, most of the time doesn't know – they just came to her, without her even realizing she wasn't making them up. Remembers how angry Mrs. Fred Garber was about *A Lost Lady;* she told Douglass she ought to have sued. Never meant to write about

Mrs. Garber, but in the shock of learning of her death the story came to her. Wrote an honest recording of feelings she evoked. Mustn't show this letter to the likes of Helen Mac! Willie.

1690. **To Sigrid Undset,** Jan. 6, 1945; Oslo.

Her Christmas remembrance was very kind and forgiving. Has thought of her so often. Living conditions deteriorate more each day. Miss Lewis can't even get a taxi to take her to Brooklyn to see her two sisters. The problem of finding servants is acute; their capable woman comes from ten until two to clean and prepare lunch, but for dinner they must cruise about town in search of food, and poor quality at that. Has been working on a story that very much interests her, but last week her right hand gave out again and she is back in Dr. Ober's brace. Isn't very philosophical about it. Will soon send Undset an early book of hers, which she thinks Undset might like despite its grave faults, which appeared in Danish and Swedish [probably 1918 edition of My Ántonia].

1691. **To Carl J. Weber,** Jan. 10, 1944 [actually 1945]; Colby, copy also at WCPM.

Can he find out where the writer of the report about Housman got his information? With a friend from Pittsburgh, called on him in Highgate at an address given them by his publisher. Saw him only the once. It was kind of him to see them. Willa Cather.

1692. **To Carrie Miner Sherwood,** Jan. 20, 1945; WCPM.

Is greatly enjoying the tulip-print dishtowel and napkins. Has been slow to write because sick with food poisoning. Has to eat most dinners out after Edith gets home about six and rests for a while. Irene's letter a special gift this Christmas. Misses Mary Virginia but enjoys having Helen Louise [Cather Southwick] nearby. Willie.

1693. **To Ferris Greenslet,** Jan. 24, 1945; Harvard.

Won't sign an agreement with a Spanish publisher now. Was ill with influenza two weeks, and hand causing trouble. Takes it out of brace two hours a day to write on a story in which she is very interested. Christmas was overeventful, so many letters from soldiers that they became emotionally wearing. Willa Cather.

1694. **To Carl J. Weber,** Jan. 31, 1945; Colby, copy also at WCPM.

No, don't try to trace the incorrect report about visit to Housman. Does not appreciate his pressing questions on her. Wishes she had not told him as much as she did. Prefers to keep her personal memories personal. Is leaving for Mexico City [not true] and this will end their correspondence. Willa Cather.

1695. **To Fanny Butcher,** Jan. 31, 1945; Newberry.

Enjoyed receiving her Christmas card. Had a nice visit to Northeast Harbor, Maine, during the summer and was able to write, but then her hand acted up again. Willa Cather.

1696. **To Mrs. George Whicher,** Jan. 31, 1945; PM.

Was glad to hear from her at Christmas. Appreciates old friends' remembrances. Yes, it was reasonable for her to quit her job. Most people's jobs are wrecked now anyway. Spends much of her time and energy writing to soldiers in foxholes who have written to her after seeing one of the Armed Forces editions. Spent the summer at Northeast Harbor, Maine, enjoying a little work. Still has occasional problems with right hand. It is tied up in Dr. Ober's brace again now, so can't write by hand. Willa Cather.

1697. **To Ferris Greenslet,** Jan. 31, 1945; Harvard.

Sorry to hear about Miss Lewison's manuscript; doesn't enjoy seeing appraisals of her work. He had better send it. Suspects the bibliography may not be complete as to translations. Probably she didn't know about the Hungarian *Shadows on the Rock,* for example. Enclosing a list for his own use. Willa Cather. [list attached]

1698. **To Elizabeth Shepley Sergeant,** Monday, Feb. 5, [1945?]; UVa.

Where is she? How is she? Worries about her during such cold weather. Hand is bad, and has many letters to write to soldiers who have read her books in Armed Forces Editions. Little time for personal letters. Please write. W. S. C.

1699. **To Stephen Tennant,** Feb. 16, 1945; Yongue.

Sorry not to have written in so long. Had many irritations during the Christmas season – numerous letters from soldiers to answer, hand very bad. Enough to make her quite misanthropic for a while. The company of Yehudi and his family cheered her up. Still can't write by hand. No need to quarrel because of differing views re. talking about books, as opposed to writing them. Finds the book he sent her at Christmas, *The Unquiet Grave*

[Connelly], excessively jaded. The frequent short quotations from Flaubert entirely misrepresent him. He was hearty and hardworking, never bored (though sometimes boring when he insists on putting in every detail). Willa Cather.

1700. To Ferris Greenslet, Feb. 26, 1945; Harvard.

Did not read the manuscript after all, and is returning it. Just having it about is bothersome. Would ask Isabelle to read it if she were still alive. Dislikes books being written about living authors. Willa Cather.

1701. To Elizabeth Shepley Sergeant, Thursday [Mar. 9 or 16, 1945?]; PM.

Hopes she can come to dinner on Saturday, March 18. Sorry to write such a scrawl; hand in brace. Glad she is in town. Willa Cather.

1702. To Ferris Greenslet, Mar. 20, 1945; Harvard.

Very nice of him to be so understanding about Miss Lewison's book. They can discuss it later. Willa Cather.

1703. To Fanny Butcher, Apr. 19, 1945; Newberry.

Very glad to hear from her. Amazing how active she is after such an illness. Wasn't up to work herself for a whole year after gallbladder operation, not until last summer in Maine. Wasn't able to write much during the winter, with interruptions and shortage of help, but did a lot of reading. Only good recent book she knows of is Hersey's *A Bell for Adano*. Wars don't nourish art. W. S. C.

1704. To Carrie Miner Sherwood, Apr. 29, [1945]; WCPM. Note: handwriting very irregular and scrawling.

Glad she used her time during Easter storm to write a letter. Is still having trouble with hand. Used brace almost all the time for four months starting a little before Christmas. Can't dictate her work, only letters. Is very interested in everything Carrie writes about grandchildren. Used Tony Luhan's last name (which he took because his Indian name would be too difficult for white people) for the owner of the mules in *Archbishop* but changed the spelling so it wouldn't be obvious. Of course, he didn't have the mules as in the book. Personally knew of a pair of white mules owned by Mexicans. Is she really overseeing all five farms, besides maintaining Red Cross work? Would very much like to come to Red Cloud, but has been emotionally weak ever since her operation. Still able to write, as evidenced by work on a new story last summer that she greatly enjoyed. With any emotional excitement has physical symptoms, can't sleep, and cries uncontrollably. Is letting Mariel Gere know she will not be coming for the fiftieth class anniversary. Excitement would be too much. Has had a happy winter, though shortage of domestic help makes life difficult. Enjoys having Helen Louise [Cather Southwick] nearby and enjoys the visits of Yehudi Menuhin and his wife. Willie.

1705. **To Stephen Tennant,** n.d.; Yongue, copy, not original.
[Quotes a sentence written by him on a postcard that she had apparently tucked into a copy of *Salammbô* eight years ago: "Marseilles in spring was wonderful – the foliage of the plane trees, the pink evening sky, the old skull-colored city: very wicked and old, with no regrets."] That sentence restores her confidence in *Lascar*. Tells more about Marseilles than anything in Joseph Conrad's *Arrow of Gold* – his weakest book, of course. This sentence is authentic. Willa Cather.

1706. **To Mariel Gere,** May 1, [1945], from New York; WCPM.
Would enjoy coming to the class reunion, but doctor forbids it. Was planning to go to Mexico City in June but had to cancel. Has had to avoid excitement since her gallbladder operation three years ago. Even a happy time would be too much for her. May come visit some time when it is quiet, nothing special going on. Tell others only that she is not well. Willa.

1707. **To Ferris Greenslet,** May 9, 1945; Harvard.
Glad to hear *My Ántonia* and *The Song of the Lark* keep selling so well. Believes *O Pioneers!* would, too, if Houghton Mifflin had not insisted on putting it out in a cheap edition a few years ago. Does he know whether Ford Madox Ford is still alive? Ford disseminated a misleading report of her and Isabelle's visit to A. E. Housman, and it keeps popping up. Members of Isabelle's family bothered by it. Expects to write her own account some time. Ford was often untruthful, but if still living won't say flatly that his report was a lie. Willa Cather.

1708. **To Sigrid Undset,** May 16, [1945]; Oslo.
The long agony is finally over, leaving a beautiful world destroyed. True peace will not return for a long time. The San Francisco "Conference" [April 25-June 26, to draft the charter of the United Nations] a pathetic

event. Her brother has been there, and everyone was irritable and hungry. Nothing to eat and journalists had to sleep on cots in the halls, but the Russians stayed on their battleships in the harbor, well provisioned with good wine and food – not taking chances, and is afraid they won't take chances in the future either. Please let them know when she plans to return to Norway; wants so much to see her again before she goes.

1709. **To Mr. Halter,** May 24, 1945; UVa.
Has no particular favorite among her books. Some carried out her plan for them better than others. Willa Cather.

1710. **To Carrie Miner Sherwood,** n.d. [1945?]; WCPM.
Leaving for Northeast Harbor, Maine very soon. Enclosing something for her to read. Willie.

1711. **To Lizzie [?],** June 14, 1945; WCPM.
Writes many letters to soldiers as a result of the Armed Forces Editions, but has meant to write to her for some time. Wonders if her son Richard is in the Army. Hasn't been very strong since the gallbladder operation. Often thinks how kind she was to her [Cather's] parents. Willa Cather.

1712. **To Dr. Garbat,** June 27, 1945; UVa.
His letter with good news about her blood count and information about the typical slow recovery from major surgery has greatly encouraged her. Won't be able to come in before she leaves town. Has been seeing her oculist and her dentist and time is full. Leaving soon for Northeast Harbor, Maine, for two months. Willa Cather.

1713. **To Whit Burnett [from Sarah J. Bloom, secretary],** July 5, 1945; Princeton.
Cather gone to California [actually Maine]. Suggests he consider "The Sculptor's Funeral."

1714. **To Ferris Greenslet,** Aug. 23, 1945, from Northeast Harbor, Maine; Harvard.
Does not object to proposed Italian translation of *My Ántonia*, though dislikes any transaction with Viking. Italian translation of *Death Comes for the Archbishop* very good. Surprisingly, French of *Archbishop* is not – at any rate, the first version, which she rejected, was not, with absurd footnote definitions of western terms such as "a religious order" for "trappers." When

back in New York will send name of woman who translated *Archbishop* into Italian. Willa Cather.

1715. To Carrie Miner Sherwood, n.d. [1945, before Sept. 25]; WCPM.
Likes the write-up "A Tribute" and suspects Carrie did it. Will send a copy to Roscoe. Willie.

1716. To Houghton Mifflin, Sept. 28, 1945, from New York, telegram; Harvard.
Will Ferris Greenslet be in Boston the first week of November? Willa Cather.

1717. To Mariel Gere, n.d. [Oct. 19, 1945?]; WCPM.
Appreciates her letter. Roscoe's death [Sept. 25, 1945] a terrible blow. Had frequent letters from his daughter Virginia, who thought he was in better health all the time. Was notified by telegram while in Maine, and the following day received a letter he had mailed the day before he died. Terribly sudden, though a blessing for him. Does she remember the day they spent in Brownsville during the severe drought? This is the most difficult ordeal she will ever endure. Willa.

1718. To Irene Miner Weisz, Oct. 22, [pm. 1945]; Newberry.
Has been ill since returning from Maine. Is broken by Roscoe's death. He was the closest to her of all her family, closer than Douglass. Does not care to write any more. Knows now that the only thing in life that matters is the people one loves. Had letters from him every two weeks for many years. Willie.

1719. To Ferris Greenslet, Oct. 30, 1945 [attached note by Leon Edel indicates that F. Greenslet gave this letter to E. K. Brown, leaving it to him to decide whether to destroy it, and at the time he died Brown had apparently made no decision]; Beinecke.
Brother Roscoe died in his sleep on September 25. He was less than two years older than she [actually four years younger] and is part of her earliest memories. Was the closest to her of all her brothers. Feels that something inside is broken. Very difficult to reply to all the letters of condolence. Thanks for sending his *Practical Cogitator*, but can't read small type due to eye trouble. Please destroy this letter. Had just finished a story she had been thinking about for a long time and was doing research for a larger project when the news came. Willa Cather.

1720. To Miss Geffen [American Academy of Arts and Letters] [from Sarah J. Bloom, secretary], Nov. 3, 1945; AAAL.

Is forwarding Cather's ballots. She has been away. Also, her brother died recently. Sarah J. Bloom, Secretary.

1721. To Carrie Miner Sherwood, n.d. [Nov. 7, 1945?]; WCPM.

Roscoe's death has hurt worse than any other grief. They had written each other weekly for years. Appreciates her thoughts. Willie.

1722. To Elizabeth Shepley Sergeant, Nov. 21, 1945; PM.

Brother Roscoe died suddenly this past summer of a heart attack in his sleep. A great shock. This was the brother with whom she rambled about in the West and Southwest. He often came to New York in the winter to see her. Two cheerful letters from him reached her after she learned of his death. Wants close friends to know, will never be the same. Please don't try to reply. Willa.

1723. To Elizabeth Shepley Sergeant, n.d. [c. Dec. 1, 1945]; PM.

Thanks for the letter, which showed a friend's love. Willa.

1724. To Irene Miner Weisz, n.d. [pm. Dec. 17, 1945], Christmas card; Newberry.

Feels homesick for small churches like the one pictured, but can get to Maine only in the summer. Doubts she will ever go to Red Cloud again, after hearing that the family home is now a rooming house. Willie.

1725. To Fanny Butcher, Jan. 3, 1946; Newberry.

Hasn't written because devastated by the death of brother Roscoe. Feels only half alive. Two cheerful letters from him arrived after she learned of his death. Wants close friends to know, will never be the same. Willa Cather.

1726. To Zoë Akins, Jan. 3, 1946; Huntington.

Hasn't written because devastated by the death of brother Roscoe. Feels only half alive. Received two lines from him, quite cheerful, after the telegram telling of his death. Wants close friends to know, will never be the same. Thanks for the beautiful peach blossoms. Hand is bad again. [no signature]

1727. To Mrs. George Whicher, Jan. 3, 1946; PM.

Hasn't written because devastated by the death of brother Roscoe. Since then has felt only half alive. Were very close. Time spent with him in the West was the most real part of her life. Received two letters from him after the telegram announcing his death. Wants a few old friends to know that she is no longer the same. Likes her book on church symbolism very much and would like another copy to send to Mary Virginia. Willa Cather.

1728. To Ferris Greenslet, Feb. 12, 1946; Harvard.

Just back from three weeks in the hospital for minor surgery. Sorry to say has not read *The Practical Cogitator* very thoroughly, but enjoyed the section called "How to Compose Your Life." Can read only larger type, at least for a while. Also, quick changes in his book from one thinker to another are jolting. Alfred Knopf says he has heard good comments on it. Willa Cather.

1729. To Carrie Miner Sherwood, Feb. 21, [1946]; WCPM.

Received a newspaper report of her accident the day she got home from the hospital. Felt utterly disheartened and lay awake that night remembering many things, including the day they met. Elsie let her know it was not quite so serious as the newspaper indicated. Hopes she and Mary are safe at home now. Willie.

1730. To Ferris Greenslet, Mar. 29, [1946]; Harvard.

Has finally finished reading *The Practical Cogitator*, first prose anthology she ever read. Enjoyed many of the individual selections, but wishes the book were shorter. Prefers to read people in historic context. Sorry for bad handwriting, but hand is in Dr. Ober's brace again. Willa Cather. P.S.: Really, doesn't he think anthologies reflect superficiality in the times?

1731. To Ferris Greenslet, May 13, 1946, telegram; Harvard.

No, will not approve radio performance of *Ántonia*. Willa Cather.

1732. To Sigrid Undset, May 20, 1946 [possibly incomplete]; Oslo.

Has read her letter many times. It must be sad to find her little town so altered and so many young men killed. But to be home, where everyone had a common cause to work for together, must be important; that feeling of working together creates hope as nothing else can. Here in the U.S. things are in a sad way. Yes, she might well lament, "Oh, if Roosevelt were still alive!" Now it seems as if John L. Lewis, President of the United Mine Workers, has more power than anyone else in the country. Is able to stop wheels turning everywhere. Nothing gets accomplished in Washington, due to squabbles and mismanagement. Everyone feels bitterly disappointed. She is fortunate to be in a place where the only "bigness" is that of the spirit. Is glad she saw America when she did, and not as it is now. Now lives, not in the present, but in old histories and great books. Is so glad her *Kristin Lavransdatter* is out in three volumes again, as it ought to be, instead of jammed into one big one. Hopes she will never let Hollywood film any of her books. Sorry to write such a hopeless letter. Maybe if they can get up to the country again, to the forests and big tides of the Maine coast, can regain her spirits.

1733. To Captain Hazlewood, June 1, 1946; Beinecke.
Thanks for his interesting letter. If her health were better, would want to talk with him about the Spanish missionary he described. His question about how an author decides what material will be artistically successful is based on misconception. The subject comes, it awakens a spark of something, and there should not be any further thought about whether the result will be successful. Suggests he read her letter to *Commonweal* about the writing of *Death Comes for the Archbishop*. Willa Cather.

1734. To Ferris Greenslet, June 1, 1946; Harvard.
Has asked Alfred Knopf to see that no radio adaptation of any of her work will ever be allowed. Legal counsel believes they could win a court case over this. If people just listen they will forget how to read. Has been kept in town by illness of several friends; otherwise would be in Maine now. Willa Cather.

1735. To Mrs. [Margaret?] Crofts, June 26, 1946; UNL.
Has tried to reach her by telephone without success. Has received the book she sent about French settlement in the U.S. Would be impossible to write a book about every such settlement. Anyway, impossible to write successfully just from information. Willa Cather.

1736. To Elizabeth Shepley Sergeant, Aug. 16, 1946, from Northeast Harbor, Maine; PM.
No, will never consent to a Portable Cather, the ultimate height of insidious anthologies. If she is writing a book she is interested in, why does she

waste her time assembling an anthology? Believes Alfred Knopf would agree and refuse permission. Please forget the idea. Willa Cather.

1737. **To Ferris Greenslet,** Aug. 28, 1946, from Northeast Harbor, Maine; Harvard. Has refused Viking's request for material for a Portable Cather, as has Alfred Knopf. The worst form the anthology has yet taken. Willa Cather.

1738. **To Helen Louise Cather Southwick,** Sept. 17, 1946, extract made by E. K. Brown; Beinecke.
First short story was published in *McClure's* [not true]. McClure also published her first volume of stories. Hopes she hasn't seen it; it wasn't very good.

1739. **To Helen Louise Cather Southwick,** Sept. 22, 1946, extract made by E. K. Brown; Beinecke.
She and Charles the only family members left with whom she can be honest and be herself.

1740. **To Carrie Miner Sherwood,** Sept. 25, 1946, from Northeast Harbor, Maine; WCPM.
Sending a check for the Red Cloud Hospital Fund but wants the donation to be anonymous. Is glad the old house is being put to this use, though doesn't see the need when Hastings so readily accessible. Not sending more because still helps a good many causes in the county as well as nieces and nephews. Some nieces and nephews help her, too – such as when Helen Louise sent butter by air mail last winter when butter was unavailable in New York. Used to bring meat to her from New Jersey, too. Are returning to New York next week and will soon have apartment redone. Much love. Willie.

1741. **To E. K. Brown,** Oct. 7, 1946; Beinecke.
Reply has been delayed by repairs of apartment. Greatly appreciates his insightful reading of her work and generally agrees with his judgments. Is not writing much nowadays because low in spirits since the deaths of her brothers Douglass and Roscoe. Yes, *Death Comes for the Archbishop* is her best. It was hard to find a structure to pull together so many disparate elements in the Southwest. It simply came to her one day when watching the sunset color the Sangre de Cristo Mountains that the essence of the early Southwest was the story of the missionaries from France. Devoted herself

to research on it from that day. Mary Austin claimed the book was written in her house, and now a woman named [Mary Cabot] Wheelwright claiming it was written in hers. Actually, mostly written in Jaffrey, New Hampshire. Has always felt disappointed with O *Pioneers!*. Tried to put together the Norwegian and the French settlers, and they never mixed. Once, not long after it was published, met Louis Brandeis on the street and he told her that what he most liked about the novel was its sincerity of feeling for the place and people. Said that one of the writers in whom he did not find that sincerity was Edith Wharton. Never saw him again. Probably he didn't find her own next two books sincere either. Kept working and trying to learn. Believes Brown underestimates the early railroad builders; Jim Hill, for example, a person of great imagination and personal quality. Never gave great care to language per se in her books, but tried to let the language come to her that would express feeling for the subject. Is pleased by his praise of My *Mortal Enemy*. Agrees that *Lucy Gayheart* isn't very good, except in the last part, after the Gayhearts themselves are dead and the book centers on the effect they have in the businessman's memory. Wishes she'd had a better sense of form earlier in her career. Willa Cather.

1742. **To Carrie Miner Sherwood**, n.d. [Oct. 1946], telegram; WCPM.
Has just received letter dated October 10. Very sorry. Will write tomorrow. Willa.

1743. **To Helen Louise Cather Southwick**, Oct. 24, 1946, extract made by E. K. Brown; Beinecke.
Believes she will be the kind of mother her grandmother was – that is, Cather's mother. Took care of her seven children but let them be their own persons and keep their own souls.

1744. **To Mr. and Mrs. Weisz**, n.d. [pm. Dec. 18, 1946], Christmas card; Newberry.
Conveys her love. Willie.

1745. **To unknown** [Carrie Miner?], prob. Dec. 1946, Christmas card; Newberry.
Thanks for not punishing her. As Sigrid Undset says, it is very easy to punish someone who is already down. Willie.

1746. To Carrie Miner Sherwood, Dec. 18, [1946]; WCPM.

Loves the comical story she sent of the first Thanksgiving, with pastry from the marrow of buffalo bones, and so on. Willie.

1747. To Dorothy Canfield Fisher, Jan. 3, [1947?]; UVt.

Was happy to receive her greeting on Christmas morning. No, can't remember translating [Heinrich] Heine's "Three Kings," but finds it amusing to think of having translated from a language in which she didn't know a bit of grammar. Very like her to have done so! Is happy and busy. Willa.

1748. To Eleanor Austerman, Jan. 16, 1947; UVa.

Sorry not to have written in so long, but often thinks of her. Last six years have been sad, with the deaths of brothers Douglass and Roscoe. Has spent the last two summers in Maine, but has never found a place where she could work so well as at the Shattuck Inn [in Jaffrey, N.H.]. Appreciates her Christmas card, with its fine photograph of the inn. Still regrets the beautiful woods were destroyed by storm. Hopes to come there again. Willa Cather.

1749. To E. K. Brown, Jan. 24, 1947; Beinecke.

Does not yet know plans for spring and summer. Anticipates being in California for part of that time to see two brothers [Jack and James]. Will hope to meet with him when he is in town. Would have many things to talk about — such as the new edition of Shakespeare that cuts out what the editor considers unimportant. Does not want writers like John Dos Passos to be legally stopped from writing as they want, but wishes law would stop editors who tamper with classics. Brandeis's death a great loss to the work of the Supreme Court. Spent many evenings at his home during years in Boston and often saw the Brandeises at the opera. Was introduced to Mrs. James T. Fields by Mrs. Brandeis, who was a fine and intelligent woman in her own right. Life sometimes seems dreary when one thinks about the people who have gone. Remembers William Archer well; remembers being in Lady Gregory's box with him the night the Abbey players made their London debut. Saw Synge's *The Playboy of the Western World*. Archer helped open her mind to new kinds of theatrical drama. Looks forward to discussing their personal values when he comes to New York. Willa Cather.

1750. To Carrie Miner Sherwood, Jan. 26, 1947; WCPM.

Sorry not to have answered her letter of last fall. Returned from vacation two weeks late, and the hall boy who usually takes such good care of her mail had left on his vacation by that time. Found most of her letters tied up together, but he had put a few into a separate folder on her desk, and cleaning woman piled books on top of it. So it was a long time before she found the letter. This might have caused a misunderstanding between them. Hopes now it is all cleared up. Has enemies in Red Cloud who are probably making the worst of her initial lack of interest in the new hospital. Still hopes to visit some day. Hasn't heard from Irene in quite a while; hopes she is all right. Willie.

1751. To Ferris Greenslet, Jan. 31, 1947; Harvard.

Please try to prevent the selling of *A Song of the Lark* [*sic*] to a moviemaker. Doesn't want the money. Has received a generous inheritance from her brother Douglass and doesn't need any more money. Willa Cather.

1752. To Mary Miner Creighton, Feb. 26, 1947; Newberry.

Is sending a letter from Sigrid Undset that she may find interesting, since she has been to Norway. Willie.

1753. To Father Maline [typographical error for Malone?], Mar. 3, 1947; UVa.

Yes, may quote the few lines about Father Noel Chabanel, whom she found very interesting, more than any of his fellow martyrs. Willa Cather.

1754. To Bishop George Beecher, Mar. 12, 1947, transcription made by Bernice Slote; UNL.

Was grieved to learn of the death of Mrs. Beecher. Delayed writing until sufficiently recovered from the strain of her right hand to do so by hand. Does not write to many people in Red Cloud any longer, but does write to Carrie Sherwood and Mary Creighton and to Sidney Florance and his wife. Glad the hospital board is making such a good use of her family's old home. Some of the people in the country out from Red Cloud have written telling her how kind her mother was to them when they came to town. These are the memories one cherishes. Prays that he can bear up under the loneliness that has come to him. Willa Cather.

1755. To E. K. Brown, Mar. 23, 1947; Beinecke.

Will let him know her plans as soon as they are made. Hephzibah Menuhin, her husband, and their two little boys were there to see her yesterday morning. Yehudi and his family arrived soon afterward. Visited happily until 11:30, then rose and quietly got the children into their wraps, went down on the elevator, and took cabs to the North River docks for lunch before sailing on the *Queen Elizabeth* at one o'clock. They never seem to get into a flurry. Yehudi and Hephzibah to give concerts in London and other cities in Europe. Have been a joy to her for sixteen years. Are people with beautiful natures. Still feels their presence in her rooms. Willa Cather. [signed by Sarah J. Bloom]

1756. To E. K. Brown [from Sarah J. Bloom, secretary], Mar. 30, 1947; Beinecke. Dictation of the enclosed letter was interrupted, and Cather left town without finishing it. Believes she should not hold it any longer.

1757. To Sigrid Undset, Apr. 8, 1947; Oslo. Has read over and enjoyed her letter many times. Past few months very difficult. Tendon in right hand relapsed in January, and since then has been immobilized in a brace. Isn't the world acting strangely now? Miss Lewis was lunching with some advanced Hindus and heard them speak absurdly, boasting and exulting about India's independence from England as an escape from despotism. When thousands die of famine in their cities and there is no Wavell [Viceroy of India 1943-47] to supervise rescue squads in Calcutta, they may change their tune. England still suffering regimentation and shortages. An elderly friend there tried to get enough lumber to repair his porch floor, but fell and broke his hip before the permission came. Doubtful he will survive the accident at his age. New York's winter was dreary and demoralizingly mild. Perhaps she knows the Irish proverb, "A green Christmas makes a full graveyard." New York has become the world's most foolish place to live. All the old women dye their hair yellow, or cut it short and frizz it wildly, and no one dresses tastefully any more. Is glad she remembers the shadbush and dogwood so fondly, and wonders if she had ever seen a Judas tree (*Cercis canadensis*) in bloom. Apologizes for writing such a foolish letter. The warm, soft winter, and the *strange deterioration of humankind* has robbed her of her spirit. Everyone seems to want to live in New York and wear outrageous outfits and drink cocktails. When she goes North, will feel better and write again.

1758. To E. K. Brown, Apr. 12, 1947; Beinecke.

Still doesn't have definite plans for summer, but will not go to California as expected. Instead, to Northeast Harbor, Maine. Hopes to be able to work some. Agrees it is good for young people to go to France, but only if they are the right kind of young people. Once saw the kind that clustered around Gertrude Stein, and not one of them has amounted to anything. Not people of force; some actually wore bracelets! Found a great force of life in John Steinbeck's play *The Moon Is Down*, but wishes he hadn't used a long quotation from Plato as the climax. Will let him know when she is leaving for Maine as soon as she knows. Willa Cather.

1759. To Dorothy Canfield Fisher, Apr. 17, 1947; UVt.

Has been wanting to write but wanted to wait until she could write by hand. Injured the tendon of right thumb again and has had it in brace. Long ago promised an editor to write an account of their visit to A. E. Housman. Wants to mention how Dorothy rescued the occasion by talking about Latin scholarship, which provided an avenue of approach to him. Wants to be accurate. Is it right that she had come directly from studying with Gaston Paris in France, for her doctorate? Recalls that Housman found it interesting. Several people have sent dreadful manuscripts about Housman. Wishes a certain type of young men would not pine for Housman as they do. The word "lad" seems to exert a magic spell for them. Recalls that she and Isabelle had just come from Ludlow, and the word "lad" was quite common there, meaning any hired boy. Willa. P.S.: Didn't Housman teach Latin at the University of London? What branch of Latin?

1760. To Dorothy Canfield Fisher [from Sarah J. Bloom, secretary], May 14, 1947; UVt.

Returning her reply to Cather's letter of April 17. She did receive it and read it before her death.

Letters for Which No Date Has Been Identified

1761. [To Mary Austin], n.d., unprinted card; Huntington.
This brings love and admiration. Willa Cather.

1762. To Nell [?], n.d.; WCPM.
Sorry to hear about her mastoid operation. Two of her friends suffered serious injuries during the Christmas season. Nell has recovered faster than most of them. Would like to have another visit in Red Cloud. A great deal has happened since she was there. Willa Cather.

1763. To Helen [Sprague?], n.d. [1935?]; WCPM.
Having a pleasant winter. Going to hear *Don Giovanni* tomorrow night. W. S. C.

1764. To Pat [Knopf?], Apr. 12, [?]; UVa.
Enjoyed the spring issue of *The Idol,* which is very lively. Errors from the French exams were too good to be true. Had tea with his mother today. Willa Cather. P.S.: Plans to investigate F. W. Croft.

1765. To Mr. Byran [sic], n.d., excerpt made by E. K. Brown, who conjectures it was written about 1936 or 1937; Beinecke.
Yes, may use the quotation so long as he does not use it to argue for translating the Bible into modern language. This was part of an interview many years ago, before she learned not to give interviews. Feels very strongly that the King James version of the Bible should remain the standard and people should not attempt to modernize it.

1766. To Mabel Dodge Luhan, n.d.; Beinecke.
Interesting how people differ in what part of Mabel's manuscript they like best. The "Green Horses" section seems to her a real work of art, much more significant than the rest, perhaps because it is drawing on early memories and a child has the artist's eye that adults lose. Buffalo is established as a world of its own. Willa Cather.

1767. To Ferris Greenslet, n.d., from Jaffrey, N.H.; Harvard.
No, doesn't want book sent to Mlle Burk but to Mme Burls. W. S. C.

1768. **To Ferris Greenslet,** n.d.; Harvard.

Just back from trip; will write soon. Willa Cather.

1769. **To Ferris Greenslet,** Thursday; Harvard.

Sending photographs. Will be staying at this hotel [the Grosvenor, New York] the rest of the month. W. S. C.

1770. **To Blanche Knopf,** Friday; HRC.

Sorry she couldn't be with them last night. Was up late the night before and tried to work yesterday, and then was worn out. Had accepted Martha Mencken's invitation for night before last some time ago. Willa Cather.

1771. **To Walter Tittle,** n.d.; HRC.

He must be thinking she has no manners, but she was called to Nebraska just after their last sitting. His box of candy carried her through blizzards. Willa Cather.

1772. **To Zoë Akins,** Tuesday; Huntington.

What beautiful roses! They and the snapdragons are still nice, after the irises have given up. Willa.

1773. Undated handwritten poem in Cather's hand, title "Equinox"; Vermont. [This poem does not appear in Joan Crane's bibliography of Cather's works.]

1774. **To Mr. Palmer,** Aug. 3, [?]; Yale.

No, never lived at 61 Washington Square and can't help with his article. Willa Cather.

1775. **To Ida Tarbell,** n.d.; Allegheny.

Must be receiving many flowers today. Shares her belief in the Bible. Willa Cather.

1776. **To Carrie Miner Sherwood,** Oct. 12, [?], from New York; WCPM.

Arrived yesterday after rough voyage that she enjoyed. Would like three more centerpieces from the Church Guild. Willie.

1777. **To Ida Tarbell,** n.d., from New York; Allegheny.

Sending a check for Mr. McClure. Willa Cather.

1778. **To Mollie Ferris,** Dec. 28, [?]; WCPM.

Delighted with her Christmas presents of washcloths and a teapot holder.

Thanks for including sprigs of cedar, and please continue to remember her in her prayers. Willie.

1779. **To Lydia [Lambrecht?],** n.d.; WCPM.

Sending her mother a quilted housecoat to keep her warm indoors on cold days. She mustn't save it but use it. Willa Cather. P.S.: Please don't give out her address.

1780. **To Mrs. C. F. Lambrecht,** n.d., from Grand Manan, postcard; WCPM.

Sending a picture of the cliffs at the island where she spends her summers. Willa Cather.

1781. **To Carrie Miner Sherwood,** n.d., telegram; WCPM.

Can't come this year but plans to be there next Christmas. Willa Cather.

1782. **To Carrie Miner Sherwood,** n.d.; WCPM.

Sending Christmas greetings [and enclosing clippings?]. Please excuse her pride in this praise. Willie.

1783. **To Edward Steichen,** n.d.; WCPM.

Sending her thanks for his care in getting two prints made for her. Knows they will have a good trip. Many things she would like to talk over with him and his wife. Willa Cather.

1784. **To unidentified recipient,** n.d., from Grand Manan; WCPM.

Glad she liked the book, but will probably like *My Ántonia* more. Willa Cather.

1785. **To Bobbie [Mrs. Roscoe Cather?],** n.d.; UNL.

Sending a review from the *Nation* that she is proud of. [Possibly referring to a review of *The Song of the Lark* in October 1915 or to one of Joseph Wood Krutch's strongly positive reviews in the *Nation*: of *A Lost Lady*, November 28, 1923; of *The Professor's House*, September 23, 1925; of *My Mortal Enemy*, November 10, 1926; of *Death Comes for the Archbishop*, October 12, 1927.] Please return it after she shows Roscoe. Willie.

1786. **To Everett L. Getchell,** Jan. 28, [?]; Colby.

Sends her greetings to his class in contemporary literature, but would prefer that nothing was called literature until it was a century or more old. Willa Cather.

1787. **To Stephen Tennant,** n.d., fragment; Yongue.

P.S.: How can he like Elizabeth Bowen's *Look at All Those Roses?* All calculation, no caring. Like an operating room. Dostoevsky may be pathological, but has intense feeling for his characters. But Bowen only plays tricks with her characters, and doesn't have very good technique either.

1788. **To George Seibel,** Mar. 13, [?], from Casper, Wyo.; WCPM.

Appreciates the book of poems. Has been busy with the family reunion, but will leave tomorrow and enjoy reading sonnets all the way to the West Coast. Willa Cather.

1789. **To Irita Van Doren,** n.d., from Jaffrey, N.H.; LC.

Shocked by Mr. Sherman's death. Can't do an article for her; has too many unkept promises already. Willa Cather.

1790. **To Hamlin Garland,** Thursday [before summer 1927], from no. 5 Bank Street, New York; USC.

Would be pleased to dine with him tomorrow, but a friend from Chicago is coming to dinner. Goes out very little when she is working, as she is now. Please come by for tea on a Friday at four. Willa Cather.

1791. **To Hamlin Garland,** Dec. 27, [?] [before summer 1927], from no. 5 Bank Street, New York; USC.

Appreciates his letter. Very glad to know her work has pleased him. Will plan to drop in for tea, though she is not often uptown. Would be pleased if he could come by for tea on a Friday at four. Must have a great deal to talk about. Willa Cather.

1792. **To H. L. Mencken,** n.d.; Baltimore.

Sending an amusing clipping from one of the Paris newspapers about Americans during Prohibition. Willa Cather.

1793. **To Zoë Akins,** Sunday; Huntington.

Name she was trying to think of was Charles Augustus Hare [error for August John Hare, 1834–1903], editor of *The Story of Two Noble Lives* [1893]. W. S. C.

1794. **To Zoë Akins,** n.d.; Huntington.

Yes, glad to have dinner with her tonight. Will be there at seven. W. S. C.

1795. **To Zoë Akins,** n.d.; Huntington.
Sending some dark hyacinths (a flower Virgil always compares to the curls of young boys in the Eclogues). She will be well long before the last one opens. Willa.

1796. **To Zoë Akins,** n.d., from Grand Manan, postcard; Huntington.
Here is where their cottage is located, overlooking the sea, and with many wildflowers.

1797. **To Carrie Miner Sherwood,** Mar. 26, [?]; WCPM.
Will always remember the time they had together last summer. Has been in bed with influenza for two weeks. Willie.

1798. **To unidentified recipient,** n.d.; WCPM.
Saw this happy surprise when she bought a newspaper on the train. Willie.

1799. **To Carrie Miner Sherwood,** Apr. 12, [?], from New York, telegram; WCPM.
Her letter cleared away a great deal of puzzlement and unhappiness. Willie.

1800. **To S. S. McClure,** Monday; Indiana.
Hopes he can come to tea on Wednesday at four. Willa Cather.

1801. **To Mrs. S. S. McClure,** Monday [before 1928]; Indiana.
Is worried about her mother and plans to go to Nebraska around the first of the year to spend some time with her. Can't go to England while she is so ill. Please let Mr. McClure know. Is still under doctor's care, but the tablets have helped the bronchitis. Father came and stayed with her for a while. Willa Cather.

1802. **To Mr. Warren,** Nov. 22, [?], from Grosvenor Hotel, New York; Harvard.
Please send copies of the *Galaxy* to the people listed. Willa Cather.

1803. **To Fanny Butcher,** Thursday; Newberry.
Terribly busy. Happy Easter! W. S. C.

1804. **To Fanny Butcher,** n.d.; Newberry.
Thanks and Happy New Year. Willa Cather.

1805. **To Malcolm Cowley,** Saturday, from no. 5 Bank Street, New York; Newberry.

Will plan to see him on Wednesday December 30 at four. Willa Cather.

1806. **To Malcolm Cowley,** Jan. 17, [?]; Newberry.

Appreciates his comments. If she resumes her Friday afternoon teas, will send him a card. Dislikes interviews in general. Willa Cather.

1807. **To Miss Vondler,** n.d.; Newberry.

Doesn't remember Blind Tom. Her character is a composite of several musicians, including Blind Boone. Willa Cather.

1808. **To Merle Johnson,** n.d.; NYPL.

The write-up is accurate except for her birth date. Was born in 1876, not 1875 [actually, 1873]. Willa Cather.

1809. **To Miss Carson,** Sunday, from Grosvenor Hotel, New York; UVa.

Please let writer of enclosed letter know that she does not allow condensations or excerpts of her books. W. S. C.

1810. **To Mr. Sterner,** n.d. [prob. between fall 1927 and Dec. 1932], from Grosvenor Hotel, New York; Penn.

He may use the sonnet, but regards it as so poor that she dropped it from the second edition of the volume [1923]. Very juvenile. Willa Cather.

1811. **To [Dorothy Canfield Fisher],** n.d. [apparently, from scrawling handwriting, very late or from one of the earlier periods when she had problems with her hand]; UVt.

Hates to admit that the grouch in the enclosed picture was one of her classmates. Doesn't actually remember him. W.

1812. **To Miss McNally,** Jan. 4, [?], from Red Cloud; BYU.

Likes the review of her book, largely because it is well written. Willa Cather.

1813. **To ?** [prob. Mr. or Mrs. George Whicher], n.d., from Shattuck Inn, Jaffrey, N.H.; PM.

Looks forward to seeing them. W. S. C.

1814. **To ? [prob. Mr. and Mrs. George Whicher]**, n.d.; PM.

Please come after five. W. S. C. P.S.: Prefers a late visit because working during the day. Do plan to stay for dinner.

1815. **To ?**, n.d., note written on a printed page showing pictures of Clement C. Moore and his house, with the beginning of the poem "A Visit from St. Nicholas"; PM.

Was Moore a real person, then?

1816. **To Mr. Sanborn**, Tuesday; UNL.

Missed receiving his letter; was spending the weekend at Cos Cob. Hasn't been to any musical events since returning except for a few by German opera performers. Has finally caught up on correspondence – probably three hundred letters! Hopes they can have dinner or tea. Olive Fremstad is away in Egypt. Willa Cather.

1817. **To Lydia [Lambrecht]**, n.d.; WCPM.

Sending a check to be used for something for her mother's birthday in May, as she will be in New Hampshire then. Willa Cather. P.S.: Ribbons in Christmas box were just to brighten it up.

Biographical Directory

This section contains information about persons addressed or mentioned in the letters, to the extent that I am able to provide it. Not everyone is identified.

Abbott, Edith. 1876–1957. Graduated from the University of Nebraska in 1901 and became dean of the University of Chicago School of Social Service Administration. Received an honorary doctorate from the University of Nebraska the same year as Cather, 1917.

Ackroyd, Rose. Granddaughter of Mary Ann Anderson, of the Back Creek area in Virginia, and niece of Enoch and Marjorie Anderson, who accompanied the Cathers from Virginia to Nebraska. Wrote to Cather on April 21, 1940, after reading *Sapphira and the Slave Girl.*

Adams, Frederick B. One-time director of the Pierpont Morgan Library.

Adler, Elmer. 1884–1962. Book designer and master of fine and art printing; designed and supervised the printing of Cather's "December Night" (excerpt from *Death Comes for the Archbishop*) and other special editions.

Akins, Zoë. 1886–1958. Writer of poetry, fiction, criticism, plays, screenplays, and radio and television scripts. Best known as a playwright. Winner of the Pulitzer Prize in 1935 for her adaptation of Edith Wharton's *The Old Maid.*

Alexander, William V. Editor of *Ladies Home Journal*, for which Cather wrote an article on Ethelbert Nevin.

Ames, Mary H. (Maysie). Classmate of Cather and of Mariel Gere.

Anderson, Edwin H. 1861–1947. Director of the Carnegie Library in Pittsburgh while Cather lived there; director of the New York Public Library, 1913–34.

Andrews, Sarah ("Auntie"). 1834–1925. Sister of Mary Virginia Cather.

Archer, William. 1856–1924. Scottish playwright and drama critic.

Armes, Ethel Marie. d. 1946. American journalist; in connection with her interest in the Robert E. Lee Foundation, wrote *Stratford Hall, the Great House of the Lees.*

Auld, Will. Banker in Red Cloud, married to Jessica Cather. They divorced in 1933.

Auld Mellen, Mary Virginia. b. 1905. Cather's favorite niece.

Austerman, George. Owner of the Shattuck Inn in Jaffrey, New Hampshire, where Cather spent fall months for many years. Austerman was married to the daughter of the original owner, whose name was Shattuck.

Axtell, Charles. Publisher and editor in chief of the *Home Monthly Magazine.*

Bain, Read. 1892–?. A professor of sociology at Miami University, Oxford, Ohio; vice president of the American Sociological Society; editor of the *American Sociological Review* 1938–42.

Bakst, Leon. 1866–1924. Russian painter who studied in Paris; began designing stage sets in 1900 and in 1906 returned to Paris to design sets for the Ballets Russes.

Balzac, Honoré de. 1799–1850. French novelist.

Barrie, J. M. 1860–1937. British playwright and novelist.

Bartlett, Alice Hunt. 1869–1949. American editor of the *Poetry Review* of London.

Bates, Herbert. d. 1931. A professor of English at the University of Nebraska who placed some of Cather's earliest work; left the university to become music critic in Cincinnati.

Bates, Rev. John Mallory. 1846–1930. Minister at Grace Episcopal Church in Red Cloud.

Beach, Sylvia. 1887–1962. Born Nancy Woodbridge Beach, she moved to Paris and in 1919 opened her bookstore, Shakespeare and Co., which attracted many English-speaking authors and had the distinction of first publishing Joyce's *Ulysses.*

Beecher, George Allen. 1868–1951. Episcopal bishop who confirmed Cather and her parents in the Episcopal Church. Bishop of Western Nebraska, 1910–43.

Benda, Wladyslaw Theodor. 1873–1948. Magazine and book illustrator chosen by Cather for *My Ántonia.*

Bennett, Arnold. 1867–1931. English novelist.

Bernhardt, Sarah. 1844–1923. Celebrated French actress.

Biddle, Francis. 1886–1968. A member of an established Philadelphia family, Biddle began the practice of law in 1917 after serving as secretary to Supreme Court Justice Oliver Wendell Holmes for one year. Attorney General under Franklin Delano Roosevelt, 1941–45, and a judge at the Nuremburg Trials.

Birtwell, Lorna. A student of Cather's at the Breadloaf School; published an article defending *One of Ours* in the *Saturday Evening Post* in 1922.

Bliven, Bruce. 1889–1977. Editor and critic born in Iowa who began his career in journalism in 1909 at the *San Francisco Bulletin* while still a student at Stanford University. Became managing editor at the *New Republic* in 1923 and its president in 1930.

Boak, Rachel Elizabeth Seibert. 1816–93. Cather's maternal grandmother, the model for Mrs. Harris in "Old Mrs. Harris."

Boas, Franz. 1858–1942. Influential German-born American anthropologist, taught at Columbia University from 1899 to 1942.

Bourda, Josephine. Cather's housekeeper and cook for many years, from Switzerland.

Bourne, Randolph. Critic associated with the *New Republic;* opponent of entry into World War I. Died in December 1918 of influenza. Favorably reviewed *My Ántonia* in the *Dial.*

Boyd, Thomas Alexander. 1898–1935. Columnist for the *St. Paul Daily News;* also a biographer and novelist.

Boynton, H. W. Favorably reviewed *The Song of the Lark* in the *New York Evening Post* and *My Ántonia* in *Bookman.*

Braithwaite, William Stanley. 1878–1962. African American editor and critic; wrote for the *Boston Evening Transcript* and edited several anthologies of poetry.

Brodstone, Evelyn (or Evelene), Lady Vesty. 1875–1941. A friend of Cather's in her youth, from Superior, Nebraska. A noted business executive, married an owner of the British firm for which she worked.

Brooks, Van Wyck. 1886–1963. A historian of literature and authors, literary critic, and biographer. Won the Pulitzer Prize for history in 1937 for *The Flowering of New England.*

Bulwer-Lytton, Edward. 1803–73. English novelist, author of *The Last Days of Pompeii* (1834).

Burnett, Whit. Editor of a volume of miscellaneous stories called *This Is My Best.*

Butcher, Fanny. 1888–1987. A graduate of the University of Chicago; reviewed books, music, and art for the *Chicago Tribune* for almost fifty years.

Butler, Nicholas Murray. 1862–1947. President of Columbia University 1902–45, President of the American Academy of Arts and Letters 1928–1941.

Bynner, Witter. 1881–1968. Poet. After graduation from Harvard in 1902, worked as an editor at *McClure's*; later lived in Santa Fe.

Calvé, Emma. 1858?–1942. French operatic soprano whom Cather reviewed on May 23, 1897 and May 12, 1900.

Canby, Henry Seidel. 1878–1961. American editor, critic, and literary biographer. A professor at Yale, he helped launch the *Yale Review* and edited the *New York Evening Post's Literary Review* and the *Saturday Review of Literature.* Editor in chief for the Book-of-the-Month Club 1926–54.

Canby, Marion (Mrs. Henry Seidel). American poet whose verses, collected in *High Mowing* (1932) and *On My Way* (1937), appeared in such magazines as *Scribner's,* the *Saturday Review of Literature,* and the *New Yorker.*

Canfield family. James Hulme Canfield, 1847–1909, was chancellor of the University of Nebraska during Cather's student days and later president of Ohio State University. Mrs. Canfield, Flavia, was a painter and a socialite greatly interested in the arts. Their daughter, Dorothy Canfield Fisher, 1879-1958, was a prolific writer of both fiction and nonfiction, a member of the first editorial board of the Book-of-the-Month Club, and a friend of Cather's from her student days on.

Cather, Charles Fectigue. 1848-1928. Father of Willa Cather.

Cather, Douglass. 1880-1938. Cather's brother, to whom she was very close.

Cather, Elsie. 1890-1964. Cather's sister.

Cather, Frances Smith. 1846-1922. Strong-minded aunt (Aunt Franc) married to Cather's father's brother George; mother of Grosvenor Cather, the model for Claude Wheeler in *One of Ours*.

Cather, James. 1886-1966. Cather's brother, married Ethel Garber.

Cather, Jessica. *See* Cather Auld, Jessica.

Cather, John (Jack). 1892-1959. Cather's youngest brother.

Cather, Mary Virginia Boak (Jennie). 1850-1931. Mother of Willa Cather.

Cather, Roscoe (Ross). 1877-1945. Cather's brother, to whom she was very close.

Cather Auld, Jessica, or Jessie (Mrs. William). 1881-1964. Sister of Willa Cather.

Conklin, Groff. 1904-68. Anthologist, especially of science fiction.

Connely, William. British collector of autographs and letters, biographer of architect Louis Sullivan.

Cousins, Margaret. 1905-? A graduate of the University of Texas, Cousins became fiction editor of *Woman's Home Companion* and managing editor of *Good Housekeeping* before serving as a senior editor at Doubleday 1961-73.

Cowley, Malcolm. 1898-1989. American critic and editor.

Crawford, F. Marion. 1854-1909. Financially successful American novelist.

Crofts, Margaret. Author of *Armed with Light* (1937). Married to Frederick S. Crofts, of F. S. Crofts & Co. Publishers.

Cross, Wilbur. 1862–1948. Professor at Yale and editor of the *Yale Review*; governor of Connecticut 1931–39.

Damrosch, Walter. 1862–1950. German American conductor and composer, elected to the National Institute of Arts and Letters in 1898 and to the American Academy of Arts and Letters in 1932. President of the Academy 1941–1948.

Dashiell, Alfred. 1901–70. Editor for *Reader's Digest*, *Scribner's Magazine*, and *Editor's Choice*. Coauthored *A Study of the Short Story* with H. S. Canby.

Daudet, Alphonse. 1840–97. French novelist.

Deland, Margaret Campbell. 1857–1945.

Dell, Floyd. 1887–1969. Illinois-born novelist, reviewer, editor, playwright, and cultural historian.

DeVoto, Bernard. 1897–1955. Historian, essayist, and literary critic; faculty member at Harvard. Edited "The Easy Chair" for *Harper's Magazine*, 1930–55; editor of the *Saturday Review of Literature*.

Dickens, Charles. 1812–70. English novelist.

Dos Passos, John. 1896–1970. American novelist of the post–World War I period; associated with the Lost Generation.

Dostoevsky, Fyodor. 1821–81. Russian novelist.

Dunne, Finley Peter. 1867–1936. Creator of popular newspaper character "Misther Dooley."

Dvořák, Anton. 1841–1904. Bohemian composer.

Dwight, H. G. Writer of fiction and poetry whose work Cather accepted (and sometimes declined) for *McClure's Magazine*.

Eliot, George (pseud.). Mary Ann Evans. 1819–80. English novelist.

Engel, Soltan. A graduate of Columbia University, a collector of art works, rare books, and manuscripts; donated a rich collection to Columbia.

Ferrero, Guglielmo. 1871–1942. Italian historian and journalist, held the Chair of History at the University of Geneva.

Ferris, Mollie. c. 1864-1941. A friend of Cather's in Red Cloud, member of Grace Church.

Feuillerat, Albert G. 1874-1953. Born in Toulouse, France; taught at Harvard, Columbia, and Yale before becoming Sterling Professor of French at Yale, 1929-43.

Fields, Annie Adams. 1834-1915. Celebrated hostess, widow of James T. Fields, noted Boston publisher. Wrote poems and edited the *Life and Letters of Harriet Beecher Stowe*.

Fiske, Minnie Maddern. 1865-1932. Noted actress interviewed by Cather in 1899.

Fitzgerald, F. Scott. 1896-1940. American novelist.

Florance, Beatrix Mizer (Mrs. Sidney). Childhood friend of Cather, studied music in Chicago.

Florance, Sidney. Banker in Red Cloud.

Foerster, Norman. 1887-? Professor and critic who was a student of Cather's in Pittsburgh; established a creative arts doctoral program at the University of Iowa.

Ford, Ford Madox (pseud.). Ford Madox Hueffer. 1873-1939. British novelist and critic.

Franklin, Christine Ladd. 1847-1930. A lecturer at Columbia University, 1914-27, in psychology and logic.

Fremstad, Olive. 1871-1951. Swedish American soprano; made her Metropolitan Opera debut in 1903 and specialized in Wagnerian roles.

Frost, Robert. 1874-1963. American poet.

Gale, Zona. 1874-1938. Essayist, novelist, and playwright. Won the Pulitzer Prize for drama in 1921 for *Miss Lulu Bett*. Active in social issues and in Progressive politics.

Gannett, Lewis. 1891-1966. Journalist, staff writer for the *Nation*, 1919-28, book critic for the *New York Herald Tribune* after 1931. The author of *Young China* (1926) and other books.

Garber, Lyra Wheeler. 1855 (prob.)-1921. Second wife of Silas Garber. Social leader in Red Cloud during Cather's childhood and adolescence. The model for Marian Forrester in *A Lost Lady*.

Garber, Silas. 1833-1905. Captain of Company D, the 27th Iowa Infantry, during the Civil War; homesteaded in Nebraska in 1870 and in 1871 founded the town of Red Cloud; governor of Nebraska, 1874-78; impoverished by the failure of the Farmers' and Merchants' Bank in Red Cloud in 1893. The model for Captain Forrester in *A Lost Lady*.

Garland, Hamlin. 1860-1940. American novelist and short story writer.

Gayhardt, Anna. A teacher at the Blue Hill school when Cather met her, a graduate of Peru Normal School.

Geffen, Felicia. 1903-94. Executive director of the American Academy of Arts and Letters, 1941-73.

Gere family. Charles Gere, 1860-1904, was the publisher of the *Nebraska State Journal*. Cather met the Geres when she went away to Lincoln for college. Among the several daughters of the family, Mariel Gere (1874-1960) became one of her best friends.

Gerwig, George. Drama critic before Cather on the *Nebraska State Journal*; M.A. University of Nebraska 1890; in 1892 moved to Allegheny, Pennsylvania, where he became secretary to the Board of Education.

Gibbon, Perceval. 1879-1926. British journalist and war correspondent; a frequent contributor to American and British magazines.

Goldmark, Josephine. 1866-1939. Protective labor law activist, research director of the National Consumer's League. Her book *Fatigue and Efficiency* is credited with helping in the fight for shorter labor hours.

Goldmark, Pauline. 1874-1962. Secretary of the National and the New York State Consumers' Leagues, and Assistant Director of Social Research for the Russell Sage Foundation. From 1919 to 1939 advisor on employment problems and health of women for AT&T. Wrote *Women and Children in the Canning Industry* (1908).

Grant, Judge Robert. 1852-1940. Member of the Department of Literature, American Academy of Arts and Letters, elected in 1915.

Greenslet, Ferris. 1875-1959. Associate editor for the *Atlantic Monthly*, 1902-7, and then, for thirty-five years, literary editor at Houghton Mifflin, where he championed Cather's early novels. His own books included *Joseph Glanville, a Study in English Thought and Literature in the 17th Century, Walter Pater, The Life of James Russell Lowell, The Life of Thomas Bailey Aldrich, The Lowells and Their Seven Worlds,* and *Under the Bridge,* a memoir of his life in publishing. He edited the collected lyrics of Louise Imogen Guiney.

Hambourg, Jan. 1882-1947. Violinist, husband of Isabelle McClung Hambourg.

Hardy, Thomas. 1840-1928. English novelist and poet.

Harris, Sarah. 1860-1917. Newspaperwoman Cather met while a student at the University of Nebraska. Co-owner and editor of the *Lincoln Courier* in the late 1890s.

Henderson, Alice Corbin. b. 1881. Santa Fe poet and editor.

Hendrick, Burton J. 1871-1949. Member of the Department of Literature, American Academy of Arts and Letters.

Hills, Laura Coombs. 1859-1952. Massachusetts painter who specialized in miniatures and flowers in pastel.

Hogan, Eugene Pendleton. b. 1907. Author of three novels in the 1930s.

Hopkins, Anthony Hope. 1863-1933. Writer of historical romances such as *The Prison of Zenda.*

Howe, Mark Antony DeWolfe. 1906-67. Editor of the memoirs of Annie Adams Fields.

Hueffer, Mrs. Ford Madox. *See* Ford Madox Ford.

Hughes, Langston. 1902-67. American poet; associated with the Harlem Renaissance.

Ibsen, Henrik. 1828-1906. Norwegian playwright.

James, Henry. 1843-1916. American novelist greatly admired by Cather.

Johnson, Burges. 1877-1963. A professor at Vassar and Union, also an editor and author. A graduate of Amherst College, where his papers are found.

Johnson, Robert Underwood. 1853-1937. Editor, poet, and ambassador to Italy under President Woodrow Wilson. Edited the *Century* and *Scribner's*. Secretary of the American Academy of Arts and Letters.

Johnson, Walter Willard (Spud). 1897-1968. Secretary and friend of Witter Bynner and of Mabel Dodge Luhan in Santa Fe and Taos; edited and published *Laughing Horse*, a magazine of satire.

Jones, Thomas S. 1882-1932. Poet whose religious themes during his later years took the form of a belief in automatic writing.

Jones, Will Owen. 1862-1928. Managing editor of the *Nebraska State Journal* and Cather's mentor there.

Kaley, Charles W. 1846-1917. From Red Cloud; president of the board of regents of the University of Nebraska at the time Cather sought a teaching job there.

Kaufman, Enit Zerner. 1908?-61. Portrait painter born in Austria who emigrated to New York in 1939.

Keeble, Glendinning. Music critic with the *Pittsburgh Gazette-Times*; read proof of *The Song of the Lark*.

Keppel, Frederick Paul. 1875-1943. Dean at Columbia University, 1910-18; president of the Carnegie Corporation, 1923-41. A member of the Board of Appeals on alien cases, U.S. State Department, 1941-43.

Kipling, Rudyard. 1865-1936. English novelist and poet.

Knopf, Alfred A. 1892-1984. Founder of New York publishing house in 1915. Published all of Cather's works from *Youth and the Bright Medusa* (1920) on.

Knopf, Blanche. 1894-1966. Wife of Alfred A. Knopf and an active participant in the publishing house. Traveled widely and was inducted into the French Legion of Honor.

La Farge, Oliver. 1901-63. American anthropologist and novelist; won the Pulitzer Prize for novel *Laughing Boy* (1929).

Lamb, Charles. 1775-1834. English essayist.

Lambrecht family. Mrs. Carl F. (Charlotte Preussner) Lambrecht and Pauline and Lydia were neighbors of the Cathers in Nebraska before they moved to Red Cloud.

Lane, Gertrude Battle. Served as a writer and editor for the *Woman's Home Companion* from 1903 to 1941, the year of her death. Also, vice president and director of Crowell-Collier Publishing Company. Was sometimes called "the dean of magazine editors" in America.

Lawler, Patrick Anthony. b. 1894. Prolific journalist and author whose books included *Confessions of a Journalist* (1935) and a book on Katherine Mansfield, *The Mystery of Maata* (1946).

Lemaitre, Jules. 1853-1914. French author and critic. Wrote essays on Flaubert and others, a book of verse, and a play (*Revoltee*). Elected to the French Academy in 1896.

Lewis, Sinclair. 1885-1951. American novelist, winner of the Nobel Prize in 1930.

Loti, Pierre (pseud.). Julian Viaud. 1850-1923. French novelist.

Lowell, Amy. 1874-1925. American poet and critic.

Luhan, Mabel Dodge. 1879-1962. A patron of the arts and literature who maintained a salon on Fifth Avenue in New York before moving to Taos, N.M., where she hosted celebrities such as D. H. Lawrence.

Mackenzie, Cameron. 1882-1921. Son-in-law of S. S. McClure, hired on the magazine in 1906, became general manager in 1908.

Mackoy, Harry Brent. Attorney in Kenton County, Kentucky.

Marlowe, Julia. 1866-1950. English actress.

Masaryk, Thomas. 1850-1937. Czech patriot and philosopher; a founder of Czechoslovakia, served as its president, 1918-35.

Masters, Edgar Lee. 1869-1950. American poet, known for *Spoon River Anthology* (1915).

Matthiessen, Francis O. 1902–50. Scholar and critic noted for *The American Renaissance* (1941). Also published books on Sarah Orne Jewett, Henry James, and Theodore Dreiser.

McAfee, Helen. Staff person and reviewer at the *Yale Review*.

McDonald (or MacDonald), James. 1870–1968. Classmate and admirer of Louise Pound; one of the founders of the *Lasso*.

McKeeby, Dr. G. E. 1844–1905. Cather family physician, mayor of Red Cloud in the late 1880s. Prototype for Dr. Archie in *The Song of the Lark*.

McNeny, Helen Sherman. Married to Bernard McNeny, an attorney in Red Cloud.

Meloney, Marie Mattingly. 1883–1943. Editor and writer; edited the *Delineator*, 1920–26, the *Sunday Magazine*, and *This Week Magazine*.

Mencken, H. L. 1880–1956. American editor and critic, noted for acerbic social comment and for *The American Language* (1918).

Menuhin, Yehudi. 1916–99. American violinist, debuted with the San Francisco Orchestra at age seven. Sisters Hephzibah and Yaltah were also concert musicians.

Meredith, George. 1828–1909. English novelist and poet.

Meynell, Alice. 1847–1922. British poet and essayist well known during late Victorian and mid-Georgian periods; transitional between Victorian and modernist styles.

Michelet, Jules. 1798–1874. French historian; author of the nineteen volume *History of France*.

Miner family. James L. Miner, 1847–1905, was a merchant in Red Cloud. He and his wife, a good amateur musician, were the models for the Harlings in *My Ántonia*, and Mr. Miner was the model for R. E. Dillon in "Two Friends." Their daughters (as well as a son, Hugh Miner) were Cather's friends Carrie Miner Sherwood, Irene Miner Weisz, Margaret Miner Gund, and Mary Miner Creighton.

Modjeska, Helena. 1840–1909. Celebrated Polish actress; appears in *My Mortal Enemy*.

Mohr, Emil. A Brother of the Holy Cross, the order that founded Notre Dame University.

Monroe, Harriet. 1860-1936. Founder of *Poetry Magazine* and its editor from 1912 to 1936.

Morison, Samuel Eliot. 1887-1976. American historian, twice winner of the Pulitzer Prize.

Morley, Christopher Darlington. 1890-1957. American writer of fiction, nonfiction, children's stories, and poetry and an editor of the *Saturday Review of Literature.*

Morris, Clara. 1848-1925. American actress known for emotional style.

Munsterburg, Hugo. 1863-1916. German-born scholar, wrote for various American magazines and wrote several books on psychology, sociology, and American culture.

Nansen, Fridtjof. 1861-1930. Norwegian Arctic explorer.

Nevin, Ethelbert. 1862-1901. American composer of art songs.

Nevins, Allan. 1890-1971. Historian and biographer; professor at Columbia University, 1928-58. Winner of two Pulitzer Prizes; editor of the *New York Evening Post* 1913-23; literary editor of the *New York Sun,* 1923-25.

Newbranch, Harvey. 1875-1959. An 1896 graduate of the University of Nebraska, Newbranch was editor of the *Omaha World-Herald* for fifty-six years and won a Pulitzer Prize in 1919 for an editorial condemning lynching.

Osborne, Evelyn. A friend and fellow graduate student of Dorothy Canfield whom Cather met in Paris in 1902; the prototype for Virginia Gilbert in "The Profile."

Ouida (pseud.). Marie Louise de la Ramée. 1839-1908. English romantic novelist.

Park, Marion Edwards. 1876-1960. President of Bryn Mawr College, 1922-42.

Pater, Walter. 1839-94. English essayist and critic, known as a stylist.

Pattee, Fred Lewis. 1863–1950. Professor at Pennsylvania State University; well-known scholar-critic.

Pearson, Norman Holmes. 1909–76. Professor of English at Yale. Was a close friend of H. D. (Hilda Doolittle) and edited the *Oxford Anthology of American Literature*.

Peattie, Elia W. Columnist for the *Omaha World Herald*; literary editor of the *Chicago Tribune* in 1901. Wrote fiction for adults and children, reviewed by Cather at least three times.

Perkins, Mrs. C. E. Wife of Charles Elliott Perkins, builder of the Burlington railway across Nebraska; president of the Burlington, 1881–1901; land owner in Webster County. Thought by her daughter Edith Perkins Hooper to have been the model for Mrs. Ogden in *A Lost Lady*.

Phelps, William Lyon. 1865–1943. American critic; professor of English at Yale for forty years. Wrote an article on Mark Twain that Cather praised.

Piercy, Josephine. Edited *Modern Writers at Work* (1930), which provided letters from writers describing their working methods along with selections of their work.

Pound, Louise. 1872–1958. College friend of Cather's who went on to gain recognition as a scholar of folklore; the first woman president of the Modern Language Association.

Puvis de Chavannes, Pierre. 1824–98. French muralist.

Rascoe, Burton. 1892–1957. Editor, author, and critic of drama and literature whose column "The Day Book of a New Yorker" was syndicated in over four hundred newspapers. Fired from his job at the *Chicago Tribune* for having written negative comments about Mary Baker Eddy, he became Associate Editor of *McCall's* in 1921. Reviewed *Death Comes for the Archbishop* in *Bookman*.

Reynolds, Paul Revere. 1864–1944. The first literary agent in New York; founded his business in 1893 and represented many well-known authors. Served as Cather's agent beginning in 1916.

Richardson, Winifred (Fred). Daughter of W. N. Richardson, the model for Mr. Trueman of "Two Friends." Married Seward Garber, son of Silas Garber and his first wife.

Rittenhouse, Jessie B. Editor of *The Little Book of Modern Verse* (New York, 1913), which included "Grandmither, Think Not I Forget."

Roberts, Althea (Allie). Classmate of Cather and of Mariel Gere. Later Mrs. Corwin Haggard.

Robins, Elizabeth. 1862-1952. Novelist, also wrote under the pseudonym C. E. Raimond.

Roe, E. P. 1838-88. A Civil War chaplain who became an author of extremely popular novels. Wrote thirty books, all with religious themes.

Roosevelt, Grace Lockwood. Author of *We Owed It to the Children* (1935).

Roseboro', Viola. 1858-1945. Fiction editor at *McClure's* 1896-1906. Author of short stories and novels.

Saint-Gaudens, Augustus. 1848-1907. Irish-born sculptor who lived in New York and later Paris. Prominent works include the Shaw Memorial (Boston), the Lincoln Statue (Chicago), and the Adams Memorial.

Saroyan, William. 1908-81. American writer of short stories, novels, and plays; in 1940, refused the Pulitzer Prize offered for his play *The Time of Your Life.*

Scaife, R. L. Production editor at Houghton Mifflin.

Scott, Evelyn. 1893-1963. American writer from Tennessee, attended Sophie Newcomb Preparatory School and Art School in New Orleans before eloping to Brazil in 1913. Her experiences became the basis for *Escapade* (1923).

Seibel, George. 1873-1958. A literary and drama critic in Pittsburgh; Sunday editor for the *Pittsburg Gazette-Times,* 1896-1911; managing editor of a German-language daily in Pittsburgh, 1912-25. Director of the Carnegie Free Library in Allegheny, Pennsylvania, 1938-54.

Sergeant, Elizabeth Shepley. 1881-1965. Author and journalist; wrote for *The New Republic* and others; met Cather in 1910 and wrote *Willa Cather: A Memoir* (1953).

Seymour, Elizabeth (Bess). 1857–1934. Lived with half-brother Will Andrews and their mother, Sarah Andrews, sister of Cather's mother, on Will's farm north of Bladen.

Sibut, Céline. A friend of Dorothy Canfield in Paris, whose mother ran a pension whether Cather stayed in 1902.

Sill, Peorianna Bogardus. 1833–1921. Directed 1889 production of *Beauty and the Beast* in Red Cloud, in which Cather took part.

Sprague, Helen McNeny. Daughter of Bernard and Helen McNeny, married attorney Leon Sprague.

Steichen, Edward. 1879–1973. Photographer famous for portraits, especially fashion and portrait photography for *Vanity Fair* and *Vogue*.

Steinbeck, John. 1902–68. American novelist, winner of the Pulitzer Prize in 1940 and the Nobel Prize in 1962.

Stevenson, Robert Louis. 1850–94. Scottish adventure novelist.

Stowell, Helen Louise Stevens. Married Eugene Alexander Stowell around 1881 in Boston, moved to a sheep ranch near Red Cloud, later moved to California.

Street, Julian. 1897–1947. Wrote *Men, Machines and Morals*.

Swinburne, Algernon Charles. 1837–1909. Victorian "decadent" poet.

Tarbell, Ida. 1857–1944. Famous "muckraking" writer. Preceded Cather as an editor at *McClure's*.

Tauchnitz, Christian Bernhard. 1816–95. Printer in Leipzig who initiated a "Collection of British and American Authors" reprint series in 1842.

Teasdale, Sara. 1884–1933. American lyric poet.

Train, Arthur. 1875–1945. Member of the Department of Literature of the American Academy of Arts and Letters. President of the National Institute of Arts and Letters, 1941–45.

Tyndale, Dr. Julius. Medical doctor in Lincoln during Cather's college years who also wrote theater reviews. Brother of Mrs. Westermann.

Undset, Sigrid. 1882–1949. Norwegian writer.

Vanamee, Grace D. 1876–1946. Public lecturer, founder of the Women's National Republican Club. Deputy/Secretary (i.e., Executive Director) to Robert U. Johnson at the American Academy of Arts and Letters, 1915–40.

Van Doren, Carl. 1885–1950. American editor, critic, and novelist; author of *The American Novel* (1921).

Van Loon, Hendrick Willem. 1882–1944. Netherlands-born American journalist who specialized in popular compendia such as *The Story of the Bible* (1923) and *Van Loon's Geography* (1932).

Van Vechten, Carl. 1880–1964. American novelist, photographer, and music and drama critic.

Vermorcken, Elizabeth Moorhead. An acquaintance from Pittsburgh who later wrote *They Too Were Here: Louise Homer and Willa Cather* (1950).

Vinsonhaler, Duncan M. A judge in Omaha; representing a group of Omaha citizens, he commissioned a portrait of Cather.

Wagenknecht, Edward. b. 1900. American literary critic and biographer. Wrote on Thoreau, Hawthorne, Sir Walter Scott, Mark Twain, Shakespeare, and Abraham Lincoln.

Weber, Carl J. 1894–1966. Literary scholar, taught at Colby College for thirty-nine years. Wrote a biography of Thomas Hardy.

Wells, Carlton F. b. 1898. Professor in the Department of English at the University of Michigan; wrote or edited a number of books.

Westermann family. Acquaintances of Cather's in Lincoln; Louis Westermann was the owner and publisher of the *Lincoln Evening News*. The departure of Fritz Westermann, 1865–1934, for the Spanish American War drew Cather's approval. Prototypes for the Erlichs in *One of Ours*.

Weston, Katherine (Kit). Friend of Cather's from Beatrice, Nebraska, whom she met at college. Her father was Chairman of the University of Nebraska Board of Regents.

Wheelwright, Mary Cabot. Founder of the Wheelwright Museum in Santa Fe.

Whicher, George Frisbie. 1889–1954. The son of a professor of classics, Whicher received his B.A. in 1910 from Amherst College, where he subsequently taught from 1915 to 1954, after having received his Ph.D. from Columbia in 1913. Author of a biography of Emily Dickinson (1935) and other literary studies.

Whicher, Harriet Fox. 1890–1966. A graduate of Bryn Mawr and Barnard, Whicher served as professor of English at Mount Holyoke from 1918 until 1944, afterward becoming a freelance copyeditor at McGraw Hill. Edited her husband's posthumous volume of essays *Poetry and Civilization* (1955).

White, William Allen. 1868–1944. Editor of the *Emporia* (Kansas) *Gazette* and winner of the Pulitzer Prize in 1923.

Wiener, Charles F. 1846–1911. Merchant who lived near the Cathers in Red Cloud when Cather was growing up; conversant in French and German, Mr. and Mrs. Wiener allowed her the use of their fine library. Prototype for Mr. Rosen in "Old Mrs. Harris."

Wiener, Fanny Meyer. 1853–93. Prototype for Mrs. Rosen in "Old Mrs. Harris."

Wilcox, Ella Wheeler. 1850–1919. American poet, sometimes called "the poet of passion" from the title of her book *Poems of Passion.*

Willard, Mary and May. Friends of Cather's in Pittsburgh.

Wilson, James Southall. 1881–1963. Professor at the University of Virginia, 1919–52; founded and edited the *Virginia Quarterly Review.*

Winter, William. 1836–1917. Critic, poet, and scholar; joined the *New York Tribune* as Assistant Editor in 1865 and was best known for theater reviews.

Woodberry, George E. Professor of English at the University of Nebraska in the early 1880s, later at Columbia University; introduced Cather to Amy Lowell.

Woollcott, Alexander. 1887–1943. American critic and radio personality, known for his wit; a member of the Algonquin Roundtable.

Wyer, Malcolm Glenn. 1877–1965. Director of the Denver Public Library, 1924–51; Director of Libraries, University of Denver, 1933–48; president of the American Library Association, 1936–37.

Wylie, Elinor. 1885–1928. American poet and novelist, known for her beauty as well as for her writing.

Index of Addressees

Index of Names and Titles Mentioned

Index of Repositories